C

D1267991

LAW AND COMMUNITY ON THE
MEXICAN CALIFORNIA FRONTIER

Law and Community on the Mexican California Frontier

ANGLO-AMERICAN EXPATRIATES AND THE CLASH OF LEGAL TRADITIONS, 1821–1846

By David J. Langum

University of Oklahoma Press : Norman and London

GALLAUDET UNIVERSITY LIBRARY
WASHINGTON, D.C. 20002

Library of Congress Cataloging-in-Publication Data

Langum, David J., 1940–
  Law and community on the Mexican California
frontier.

  Bibliography: p. 287
  Includes index.
    1. Law—California—History and criticism.
  2. British Americans—Legal status, laws, etc.—
  California—History.   3. Mexican Americans—
  California—History.   I. Title.
  KFC78.L33   1987   349.794′09   86–19341
  ISBN 0–8061–2037–1 (alk. paper) 347.94009

The paper in this book meets the guidelines for permanence and
durability of the Committee on Production Guidelines for Book
Longevity of the Council on Library Resources, Inc.

Copyright © 1987 by the University of Oklahoma Press, Norman,
Publishing Division of the University. Manufactured in the U.S.A.
First edition.

349.794
23ℓ
1987

This book is dedicated with love and gratitude to my father, John Kenneth Langum, and to the memory of my mother, Virginia Anne de Mattos Langum.

027516

025316

Contents

Illustrations

ix

Acknowledgments

The debts of gratitude I incurred while writing this book are owed to so many persons and institutions that I am reluctant to begin for fear I might neglect someone. With that risk I must try.

I wrote this book over many years and at three different schools, Detroit College of Law, Nevada School of Law, Reno, and now, Cumberland School of Law, Samford University, Birmingham. All three provided wonderful institutional support in many direct and indirect ways. John S. Abbott was especially kind to allow me a teaching schedule at Detroit flexible enough to permit my initial research. The librarians at Bancroft Library and Huntington Library showed consistent courtesies. William Mason, of the Los Angeles County Museum of Natural History, shared his personal guide to the Los Angeles alcalde records.

I am especially grateful to Norman Borchert, formerly the Assistant County Recorder of Monterey County, now retired. He was the custodian of the Mexican judicial records of the Monterey courts during the summers I was reading them. Mr. Borchert and his kind assistants provided me with desk space and freedom to use the documents without restriction and, in the midst of reading nearly illegible papers, offered me an occasional word of encouragement. Without their help it would have been far more difficult to do the necessary research.

Thomas A. Green of the University of Michigan Law School gave me a considerable number of suggestions. He was my principal doctoral adviser at Michigan, and an earlier version of this work was submitted in partial fulfillment of the requirements of the S.J.D. degree.

Many faculty colleagues read chapters and gave me the benefits of their counsel. These included Robert A. McCormick, Robert A. Riegert, David G. Stankow, and Bradford Stone. Other friends and scholars who have read portions include David J. Boden-hamer, Tony Freyer, Benjamin F. Gilbert, Joseph W. McKnight, and John R. Wunder.

Laura J. Redoutey read the entire manuscript and made many helpful editorial suggestions. Substantial portions of the domestic relations material in chapter 9 were first published in the *Pepperdine Law Review* for 1979, and are republished here through its courtesy. Good friends Stanley F. Siddle and Joan Veit Lavin both put me up and put up with me during many research trips to the Bay Area.

I have three special thanks. First is to my father for his continual encouragement. Second is to my wife, JoAnne, and children, who were usually patient and forbearing. My four-year-old daughter, Virginia, was always enthusiastic in urging me to work hard. Third, I must thank a deceased writer I never knew, Bernard De Voto. His *The Year of Decision: 1846,* read over twenty years ago, first introduced me to the pleasures of Mexican California. They have proved to be of unfailing interest and enjoyment.

Notwithstanding all this help, any errors of judgment or fact remain my sole responsibility. In the nature of things there must be some; I hope there are not many.

David J. Langum
Birmingham, Alabama

LAW AND COMMUNITY ON THE
MEXICAN CALIFORNIA FRONTIER

Introduction

Americans had peacefully invaded California, bringing with them their preconceptions of the proper legal order, long before their government's official seizure in 1846. The generation that migrated to the soon-to-be Golden State in the 1830s and 1840s was a highly legalistic one. These Americans, and their British cousins as well, spoke, wrote, and thought in legal terms. The law was deeply revered and was an ingrained and inextricable part of their culture.[1]

Upon their arrival in California, these American and British expatriates were immediately confronted with the knowledge that it was *Mexican* California they had entered. Not only was Spanish the language but the country had a legal system quite different from their accustomed and much-esteemed common law. The Mexican legal system had its traditions and normative concepts of justice that were different from those the immigrants thought a legal system should embody, and these notions of justice were delivered through procedures far different from those employed by the Anglo-American system.

This book addresses four distinct topics that arise from these basic facts. The first is a description of the legal system of Mexican California between the years of 1821 and 1846, as actually practiced and as viewed from the local level, rather than from the idealized heights of legislation in Mexico City. Second is the question of how the Anglo-American expatriates who lived in Mexican California were treated by the legal system. The third theme is

---

[1] For a detailed study of the overland immigrants and property law, see J. REID, LAW FOR THE ELEPHANT: PROPERTY AND SOCIAL BEHAVIOR ON THE OVERLAND TRAIL (1980). Reid suggests that law had become a behavioral part of America's culture and that Americans of the mid-nineteenth century were reasonably familiar with legal concepts.

3

the clash between the Hispanic and the Anglo-American legal traditions that caused the foreigners' hostility to the Mexican system. The fourth topic is a review of the methods by which the foreign residents handled their legal affairs on a frontier without lawyers and in a legal setting that they viewed with contempt.

Some readers may be more interested in one part of the book than another. Historians of California, Mexico, or the West may be more concerned with the first two topics and legal historians with the second two themes. The subjects are related but different, and the reader's indulgence is requested respecting material of more interest to someone else. Moreover, general historians may think the footnote citations excessively abbreviated. They are not in standard academic style, but they do conform, with minor eccentricities, to the Uniform System of Legal Citation. The bibliography is prepared in accordance with general academic usage, and the additional information that general historians are accustomed to finding in footnotes is readily obtainable there.

This study involves not only law on the Mexican frontier but also the relationship of that law with the foreign residents. This duality of purpose has required the exclusion of some material that might otherwise have been interesting and helpful. The focus is on Mexican law as applied on only one frontier, that of Alta California. Some comparisons are made occasionally with New Mexico, but no systematic effort is made to study the legal experiences of the Mexican borderlands generally. New Mexico and Arizona had very few foreign residents during the period of 1821 to 1846. In contrast, Texas had a massive influx of foreigners, primarily from the United States, between 1825 and its independence in 1836. By 1830, American immigrants in Texas were twice the numbers of the local non-Indian population, and by 1834 Americans outnumbered the tejanos by five to one. Mexican law applied in Santa Fe, Tucson, and San Antonio, as well as in Monterey. Yet neither New Mexico, Arizona, nor Texas seem suited to study the interaction of Anglo-Americans with a foreign legal culture. New Mexico and Arizona had too few expatriates; Texas had too many.

The desire to analyze the relationship of Mexican law to Anglo-Americans led to a second limitation. Public law has been de-emphasized. Such legal areas as municipal law, licensing, water allocation, and forest regulation, to name a few, have been touched upon only lightly. They did not have much impact on the expatriates. Criminal law did affect the foreigners considerably, however, and a chapter is devoted to the system of criminal justice. With that exception, private law is in the forefront.

The expatriates roundly criticized the California courts and called them corrupt and inefficient. With allowance for a rare individual judge, the charge of corruption cannot be sustained. From the British and American viewpoints, however, the Mexican California courts were certainly inefficient. The briefest glance at the system reveals massive, but explainable, structural inefficiency. If judges were sometimes unwilling to resolve disputes, it may have been because they served involuntarily and without compensation. Confusion over authority to render firm decisions and judgments was rampant, in part because the formal, statutory role of the only lower courts in California was merely preliminary and conciliatory. The regular Mexican trial courts were not established in California. Nevertheless, civil judgments were rendered but once obtained were uncertain of collection. This was because California practice permitted modification of judgments to alter time for payment. Moreover, there was no official, such as a sheriff, designated to seize a judgment debtor's property.

For all its inefficiencies the California legal system was well calculated to advance its own ideals and jurisprudence of dispute resolution. These ideals included culturally based goals of conciliation of the parties and, where that was impossible, the use of community pressures, rather than force, to compel adherence to a judicial resolution of a dispute. Legal historians have been blinded too long by the positivist concept of law as the command of the sovereign and by the more recent concept of law as a manipulative instrument wielded by the holders of economic and social power. We are rediscovering that there are justice systems that are communally based and which often have few of the accoutrements of formal law.[2] This is especially true of isolated and

[2] A number of recent studies suggest that in many contexts, usually of a closely knit, homogeneous society, law can be more dependent on custom and societal consensus than on force or direct, formal sanction. See J. AUERBACH, JUSTICE WITHOUT LAW? (1983); M. BARKUN, LAW WITHOUT SANCTIONS: ORDER IN PRIMITIVE SOCIETIES AND THE WORLD COMMUNITY (1968); W. NELSON, DISPUTE AND CONFLICT RESOLUTION IN PLYMOUTH COLONY, MASSACHUSETTS, 1725–1825 (1981). The de-

homogeneous societies, such as California before the immigration of the American and British expatriates. Exploring the workings of the Mexican California law offers an opportunity to examine such a community-based legal system.

The ideals of conciliation and community were of little interest to the individualistic expatriates. Their concept of the role of law, fostered by common law traditions and the quickening pace of the commercial era, was far different. At the same time the Americans and the British were denouncing the California legal system, their strong impulses for legality impelled them toward a search for legitimacy. Law and regularity were important to this generation, far more than for our own. This put the expatriates in a dilemma. Their own cultural presuppositions told them to use the established legal system, but they had difficulty doing so because it ill-served their needs.

The resolution of this dilemma could almost be described as schizophrenic. The expatriate community avoided the local legal system in some situations and used it for others. Their solutions were too complex for easy generalization, and they varied, not only as to the kind of law, for example, domestic relations or dispute resolution, but also as to class of expatriate immigrant.

The evidence suggests many historical questions. The jurisprudential assumptions behind the California legal system and the individualistic Anglo-American concept of law and how these conflicts were resolved have been mentioned. An examination of the Mexican California legal system in its own right, how it operated and how the foreigners were treated within it, is equally interesting. On the local level it was conducted in a far different manner than the Mexican statutory provisions would suggest. Notwithstanding the Anglo-Americans' disdain for the system, they often found themselves in the local courts as either criminal or civil defendants, especially when the plaintiffs were Californian or Mexican. How the foreigners fit in is of great interest, especially when viewed from the perspective of court records and not Anglo-American rhetoric. Were they treated poorly or with preference in the California alcalde courts? As will be seen, the expatriates' subjective perceptions of the Mexican California

---

vices alternative to force to secure compliance with judicial orders and how they were employed in California are discussed in Chapter 5.

legal system were not the same as the objective realities of their experiences. To the extent that the expatriates relied on their own devices in avoidance of the local law, a review of their methods helps describe something else as well. There were no resident lawyers in the American or British communities. Occasionally an attorney would travel among them and stay for a few months, but these lawyers engaged in little legal practice while they were there.[3] When an expatriate wrote a contract or settled a dispute, he did so without any lawyer to guide him. The extent to which the foreigners correctly used law suggests the degree to which legal norms had become a part of their general culture. In turn, this suggests the means whereby Anglo-Americans were able to conduct their legal relationships in a frontier setting without the support of lawyers and a sophisticated judicial system.

When reading a disputatious letter sent by an American merchant in Monterey to another American merchant in San Diego, the opportunity exists to learn a great deal. If the writer made an appeal to legalized notions of his "rights," as opposed to his position of power for retaliation, there is evidence of an engrafting of notions of "law" carried beyond the territorial limits of formal jurisdiction and into the realm of cultural norm. If a legal argument was well made or if there was evidence of merchants applying such legal concepts as merchantability or setoffs, then the accuracy of that group's familiarity with legal principles, of law remembered from their homes, can be gauged. Likewise, if an immigrant farmer decided to divorce his wife and did so by rescinding the marriage by mutual agreement, the naivete of that procedure should not obscure the interesting reality that here is a common man of the mid-nineteenth century who was aware of relatively recent legal developments redefining the nature of marriage as contractual rather than sacramental. The same could be said of so-called common law marriages. Thus the California ex-

---

[3] One lawyer who arrived in 1840 and stayed but briefly, Thomas Jefferson Farnham, published a book, TRAVELS IN THE CALIFORNIAS, AND SCENES IN THE PACIFIC OCEAN (New York, 1844), reprinted as TRAVELS IN CALIFORNIA (1947). Another lawyer, Lansford W. Hastings, stayed for a longer time and engaged in some minimal legal work. He was in California for a few months in 1843–44 and again for a few months in 1845–46, and he published THE EMIGRANTS' GUIDE TO OREGON AND CALIFORNIA (Cincinnati, 1845), reprint ed. (1969).

perience raises the question of the extent to which law had become a cultural norm of the American and British people by the mid-nineteenth century and how accurately they were aware of its contours.

A brief account of the organization of the book and the sources and methodology involved will be of help to the reader. Chapter 1 is a sketch of the general history of California before the Mexican War of 1846. This concerns only Upper California (Alta California). Baja California was very lightly populated and was administered separately from Alta California during most of the Mexican period. There were extremely few foreign residents in Baja California, and no part of that region became American territory. References to California, then, will be to the area now familiar as the American state.

The next three chapters concern the Mexican California judicial system itself and how the Anglo-Americans were treated within it. Chapter 2 describes the system's structure and the Spanish and Mexican background. Chapters 3 and 4 treat the processes of litigation, criminal and civil, respectively, before the California courts. How litigation was commenced, its conduct and procedure, the kinds of cases litigated, postjudgment remedies, sentencing in criminal matters, and appellate review are among the topics examined.

Chapter 5 analyzes the differing values held by the Californios and the Anglo-Americans, which were reflected in their respective legal systems. Different legal values formed the bases for the expatriates' harsh perceptions and criticisms of the local courts. Chapters 6 through 9 discuss how the foreigners, and to a lesser extent the Californios as well, conducted their legal business in the areas of contract formation, credit creation and debt collection, dispute resolution, and domestic relations. The expatriates' activities reflect their reactions to a distrusted local legal system through which they nevertheless wanted to legitimate their conduct. Equally, the legal arrangements adopted reflect a reaction to the geographic and economic realities of the frontier in which they lived.

The final chapter attempts to tie these themes together. The discussion also suggests that there may be a deeper dimension to the clash between Mexican California and Anglo-American legal values beyond that of traditions. In the Anglo-American critique of the communal-based justice system of Mexican California, a deeper conflict can be seen. The more fundamental clash was between the traditional values and the languid procedures of a pre-industrial, pastoral people and the atomistic, individualist energies of those in the very throes of the Industrial Revolution.

The years covered by this study are 1835 to 1846, although helpful information is drawn from outside the primary period. The dates are not chosen arbitrarily. The year 1846 was the year of the American invasion and conquest of California, which makes it an obvious ending. The year 1835 is more practical than logical. Mexico achieved its independence in 1821, but not until the 1830s did significant numbers of American and English merchants and seamen settle in California. Not until the mid-1830s did they began having much legal involvement with each other and with the official legal system. The economic life of California blossomed in the 1830s with the secularization of the missions and the consequent growth of private ranches. The expansion of private economic interests and the pace of trade of the 1830s led to more litigation and more extrajudicial legal activity. Not only are there more materials from the mid-1830s onward, but of those materials that were generated before 1835 the amount still extant is minimal.

There are many varied sources of primary materials for this study. Spanish and Mexican legislation, decrees, and orders provide a starting point for understanding the California legal system. Yet California was so intellectually and geographically isolated from the mainstream of Mexican life that merely to look at the legal system that functioned in the Mexican heartland would be misleading. California must be viewed in its own right, as well as being a portion of the Republic of Mexico. The methodology of this book is therefore somewhat anthropological in nature because the description and analysis of the California legal system is constructed from the ground up, supported by an examination of the local documents. This is particularly true of chapters 2 to 4. The disparity between the Mexican statutory mandates and the actual functioning of the local courts is so great that an accurate picture of how litigation was conducted can be constructed only through a background of thousands of pieces of judicial minutiae. In examining this minutiae we need to bear in mind the monetary equivalents. Throughout the period the Mexican peso was equal in value to the American dollar. The American dollar of 1835–46 is roughly equivalent to eleven dollars of 1987.[4] Monetary amounts in this book are always rendered in the original peso or dollar amounts, interchangeable to contemporaries, except where a modern equivalency is expressly noted.

Unfortunately, the pieces of judicial minutiae are widely scattered throughout several repositories, much is no longer extant, and what can be located is often disorganized in the sense that not all the materials relating to the same lawsuit are grouped together. Much of it is written in obscure abbreviations, illegible handwriting, and ungrammatical Spanish. It is altogether unlike the neat and tidy files maintained by modern courts, where everything pertaining to a particular case is kept in a single jacket. California judicial documents for civil cases were maintained according to the kind of procedure or stage of proceeding, not by individual case.

The English language of the period was not always of the best either. The letters of the expatriates are colorful in their misspellings and grammatical misuses, but the use of [sic] in quotations would have been nearly constant; therefore, it is not used at all. The quotations are correct, however.

The conclusions of this book are based in large measure on the judicial documents for the Monterey District, 1835–46. There are several reasons for this concentration. First, Monterey was California's second largest town during this period, only slightly smaller than Los Angeles. Moreover, it was the departmental capital and the location of the customhouse, the largest source of government revenue. In short, it was an important place. Second, of the settled California areas with large populations, Monterey had the most expatriates. Since the focus of this book is on the Anglo-Americans and their relationship to the official system, this concentration seemed an advantage. Third, the Monterey records for this period are, by far, more nearly complete than those for any other California localities and are largely contained in one collection, the Monterey Archives, now maintained by the Mon-

---

[4] This is based on the United States government's statistical series, "Consumer Price Indexes—All Items 1800 to 1970," published in HISTORICAL STATISTICS OF THE UNITED STATES, and brought up to date through supplements. A comparison of the price levels for 1835–1846 with that of 1987 yields roughly the ratio of eleven to one.

terey County Historical Society. Last, the Monterey Archives has a serviceable plaintiff-defendant index that was of enormous help. Documents from other California localities have been used as well. Much judicial material found its way into the papers of various prefects—executive officials and subgovernors—who had major roles in the legal process. Prefecture records are scattered and most often are found in the collected papers of various individuals who on different occasions held one of the two offices, one for northern California and another for southern California. The most complete collection of prefecture records are those of the Los Angeles District, held by the Huntington Library. These proved to be an interesting counterpoise to the Monterey records. They are from a different part of California and reflect somewhat different procedures, and the perspective is different since the prefect was most frequently involved in appeals or complaints about trial judges, whereas the bulk of the Monterey records are of the trial courts themselves.

Many other primary records were examined; they were from all levels of the California government and were held in many repositories. The Monterey trial records and the Los Angeles prefect records are merely the documents upon which the greatest reliance has been placed. The Los Angeles trial records were also briefly reviewed and supported conclusions drawn from their Monterey equivalents. These alcalde files, called the Los Angeles Archives, are in the Los Angeles County Museum of Natural History, Los Angeles. In addition, and especially concerning expatriate reactions to and evasions of the California law, the private papers of leading merchants have been helpful. The most helpful have been the Fitch Documents and the Larkin Papers, both at the Bancroft Library in Berkeley.

1

The Historical Setting

California was a Spanish colony until the success of the Mexican Revolution in 1821, but it had been settled so late, in 1769, that many of the traditional Spanish colonial institutions never appeared. California never experienced the large agricultural holdings with their systems of forced Indian labor known as the encomiendas, nor an aggregation of native Spaniards sufficiently large to form an educated, cultured elite. In Spanish California there were no presses, no theaters, no law courts, and no attorneys. A few natives of European Spain, *peninsulares,* were scattered about as commandantes of the four forts, or presidios, at San Francisco, Monterey, Santa Barbara, and San Diego, and as Franciscan missionaries in the twenty missions founded during the Spanish period. Many of these native Spaniards would leave after independence. The civilian settlements, the two pueblos of San Jose and Los Angeles and the lesser village of Branciforte, were small and struggling. Their populations were composed primarily of Mexican mestizos of mixed Indian blood, retired junior officers and privates, their families, and a few artisans.

The term "Spanish land grant" is a misnomer. Almost all the California land grants date from the Mexican years. Spain was closefisted and, except for small town plots, the few handfuls of grants unloosed by Spanish authorities in California were usufructuary. They did not represent ownership but merely a right to cultivate crops or raise cattle—a license to use the king's land, conditioned upon payment of royalties to the Crown. A few other settlers, artisans from Mexico and farmers, clustered about the presidios. Most of the non-Indian population was composed of soldiers, retired soldiers, missionaries, and servants and families of these groups.

Americans have romanticized Hispanic California, mentally populating it with kindly padres, submissive yet well-cared-for Indians, dashing horsemen, dark-haired women with flirtatious eyes and flowing skirts, all accompanied by guitar music and roses of Castile.[1] It is mostly myth. Spanish California in fact was an underpopulated military frontier. Were it possible to be transported back in time to a Spanish California community, or to a Mexican California community for that matter, most Americans would find it to be dusty, dirty, flea-ridden, and squalid. California's strength was its largely homogeneous population, Mexican mestizos from the middle and lower classes, with a small seasoning of native Spaniards and blacks. There was some intermarriage with the native Indians, which contributed even more to the homogeneity of society. The Californios were loyal to the Crown and never swore fealty to Mexico until Spain had abandoned the field of combat and the revolution had been won. This early homogeneity of population was to have an impact on the later California legal system.

General Spanish distrust of foreigners and traditional colonial mercantile policies combined to close California ports to all but carefully screened foreign visitors and to close them absolutely to foreign trade. Scientific and exploratory expeditions of all friendly powers were welcome, but trading or hunting vessels were not, except for short visitations under conditions of extreme distress such as a need to repair a mast or to take on water. In times of extreme scarcity, expecially during the Mexican wars of independence, 1810 to 1821, when the annual supply ships failed to appear, local authorities did trade with foreign vessels.[2] Generally,

---

[1] This favorable postconquest romantization contrasts sharply with a judgmental and critical view of California held by many Americans before the 1846 invasion. *See* J. HART, AMERICAN IMAGES OF SPANISH CALIFORNIA (1960); Clark, *Their Pride, Their Manners, and Their Voices: Sources of the Traditional Portrait of the Early Californians*, 53 CAL. HIST. Q. 71 (1974); Langum, *Californios and the Image of Indolence*, 9 W. HIST. Q. 181 (1978). The American historical and literary interpretation of Hispanic California shifted dramatically after the conquest. For an interpretation of this and a suggestion of possible reasons, see Langum, *From Condemnation to Praise: Shifting Perspectives on Hispanic California*, 61 CAL. HIST. 282 (1983). A realistic study of Hispanic society in Alta California is O. JONES, LOS PAISANOS: SPANISH SETTLERS ON THE NORTHERN FRONTIER OF NEW SPAIN (1979).

[2] The best descriptions of the Spanish efforts to provide supplies to California

Spanish California was stubbornly closed to foreign trade, and such foreign commercial ships and personnel as sought entry to California did so at their peril. The earliest Californian economic activity to catch the eye of the world was the hunting of sea otters off the coast. Beginning in the 1790s this became an international sport as Americans, Englishmen, and Russians hovered off the California harbors and bays, moving in surreptitiously to catch their prey. This violated Spanish law and the California authorities did make efforts to stop the practice, but without a naval force it was difficult to make much headway.[3] Some captured Russian hunters were imprisoned,[4] and an American ship, the *Lelia Byrd*, was obliged to shoot its way out of the San Diego harbor in 1803 after its crew had been apprehended in an illegal attempt to buy furs.[5] The hunters had abundant freedom, however; only the near extinction of the otters and changing market conditions stopped them. The peak period of activity was 1810 to 1820, although otter hunts continued with diminished success throughout the Mexican period. Several of the early American residents in California, such as John B. R. Cooper and Nathan Spear, were first attracted to California because of involvement in the otter hunt. The later hide-and-tallow trade and the still later overland migrations were far more significant sources of foreign entry.

Once it was independent from Spain, Mexico opened its California ports to foreign commerce, but this had very little immediate impact on the introduction of foreign manufactures into California society. The Franciscan missions held a virtual monopoly on what had replaced the otters as the leading and most valuable export products of the country, cattle hides and tallow. In 1823

are M. THURMAN, THE NAVAL DEPARTMENT OF SAN BLAS: NEW SPAIN'S BASTION FOR ALTA CALIFORNIA AND NOOTKA, 1767–1798 (1967) and Chapman, *The Alta California Supply Ships, 1773–1776*, 19 Sw. HIST. Q. 184 (1916). A small amount of supplies for California were also carried on the Manila galleons which called at Monterey for servicing. *See generally* Schurz, *The Manila Galleon and California*, 21 Sw. HIST. Q. 107 (1918).

[3] The best account of the hunting of sea otters in California is A. OGDEN, THE CALIFORNIA SEA OTTER TRADE, 1784–1848 (1941).

[4] *See, e.g.,* V. TARAKANOFF, STATEMENT OF MY CAPTIVITY AMONG THE CALIFORNIANS (Early California Travels Series, vol. 16) (1953).

[5] R. CLEVELAND, A NARRATIVE OF VOYAGES AND COMMERCIAL ENTERPRISES 194–198 (Cambridge, Mass. 1842).

an enterprising Englishman named William Hartnell engaged the Franciscans in a three-year contract for the trade of hides and tallow derived from the huge herds they maintained on the far-flung missionary ranches. The hides and tallow were exchanged for manufactured items needed by the missionaries and their Indian wards. At the expiration of the contract, competitive foreign traders entered the field and each mission traded for itself. The missions, however, had relatively little demand for foreign products, and this restricted both the size and the profitability of this trade until the mid-1830s.[6]

During the years 1834 to 1836 the missions were secularized. By this process they were reduced to the status of parish churches, and their vast landholdings were redistributed by the California government through land grants to hundreds of private ranchers. Although considerable economic chaos, destruction, and corruption resulted from the transition,[7] the private entrepreneurs soon increased their herds to a point rivaling or exceeding those previously maintained by the Franciscan fathers.[8] With the growth of private ranches, and for the first time in California's history, individual desires for manufactured goods and the luxuries of life were coupled with private means to pay for them.

Adding to consumer demand by the mid-1830s was a considerable increase in population, due primarily to the fecundity of the California women rather than immigration. It is to these native sons and daughters that the term "Californios" is properly applied. They certainly would not have referred to themselves as Mexicans, which indeed was a term, to the natives, of some deri-

[6] The early hide-and-tallow trade and its financial difficulties can be examined through the biography of the pioneer of the field, William Hartnell. S. DAKIN, THE LIVES OF WILLIAM HARTNELL 33–88 (1949). A more academic and analytical study of this early period is Ogden, *Hides and Tallow: McCulloch, Hartnell and Company, 1822–1828*, 6 CAL. HIST. SOC'Y Q. 254 (1927).

[7] There is considerable historical controversy concerning the secularization program. For temperate statements of the conflicting viewpoints, *compare* G. GEARY, THE SECULARIZATION OF THE CALIFORNIA MISSIONS (1934), *with* Servín, *The Secularization of the California Missions: A Reappraisal*, 47 SO. CAL. HIST. Q. 133 (1961). The agricultural boom of the late 1830s and the 1840s, however, is a fact of which all historians have taken account, and it was primarily from former mission lands that the land-grant ranchos were carved out.

[8] J. FRANCIS, AN ECONOMIC AND SOCIAL HISTORY OF MEXICAN CALIFORNIA 509–38 (1976).

sion. In this book, however, unless specified to the contrary, the terms "Californio" and "Mexican" are used interchangeably. The market responded generously to the increase in population and growth of consumer demand. California had no manufacturing of its own, but throughout the late 1830s and early 1840s hundreds of foreign ships brought manufactures to California and sailed away with the hides and tallow sold in exchange.[9] This steady stream of shipping served as a pipeline through which all the goods and effects, luxuries and necessities, of nineteenth-century civilization flowed to this languid, underdeveloped region. Richard Henry Dana, Jr., a young sailor working in this trade, graphically reported in his classic account, *Two Years Before the Mast:*

Our cargo was an assorted one; that is, it consisted of everything under the sun. We had spirits, of all kinds, (sold by the cask,) teas, coffee, sugars, spices, raisins, molasses, hard-ware, crockery-ware, tin-ware, cutlery, clothing of all kinds, boots and shoes from Lynn, calicoes and cottons from Lowell, crapes, silks; also, shawls, scarfs, necklaces, jewelry, and combs for the ladies; furniture; and in fact, everything that can be imagined, from Chinese fire-works to English cart-wheels—of which we had a dozen pairs with their iron rims on.[10]

The bulk of this vital commerce was controlled by Americans, especially through such New England firms as Bryant, Sturgis & Company and William Appleton & Company. Most of the trading ships that touched the California shores in the period 1835 to 1846 were American.[11] The hide-and-tallow trade contributed

---

[9] Of necessity, the hide-and-tallow trade is discussed by every historian dealing with the period. Yet it is surprising how little has been written in depth concerning this single most important economic activity of pre–American California. The fullest scholarly treatment is Dallas, "The Hide and Tallow Trade in Alta California, 1822–1846" (Ph.D. dissertation Indiana University, 1955). The classic contemporary account, but from the limited perspective of a sailor, is R. Dana, Two Years Before the Mast (New York, 1840), (Kemble ed. 1964) (2 vols.). This work has appeared in many reprint editions, but there is an emerging consensus that Kemble's edition will be the scholarly standard. *See also* Ogden, *Boston Hide Droghers Along California Shores,* 8 Cal. Hist. Soc'y Q. 289 (1929); Ogden, *New England Traders in Spanish and Mexican California,* in Greater America: Essays in Honor of Herbert Eugene Bolton 395 (1945).

[10] 1 Dana, *supra* note 9 (Kemble ed. 1964), at 82.

[11] This may be seen from an examination of the lists of the 76 vessels visit-

significantly to the increase of foreign residents, largely American, but with large numbers of British and some Frenchmen as well. Much of the trading of goods for hides was done on shipboard. Once a ship arrived at port and cleared customs, it became a floating bazaar. Swarms of ranchers and their families would come in from the countryside in a festive mood to order goods. Most of the transactions were based on credit. This required the trading companies to maintain resident agents. Some managed warehouses for the reception of hides and tallow brought in as payment, while others wandered throughout the country, showing new wares and dunning payment from improvident ranchers at the critical time following the seasonal slaughters. Many of the leading foreign residents of Mexican California, including such Americans as Henry Fitch, Alfred Robinson, Alpheus B. Thompson, and David Spence, a Scotsman, arrived as employees of companies engaged in the hide-and-tallow trade.[12]

The wealth generated by this activity also allowed for the creation of an intermediate class of independent and fixed merchants who, acting as middlemen between the trading ships and the native purchasers, maintained a permanent market in goods and hides. As early as 1835 these expatriate traders dominated the California market. In that year, Dana observed:

> In Monterey there are a number of English and Americans . . . who have married Californians, become united to the Catholic church, and acquired considerable property. Having more industry, frugality, and enterprise than the natives, they soon get nearly all the trade into their hands. They usually keep shops, in which they retail the goods purchased in larger quantities from our vessels, and also send

---

ing California ports, 1836–40, and the 148 for 1841–45, that are described in 4 H. BANCROFT, HISTORY OF CALIFORNIA 100–6, 562–70 (1886) (1884–1890) (7 vols.) [hereinafter cited as HISTORY OF CALIFORNIA].

[12] For Fitch, see Miller, "Henry Delano Fitch: A Yankee Trader in California, 1826–1849" (Ph.D. dissertation, University of Southern California, 1972). Robinson wrote an interesting and popular contemporary account of Mexican California. A. ROBINSON, LIFE IN CALIFORNIA (New York, 1846), which has appeared in many reprint editions. *See also* Ogden, *Alfred Robinson, New England Merchant in Mexican California*, 23 CAL. HIST. SOC'Y Q. 193 (1944); OGDEN, *Business Letters of Alfred Robinson*, 23 CAL. HIST. SOC'Y Q. 301 (1944). Some of Thompson's papers have been collected in CHINA TRADE DAYS IN CALIFORNIA: SELECTED LETTERS FROM THE THOMPSON PAPERS, 1832–1863 (Brown ed. 1947).

a good deal into the interior, taking hides in pay, which they again barter with our vessels. In every town on the coast there are foreigners engaged in this kind of trade, while I recollect but two shops kept by natives.[13]

The most influential foreigners in Mexican California were among this class of independent merchants, including Thomas O. Larkin in Monterey and Abel Stearns in Los Angeles.[14] The commercial ventures of these expatriate merchants went far beyond a retail trade of consumer goods for hides and tallow. They traded with one another and with merchants in the Sandwich Islands (Hawaii), and they formed combinations and joint ventures for far-flung commercial adventures. Some foreigners who arrived while pursuing the otter trade or as employees of a trading ship also joined this group of independent merchants. The most interesting legal disputes arose out of this class of independent merchants.

Americans are a wandering people, and throughout the 1830s and 1840s several Americans arrived in California by means other than the sea route used by the early merchants and traders. As early as 1826, Jedediah Smith had led a trapping party from Saint Louis to California in search of beaver. Throughout the next ten years several hunting parties explored the various mountain passes leading to California. Most of these trappers stayed but briefly in California and had minimal but unpleasant contact with the local authorities, who smarted from the impudent intruders' disregard for the necessity of entrance passports and disdain for the inconvenience of hunting licenses.

---

[13] 1 DANA, *supra* note 9 (rep. ed. 1964), at 88. It has been suggested, however, based upon the Mexican Census of 1836, that only 61 percent of the merchants in the capital of Monterey in 1836 were born outside of California. Tucey & Hornbeck, *Anglo Immigration and the Hispanic Town: A Study of Urban Change in Monterey, California, 1835–1850,* 13 SOC. SCI. J. 1, 3 (1976) (No. 2 separately paginated).

[14] Larkin was the foremost merchant in northern California and served as American consul from 1843, yet there is no adequate biography of his life. R. UNDERHILL, FROM COWHIDES TO GOLDEN FLEECE (1939), serves by default. T. LARKIN, CHAPTERS IN THE EARLY LIFE OF THOMAS OLIVER LARKIN (Parker ed. 1939), provides information about him before his 1832 arrival in California. For Stearns, see D. WRIGHT, A YANKEE IN MEXICAN CALIFORNIA: ABEL STEARNS, 1798–1848 (1977). This is an excellent biography, filled with details evocative of the mood and temper of the times.

A few of the trappers stayed on in California, notably J. J. Warner, who ultimately obtained a ranch in the San Diego area, and Isaac Graham, who in 1836 built a distillery in Natividad, near present-day Salinas. Later, in 1841, Graham operated a sawmill in the Santa Cruz Mountains, north and east of the city of Santa Cruz. The image of the "mountain men," the Rocky Mountain trappers, as uncouth drunkards and filthy hell raisers is not entirely accurate. It is substantially so, however, for Graham. As the preeminent California historian, Hubert Howe Bancroft, said, Graham was "a loud-mouthed, unprincipled, profligate, and reckless man, whose only good qualities seem to have been the personal bravery and prodigal hospitality of his class, with undoubted skill as a hunter, and a degree of industry."[15] Graham quartered a gang of ruffians, mostly deserted sailors and illegally entered trappers. They were a wild group, often drunken and disheveled. Their playing of armed politics in helping one California governor unseat another, coupled with loose talk of an American-inspired, Texas-style takeover of California, led to their expulsion to lower (mainland) Mexico in 1840 in an international incident known as the "Graham Affair." They were not repatriated to the United States, however, and the central authorities in Mexico permitted the men to return to California.

The number of trappers and deserted sailors in California was relatively small. Forty-seven had been banished to Mexico in the Graham Affair, and these represented most of the Americans and British in California as of 1840 who were not engaged in some facet of commerce or ranching. The American consul, Thomas O. Larkin, estimated retrospectively in 1846 that there had been two hundred to three hundred foreigners in California as of 1832.[16] Bancroft estimated a total of 380 male expatriates as of 1840.[17] Almost all had arrived in California as sea captains, mates, employees in the otter or hide trade, or as merchants or commercial agents. Whatever their original purpose in migrating, by 1841 these Anglo-Americans were primarily engaged in mer-

[15] 3 HISTORY OF CALIFORNIA, *supra* note 11, at 763.

[16] Official Correspondence, Apr. 20, 1846, 4 THE LARKIN PAPERS: PERSONAL, BUSINESS, AND OFFICIAL CORRESPONDENCE OF THOMAS OLIVER LARKIN, MERCHANT AND UNITED STATES CONSUL IN CALIFORNIA 306 (Hammond ed. 1951–1968) (10 vols. & index) [hereinafter cited as LARKIN PAPERS].

[17] 4 HISTORY OF CALIFORNIA, *supra* note 11, at 117.

cantile or ranching pursuits. The 380 expatriates, divided about equally between Americans and subjects of Great Britain with a smattering of Frenchmen, exhibited far different characteristics from those of the arrivals after 1841; they are therefore referred to collectively as the "older residents."

Few Anglo-Americans became more thoroughly assimilated into a foreign culture than these male expatriates, who, as John Caughey succinctly wrote, "professed the Catholic faith, took California wives, learned and used the Spanish language, adopted California dress, Hispanicized their names, applied for naturalization as Mexican citizens, and conformed to the mores of their adopted land."[18] Their industriousness may have led to commercial success for these immigrants far greater than that of the native Californios. Yet, so thoroughly assimilated were they that Dana was moved to remark in 1835, with some hyperbole, that "their children are brought up Spaniards, in every respect [i.e., Mexicans], and if the 'California fever' (laziness) spares the first generation, it always attacks the second."[19]

Beginning in 1841 a new wave of population settled into California. This migration came overland from the East. Although coming from the same direction and through the same mountain passes as the earlier beaver trappers, the newer movement was entirely different from that of either the trappers or the older residents. These immigrants came in wagon trains, loaded with possessions and agricultural implements. This new immigration began slowly in 1841, when the thirty-two men, one woman, and one child who comprised the Bidwell-Bartleson party left Sapling Grove, Kansas, in May and arrived on the Sacramento River in central California in October.[20] Thereafter, the foreign arrivals in California swelled. Some continued to travel by sea. After the feasibility of overland travel had been demonstrated, however, the

---

[18] J. CAUGHEY, CALIFORNIA: A REMARKABLE STATE'S LIFE HISTORY 139 (3d ed. 1970). A recent study has suggested that early Anglo contact in New Mexico represented more of a "cooperative fusion" than a "clash of cultures" because of intermarriage with Hispanic women. *See* R. CRAVER, THE IMPACT OF INTIMACY: MEXICAN-ANGLO INTERMARRIAGE IN NEW MEXICO (1982).

[19] 1 DANA, *supra* note 9, (rep. ed. 1964), at 172.

[20] Firsthand accounts of this first overland migration include J. BELDEN, JOSIAH BELDEN 1841 CALIFORNIA OVERLAND PIONEER: HIS MEMOIR AND EARLY LETTERS (Nunis ed. 1962); J. BIDWELL, LIFE IN CALIFORNIA BEFORE THE GOLD DISCOVERY (1966).

numbers of overlanders from the East increased dramatically, from 38 in 1843 to 260 in 1845 and then to 1,500 in 1846, although the immigrants of that year arrived after the American invasion.[21] In addition, Americans traveled to California from Oregon in the early 1840s.

Bancroft estimated that the foreign males who arrived in California from 1841 to 1845 totaled 420, and that in the same period 120 departed or died, from both the older residents and the newcomers, for a net gain of 300.[22] Many of the new arrivals who remained had families. Population analysis for the opening months of 1846, on the eve of the American conquest and before the arrival of the extraordinarily large migration of 1846, must necessarily be approximate. An attempt is made in Table 1 and the accompanying explanatory note.[23]

The people arriving from 1841 to 1845 were different from the older residents in ways beyond their mode of travel. Most were farmers; many were crude in manner and, caught up in the heady emotions of manifest destiny, they became increasingly impatient with Hispanic institutions. Many brought wives and children. Certain that California would soon be American, they came

---

[21] J. UNRUH, THE PLAINS ACROSS: THE OVERLAND EMIGRANTS AND THE TRANS-MISSISSIPPI WEST, 1840–60, 119 (Table 1) (1979).

[22] 4 HISTORY OF CALIFORNIA, *supra* note 11, at 588.

[23] The estimates shown in Table 1 are higher than most others. Larkin estimated the foreign population including families at 1,000 to 1,200 as of April 1846. 4 LARKIN PAPERS, *supra* note 16, at 306. It is unclear whether he included Hispanic wives and children of the older residents in this total. Bancroft put the total non-Indian population at 6,900 for 1845. 4 HISTORY OF CALIFORNIA, *supra* note 11, at 649. Bancroft made a detailed bibliographic dictionary of persons present in California before 1848, encyclopedic as regards foreigners and a register of "all who acquired any sort of prominence in territorial or local affairs," as regards Spaniards, Mexicans and native Californios. H. BANCROFT, CALIFORNIA PIONEER REGISTER AND INDEX, 1542–1848, 23 (1964) (extracted from HISTORY OF CALIFORNIA [1884–90]). My detailed examination of local court records has revealed many, many persons, primarily Mexicans and Californios but foreigners as well, who were obviously present in California but not identified in Bancroft's lists. I am therefore convinced that his estimates are too low.

My figure of 10,000 non-Indians in spring 1846 is supported by the estimate of the well-informed military commander, Mariano Vallejo, who estimated 6,000 non-Indians in December 1841. This was after the arrival of the first small overland party but before the major surge of family travel from the East and Oregon. Letter of M. Vallejo to Minister of War and Navy, Dec. 11, 1841, in CINCO DOCUMENTOS SOBRE LA ALTA CALIFORNIA 11 (Mexico City 1944).

Table 1. Estimated California Population, Spring 1846

	Population	
Foreign-born		
Older male residents (wives and children not included)	360	
Male overlanders	320	
Wives and children of male overlanders	620	
Total foreign-born	1,300	
Wives and children of older residents	1,700	
Hispanic-Californio population	7,000	
Total non-Indian population		10,000
Indians and half-bloods in towns and ranches		7,000
Total California population excluding unassimilated Indians		17,000

to settle, to acquire land—if necessary, to steal it—and they had no desire to assimilate. Larkin noted that "many of them never expect to speak the prevailing language of the Country."[24] The overlanders tended to keep to themselves and not to mingle with the Californio population. Most did not even bother to apply for the passports legally required to maintain residence in the Mexican department.

Whereas the older residents were unfailingly polite and courteous to the local leaders, despite any private reservations or desire for a better-ordered government, these newer arrivals were brash and insolent in the limited contact they had with the Californios. Most of the historians who have studied this period have remarked on these differences between the newer, mostly overland immigrants and the more easily assimilated earlier expatriates who arrived by sea.[25] A well-educated contemporary ob-

[24] 4 LARKIN PAPERS, *supra* note 16, at 306.
[25] *See, e.g.,* CAUGHEY, *supra* note 18, at 144; L. PITT, THE DECLINE OF THE CALIFORNIOS: A SOCIAL HISTORY OF THE SPANISH-SPEAKING CALIFORNIANS, 1846–1890,

server also noted this contrast. Naval surgeon William Maxwell Wood wrote the secretary of the navy in early June 1846 that:

The ceremonious courtesies which characterize all classes of Spanish population place them in strong contrast with the rude simplicity of our emigrating frontier population, and from this rudeness of manner they infer ferosity of character. But those who visit their territory in ships are regarded with much more kindly feelings because from previous association with similar people, they have generally acquired something of the manner adopted to Californian intercourse.[26]

The differences in these groups have been stressed deliberately. Obviously they have important ramifications for the two elements of the expatriate community's dealings with the official legal system and for their own internal legal arrangements.

In the spring of 1846, Larkin estimated that three-quarters of the expatriates were Americans and of the balance the majority were subjects of Great Britain.[27] To speak of the expatriate community as an Anglo-American colony is not misleading. Arriving by sea, the older residents tended to live in the coastal areas, where many retained occupations dependent upon seaborne commerce. They were scattered throughout the department but were concentrated in the northern areas surrounding Monterey and San Francisco. The recent overlanders were almost entirely Americans, although they included among them a good number of German families who had previously immigrated to the United States and had since strongly identified with American ways, at least as contrasted to the Californios and Mexicans. In general, these newer arrivals avoided the settled regions and concentrated in the interior valley near Sacramento and along a line extending to San Francisco, then a small village called Yerba Buena.

A considerable number of the overlanders were employed by John Sutter in his establishment in present-day Sacramento, located at the confluence of the Sacramento and American rivers.

---

at 18–19 (1971); Hawgood, *The Pattern of Yankee Infiltration in Mexican Alta California, 1821–1846,* 27 PAC. HIST. REV. 27–31 (1958).

[26] Report of William Maxwell Wood to George Bancroft, Secretary of the Navy, June 4, 1846. Naval Records Collection of the Office of Naval Records and Library, Record Group 45, Records of the Office of the Secretary of the Navy, Letters from Officers Commanding Squadrons, 1841–86, Pacific Squadron, 1841–86, File 10–43–2. National Archives, Washington, D.C.

[27] 4 LARKIN PAPERS, *supra* note 16, at 306.

Some of the earliest overland immigrants had obtained land by grant from the government, but it became more difficult to procure grants after 1843. In addition, most of the recent arrivals were unwilling to acquire Mexican citizenship, a requirement for a government land grant. Thus most of the immigrants of 1844 and 1845 worked for other expatriates as foremen, loggers, and laborers, or farmed by squatting on public or private lands. The California ranches were huge by modern standards, a ranch of 10,000 acres being small. But to Americans accustomed to more intensive agricultural methods, many of the California ranches must have seemed unoccupied or abandoned.

Two of the foreigners deserve detailed description. They are Thomas Oliver Larkin, an American, and John Augustus Sutter, a Swiss. Sutter was born in 1803 but left Europe in 1834, one step ahead of his creditors.[28] After traveling through such varied places as Saint Louis, Santa Fe, Hawaii, and Alaska, he arrived in California in 1839, armed with letters of introduction to the Californio authorities. He quickly established a friendly rapport with Governor Alvarado, who viewed with favor Sutter's scheme to found a large colony and fort in the interior valley. Such an establishment might serve to check the Indians of the interior valley, who frequently raided outlying settlements, and at the same time block the power of a local political opponent, Mariano Guadalupe Vallejo, who had a large ranch and military establishment in nearby Sonoma.

In 1840, Alvarado granted Sutter a ranch of 11 leagues, approximately 50,000 acres or 76 square miles. He quickly converted his large holding into a heavily armed and nearly feudal fiefdom, which he named New Helvetia, or New Switzerland. In addition to the usual cattle operations, he trapped furs, planted an extensive acreage of wheat, built a distillery and a tannery, and devoted his considerable energy to a wide range of related economic ventures. After 1841, New Helvetia buzzed with the activity and comings and goings of Sutter's many Indian, Hawaiian, and American employees. Among his miscellaneous enterprises was a sawmilling operation at Coloma, California. In early 1848, during the

---

[28] 5 HISTORY OF CALIFORNIA, *supra* note 11, at 738. The best biographies are R. DILLON, FOOL'S GOLD: THE DECLINE AND FALL OF CAPTAIN JOHN SUTTER OF CALIFORNIA (1967); J. ZOLLINGER, SUTTER, THE MAN AND HIS EMPIRE (1939).

construction of this mill, one of Sutter's associates named James Marshall discovered the yellow flecks that set off the gold rush. The influx of gold seekers led to Sutter's ruin through the desertion of his employees and the looting and appropriation of his properties by squatters. He died in poverty in 1880.

In the early 1840s, however, Sutter was a private potentate of a personal empire. In addition, he held political status from the California government. He was appointed a local military commander and judge, with authority "to represent in the Establishment of New Helvetia all the laws of the country, to function as political authority and dispenser of justice, in order to prevent the robberies committed by adventurers from the United States, to stop the invasion of savage Indians and the hunting and trapping by companies from the Columbia."[29]

The American adventurers originally contemplated by the Californio authorities were the trappers, but beginning in 1841 the overland immigrants became a larger and much more dangerous horde of adventurers. Sutter was particularly well situated with regard to the new arrivals because his establishment in Sacramento stood athwart both the overland trail from the East and the southbound trail from Oregon.

Virtually every American overland immigrant had to pass through Sutter's domain. His distance from the Californio authorities and his military muscle enabled Sutter to treat the exhausted immigrants exactly as he wished, to aid them or to expel them. Sutter saw economic advantage to the influx of foreigners as increasing the value of his lands and as a source of inexpensive skilled labor. As a private landowner and entrepreneur he provided employment and dispensed advice ranging from methods of dealing with Californio officials to where and how to obtain land suitable for settlement. As a Mexican official himself, Sutter issued passports—until prohibited—permitting the immigrants to remain in California, conducted marriages, and resolved disputes. He sent out relief expeditions, as in 1846 for the ill-fated Donner party trapped in the Sierra Nevada, and gave emergency food and raiment to many arriving overlanders. Regardless of the motives behind Sutter's hospitality, the overlanders viewed his

[29] His commission is quoted in W. BEAN, CALIFORNIA: AN INTERPRETIVE HISTORY 83 (2d ed. 1973).

generosity as providential and many settled on the Sacramento River near Sutter's Fort. Not only were they near a protector and a source of employment, they were far removed from the ill-regarded Californio authorities and had as much daily independence as expatriates within a foreign land could expect.

Thomas Oliver Larkin arrived in California in 1832. A native of Massachusetts, born in 1802, he originally came to Monterey at the invitation of his half-brother, John B. R. Cooper, by whom he was initially employed. Within a year Larkin started in business for himself. Prospering from the first, he became one of the largest of the expatriate merchants and certainly the wealthiest in northern California. Conservative in nature, tight with money, Larkin nevertheless seized the opportunity his location in the capital afforded him and became intimate with the various California governors. In time he became well respected by the most influential and prominent Californios throughout the department. He also capitalized on his position at the seat of government by operating as a clearinghouse for many of the commercial obligations of the expatriate community. In a country without financial institutions, he operated much as a bank.

In two very important ways Larkin was different from the other older expatriate residents. First, he had an American wife. En route to California he had made the acquaintance on shipboard of an American woman, Rachel Holmes, who was traveling to join her husband. After they arrived, she learned that she had been widowed, and Larkin married her the following year. Their wedding, the first in California between two Americans, was performed on a ship off the port of Santa Barbara by the American consul to Hawaii. The second important difference is that Larkin never became a naturalized Mexican but remained an American citizen as a matter of principle. He relied on an annually renewed immigration permit for legal authority to remain in California. That lack of Mexican citizenship precluded him from a land grant, although he was able legally to acquire land by purchase. By careful trading and then skillful land purchases and management Larkin became a wealthy man. Unlike Sutter's experience, the gold rush magnified Larkin's riches. Fitting perhaps to his habit of constant work and display of nervous energy, Larkin had little time to enjoy his wealth, dying at the age of fifty-six in 1858.

Larkin's influence grew among the resident Americans as well as among the Californios, and in 1843 he was appointed the first, and as it developed the only, American consul to California. From that time until the conquest Larkin worked steadfastly for American interests, aiding individual American residents and visitors and attempting to persuade Californios that their best interests lay not with Mexico but in a close tie with the United States. He was appointed a secret and confidential agent of the United States in 1845, charged with inducing the Californios to transfer voluntarily their allegiance from Mexico to the United States.[30] Throughout the period between 1835 and 1846, Larkin remained on the best of terms with the Californio governors and frequently extended loans of cash and credit to the nearly bankrupt departmental treasury.

Larkin was frequently asked for legal advice by American expatriates, although as consul Larkin had no judicial powers other than in narrowly circumscribed disputes between seamen and masters of ships, a topic beyond the scope of this book.[31] As a young man, Larkin had served as a justice of the peace, but the matters he had handled, by his own account, were trivial.[32] Larkin should not therefore be regarded as a resident font of legal expertise. Indeed, it is to Larkin's credit that he generally refrained from giving legal advice and, even when pressed for an opinion, he declined to throw the mantle of his office about what he presented as personal views.

The expatriate community and two of its principal members have now been described. An account will next be made of the

---

[30] An excellent account of Larkin's official activities can be found in R. KELSEY, THE UNITED STATES CONSULATE IN CALIFORNIA, in 1 PUBLICATIONS OF THE ACADEMY OF PACIFIC COAST HISTORY 161–358 (1910). See also Beers, *The American Consulate in California,* 37 CAL. HIST. SOC'Y. Q. 1 (1958). For other biographical works concerning Larkin, see note 14, *supra.*

[31] "As a general rule principles of international law afford no warrant for the exercise of judicial powers by consuls; and their rights and duties in that capacity, both as to authority and extent, are dependent upon treaties," 2 C.J. *Ambassadors & Consuls* §42 (1915). The then current treaty with Mexico did not confer judicial powers to American consuls. Treaty of Amity, Commerce and Navigation, Apr. 5, 1831–Apr. 4, 1832, United States–Mexico, 8 Stat. 410, T.S. No. 203. Nor was a consular convention, contemplated by article 31, ever formed within this period.

[32] *See* LARKIN, *supra* note 14, at 48–50.

Mexican legal system itself, its Spanish origins, and its California variations. Organizational convenience requires that the California legal procedures be treated separately, and that the clash of values between the official system and the expatriates be deferred to a later chapter. Yet it will be helpful for the reader to keep in mind that these Anglo-American immigrants came from a culture that fostered individualism, and that their accustomed legal creeds fostered these values. The same certainly cannot be said of the Mexican judicial system.

2

The Mexican California Legal System

Spain had been conquered by the Arabs as early as A.D. 711, and it was not until the conclusion of a two-century struggle of *reconquista,* in 1492, that all of Spain was freed from Moorish domination. Naturally, this Arabic control for such a lengthy period made a permanent impression on the culture and institutions of Spain. The most enduring Arab influence on Spain's legal institutions was the local governmental official known to the Arabs as the *cadi* and to the Spanish as the alcalde.

As the office evolved in Spain the alcalde was a locally elected community official who served as both a mayor and a town judge. Additionally, he had some legislative duties and often presided over municipal councils. Almost always the town alcalde was the most respected figure in the community. He was usually a revered village elder, and his administration of justice was paternalistic and benevolently dictatorial. In municipal matters and local disputes the alcalde's word was literally the law itself, unfettered by substantive standards (legal rules) for the resolution of conflicts. He could decree as he thought fit, confined only by the cultural and religious mores of the local village in which he sat. Alcalde justice has been described appropriately as "a formalistic administration of law that was nevertheless based on ethical or practical judgements rather than on a fixed, 'rational' set of rules." [1]

The alcalde system was popular in Spain for the same reasons it would be later in the Spanish colonies. It offered a locally controlled justice system with extremely easy access, and it was not

---

[1] Hay, *Property, Authority and the Criminal Law,* in ALBION'S FATAL TREE 40 (Hay ed. 1975). Here, Hay is paraphrasing Max Weber's characterization of "khadi justice" and its comparability to that of the English justices of the peace.

burdened by legal technicalities. Any peasant could feel comfortable relating his viewpoint of a dispute to the alcalde.

Spanish colonial administration developed a many-tiered system of courts for New Spain and generated a confusion of conflicting jurisdictions. This abundance of courts administered a considerable body of formal substantive law. There was the famous *Recopilación de leyes de los reynos de las Indias* of 1680, which extracted more than 400,000 royal orders into a codification of 6,400 laws arranged into nine books.[2] There was also the *Novísima recopilación* of 1805 and many lesser-known compilations and digests of laws. In the commercial field a specific set of ordinances, the *Ordenanzas de Bilbao,* was made applicable to Mexico in 1792.[3]

The Spanish also introduced the alcaldes into the colonies and at the village level; for localized disputes between litigants of average means, the ordinary alcalde, alcalde ordinario, functioned in the same paternalistic manner, free from formal law, as in Spain.[4] On the eve of colonization, in the fifteenth century, Spanish villages were losing their rights to choose their own alcaldes, and at the same time there were pressures to reduce the alcaldes to a more minor status with a reduced jurisdiction. This was not firmly established, however; there were protests and some exceptions existed from town to town.[5]

This ambiguity, fitted to a period of transition, was carried over into the colonies and even much later into republican Mexico. The existence of the alcalde was always taken for granted in Spanish New Spain and the Mexico of our period. Many disputes

[2] A good general history of Spanish colonial law, especially as applied to Mexico, and of early Mexican law, is J. PALLARES, CURSO COMPLETO DE DERECHO MEXICANO (1901). More recent histories and compilations include G. FLORIS MARGADANT, INTRODUCCIÓN A LA HISTORIA DEL DERECHO MEXICANO (1971), and J. VANCE, THE BACKGROUND OF HISPANIC-AMERICAN LAW: LEGAL SOURCES AND JURIDICAL LITERATURE OF SPAIN (1943).

[3] Barker & Cormack, *The Mercantile Act: A Study in Mexican Legal Approach,* 6 SO. CAL. L. REV. 1, 6–7 (1932); Clagett, *The Sources of the Commercial Law of Mexico,* 18 TUL. L. REV. 437, 438–40 (1944). Both contain information on the promulgation and effect of the Ordinances of Bilbao.

[4] A good description of local Spanish colonial institutions is the chapter on the cabildo, or municipal corporation, in C. HARING, THE SPANISH EMPIRE IN AMERICA 147–65 (1963 ed.).

[5] J. ELLIOTT, IMPERIAL SPAIN, 1469–1716, at 93–94 (1963).

and changes as to the selection of the alcaldes and the extent of their jurisdiction took place, however.

When Alta California was first colonized in 1769 the colony was run entirely as a military outpost. The only settlers were soldiers, families of soldiers, missionaries, and a few artisans. Gradually the civilian population expanded, especially with the founding of the San Francisco presidio, which had a large civilian component, in 1776, and the beginnings of the civilian towns, or pueblos, of San Jose and Los Angeles in 1777 and 1781, respectively.

Felipe de Neve, the governor of Spanish California from 1777 to 1782,[6] issued the first detailed set of instructions for the governance of the civilian population in 1779. The king approved them two years later. This *reglamento* provided California with alcaldes, but with the proviso that the governor would appoint them for the first two years. Thereafter the settlers of each pueblo could elect their own alcaldes, but the individuals selected were subject to annual confirmation by the governor and his leave for continuation in office.[7]

Spanish California really never grew out of the stage of military outpost. Although the citizens of the pueblos gained more control over the selection of their alcaldes, the Spanish governors, who were also the military commanders of the province, continued their power over the alcaldes by a different route. They appointed direct military representatives, called *comisionados,* in each town, and empowered them to annul acts of town councils and decisions of the alcaldes. The office of the *comisionado* did not end until the success of the revolution in 1821.[8]

The alcalde system was popular in Spanish California. In the ordinary dispute there would be no need for military interference on the local level by the *comisionados,* although if a rare appeal

[6] The best biography is E. BEILHARZ, FELIPE DE NEVE: FIRST GOVERNOR OF CALIFORNIA (1971).

[7] These provisions are contained in title 14, section 18 of the Neve regulations, which are reprinted in translation as an appendix of R. POWELL, COMPROMISES OF CONFLICTING CLAIMS: A CENTURY OF CALIFORNIA LAW, 1760 TO 1860, at 235–50 (1977).

[8] Grivas, *Alcalde Rule: The Nature of Local Government in Spanish and Mexican California,* 40 CAL. HIST. SOC'Y Q. 11, 12–13 (1961), also appearing in T. GRIVAS, MILITARY GOVERNMENTS IN CALIFORNIA, 1846–1850, at 153–54 (1963); Guest, *Municipal Government in Spanish California,* 46 CAL. HIST. SOC'Y Q. 307, 312 (1967).

were taken it would be made directly to the military governor. Towns were extremely small. In 1820, Los Angeles had a non-Indian population of about 650 and San Jose, about 240.[9] Access to the alcaldes was easy, with no tangled legal formalities. There were no lawyers and no one expected the pueblo alcalde to know anything about the intricacies of Spanish law. He continued to function as the benevolent village elder, much as his fellow magistrates in the neighboring province of New Mexico have been described:

In legal proceedings, little attention was paid to any code of laws since, in fact, the magistrates had no law books or written statutes to guide them. Many were perhaps unaware that such existed. . . . By and large, judgment of the alcaldes, when it was not corrupted by personal interest or sheer malicious obstinacy, conformed to the prevailing customs of the country.[10]

Following the success of the revolution in 1821, Mexico moved slowly to implement a modern judicial system. After the brief period of Iturbide's empire had passed, Mexico adopted its first constitution in 1824. This established a federal system of government, with the various constituent states holding considerable power, and the national government having only enumerated functions. The dual sovereignties were patterned after the United States Constitution. Title V of Mexico's first constitution empowered district trial courts, circuit courts of appeal, and a national supreme court to deal with matters of national law.[11] The states were presumably to work out their own judicial systems. The geographic areas not yet sufficiently populated for statehood, including the Territory of Upper California, were under national control. Yet the constitution was curiously silent as to courts for the territories.[12]

Thus California began its Mexican period as a national territory, but without any national courts. To remedy this situation,

[9] 2 BANCROFT, HISTORY OF CALIFORNIA 349, 377 (1886) (1884–1890) (7 vols.) [hereinafter cited as HISTORY OF CALIFORNIA].

[10] M. SIMMONS, SPANISH GOVERNMENT IN NEW MEXICO 176 (1968).

[11] The 1824 Mexican constitution may be found in English translation in J. WHITE, A NEW COLLECTION OF LAWS, CHARTERS AND LOCAL ORDINANCES. . . . (Philadelphia 1839) (2 vols.).

[12] See discussion of this in H. CLAGETT & D. VALDERRAMA, A REVISED GUIDE TO THE LAW AND LEGAL LITERATURE OF MEXICO 222–23 (1973).

the National Congress by Act of May 20, 1826 provided for a legally trained district trial judge for Upper California. For appeals, California was joined to the state of Sonora as the Sixth Judicial Circuit and appeals could be taken to the circuit court, which sat in Rosario.[13] There is no evidence that a district judge arrived until 1834 or that any appeals from California were actually filed with the circuit court in Sonora.[14]

Meanwhile in California itself a plan was developed in 1824 for the disposition of both civil and criminal cases. The idea was to continue to try cases to the alcaldes with an appeal to the local military commander, with ultimate appeal, if desired, to the territorial governor.[15] The proposal sparked complaints of excessive military interference in the administration of justice and satisfied only a few.[16]

In 1834, Antonio Santa Anna, the recurrent dictator of Mexico, issued a decree for the establishment of district trial judges and circuit appellate courts, essentially based upon the 1826 legislation.[17] In that same year of 1834 a trained lawyer, Luis del Castillo Negrete, arrived in California to assume his duties as the district judge of California. Unfortunately, he became embroiled in local politics and left after only two years in office.[18] No national judge replaced him during all the remaining years of Mexican California.

Although other judges for California were appointed from time to time, there is no indication that any nominee actually was present and served as a judge. Throughout the Federalist period, California not only lacked trained trial judges but, until 1842, the legal procedures were merely a modification of the old Spanish

[13] The location of the appellate court, Rosario, is actually in Sinaloa and not modern Sonora. Sonora and Sinaloa were consolidated into one state during the years 1825 to 1831. The law in English translation appears in THE COMING OF JUSTICE TO CALIFORNIA 77–80 (Galvin ed. 1963).

[14] 2 HISTORY OF CALIFORNIA, *supra* note 9, at 677.

[15] *Id.;* W. HANSEN, THE SEARCH FOR AUTHORITY IN CALIFORNIA 7 (1960).

[16] Speech of Carlos Antonio Carrillo, Deputy for the Territory of Upper California, before the Chamber of Deputies, Oct. 18, 1831, translated and reprinted in THE COMING OF JUSTICE TO CALIFORNIA, *supra* note 13, at 52.

[17] *Id.* at 62–73.

[18] 3 HISTORY OF CALIFORNIA, *supra* note 9, at 466; H. BANCROFT, CALIFORNIA PIONEER REGISTER AND INDEX, 1542–1848, at 89 (1964) (extracted from HISTORY OF CALIFORNIA) (1884–1890).

system—alcalde trials with appeals to the California governor.[19] There was little innovation in the substantive law either. Old Spanish procedures and most of the Spanish substantive law remained in place. In 1835 a political faction known as the "Centralists" gained ascendency in Mexico. As the name implies, they favored concentration of federal power at the expense of state and territorial powers. Insofar as the justice system was concerned centralism meant less local and popular control over judges and more executive power over their selection and retention. By the end of 1836 the Centralists had consolidated their power and the Constitution of 1824 was replaced by a new charter called the Seven Laws. Military departments, of which California was one, replaced the states, and governors were appointed by the central government.[20] It was as a product of centralism that the most significant judicial legislation of the period was enacted, the laws of March 20, 1837 and May 23, 1837.

The first law, that of March 20, 1837, reorganized the office of the alcalde, stripping it of its traditional judicial authority and converting the alcaldes to local executive officials similar to mayors.[21] Their only vestige of judicial authority retained by this statute was over vagrants and disturbers of the peace. This same act established justices of the peace, and their judicial duties, together with some revived judicial responsibilities of the alcaldes, were clarified by the May 23 legislation.

---

[19] HANSEN, *supra* note 15, at 9; D. WEBER, THE MEXICAN FRONTIER, 1821–1846; THE AMERICAN SOUTHWEST UNDER MEXICO 38 (1982).

[20] In fact, centralism became even more despotic in 1843 with a new plan adopted under the name "Bases for Political and Constitutional Organization." See a general discussion of constitutional theory and the history of centralism in CLAGETT & VALDERRAMA, *supra* note 12, at 7–8.

[21] The complete Spanish text may be found in B. ARRILLAGA, 19 RECOPILACIÓN DE LEYES, DECRETOS, BANDOS, REGLAMENTOS, CIRCULARES Y PROVIDENCIAS DE LOS SUPREMOS PODRES . . . TODO EL AÑO DE 1837, at 202–34 (Mexico City 1839), and also in the appropriate volume of M. DUBLÁN & J. LOZANO, LEGISLACIÓN MEXICANA; Ó, COLECCIÓN COMPLETA DE LAS DISPOSICIONES LEGISLATIVAS . . . 1687–1910 (Mexico City 1876–1912). An English translation, although incomplete, is in Wilson, *The Alcalde System of California,* 1 Cal. 559, 560–66 (1852) (printed as an appendix). The problems with the translation are that the sections have been renumbered, not all sections of the statute are translated, and those sections that are translated are not all complete.

The most significant accomplishment of the March 20 enactment was the creation of the *prefectura,* the office of the prefects, and their deputies, the subprefects. These were the local representatives of the central government. Governors were appointed by the central government. In turn, the governor would appoint one or more prefects to serve for four years, subject to confirmation by the central government. The prefects in turn were to appoint subprefects to serve two years, subject to confirmation by the governor. During the Centralist period Alta California locally created two prefectures, one for the San Francisco District and another for the Los Angeles District. These prefectures usually had two subprefects each.

The work of the prefects and the subprefects was primarily administrative and executive in nature. Essentially they were subgovernors and deputies of subgovernors. The prefect could impose a fine of up to 100 pesos, or up to fifteen days of confinement at public works for those disobeying his orders, showing lack of respect, or disturbing the public peace. This was not a general criminal jurisdiction, obviously, but in aid of his executive powers. The subprefect had similar powers but was limited to fifty pesos in fines or eight days' confinement.

Beyond this, however, the subprefects were to propose candidates to serve as justices of the peace, who were then named to office by the prefect and confirmed by the governor. The justices of the peace could be removed by the governor, with the advice of the departmental legislative assembly. The prefects served as the repositories of laws, decrees, and miscellaneous orders and served as the means whereby new orders and laws were disseminated to the local level.

One particularly ambiguous duty of the prefect in relation to the courts should be noted. Article 70 of the Act of March 20, 1837 provided that the prefects "will arouse the courts to the most prompt and honest administration of justice, advising the governor of the faults they may observe in the judges; but they are not to meddle in the judges' functions." It would be difficult for any government official of any nation to properly discharge these sweeping responsibilities without some degree of meddling; the duties and the prohibition were inconsistent. Of course, to a society accustomed to the direct controls of a Spanish provincial governor, the provision would seem neither unusual nor bothersome. Nevertheless, it is important as background to the actual degree of prefect supervision over the California courts and the resulting Anglo-American criticism of the "improper" violation of their concept of the separation of judicial and executive powers.

The second significant act of 1837, that of May 23, expressly concerned judicial organization.[22] The provisions for the National Supreme Court can be passed over because that never concerned California. Each department, however, including California, was to have its own system of courts. At the head of the departmental judiciary was the Tribunal Superior, which, in the case of California, was to have four justices. They were divided into panels with the most junior member to serve as an intermediate appellate body, known as the "Second Instance," the trial courts being of the "First Instance." The three most senior members of the Tribunal Superior constituted the body that heard second appeals, or judicial actions in the "Third Instance."

Trial courts of general jurisdiction in both civil and criminal matters were established under the name "Courts of the First Instance." They were to be located in the capital of each department and in the chief town of every *subprefectura* that had a population more than twenty thousand. Since this was more than the total California population, by the express terms of the act a Court of First Instance should have been created only in Monterey. The departmental governor and Tribunal Superior were to designate the number of judges for each Court of First Instance, and, where there were more than one, civil and criminal jurisdiction was to be divided. The Courts of First Instance had jurisdiction only over the residents of their respective districts, which led to serious problems for interdistrict civil litigation.

The legislation contemplated that major litigation involving values of more than 200 pesos would be conducted by written process. This would entail significant formality, with pleadings

---

[22] The Spanish text is in Arrillaga, *supra* note 21, at 399–441 and in the appropriate volume of Dublán & Lozano, *supra* note 21. English translations are in J. Halleck & W. Hartnell, Translation and Digest of Such Portions of the Mexican Laws of March 20 and May 23rd, 1837, As Are Supposed to Be Still in Force and Adapted to the Present Condition of California 18–26 (San Francisco 1849), and Wilson, *supra* note 21, at 566–73. The cautions mentioned in note 21 as to the English translations of the first act are equally applicable to the translation of that of May 23.

and testimony reduced to writing. The Courts of First Instance had a somewhat abbreviated procedure, still involving a written process, for suits between 100 and 200 pesos. Litigants in this process would waive appeal except as to matters of procedure and jurisdiction.

As a condition to commencement of a lawsuit before the Court of First Instance the plaintiff had to show by a certificate that an attempt at conciliation had first been attempted in an effort to resolve the dispute. This relates to the alcaldes and justices of the peace since this same act of May 23 gave them the exclusive authority in their districts to act as conciliators. We review the conciliation procedure in a later chapter. It was itself a formal process with a summons and a judicial hearing. It was a Spanish concept, although perhaps Germanic in ultimate origin, and was designed to avoid formal litigation. The process had been codified by the Cortes, the Spanish legislative body, in 1812, from which legislation the Mexican enactment drew heavily.[23]

Unless the case were one not requiring conciliation—tax collections, bankruptcies, uncontested probates, and emergency matters such as injunctions were the most significant exceptions—even the most serious lawsuits would be commenced before an alcalde or justice of the peace. These lesser courts were also given emergency injunctive powers, but only as an aid to effectuate the conciliation process.

The act of May 23, 1837 also gave the alcaldes and justices of the peace a general civil jurisdiction over complaints that did not exceed 100 pesos and over criminal cases involving only "slight injuries and other similar faults" that warranted only "light rebuke or correction." Both of these jurisdictions, civil and criminal, were conducted by the verbal process and the procedures were quite informal.

In California, thousands of miles from Mexico City, the situation was quite different. California did not put into operation the prefecture system ordained by the 1837 statutes until early 1839, and the Tribunal Superior did not function until 1842. Before

---

[23] The Spanish text is in M. GALVAN, COLECCIÓN DE LOS DECRETOS Y ORDENES DE LAS CORTES DE ESPAÑA, QUE SE REPUTAN VIGENTES EN LA REPUBLICA DE LOS ESTADOS–UNIDOS MEXICANOS 50–51 (Mexico City 1829). English translations are in WHITE, *supra* note 11, at 419–20 (complete translation) and THE COMING OF JUSTICE TO CALIFORNIA, *supra* note 13, at 75–76 (fragmentary).

that time the traditional method of judicial operation—trial to alcalde, appeal to governor—functioned as it always had.[24]

Moreover, the differentiated system of trial courts never took effect in California. Distinct Courts of the First Instance were not established as entities separate from the traditional town judge. The chief impact of the legislation was to cause considerable confusion in nomenclature. Most town judges called themselves by the correct term of "justice of the peace." Others continued to call themselves "alcaldes," and some used the title of "judges of the First Instance." A few created hybrids, for example, "alcalde of the First Instance."

Only rarely would a civil defendant contend that the local judge trying his case had no jurisdiction because the judgment exceeded 100 pesos and demand that trial be held before a judge of the First Instance.[25] Equally infrequently would a smalltown justice of the peace refuse to hear a case seeking damages above 100 pesos and refer the case to a court in a larger town, such as Monterey.[26] These were unusual instances and the traditional town judges, the justices of the peace, in fact exercised the pow-

[24] For the beginning of the prefecture system, see 3 HISTORY OF CALIFORNIA, *supra* note 9, at 585–86. Appeals continued to the governor notwithstanding a provision in the May 23 statute that the National Supreme Court in Mexico City would pass on appeals until California had a Tribunal Superior.

[25] In a lawsuit over the outcome of a horse race, after an abortive attempt at conciliation, a Los Angeles justice of the peace appointed neutral experts and found for the plaintiff. The defendant appealed to the governor on the theory that the justices of the peace had no power in a case involving more than 100 pesos and asked that the matter be tried before a judge of the First Instance (knowing that there was none in Los Angeles). There was an issue of fact as to whether the bet involved was more than 100 pesos (how to evaluate a property bet; should side bets dependent on race results at issue in the lawsuit count toward the 100 pesos). The entire file was passed on to the governor with no indication of result. This was highly unusual. 2 Prefect Records of Los Angeles, at 4–28 (1839) [hereinafter cited as L.A.P.R. in style of L.A.P.R. 2:4–28]. These records are on deposit with the Henry E. Huntington Library in San Marino, California.

[26] An example is in letter of Jacob P. Leese to Thomas Oliver Larkin, May 23, 1845, 3 THE LARKIN PAPERS: PERSONAL, BUSINESS, AND OFFICIAL CORRESPONDENCE OF THOMAS OLIVER LARKIN, MERCHANT AND UNITED STATES CONSUL IN CALIFORNIA 191 (Hammond ed. 1951–1968) (10 vols. & index) [hereinafter cited as LARKIN PAPERS]. Justices of the peace were frequently ordered to serve against their will. It could well be in these rare situations of jurisdiction denial that a justice of the peace was as much trying to rid himself of a difficult case as to register a principled objection to jurisdiction.

ers of general trial jurisdiction, just as they had when known as alcaldes. This reality was recognized by a decree of March 2, 1843 authorizing alcaldes and justices of the peace in Alta California, Baja California, New Mexico, and Tabasco—Mexico's underpopulated frontiers—to act in the capacity of judges of the First Instance.[27]

To confuse matters further, local California politics, revolving around the dispute between the Centralists and the Federalists, resulted in the suppression of the prefecture system effective the beginning of 1844, but with a revival as of July 1845.[28] The judges' titles thus reverted to alcaldes for 1844 and the first half of 1845, returning in July 1845 to justice of the peace. During the temporary absence of the prefecture system the judges were elected and no longer appointed.

These changes in title and conundrums of jurisdiction have no great importance, and the reader need not follow them exactly. The prefect system, with its subordination of the alcaldes, was not part of the traditional Spanish-American legal system; it was not popular in California and had little real impact.[29] Regardless of title and how selected, throughout this period the California trial judge was the paternalistic town judge who had always functioned on the Spanish colonial frontiers. For practical purposes, the terms "alcalde" and "justice of the peace" are interchangeable and will be used indistinguishably hereafter unless a specific reference is indicated.

The Tribunal Superior, also required by the 1837 legislation, had a California career as checkered as that of the trial courts. Appointments were not made until March 1840,[30] and the tri-

---

[27] J. LARA, 2 COLECCIÓN DE LOS DECRETOS, Y ORDENES DE INTERES COMÚN, QUE DICTO EL GOBIERNO PROVISIONAL 357 (art. 28) (Mexico City 1850). The American California Supreme Court later recognized this authority in the alcalde and the justice of the peace. "[B]y articles 26, 27, and 28, of a decree made on the 2d day of March, 1843, Alcaldes and justices of the peace in the Departments of California, New Mexico and Tabasco, were empowered to perform the functions of judges of First Instance in those districts in which there were no judges of First Instance." Mena v. LeRoy, 1 Cal. 216, 220 (1850).

[28] 4 HISTORY OF CALIFORNIA, *supra* note 9, at 358–59, 533.

[29] Robertson, "From Alcalde to Mayor: A History of the Change from the Mexican to the American Local Institutions in California," May 1908, at 40 (Ph.D. diss., University of California at Berkeley, 1908).

[30] 3 HISTORY OF CALIFORNIA, *supra* note 9, at 605.

bunal did not begin its functions until May 1842.[31] Its chambers were in Monterey, which meant that it operated in the midst of the considerable political rivalry between Monterey and Los Angeles.[32] That made it difficult to convene a meeting of the court.

The appellate court did render several decisions and devoted considerable attention to judicial supervision during the years 1842–44. It seems to have been much less active thereafter, although the records of the tribunal are inadequate because many were scattered or destroyed. Perhaps it had become moribund by mid-1845; there were efforts in July of that year to call the court into session and to reorganize it, both of which efforts seem to have failed.[33]

There were few appeals in the Mexican California judicial system, and most of the judicial supervision was conducted by the prefects. The Tribunal Superior, perhaps unfortunately, played but a minor role. A profile of the justices and their backgrounds

[31] Circular Letter of Prefect of Los Angeles District, May 21, 1842, that the governor has announced that on May 20, 1842 the "Superior Court of Justice" (Tribunal Superior) was established. L.A.P.R. 2:708 (1842).

[32] 4 HISTORY OF CALIFORNIA, *supra* note 9, at 193, 295–96 has some of the details of the court politics. So also does 4 J. ALVARADO, HISTORIA DE CALIFORNIA, ch. 36, on file with the Bancroft Library, University of California, Berkeley, California. This history was written by Juan B. Alvarado, the governor who made the initial appointments.

[33] *Id.* at 4:531–32. But in the summer of 1845 Justice Malarín, of the California Tribunal Superior, opposed the judicial reorganization because the proposed plan included personnel changes that would deprive him of his position. On August 20, 1845, he protested that he had been "stripped of his employment." 42 Archives of California, at 394–97 (1845) [hereinafter cited as A.C. in style of A.C. 42:394–97]. These documents are on file with the Bancroft Library, University of California, Berkeley, California. This implies that until that time he had been working as a justice. It may be rhetoric, however. Malarín issued orders as late as December 25, 1844. *Id.*, 43:375–76. In July of 1845 a petition was addressed to the tribunal complaining of a particular trial judge's behavior. *Id.*, 42:189 (1845). Perhaps it could be said that there was still some minimal activity in 1845, although no opinions or orders from that year were found. One of the proposals in 1845 was to reduce the number of justices to two. As there is no evidence the court met as a body in 1845 or 1846, it is not clear nor is it important, whether the reduction was accomplished. For information on general judicial supervision in civil cases, *see* Chapter 4, notes 63–65 and accompanying text, and for criminal cases, *see* Chapter 3, notes 31–33, 37, 39, 41, and accompanying text, *infra*.

Table 2. Justices of the California Tribunal Superior
1840 Appointments

Justice	Background
Juan Malarín, Presiding Justice	Native of Peru; arrived in California in 1820; sea captain and later ranch owner. No legal training; no prior judicial experience. Wealthy.
José Antonio Carrillo	Born 1796 at San Francisco. Politician, government office holder. No legal training; brief judicial experience as alcalde before appointment.
José Antonio Estudillo	Born 1805 at Monterey. Government office holder, ranch owner. No legal training; brief judicial experience as alcalde before appointment.
Antonio María Osio	Native of Baja California. Government office holder. No legal training; no prior judicial experience.

appears in Table 2. It is apparent that most appointments to the positions, which paid well at 4,000 pesos annually, came from the ranks of politicians and government office holders. None had formal legal training and only two of the four had even brief prior service as a trial judge. Their appointment violated an express provision of an 1836 statute requiring every member of a Tribunal Superior to be a lawyer with at least six years of practice.[34]

Pursuant to the 1837 legislation, the town judges were appointed by the prefects, usually at the end of the year to serve for the following year.[35] The prefect then forwarded the names to the

[34] The biographical information is extracted from BANCROFT, CALIFORNIA PIONEER REGISTER *supra* note 18. The requirement for a position of justice on a Tribunal Superior may be found in ARRILLAGA, *supra* note 21, at 18:361–66 (1837).

[35] The prefect appoints two justices of the peace for Los Angeles, who will work pending approval by governor. L.A.P.R. 1:106 (1841); justices of the peace appointed for 1842, subject to governor's approval for San Luis Rey, Los Angeles, Santa Barbara, and San Diego. *Id.*, 1:265–67 (December 1841).

governor, who confirmed the choices.[36] At times the governor simply continued all existing judges in office for an additional year. This was done for the year 1840 by Governor Alvarado and for 1843 by Governor Micheltorena.[37] Local elections were ordered held in December 1843 for the selection of alcaldes during the brief suspension of the prefecture system.[38]

Major towns such as Los Angeles and Monterey had two justices of the peace (or whatever title they used) from the mid-1830s, as did even such lesser towns as Santa Barbara and San Jose from around 1840. By the 1840s even very small towns had at least one justice of the peace. In addition, there were substitute judges for any times of illness or absence of the regular justices of the peace. These men were often nominated by the judges themselves, subject to prefect approval,[39] as were the subordinate rural judges, who settled cattle-branding disputes and came into prominence at the spring brandings and late summer slaughters.[40]

One of the most interesting features of the Mexican California judicial system, and true throughout most of Mexico at this time, was that the appointed judges were compelled to serve without compensation and to serve for at least a year. Accordingly, there was much shuffling around to get out of the job. Requests to be excused were frequent,[41] but they could be and generally were re-

[36] The prefect writes the governor's secretary seeking approval of judicial nominations. 10 Monterey Archives, at 653 (1841) [hereinafter cited as M.A. in style of M.A. 10:653]. These records are on file with the Monterey County Historical Society, Salinas, California. The governor transmits approval of certain justice of the peace appointments. L.A.P.R. 1:509B (1841).

[37] Circular letter, prefect to justices of the peace, M.A. 9:755 (1840); Notice to the public, M.A. 16:615 (1843).

[38] 4 HISTORY OF CALIFORNIA, *supra* note 9, at 358.

[39] *See, e.g.,* M.A. 10:419 (1841). Prefect to justice of the peace of Branciforte approving justice's appointment of substitute judge.

[40] Prefect to justices of the peace of Los Angeles approving their nomination both of watchmen and a rural judge. Advise them that in judicial cases to follow your orders and in cases of policing to follow prefect's orders. L.A.P.R. 1:671A (1843). For a brief discussion of the role of the rural judge, see Robertson, *supra* note 29, at 75.

[41] *See, e.g.,* requests to be excused by Manuel Díaz of Monterey and Dolores Pacheco of San Jose, both in January 1846. Manuel Castro, *Documentos para la historia de California.* Documents 270–71 and 272–75. These documents are on file with the Bancroft Library, University of California, Berkeley, California. Manuel Castro was the prefect of the San Francisco District in January 1846.

fused by the prefects and governors.[42] A recalcitrant nominee could then be fined for refusing to act as justice of the peace. The necessity of pressure to induce persons to occupy public office may be a broader frontier phenomenon. For example, in eighteenth-century Plymouth County, Massachusetts, 7 percent of the public prosecutions in the Court of General Sessions were for refusals to serve in office.[43]

The governors made it clear to the prefects that a prospective justice of the peace had to justify with documents any claimed incapacity.[44] The only formal requisites of the statute were that a judge be at least twenty-five years of age, live in the district to which he was appointed, and be a Mexican citizen under no civil incapacity.[45]

Illiteracy was not a sufficient excuse, at least for a substitute judge. Although it is true that most of the justices of the peace were in fact semiliterate, since so much of their work involved the creation of written records,[46] at least one prospective substitute judge was informed by the Los Angeles District prefect in December 1841 that illiteracy was not enough to excuse appoint-

[42]See, e.g., A.C. 43:284 (1842); and discussion of Governor Pico's refusal to allow alcaldes in Sonoma to resign in 1845, in Albertson, "Jacob P. Leese, Californio," 157 (master's thesis, University of California at Berkeley, 1942); 4 HISTORY OF CALIFORNIA, supra note 9, at 632 (fines for refusing to serve).

[43]W. NELSON, DISPUTE AND CONFLICT RESOLUTION IN PLYMOUTH COUNTY, MASSACHUSETTS, 1725–1825, at 23 (1981) (prosecutions for refusal to serve).

[44]Prefect José Estrada writing on instructions of governor. M.A. 10:1089 (1842).

[45]Article 178 of Act of Mar. 20, 1837. For locations of text and translation, see note 21, supra. The formal requisites to be a judge of the First Instance were established in Law of Dec. 29, 1836. Such a judge must be: (1) Mexican through birth, with some exceptions, (2) a citizen in exercise of his rights, (3) free of conviction of any crime, (4) at least twenty-six years of age, and (5) a lawyer with at least four years of practice. These were the same formal requirements for the position of justice on a Tribunal Superior except that the candidate for that position had to be at least thirty years of age and a lawyer with at least six years of practice. ARRILLAGA, supra note 21, at 18:361–66 (1837).

[46]"The Mexican period of California has been neglected by historians, perhaps for two reasons. First, there is a language barrier. Most of the source materials are in Spanish, and a special kind of Spanish at that—often ungrammatical, misspelled, and full of commercial and legal terms. In addition, the research worker must deal chiefly with manuscripts, a fact that presents several problems. But the Mexican era is so important, and so interesting, that it is worth the extra effort to discover it." D. WRIGHT, A YANKEE IN MEXICAN CALIFORNIA: ABEL STEARNS, 1798–1848, at 1 (preface) (1977).

ment. "Even though in your former letter you stated that you could not read or write, I am informed by you yourself that you know how to sign your name . . . and this [is] sufficient, since your duty is nothing more than to substitute for the regular Judge, during his temporary absences when the necessity arises."[47]

Nor was economic hardship enough to be relieved of duty. When Joaquin Carrillo demurred to his appointment as judge for Santa Barbara, the prefect wrote in a huff to an associate, complaining of Carrillo:

[T]he reasons he gives to excuse himself from the office of Justice of the Peace of that District, to which he has been appointed, are not legitimate. . . . [H]e is ordered to appear without any further excuses and to take the oath of office in the usual manner. . . . [S]hould he consider himself injured, he may present his claims after taking the oath. . . . [H]is duty is to serve his country without fail.[48]

It was sometimes pointed out by Anglo-American contemporaries that there were no lawyers in Mexican California.[49] That is true for most of the period, but a little misleading. During the 1830s there were several trained and licensed Mexican lawyers present in California. As noted, Luis Castillo Negrete served as district judge from 1834 to 1836, and then left California. Even earlier, in 1830, another lawyer, Rafael Gómez, came to take up duties as the *asesor,* or legal adviser, to the California government. Gómez was replaced in 1834 but stayed on in California, dying in a ranching accident in the late 1830s. He was never given a judicial appointment.

An attorney named Cosme Peña replaced Gómez in 1834. Peña served as the legal adviser for about two years and then became a government secretary. He left California when his 1839 appointment as Los Angeles prefect was not confirmed by the central government. He likewise was never given a judicial appointment in California.

[47]L.A.P.R. 1:272 (1841).
[48]*Id.* at 221.
[49]W. COLTON, THREE YEARS IN CALIFORNIA 47 (reprint ed. 1949) (no "young" lawyers in Monterey in September 1846); W. DAVIS, SEVENTY-FIVE YEARS IN CALIFORNIA 85 (1929) ("The alcalde exercised the office of judge, jury, lawyers and all, inasmuch as no lawyers were employed; in fact there were none in the department."); G. SIMPSON, NARRATIVE OF A VOYAGE TO CALIFORNIA PORTS IN 1841–42, at 75 (1930) (no professional bar in California).

José Mariano Bonilla was another Mexican lawyer, very well educated, who arrived in 1834. He held a few governmental positions and was appointed as secretary to the Tribunal Superior, but served only temporarily. During the Mexican period his only judicial appointment was as a substitute judge for the small former mission village of San Luis Obispo. He later served as a regular judge during the American military occupation and under statehood he became a county judge.[50]

All this represented an unfortunate waste of talent. Many of these men could have made fine town judges or even justices on the Tribunal Superior. By the 1840s fewer lawyers were available to California. Manuel Castañares, California's deputy to the Mexican Congress, issued a detailed document concerning California in September 1844. He complained that there were no trained lawyers in California who could be appointed to the Courts of First Instance and the Tribunal Superior. With allowance for slight exaggeration, he was correct. Castañares went on to say that in the entire department there was not a single judge who was an attorney. In this he was absolutely right.[51] The lack of trained lawyers was chronic throughout Mexico. In the early Federalist period some Mexican states had as few as two or three attorneys within their entire jurisdiction.[52] The situation was worse on the frontiers. Neighboring New Mexico, with perhaps six times the population of Alta California, had only two attorneys during the entire Mexican period. One served as *asesor* for two years and left in 1834. The other was a district judge from 1832 to 1836. After that, there were none.[53] California was fortunate to have had as many as it did.

These judicial lapses—the failure to create appropriate courts, the confusion of jurisdiction, and the lack of trained personnel—

---

[50] Biographical information for these lawyers is from BANCROFT, CALIFORNIA PIONEER REGISTER, *supra* note 18.

[51] M. CASTAÑARES, COLECCIÓN DE DOCUMENTOS RELATIVOS AL DEPARTMENTO DE CALIFORNIAS (Mexico City 1845), reprinted in NORTHERN MEXICO ON THE EVE OF THE UNITED STATES INVASION (no pagination but under section "Poder Judicial") (Weber ed. 1976).

[52] CLAGETT & VALDERRAMA, *supra* note 12, at 211.

[53] Letter dated 1 January 1982 from Janet Lecompte to author, in author's possession. Ms. Lecompte has researched and published on the subject of the alcalde courts of New Mexico.

were much criticized by the Anglo-American expatriates. It is important to note here that the Californios were themselves displeased. When Santiago Argüello took the oath of office as prefect of the Los Angeles District in 1841, he referred in his inaugural address to the "lack of competent tribunals" and the "disadvantages which are the outcome of the state of the administration of justice at present."[54] California's representatives to the Mexican Congress repeatedly scolded the central government for the deplorable lack of California courts. Carlos Carrillo, in an 1831 address to the Congress, bemoaned that "it is easy to imagine, under such conditions, the tortures endured day after day by those wretched people [the Californios] for lack of Courts of Justice. They must accept unalterable decisions, from which there is no appeal, usually imposed by men who are absolutely ignorant of the simplest ideas of law."[55] Thirteen years later, although this was after the establishment of the appellate court, another California representative would likewise assert that California needed attorneys for its courts and that "the influence of a good administration of justice is not known in the country."[56]

Another interesting feature of the Mexican California judicial system was the number of foreigners who were appointed as judges or who were elected in the years before 1839 or for 1844. To be sure, they were naturalized Mexican citizens and drawn almost entirely from the ranks of the older residents. They were still foreigners. Table 3 shows the names of foreign judges and their nationalities for the towns of San Diego, Los Angeles, Santa Barbara, Monterey, San Jose, and San Francisco. It is probably incomplete in not including several short-term appointments of only a few months.

In addition, there were foreign alcaldes in San Gabriel (Reid, Hugo; Scot, 1843), Sonoma (Leese, Jacob P.; American, 1844–45), and doubtlessly in other of the lesser towns. Foreigners even reached the ranks of the prefectures, David Spence (Scot) being appointed a prefect in early 1846 and Abel Stearns (American) a

[54] L.A.P.R. 1:108–11 (1841).
[55] C. CARRILLO, EXPOSICIÓN . . . (Mexico City 1831), Speech of Carlos Antonio Carrillo before the Chamber of Deputies, Oct. 18, 1831, translated and reprinted in THE COMING OF JUSTICE TO CALIFORNIA 52 (Galvin ed. 1963).
[56] CASTAÑARES, supra note 51.

Table 3. Foreign Alcaldes and Justices of the Peace in Selected
California Towns, 1835–1846 (July)

Town and Alcalde or Justice	Period
San Diego:	
Fitch, Henry Delano (American)	1840 (first few months)
Ridington, Thomas (American)	1844 (substitute judge)
Los Angeles:	
Leandry, Juan B. (Italian)	1840
Wilson, Benjamin Davis (American)	1846 (auxiliary judge for distant areas)
Jordan, Louis (nationality unknown)	1846
Santa Barbara:	
Dana, William G. (American)	1836
Den, Nicholas A. (Irish)	1845
Monterey:	
Spence, David (Scot)	1835, 1839, 1840
Gilroy, John (Scot)	1835 (auxiliary alcalde for outlying area)
Allen, George (Irish)	1842 (auxiliary for outlying area)
San Jose:	
Burton, John (American)	1837 (acting judge for much of year)
San Francisco:	
Coppinger, John (English)	1839 (auxiliary for outlying area)
Hinckley, William (American)	1844
Ridley, Robert (English)	1846 (substitute judge) (briefly second justice of the peace in 1845)

subprefect, likewise in 1846. Larkin claimed that in 1844 the alcaldes of three-fifths of the towns in California were foreigners, although that appears a great exaggeration.[57]

The foreigners who served as judges were indistinguishable in actions from the natives. Leese, the American justice of the peace of Sonoma, at one point jailed another American for publicly criticizing the Mexican California government.[58] The expatriate judges administered their offices as Mexican institutions.[59]

The alcaldes also had legislative and executive roles and functioned in nonadversarial judicial actions such as bankruptcy and probate. Their authority in civil and criminal litigation is discussed in succeeding chapters.

During most of the Mexican period the usual municipal legislative functions, such as setting policy on streets, cemeteries, liquor regulations, street lights, and so forth, were controlled by the municipal council known as the ayuntamiento. This governing body was also directly concerned with water allocation within a pueblo and its outlying areas.[60] The local alcalde was its presiding officer and had both voice and vote.[61] After the establishment of the prefecture system, the ayuntamientos were abolished and the justices of the peace assumed their functions under the direction of the prefects and subprefects.

The alcalde was the chief executive officer of the municipality and was charged with the responsibility of carrying out municipal legislation and departmental decrees and statutes, as well as the national laws. On the local level he was particularly concerned with issuing passports and permits for dances, cattle slaughters, timbering, and other locally regulated activities. The alcaldes and justices of the peace engaged in correspondence with the prefects and were active in a variety of governmental concerns: monitor-

[57] Letter, Larkin to William Hooper, Mar. 22, 1845, 3 LARKIN PAPERS, *supra* note 26, at 84. Biographical information is from BANCROFT, CALIFORNIA PIONEER REGISTER, *supra* note 18.

[58] Albertson, *supra* note 42, at 144.

[59] See discussion in Robertson, *supra* note 29, at 93. The biographical information in Table 3 is from BANCROFT, CALIFORNIA PIONEER REGISTER, *supra* note 18.

[60] For an excellent study of water allocation, *see* M. MEYER, WATER IN THE HISPANIC SOUTHWEST: A SOCIAL AND LEGAL HISTORY 1550–1850 (1984).

[61] Further discussion of the alcalde's legislative and executive functions may be found in Grivas, *supra* note 8, at 17–19 and Robertson, *supra* note 29, at 60–86.

ing the activities of foreigners in their districts, gathering horses for a militia's retaliatory raid against marauding Indians, receiving complaints concerning the condition of roads, recording brands, investigating missing military weapons, or impounding liquor for nonpayment of taxes.[62]

A major portion of the alcalde's executive duties related to land grants. To be sure, there was litigation concerning land, and this is considered in the civil litigation chapter. There were non-judicial functions concerning land, as well. Town lots, or *solares,* were often granted to private individuals out of the town's commonly owned lands. This was an alcalde function in fact, although its questionable legality under the formal Mexican law was to occasion much litigation in the American years over the legitimacy of alcalde grants.

There was, however, no question of the legality of general land grants by the governor and the legislative body for ranches. Here also the alcalde had a role. The alcaldes usually put the grantees into formal possession. After the receipt of a written grant by the grantee, the local judge would survey the land with the new owner, mark the boundaries, and put the grantee into what was called "judicial possession." The town judges were also used to investigate uncertain factual issues regarding land grants. The maps used to plot the large ranches were so sketchy that when an applicant filed for a grant, disputes often arose as to whether in fact the land was vacant or whether it had been included in a previous grant and therefore was already taken. The purpose of the Mexican land grants, as with the later American homestead grants, was to foster economic development. Therefore, the Mexican grants all had conditions of improvement and cultivation attached to them. There could be an issue whether the conditions

---

[62]Activities of foreigners: justice of the peace of Branciforte to prefect, M.A. 11:347 (1843) (foreigners are going into the valley without permission); *id.,* 12:289, 559 (1844) (correspondence regarding lists of foreigners in their territory); gathering horses, *id.,* 9:887, 905 (1840); condition of roads, *id.,* 11:653 (1843) (military complains that someone is obstructing a street in Monterey); recording brands, *id.,* 15:260–61 (1838); missing weapons, L.A.P.R. 1:91–92 (1840) (San Diego); impounding liquor, M.A. 10:541 (1841). The reader should understand that the instances cited are simply examples which could be easily multiplied. Of particular interest to visiting expatriate sea captains was the alcaldes' occasional help in capturing runaway sailors.

of a previous grant had been met, for example, sufficient cultivation, so that it might be now available to another applicant. These
land grant questions, and any related problems such as water or
ditch rights, were handled on an administrative basis, not judicial, by the prefects and governors. In resolving disputed issues of
fact, they generally turned to the alcaldes and justices of the
peace as investigatory arms of the administrative process.[63]

It is clear that the alcaldes and justices of the peace were far
more than mere local judges. Their multiplicity of function added
to the foreigners' charges of "violation" of separation of powers.
"The fact that the alcalde combined in one man, judicial, legislative and executive powers seemed 'wrong' to the infiltrating immigrants from the United States, who had grown up under the belief that these three varieties of power 'should' be exercised by
different branches of government."[64] It was, nevertheless, a common frontier practice to combine these functions so as to achieve
economies of operation. Americans themselves had practiced it
in the New England colonies where

separation of powers was notably absent. Functions were assigned to
institutions without regard to the idea that courts ought to be independent bodies, distinct from the legislature and the executive. . . .

The county courts, as in Massachusetts, were more than courts;
they handled a wide range of what would now be considered administrative matters—tax collecting, road building, regulation of taverns
and ferries. They also handled probate affairs. This feature of county

---

[63] Two examples of this sort of land dispute: L.A.P.R. 1:182–95 (1844) (issue of
whether land was vacant); *id.,* 1:392–93 (1843) (joint petition of conflicting
claimants). The Los Angeles Prefect Records contain much more correspondence
and reports concerning land grants than do the Monterey records. Perhaps these
kinds of documents were removed from the Monterey records during the decades
of American land litigation, which was more pressing in northern California during the early years of United States administration. The best description of the
actual procedure of obtaining a land grant, the investigative roles of the prefects
and other subordinate officials, including the justices of the peace, and the conditions attached to grants is in R. Lounsbury, "Mexican Land Claims in California,"
2–15 (1940) (unpublished manuscript in National Archives, Washington, D.C.,
copy in possession of author). The process of using the alcalde as a kind of fact-
finder in land grant disputes apparently prevailed in New Mexico as well. Ebright,
*Manuel Martinez's Ditch Dispute: A Study in Mexican Period Custom and Jus-
tice,* 54 N.M. HIST. REV. 21 (1979).
[64] POWELL, *supra* note 7, at 30.

courts was quite typical in colonial America. It was replicated in other colonies too.[65]

There are two areas in which the California town judge functioned that are judicial in nature yet are not necessarily litigious: bankruptcy and probate. There were hundreds of lawsuits to collect debts in Mexican California, but very few bankruptcies in the sense of a formal administration of a debtor's assets for the benefit of creditors. There were also many insolvents. Perhaps it was because of the weakness of postjudgment remedies that debtors felt little pressure to initiate any creditor composition arrangements, while creditors simply sought whatever individual remedies they could arrange.

Two bankruptcies supply examples of the available techniques. One was in Monterey, where on April 21, 1844, George Allen, an Irishman, reported to the alcalde that Alexander Frere, an American, had just departed on a ship, leaving debts and creditors behind. The alcalde immediately ordered an inventory of Frere's assets; claims were submitted; some tools and 150 pounds of iron were turned over to a principal creditor, an Irish carpenter; and the alcalde ordered an auction of the remaining goods. The administration of the estate took about one and one-half months.[66]

Of course, not all insolvents fled, and an example from Los Angeles in 1845 is probably more representative. Here the insolvent petitioned the alcalde himself. The petitioner was Rafael Gallardo, a Californio who had held various local governmental jobs, including a year's service in 1843 as the Los Angeles justice of the peace.[67] He had no large land grant and therefore no signifi-

---

[65] L. FRIEDMAN, A HISTORY OF AMERICAN LAW 36–37 (1973); for additional discussion of the undifferentiated nature of the courts' duties in colonial Massachusetts, see Hartog, *The Public Law of a County Court; Judicial Government in Eighteenth-Century Massachusetts,* 20 AM. J. LEGAL HIST. 282 (1976). Aside from frontier practice, however, the Spanish had an almost especial disinterest in the notion of separation of powers. In both the Continental Spanish system and in New Spain, "from the highest government authority down to the municipal level, many officials were empowered to wield executive and judicial powers simultaneously and, in some instances, were even given legislative functions," CLAGETT & VALDERRAMA, *supra* note 12, at 101.

[66] M.A. 11:1182–85 (1844). A contemplated judicial bankruptcy of William S. Hinckley is mentioned in Letter, Larkin to Hinckley, October (n.d.) 1845, 4 LARKIN PAPERS, *supra* note 26, at 15.

[67] L.A.P.R. A:205–7A (1845).

cant wealth, but he did own and operate an orchard. It is fair to categorize him as within the respectable middle class, although such concepts are somewhat difficult of application to this pre-industrial society.

Gallardo told the court that he had no assets other than his orchard and his home, that creditors were pursuing him, and he asked the alcalde to call a meeting of creditors and to give him a year's extension of time for payment. He was careful to point out that his financial problems were not caused "by my idleness or tardiness" but only by the poor crop of the current year. He also had taken the precaution of getting the advance approval of two of his creditors. It is an interesting petition in many respects, but unfortunately there is not a clue of the final disposition. Gallardo owed a total of 2,289 pesos, about $25,000 in today's dollars, to nine different persons, as individuals and as representatives of various businesses. The analysis of the nationality and occupation of the creditors shown in Table 4 reveals the rich, cosmopolitan nature of commercial activity in Mexican California.[68]

In the tasks of settling estates, the town judges had three primary responsibilities. The first was as a holder of wills in the same manner that he was a holder of contracts, a function to be reviewed later. Second, he had general supervision over executors' administration of decedents' estates, in much the same manner as modern courts. Third, as a judge he would try litigation to settle inheritance disputes. This last aspect will be reserved for the civil litigation chapter.

In his function as a notary, contracts and other written documents could be created before the alcalde or written elsewhere and left with him as public documents. They then became automatically authenticated if needed for subsequent use. This procedure was used most frequently for land titles and contracts, for which the alcaldes functioned much like a modern recording office.

Although the practice of leaving wills with the alcalde was more frequently engaged in by the native Californios, some expatriates also deposited their wills with the alcalde or justice of the peace.[69]

---

[68] Biographical information is from BANCROFT, CALIFORNIA PIONEER REGISTER, *supra* note 18.

[69] Wills of Edward Manuel McIntosh (Scot), M.A. 11:569 (1842); José María Watson (English?), *id.,* 15:627 (1841). The dates indicated are the dates of the

Table 4. Names, Sums Owed, Nationalities, and Occupations of
Creditors of Rafael Gallardo, April 1845

Name	Sum Owed, Pesos	Nationality	Occupation
Narciso Botello	684	Mexican	Trader-rancher
Josefa Cota	600	Californio	Ranch owner
James McKinley	101	Scot	Trader
William Howard	49	American	Ship's commercial agent
Alexander Bell	142	American	Trader
Guillermo Celaya	200	Unknown	Unknown
Miguel Pedrorena	57	Spanish	Ship's commercial agent
Louis Lamoreux	56	Canadian	Carpenter
Jacob Frankfort	400	German	Trader

Judicial probate administration could be as formal as any today,
as shown in Pio Pico's service as executor of the estate of José A.
Yorba. A complete inventory was filed, as were many creditors'
claims and receipts for payment, a report by Pico to the alcalde
on distribution, and a judicial order.[70] Expatriate decedents' estates were also judicially administered, often by expatriate executors or administrators. William Hartnell (English) was the executor of the estate of John Mulligan (Irish); James Alexander Forbes
(English) acted in the same capacity for William Rae (Scot); and
Richard Laughlin (American) was appointed "receiver" of the
goods of another deceased American, Samuel Loring.[71]

wills lodged with the justices of the peace and the deaths of these individuals occurred years later.

[70] L.A.P.R. 2:189–203 (1844). Another formal probate procedure with estate
liquidation, creditors' claims, inventory, and wife's petition for allowance, is in
M.A. 5:542–72 (1842).

[71] Estate of Mulligan, Manuel Castro, *Documentos, supra* note 41, Document
12 (1834); Rae, A.C. 38:446–53 (1845); Loring, L.A.P.R. 2:108–13 (1842). Another example of an American taking charge of the estate of a fellow American is
John Temple's acting as depository of the goods of William Church, who died in-
testate in 1843. A.C. 33:120 (1844).

As American consul, Thomas O. Larkin played a special role in the settlement of American decedent estates. He notified parents and wives of their loved ones' deaths, assisted in the settlement of the small estates of American sailors who died in California in the midst of a voyage, and on one occasion counseled a dying American to make a will and thereafter forwarded the net proceeds of his estate to the man's family in Virginia.[72] In taking charge of these estates, Larkin was acting pursuant to his express statutory duties as consul,[73] and also in the tradition of one of the very earliest functions of a consul in a foreign land—a role going back to the Middle Ages.[74]

[72] R. KELSEY, THE UNITED STATES CONSULATE IN CALIFORNIA, *reprinted in* 1 PUBLICATIONS OF THE ACADEMY OF PACIFIC COAST HISTORY 199 (1910). Larkins was looked to by the Californios as responsible for the disposition of the effects of deceased Americans. For example, letter, Pedro C. Carrillo to Larkin, Nov. 14, 1844, in 2 LARKIN PAPERS, *supra* note 26, at 284. For other general discussion of Larkin's activities as consul, *see* Beers, *The American Consulate in California,* 37 CAL. HIST. SOC'Y Q. 1 (1958).

[73] It is a consular officer's duty to take possession of the personal estate left by any citizen of the United States dying within his consulate, to inventory the same, to pay debts owing, to collect debts due, and so on, providing local law or treaty permits and the decedent has no legal representative. 22 U.S.C. §4195 (originally enacted as Act of Apr. 14, 1792, ch. 24, §2, 1 Stat. 255).

[74] Irizarry y Puente, *Functions and Powers of the Foreign Consulate—A Study in Medieval Legal History,* 20 N.Y.U. L. REV. 57, 86–90 (1944).

3

Criminal Litigation

Of the hundreds of Americans and Englishmen present in Mexican California, it was inevitable that some would become enmeshed in the criminal justice system. For many it was because of their violation of the criminal norms. Others had their rights violated. They had been robbed or assaulted and sought vengeance through the local courts against the Mexicans, Californios, or other expatriates who had wronged them.

Fascinating questions arise about the experiences of these Anglo-Americans. Were they treated more harshly or more leniently than the local citizenry? Were the local authorities less careful in their investigations, less zealous in their prosecutions, when a foreigner was the victim of a crime? These inquiries cannot be answered accurately until the structure of the Mexican and Californian law of crimes and criminal procedure is studied and we understand how the system operated internally and without regard to expatriates.

The simple structure of all litigation in the period of Spanish California was well-reflected on the criminal side of the judicial docket. The hard-working town alcalde was relied upon for the investigation of crimes, for the trials, and for the sentencing of offenders. This elected, venerable, multifunctional official was often assisted by an investigatory commission, especially in such serious crimes as murder. The ultimate judicial responsibility at the trial level was the alcalde's. Procedural rules were simple, with substantive criminal law only vaguely defined—at least on Spain's frontier—and appeals were to the provincial governor and almost always limited to the degree of sentencing. Appeal beyond the limits of California was rare except in capital cases where the sentence was often reviewed by the viceroy in Mexico City or by the court of the audiencia.

The Mexican Revolution's success in 1821 did not produce

much change in substantive criminal law, that portion of the law defining what conduct amounts to a crime. Although the Mexican congresses passed a variety of penal regulations between 1821 and 1857, the bases of the criminal law are not found until the constitution of 1857, well after the American conquest in 1846. In fact, the first Mexican criminal code did not appear until 1871.[1]

Courts in Mexican California rarely articulated their views as to substantive criminal law. For a higher level of offense they proceeded on the basis of community understanding as to what was a *malum in se,* an inherently wrongful act; murder, rape, robbery, assault, or misbranding cattle are examples. For less severe offenses, there was a mass of regulations issued by the alcalde and the ayuntamiento (city council). Following the suppression of the Federalist system by the legislation of 1837, the prefects, subprefects, and justices of the peace assumed the task of local regulation.

There was tight local control: licenses were to be obtained before holding a private dance; passports issued before leaving the town's vicinity; lights kept at night in front of stores; cattle slaughtered only at prescribed times; and liquor sold only at approved times and in regulated amounts. These local ordinances were endless. If Mexican California suffered from weak government at its departmental level, it was fairly tied by an excess of government in its localities. Offenses against these kinds of regulations were handled summarily and usually resulted in a small fine, with perhaps a day or two in jail for repeat offenders. Many of these punishments were given by the prefects and subprefects pursuant to their summary powers, as well as by the justices of the peace.

The law of criminal procedure is distinct from the crime-defining substantive law. Here the Mexican law was clear, at least in theory. The two major statutes of 1837 thoroughly reformed and clearly defined the appropriate procedures for Mexican courts, including those in California. Both were a product of the ascendency in Mexico of a political faction, the Centralists, dedicated to stronger executive and more concentrated political power, over the Federalists, whose principles called for decentralization and dispersal of power.

The March 20, 1837 law deprived the alcaldes of most of their

---

[1]H. CLAGETT & D. VALDERRAMA, A REVISED GUIDE TO THE LAW AND LEGAL LITERATURE OF MEXICO 172 (1973).

traditional judicial authority and converted them to local executive officials comparable to mayors. This was as true for their criminal jurisdiction as for their civil. Notwithstanding, they still retained authority to punish breach of the peace, drunkenness, and contempt of their own executive authority by fines of up to twenty-five pesos and as much as four days at public works.[2]

The May 23, 1837 law dealt specifically with the judiciary and created an entire panoply of courts. The lowest courts of general jurisdiction, criminal as well as civil, were denominated Courts of the First Instance.[3] Criminal sentences were reviewable by Courts of Second Instance and Third Instance, and theoretically one appeal as to sentence was mandatory. Each department, including California, was to have its own system of courts of First, Second, and Third Instance.

Alcades and justices of the peace held inferior jurisdictions limited to trial of only those criminal matters "respecting trifling injuries and other similar faults that do not merit any other punishment than a slight reprehension or correction." These offenses were nowhere cataloged by conduct, with the result that a justice of the peace's personal view of culpability and appropriate punishment could, in theory at least, concurrently determine his jurisdiction. Additionally, the May 23 legislation provided that alcaldes and justices of the peace were to handle the conciliation procedures prerequisite to private prosecution for personal injuries and were empowered in emergencies or under authorization from the Court of the First Instance to undertake the "first steps" in other criminal cases, a phrase that is not clear but probably

[2] Law of Mar. 20, 1837, *reprinted in* Wilson, *The Alcalde System of California,* 1 Cal. 559, 560 (1852) (incomplete text printed as an appendix). A printing of the complete Spanish text may be found in 19 B. ARRILLAGA, RECOPILACIÓN DE LEYES, DECRETOS, BANDOS, REGLAMENTOS, CIRCULARES Y PROVIDENCIAS DE LOS SUPREMOS PODERES . . . TODO EL AÑO DE 1837, 202 (Mexico City 1839), and also in the appropriate volume of M. DUBLÁN & J. LOZANO, LEGISLACIÓN MEXICANA; Ó, COLLECIÓN COMPLETA DE LAS DISPOSICIONES LEGISLATIVAS . . . 1687–1910 (Mexico City 1876–1912).

[3] Decree of May 23, 1837. The incomplete text is reprinted in J. HALLECK & W. HARTNELL, TRANSLATION AND DIGEST OF SUCH PORTIONS OF THE MEXICAN LAWS OF MARCH 20TH AND MAY 23RD, 1837, AS ARE SUPPOSED TO BE STILL IN FORCE AND ADAPTED TO THE PRESENT CONDITION OF CALIFORNIA 20 (San Francisco 1849). This decree was likewise reprinted in English in Wilson, *supra* note 2, at 566–73, and in Spanish in ARRILLAGA, *supra* note 2, at 19, 399–441. It may also be found, in Spanish, in DUBLÁN & LOZANO, *supra* note 2.

was intended to include such matters as autopsies, preliminary depositions, and initial incarcerations.[4]

This elaborate judicial structure was imperfectly implemented in California. The appellate court designated as that of the Third Instance in the May 1837 legislation, the Tribunal Superior, was not actually functional in California until 1842. Until it was organized, appeals as to sentence continued to be made to the governor. General supervisory powers over the trial courts were in the prefects and subprefects.

The trial courts were even less affected by the 1837 Centralist legislation than the appellate tribunal. The courts of First Instance were never formally established, and the low-level town judges continued to adjudicate all criminal matters without limitations of jurisdiction. They sometimes called themselves "judges of the First Instance," but other times they referred correctly to themselves as *jueces de paz* (justices of the peace), or less frequently by the traditional title of alcalde. The titles were sometimes mixed, but it was the same position whatever it was called. The larger towns of Los Angeles and Monterey frequently had two judges. When this was so, one of the judges, called the second *juez de paz,* would supervise initial incarceration, investigation, and guilt determination, while the first justice of the peace would pronounce sentence. When a serious criminal case arose in one of the smaller towns near Monterey that had only one justice of the peace, the local judge often would confine his activities to the taking of depositions and other investigation, and would then remand the defendant and the completed investigation to the judge in Monterey.

Criminal matters typically were initiated by a complaint to the *juez.* The accusation could be made by a private citizen,[5] or by the prefect.[6] Occasionally these prefects, the subprefects, or even

---

[4] A set of 1824 instructions for California alcaldes indicates that these are within the preliminary matters. H. BANCROFT, CALIFORNIA PASTORAL 576–80 (1888).

[5] See, for example, Castro's complaint of assault made to the alcalde in 1837. 7 Monterey Archives, at 1462 (1837) [hereinafter cited as M.A. in style of M.A. 7 : 1462]. These records are on file with the Monterey County Historical Society, Salinas, California.

[6] For example, the report of the prefect to the justice of the peace of the first Instance of Los Angeles on Mar. 21, 1842: "Yesterday I saw Señor Enrique Sepúlveda beat an Indian named Tomás, a servant of Señor José María Aguilar, with his sword and trample him with his horse. I report the above to you in order that you

the governor himself, would simply order the *juez* to initiate a criminal action against a defendant.[7] This was not as common as a citizen complaint, however.

If the alleged culprit were within the judge's territorial district, the *juez* would simply summon him for detention or bail, but in either event would begin the investigatory process. If the defendant had fled, the judge requested aid in making an arrest. Judges could request that a military commander[8] or the governor[9] make an arrest and return a defendant to the court in which an accusation was pending. This cooperation was routine, and there is frequent correspondence in the judicial records from military commanders relating to the transportation of prisoners wanted by the civilian criminal courts.[10] The prefects were also involved in arrests out of a judge's district, and there is much correspondence back and forth between prefects and judges about the whereabouts of various culprits and requests from prefects to alcaldes to make arrests on behalf of a different district.[11]

There were no professional police, but there were citizen patrols in the larger towns and in certain rural areas. Presumably the alcaldes and prefects could call on their services to make arrests.[12] A frequent form of requested aid in arrest was therefore

---

may make the necessary investigations as to who was the provoker or guilty one in this quarrel." 1 Prefect Records of Los Angeles, at 596–97 (1842) [hereinafter cited as L.A.P.R. in style of L.A.P.R. 1:596–97]. These records are on deposit with the Henry E. Huntington Library in San Marino, California.

[7]The prefect of the Northern District reported complaints of theft by one Agustín Hernández, and in consequence ordered the justice of the peace in Branciforte (Santa Cruz) not to permit him to sow crops. M.A. 10:9, 13 (1841). For examples of communications, governor to prefect and governor to judge, ordering arrests, see 43 Archives of California, at 255, 257 (1841) [hereinafter cited as A.C. in the style of A.C. 43:255, 257]. These documents are on deposit with the Bancroft Library, University of California, Berkeley, California.

[8]M.A. 10:1263 (1842).

[9]L.A.P.R. A:32 (1835).

[10]For example on July 23, 1842, the commander of the Monterey guard, Floriano Silva, reported to the Monterey judge that a soldier had been dispatched to the nearby community of San José Castro to conduct a prisoner to Monterey as the judge had requested in his note of the previous day. M.A. 10:1307 (1842).

[11]*See, e.g.,* Santa Cruz judge to prefect, July 20, 1840 (the man you wanted is not here; he left for Monterey), *id.,* 9:877 (1840); prefect to Monterey judge, Sept. 25, 1840 (Ygnacio Acedo wanted from your jurisdiction; put him in prison, seizing any arms you find in his control), *id.,* 9:1085 (1840).

[12]For example, a force of twenty men was established in July 1840 to prevent

from one judge directly to another. Thus, for example, the *juez* of Santa Cruz wrote his equivalent in Monterey in 1839, requesting the appearance of a defendant;[13] the "Justice of the Peace of the First Instance" of Santa Barbara cautioned the second justice of the peace of Los Angeles in 1842 that a named foreigner from New Mexico had stolen mules and was headed toward his city;[14] and in 1844 the San Jose judge advised his counterpart in San Francisco that it was "indispensable" that a certain defendant "appear in this court in order to respond to accusations."[15]

Upon the arrest and incarceration of the defendant, the judge had two immediate responsibilities. The first was the question of whether to release the defendant upon sufficient surety bond. The second and more important responsibility was that of investigation of the crime itself, a function which, far contrary to common law notions, was undertaken by the judge.

The law required that within three days following arrest the prisoner be given a declaration of the cause of the proceedings against him and, if possible, the names of his accusers. Mere suspicion was enough to authorize an arrest, but thereafter a further step was necessary. When the judge's investigation disclosed both that a crime had occurred that merited bodily punishment and not merely a fine, and second, that there were motives or indications sufficient to believe that the prisoner had committed the criminal act, then the judge declared the prisoner *bien preso,* meaning that he was properly imprisoned.[16]

After the formation of the Tribunal Superior these arrest procedures were closely followed, and defendants were released because of their violation. Most societies produce at least a few extraordinarily conscientious judges and Mexican California was no exception. On Christmas Eve, 1844, Juan Malarín, the presiding

robberies by a patrol between San Jose and San Juan de Castro. A.C. 43:172 (1840). Analogously, the prefects from time to time appointed citizens to make specific investigations. For example, on Oct. 21, 1840 the Los Angeles prefect ordered certain named citizens to go to Abel Stearn's house to search for smuggled goods. L.A.P.R. 1:67 (1840).

[13] M.A. 9:575 (1839).

[14] L.A.P.R. 2:451 (1842).

[15] Official Documents Relating to Early San Francisco. 1835–1857. Document 84 (1844) [hereinafter cited as O.D.R.E.S.F.]. These documents are on file with the Bancroft Library, University of California, Berkeley, California.

[16] 18 ARRILLAGA, *supra* note 2, at 361–66 (1837).

justice of the Tribunal Superior, visited the Monterey jail where he encountered a prisoner by the name of Pablo Juan. Pablo had been imprisoned for nineteen days and not notified of the cause for which he was jailed or whether he had been declared *bien preso*. The next day, on Christmas, Malarín penned an order to the judge of the First Instance, in which he cited the law that prohibited detention for more than three days without a declaration of *bien preso*, ordered the judge to put Pablo Juan at liberty immediately, and expressed the "hope that there will be no repetition of this fault."[17]

In theory a defendant was subject to imprisonment pending final guilt determination and sentencing if the ultimate sentence could be greater than a fine. After arrest, if the evidence suggested that the prisoner should not be punished with a bodily punishment but only a fine, the defendant was entitled to be released forthwith.[18]

Most jails were filthy, however, and they were also unreliable places of detention because of the ease of escape. Probably for these reasons defendants charged with less heinous crimes were frequently admitted to bail even though the charges carried potential sentences of more than fines. The bail process required one or more responsible persons in the community to give surety in a stated sum for the defendant's return, together with the promise to keep control of the defendant in the interim. Release on surety was permitted, for example, on charges of assault with a knife, robbery, and embezzlement.[19]

Even if bail were not granted, a defendant could subsequently ask for a pre-guilt-determination release based upon various equitable factors. Thus one San Francisco man, apparently charged with beating his wife, sought release in 1846 because his wife had recovered and, in any event, it was time for him to sow his crops. The judicial response to this plea was not recorded. A prisoner in the Los Angeles city jail petitioned for freedom in 1844 because his sons were sick and "being cared for out of charity." He was

[17] A.C. 43:375–76 (1844); another prisoner was freed by Malarín in November 1844 because of excessive time of detention. A.C. 43:377 (1844).

[18] 18 ARRILLAGA, *supra* note 2, at 361–66.

[19] M.A. 4:97 (1843); *id.,* 8:313 (1845); *id.,* 3:527–28; and *id.,* 4:178–243 (1843). This last case, the embezzlement matter, involved an expatriate victim, an expatriate defendant, and an expatriate surety.

released on surety bond for the duration of their illness.[20] In a robbery case a Monterey defendant was released to his home after five months in jail because of extreme illness.[21]

The process of investigation went on simultaneously. This was conducted by the *juez,* primarily by obtaining oral statements from the defendant, the victim, and any witnesses, which were transcribed by the judge or an assistant into a dossier on the case. This dossier was known as the *sumaria.* Neither prosecutor nor defense counsel was involved at this level. There was very little legal maneuvering at this stage, which was primarily one of simple fact gathering.

Occasionally, however, the rare legal issue was interjected into the investigatory process. In 1842 a murder defendant attempted to disqualify the judge for bias in the opening phase of his investigation because of an earlier civil case in which the same judge had ordered the defendant's goods seized. The alcalde referred the question of disqualification to the prefect, who advised this was an insufficient excuse for challenge and that the alcalde's judicial investigation should go forward.[22] California had no professional bar but usually enjoyed the services of a single professional lawyer, the *asesor,* who served as an adviser to the departmental government. It does not appear that the *asesor* ever served as a regular prosecutor, but limited his involvement in criminal matters to advice as to sentencing. On at least one occasion, however, the *asesor* advised the investigating judge that no crime had been committed and that there were defects in the investigatory process in that a declaration had been taken from a witness under the age of twenty. Relying on this, the alcalde dismissed the pending charges.[23] This involvement was highly unusual, however.

Crimes tended to be localized in the rural society of Mexican California. Generally the alcalde had only to summon witnesses from the area surrounding the town in which he held his office to require their appearance and the giving of a declaration. If a witness lived in a different geographical jurisdiction, the statement

[20] O.D.R.E.S.F. Document 138 (1846) *supra* note 15, (wife recovered); L.A.P.R. A:201–2 (1844) (children ill).

[21] M.A. 3:829, 878–79 (1843).

[22] *Id.,* 10:1005, 1007 (1842 prosecution of Manuel Gonzales, who was subsequently executed).

[23] *Id.,* 2:46–62 (1835). The crime charged is illegible in the *sumaria.*

would properly be given before the judge of the town in which district the witness resided, and the May 23 law specifically so provided. Unless the witness voluntarily cooperated by traveling to the requesting *juez,* the investigating judge would have to ask the other district's alcalde to take a statement or, failing that, ask the prefect for help in getting witnesses to appear for declarations. This cumbersome procedure generated considerable correspondence and confusion.[24]

No counsel was appointed until the judge was convinced of the probability of the defendant's guilt and declared him *bien preso,* or properly imprisoned. Then both defensor and fiscal (prosecutor) were appointed, at least if the case were capital or potentially so. The defendant apparently could nominate his own defense attorney.[25] Because there were no trained lawyers, an appraisal of two representative persons appointed as prosecutors in serious cases is instructive: the prosecutor of Manuel Gonzales, charged with murder, was José Abrego, a hatter, merchant, and departmental treasurer, and for William Day, charged with a nearly fatal knife assault, it was Felipe Castillo, a cigar maker and trader.[26]

The import of this is not that these were bad choices but simply that legal expertise was not readily available. Unlike judges, who were required to accept appointment as a *juez,* individuals could decline to act as defense counsel or prosecutor.[27] Apparently there were a significant number of refusals because the Los Angeles prefect complained to the governor in July 1835 that there were several criminal cases pending, but "no one here willing to accept the nomination and truly capable of performing" as a prosecutor.[28]

[24] For examples, both from murder cases, letter from *juez* to prefect asking for help in getting witnesses in for declarations, M.A. 16:386 (1842) and letter of *juez* advising that a particular witness is not in Monterey and the judge to ask for help is the one in Santa Cruz. *Id.,* 10:1337 (1842).

[25] Gil Sánchez, charged with murder, nominated an individual as defense attorney who was thereafter appointed by the court. *Id.,* 10:1293 (1842).

[26] Gonzales, *id.,* 3:371 (1842); Day, D. WRIGHT, A YANKEE IN MEXICAN CALIFORNIA, ABEL STEARNS: 1798–1848, at 68–70 (1977) (1835 incident). Biographical information from H. BANCROFT, CALIFORNIA PIONEER REGISTER AND INDEX: 1542–1848, at 26, 89 (1964) (extracted from HISTORY OF CALIFORNIA (1884–1890)).

[27] Letter of Pablo de la Guerra, May 28, 1842, declining to defend a prisoner, M.A. 10:1213 (1842). Letter of appointment of prosecutor, July 7, 1835, containing language "should you accept this appointment." L.A.P.R. A:34 (1835).

[28] L.A.P.R. A:36 (1835).

Both prosecution and defense were based on the dossier accumulated during the investigation, not on a trial in the common law sense. The only issue that appears to have been vigorously argued was sentence, not guilt itself, which was not often in serious dispute. This does not mean that the representation by counsel was a sham. Communal mores and standards were in the forefront. In the murder case of Manuel Gonzales the defense argued that the defendant was provoked and angered and asked for mercy, and the fiscal just as vigorously pointed out that the victim was a hard worker and a family man. The result was the defendant's execution.[29] Gil Sánchez was tried for a different murder at about the same time. His defensor argued that the defendant was honorable and quiet, and the decedent was much complained of in the community as a bully. He had insulted and hassled the defendant and had even robbed Sánchez's assistant. The defensor probably did not need to mention, and he did not, the fact that Sánchez, unlike Gonzales, was significantly propertied and the owner of a land grant rancho. The result in this case, unlike that of Gonzales, was a sentence to the time already served, approximately six months.[30]

After the sentence by the justice of the peace, the defendant could appeal. Indeed, one appeal was required by the 1837 legislation in criminal matters. It is easier to understand the Californian criminal appellate procedure and judicial supervisory process in the light of two very different factors: an ambiguous statute and some specific history.

According to the March 20, 1837 law, the local judges were to be named by the prefects on the recommendation of the subprefects. That same law charged the prefects with the responsibility to stimulate the courts to a prompt and correct administration of justice, with a duty to report all defects in the judges to the governor. At the same time, however, the prefects were specifically enjoined not to meddle with the functions of the judges. These ambiguous general duties and the specific prohibition against meddling are, of course, somewhat inconsistent.

During its Spanish period California had been governed as a military frontier. The governor was also the military comman-

[29]M.A. 3:314–418 (1842).
[30]Id., 3:649–715 (1842).

dant. Although village alcaldes were established as early as 1781, twelve years after the colony's founding, any criminal matter of real importance was appealed to and ultimately decided by the governor. The tradition of executive review of judicial acts continued after independence through the governors and the prefects.

There was a significant blending of judicial and executive functions, or what the common law legal mind would regard as such, at least until the 1842 founding of the California appellate court, the Tribunal Superior. Given the broad supervisory powers over the courts allowed to the prefects by the 1837 legislation, the requirement in this same act that there be at least one appeal in criminal causes, and the earlier Spanish pattern of procedure in frontier California, what would be more natural than to have constant appeals to, and review of the alcaldes' work by, executive officials—the subprefects, the prefects, and the governors.

The judicial cases before the establishment of the Tribunal Superior contain many writings from the judges to the prefects asking for their opinions or requesting consultations about proposed courses of action. The prefects and subprefects kept a tight rein on the alcaldes, requiring performance of their administrative duties, such as reporting lists of prisoners or outlining for a judge the law applicable to a particular case. Alcaldes were fined for such misfeasances as permitting card playing in a tavern on Sunday, and, in one instance, a special judge was appointed where a defendant was alleged to have physically attacked the local *juez*.[31] The governor was equally involved in this supervision, fining judges for failure to fulfill their duties,[32] or appointing a special judge where the regular alcalde might have a personal interest in a pending criminal matter.[33]

More important than these general supervisory controls, the executive officials routinely approved or disapproved judicial sen-

[31] Requiring performance: L.A.P.R. 1:606–8, 609B–9C (1842); outlining the law: *id.*, 1:567–68B (1841); fining alcaldes: 3 H. BANCROFT, HISTORY OF CALIFORNIA 639 (1886) (1884–1890) (7 vols.) [hereinafter cited as HISTORY OF CALIFORNIA] (1839 incident); appointing special judge: 4 HISTORY OF CALIFORNIA, *supra,* at 632 (1841 incident).

[32] A.C. 43:238 (1839); 4 HISTORY OF CALIFORNIA, *supra* note 31, at 684 (1841 incident).

[33] An 1838 petition of the governor asked that he order the prefect of the Second District to appoint another judge to preside because the Los Angeles judge was related to the suspected thief. A.C. 39:380–81 (1838).

tences arising in particular cases. Particularly is this true of southern California, where the prefect of the Second District had more control over the judiciary than in the north. Alcaldes regularly asked the subprefect, who in turn asked the prefect, to approve even such minor sentences as banishment from one community to another area of California.[34] There would be no counsel in these kinds of cases. The same seeking of executive approval of sentence occurred in serious cases and, although less frequently, in the north as well. In December 1841 the Monterey judge convicted an Indian for the slaying of another Indian and sentenced him to six years at daily public works in the local presidio. Thereafter the judge referred the matter to the prefect for approval of the sentence. The prefect wrote back to the judge in February of 1842 that "I ratify your judgment as in conformity with justice."[35] Felony convictions prior to 1842 were sometimes sent by the governor to the National Supreme Court in Mexico City for review.[36]

After the seating of the Tribunal Superior in May 1842, that body decided appeals, that is, by approving or modifying sentences, sentencing still being the significant issue on appeal. Additionally, the appellate court took general supervisory charge of local courts by way, for example, of ordering compliance with the jail inspection duties of local judges and organizing meetings of town alcaldes.[37] Thereafter the executive authorities confined themselves primarily to supervisory and oversight review. The governor retained a pardoning power.[38]

Because of the former pattern and general confusion, some individuals continued to petition the executive officials concerning judicial matters. For example, Louis Gasquet, the French consul, wrote the governor in October 1845 on behalf of José Arnas, a

[34] L.A.P.R. 1:438 (1840); id., 1:436B–37B (1840); id., 1:605A (Jan. 1842).

[35] M.A. 3:591–626 (1841); id., 10:933 (Feb. 3, 1842).

[36] L.A.P.R. A:36, 41 (1835) (murder); A.C. 43:352–53 (1832 & 1833) (seven cases, including four murders).

[37] Letter of Bonilla, a temporary official of the Tribunal Superior, to second alcalde of Monterey, Sept. 24, 1844. M.A. 11:1647 (1844); an order in A.C. 43:353–54 (1842), wherein the Tribunal Superior stripped a judge of his office and rendered him ineligible for public duty for three years because of a failure to control a disorder that had led to a murder. For information on the Tribunal Superior's supervisory functions with regard to civil litigation, see chapter 4, notes 63–65 and accompanying text, *infra.*

[38] Examples of gubernatorial forgiveness may be found in A.C. 43:429 (1843) and *id.,* 43:288 (1844).

Spanish subject, Spain not yet having a consulate in California and France representing its interests. He complained that the Los Ángeles alcalde had arbitrarily jailed Arnas for a personal dispute between the two.[39] But review of individual judicial sentences was gone. More typical was a circular letter from Governor Pio Pico to all California alcaldes in March of 1845 warning of the need to crack down on criminals, complaining of the lack of energy of local officials, and threatening that "the government will not tolerate any omission in the fulfillment of your duties."[40]

Hortatory proclamations by executive authority and occasional suspensions of errant judges for misconduct seem well within the scope of the 1837 legislation, but still independent of the actual exercise of judicial authority.[41] The separation of executive and judicial power came slowly to California. It was present at least in theory as early as 1836, when an overbearing American naval commander demanded an explanation of the governor concerning the arrest of several Americans. Governor Nicolás Gutiérrez responded that "this class of affair belongs to the judicial power, which power in all free countries, such as mine, acts independently of the executive power . . . without my being able to do anything else but to stimulate it in a general way in the performance of its duty."[42]

The understanding of separation of powers, if not always its practice, was seen in other criminal contexts as well. In November of 1842, Governor Juan B. Alvarado peremptorily ordered the Monterey *juez* to banish from the area a woman named Guadalupe Castillo, who was, for complicated reasons, a political thorn. The judge cautiously responded that he did not have any formal complaint, and that "I do not think it just to sentence Castillo when she has not been accused." The law demanded various procedures, he politely explained to the governor; there were pen-

---

[39] *Id.*, 31:201–2 (1845). *See also id.*, 43:432 (1844) (complaint to governor that a second alcalde had insulted complainant); O.D.R.E.S.F. Document 148 (1846), *supra* note 15, (letter to first alcalde: "[I]f there is no way to obtain justice in this place, I will write to the office of the Subprefect and the Governor.")

[40] Copy of letter in M.A. 11:155 (1845).

[41] An Englishman who was the second alcalde of San Francisco in early 1846 was suspended by the prefect for fighting with the American vice-consul. 5 HISTORY OF CALIFORNIA, *supra* note 31, at 648.

[42] Tays, *Commodore Edmund P. Kennedy, U.S.N., Versus Governor Nicholas Gutiérrez: An Incident of 1836*, 12 CAL. HIST. SOC'Y Q. 137, 145 (1933).

alties for arbitrary judges, and it was "not a governor's legal decision." Reluctantly, he said he would comply but only if the governor with "more reflection orders me to complete that which you proposed." The governor backed down, declaring with typical Californio grandiloquence that "my honor and esteem and all that is conducive to respect the dignity of the office you occupy obliges me to prevent you from executing that which I ordered in my first note, that being within your more narrow responsibility."[43]

The theory of separation of powers was necessarily vague until a judicial superintending body was established. Although never as firmly established as in the United States, the seating of the Tribunal Superior made it more of a reality, at least in the criminal arena.[44]

The Californio process of criminal justice involved arrest and an investigation to determine guilt. Critical to it was the building of a consensus for punishment. The representation by counsel, concerned primarily with the issue of punishment or what to do with the offender, and the appeals and seeking of advice from various executive officials, all should be viewed as building a community consensus on how to treat the offender.

The entire procedure was deeply resented by Anglo-American expatriates. It deprived them of three features they thought essential to a properly ordered criminal justice system: prompt bail, a jury trial with confrontation of accusers, and a separation of judicial and executive functions. The expatriates might have been relieved that so many offenses regarded elsewhere as very serious (such as theft, cattle rustling, or nonmaiming assault) were not of such high consequence in California as to invoke any significant punishment. That was, however, a source of another criticism, described hereafter, that the enforcement of the criminal laws was too lax. In those matters considered serious enough to invoke the formal investigatory process, the delays, the lack of bail, and the absence of trial were especially condemned. A contemporary English visitor complained:

[43] M.A. 3:943–52 (1842). The Los Angeles prefect mentioned in 1840 that he could not interfere with a judge's judicial activities. L.A.P.R. 1:340. Yet at the same time, by today's standards, prefects did so with some regularity.

[44] Executive interference continued more actively in civil matters, even following the installation of the Tribunal Superior. See discussion in chapter 4, notes 72–75 and accompanying text, *infra.*

In California . . . the judicial system is rotten to the core. Even the
fundamental distinction between executive and judiciary is practically unknown. In cases of real or fictitious importance, the alcalde
reports to the prefect of his district, the prefect to the governor of the
province, and the governor to the central authorities of Mexico; and
while all this tedious process advances at a Spanish pace, the accused party, even if innocent, is enduring, in some dungeon or other,
a degree of mental torture more than adequate, in most instances, to
the expiation of his alleged guilt.

But this is only a small part of the evil. The ordinary result, when
time and tide have done their worst, is a rescript either for dismiss-
ing or for punishing without trial, perhaps for punishing the innocent
or for acquitting the guilty.[45]

This quotation is especially apt as it contains all three of the
most frequent criticisms: lack of bail, lack of common law style of
trial, and confusion between executive and judicial roles. The
comment was made before the seating of the Tribunal Superior,
but beyond that it reflects a lack of appreciation for the unfamiliar situations in which the Californio officials were placed.
Recall that the judges were all lay personnel, thrust into their
judgeships often against their will by threats of fines if they refused to accept the appointment. Aside from the other historical
and legal reasons for the judges to have occasion to consult frequently with executive officials, it would be a normal procedure
for them to seek help with their unfamiliar jobs.

The expatriate criticism of lack of bail and lack of trial also reflected a cultural misunderstanding and an absence of knowledge
that they were witnessing a different legal *system* in operation.
The process of investigation, the building of a dossier, the absence of bail, and the recommendation of sentence—all in lieu of
a formal trial—had a shadowy similarity to the usual Continental
civil law procedure for criminal process. It was an outgrowth of
Mexico's heritage from Spanish civil law, but it furnished procedures totally alien to the common law culture of the expatriates.

The Continental criminal procedure, to generalize, historically
provided for preliminary examinations before a judge of investigation who took witnesses' testimony and other evidence and

---

[45] G. SIMPSON, NARRATIVE OF A JOURNEY ROUND THE WORLD, DURING THE YEARS
1841 AND 1842 (London 1847), reprinted as NARRATIVE OF A VOYAGE TO CALIFOR-
NIA PORTS IN 1841–42, at 75 (1930).

compiled a dossier of proof. The initial proceedings were inquisitorial in nature and often secret. After the investigation was complete, however, the file was referred to a different judge and opportunity made available for a public hearing.

Mexico adopted this model, but only imperfectly. Until its revolution, the Spanish system of justice practiced in Mexico was almost entirely inquisitorial.[46] The first criminal procedure law (that of May 23, 1837) amply provided for the *sumaria,* or investigative level. Although one section did contemplate the possibility of a *plenario,* or public plenary hearing, this second stage of the Roman-derived criminal procedure was significantly weakened in the Mexican law. Section 128 gave the judge the power to proceed directly to sentencing after the *sumaria,* without a public trial, if he determined that the defendant's pleas either had no relation to the crime, they would not diminish its gravity, or they were improbable.

Nor does the neglect of the public phase of trial appear to be inadvertent. Instructions for the use of the alcaldes in California were drafted by the territorial legal adviser in 1824.[47] Paragraphs four through seven provided that the alcalde must make an initial determination of guilt (*bien preso*) within sixty hours following incarceration. Therefter a defense counsel was named by the defendant or appointed by the alcalde. The complete dossier was to be provided to counsel, who had the opportunity to argue whether the offense had been proven. Assuming guilt, the matter was referred to the legal adviser for consultation as to sentence. Again the public trial was omitted.

Mexico's neglect of the public portion of the twofold Continental procedure has continued until recent times. The Mexican commissioner to the United States–Mexican Claim Commission indicated in 1927 that, following the completion of the dossier,

the public hearing is held, in which the parties very often do not have anything further to allege, because everything concerning their interests has already been done and stated. In such a case, the hearing is limited to the prosecuting Attorney's ratification of his accusa-

[46] CLAGETT & VALDERRAMA, *supra* note 1, at 194. For an overview of the chaotic conditions of Mexican criminal justice in the eighteenth century, see C. MAC-LACHLAN, CRIMINAL JUSTICE IN EIGHTEENTH-CENTURY MEXICO: A STUDY OF THE TRIBUNAL OF THE ACORDADA (1974).

[47] BANCROFT, CALIFORNIA PASTORAL, *supra* note 4, at 576–79.

tion, previously filed, and the defendants and their counsel also rely on the allegations previously made by them, these two facts being entered in the record, whereupon the Judge declares the case closed and it becomes ready to be decided.[48]

The Mexican law of 1837 did not provide that the determination of guilt be made by a judge other than the investigating magistrate. The only express reference to the interplay of different courts related to appeals from sentences. Appeals were almost entirely concerned with sentences and only an interlocutory sentence was to be given by the Court of First Instance, which was followed by automatic appeal to the Court of Second Instance for a definitive sentence. Although the law did not provide for either a public hearing or a division of judicial responsibility for investigation separate and apart from decision and sentencing, the latter was often accomplished in fact. In the larger California towns, and especially in the 1840s, there were usually two alcaldes or justices of the peace. As mentioned before, it was usual for the second or junior alcalde to handle preliminary decisions

[48]United States *ex rel.* Chattin v. United Mexican States, 4 U.N.R.I.A.A. 282 (1927) (dissent of G. Fernández MacGregor). A five-minute pro forma *plenario* hearing and sentencing conducted by the same judge as had collected the evidence in the investigatory stage, with no real opportunity for the accused to speak freely in open court held to constitute a criminal procedure "far below international standards of civilization."

A more idealistic view of the Mexican procedure was given in 1895 by the Mexican jurist Matías Romero:

"It is the practice in Mexico that all the preliminary proceedings in a criminal case shall take place before the judge who presides over such proceedings, without a jury, but when this is finished, then the jury is convened and they hear the statement of the District Attorney, the defense of the accused, and such witnesses as they desire—both their direct testimony and their cross-examination—and finally give their verdict, declaring the accused innocent or guilty.

"[The Mexican law, following that of the Roman, provides that] every criminal trial is divided into two stages: the summary [*sumaria*], which is secret, and the purpose of which is to find out the facts connected with the case, the testimony of the accused being taken down when he may not know who appears against him, and sometimes not even of what crime he is accused; and the plenary [*plenario*], or second stage, in which the proceedings of the summary are made public, and all the other proceedings are public, and then the accused has the same rights as are guaranteed to him by the common law. He is allowed to go out on bail only in a very few limited cases, determined by law, and never if he is liable on conviction to bodily punishment. He is not allowed to hear the testimony against him until after the summary is over."

Printed in W. LOGAN, A MEXICAN LAW SUIT 39, 40 (1895).

as to bail and to conduct the investigation, and then to allow the first alcalde to make the final decision of sentencing.

Regardless of how close or how far the Mexican law was from Continental notions, it is clear that the procedure was a long distance from the expatriates' remembered common law. The California criminal procedure provided for the accumulation of a dossier of statements as the basis upon which to make judgment, rather than a public trial. The expatriates resented the process. So far removed was the procedure from the common law tradition that section 124 of the 1837 legislation enjoined that "the confrontation of witnesses with the culprit shall only be practiced when the judge considers it absolutely necessary in order to find out the truth." The following section makes it clear that this necessity is for identification of the defendant by witnesses and not for the purpose that would come immediately to a mind imbued with the common law, that is, cross-examination.

Criminal conduct within Mexican California ran the entire course of human experience. Although sanctions were generally moderate by modern standards, they were somewhat erratic, as one might expect of a legal system lacking professional judges, prosecutors, or substantive standards.

The variability of punishment also reflects the highly discretionary, community-based nature of the alcalde system. The judicial records seldom indicate when a particular defendant was sentenced whether it was for a first offense or whether the alcalde was dealing with a recidivist. The communities were quite small, however, and the judges were probably personally familiar with almost every defendant they sentenced.

The Monterey criminal records are unindexed and probably incomplete, making it difficult to draw any generalization from them as to the distribution of crimes. There is an index to the Criminal Branch of the Court of the First Instance of Los Angeles for the years 1830 to 1846. This index is likewise incomplete, at least for the early years,[49] but there is no reason to believe it is not representative of the range and kind of criminal activity, both

---

[49] This *Yndice Juzgado la Instancia de la ciudad de los Angeles, Ramo Criminal* was apparently prepared in 1846 by Abel Stearns and is on deposit with the Huntington Library, San Marino, California. One aspect of its incompleteness is ironic in that the criminal charges against William Day for his serious 1835 stabbing of the same Abel Stearns are not included in the index.

Table 5. Distribution of Crimes Shown in Index to Criminal Branch of Court of First Instance of Los Angeles, 1830–1846

Crimes	Percent
Wounding (assault)	26
Theft and robbery (unspecified)	24
Cattle theft	18
Murder	14
Adultery	4
Rape	2
All other crime	12
Total	100

for Los Angeles and Monterey. These constitute a record of only those crimes sufficiently serious to reach the first *juez*. Excluded are such minor offenses as drunkenness, gambling on Sunday, or failure to obtain a license for a dance, the kinds of matters that would have been handled for most of this period by the second *juez*. Also excluded would be those minor crimes for which no formal investigation, or *sumaria,* was undertaken.

The index shows 166 items, including 127 charges of serious crimes where the charge is designated. Although incomplete as to total number, the percentage breakdown of the designated crimes gives us a good idea of the range of criminal activity.

The representativeness of this may be tested by comparison with a July 1840 list of prisoners in the Los Angeles jail. Of twenty-two prisoners the charges were distributed as shown in Table 6.[50]

Economic crimes, theft, and especially cattle theft, clearly were significant to Mexican California society, as were crimes of violence, wounding, and murder. Prosecutions for sex crimes, by way of contrast, were relatively few in number.

Minor criminal activity, not within the purview of the first *juez* and not included in these figures, generally drew only moderate punishment. Thus in 1838 a Scotsman was fined five pesos for being drunk and making threats, and in 1846 an Englishman was

[50] A.C. 33:118 (1840).

Table 6. Distribution of Charges for Prisoners in Los Angeles Jail, July 1840

Charge	Number
Robbery	3
Petty larceny	3
Cattle theft	10
Murder	3
Assassination	2
Violence on a mate	1

fined two pesos and sentenced to two days in jail for insults to authorities.[51] Slander, however, could be more serious. In July 1841 a Montereño, José Alvarado, was sentenced to one month in the chain gang for slandering the daughter of Miguel Avila, although in 1845 in the same town another defendant was let off with a warning.[52]

The typical sentence for minor criminal activity was banishment. Banishment did not mean that a defendant was ordered to live in a remote hinterland but simply that he leave the town. The Monterey judicial records are replete with alcalde orders that someone be expelled from town, at times with little or no specification of the criminal activity involved.[53]

Banishment was a particularly popular punishment for adultery, and it well illustrates the function of banishment as a community-based device, not so much to punish but to rid the community of a disruptive influence. Thus the *juez* of Santa Cruz in 1840 ordered an adultress to leave the city in order to avoid scandal,[54] and the prefect of Los Angeles approved the banishment of another adultress in 1842 because "it may serve as an example to other women of bad character."[55]

Punishment for adultery could be other than banishment, as when a San Francisco judge ordered a male culprit to jail for two

[51]M.A. 6:311 (1838); *id.,* 6:1170 (1846).
[52]4 HISTORY OF CALIFORNIA, *supra* note 31, at 653 (1841); M.A. 6:1116 (1845).
[53]Examples are found in M.A. 6:267 (1837); *id.,* 6:275 (1837).
[54]L.A.P.R. 1:447B (1840).
[55]*Id.,* 1:605A (1842).

months in 1838, but apparently released him early.[56] Furthermore, the banishment ordered for adultery could include an order for relocation in a specific area. The Monterey alcalde banished an adulterous Irishman specifically to the northern frontier of Sonoma in 1842.[57]

The procedure of banishment often had the practical effect of Los Angeles depositing its miscreants with Monterey and Monterey returning the favor. For example, in 1836 the Monterey judge ordered a ne'er-do-well specifically to leave town and go to Los Angeles.[58] In 1843 another Monterey jurist banished a vagabond, and on the day of sentencing deposited the defendant on board a ship departing immediately. He then wrote the Los Angeles *juez* to expect him.[59] Still another Monterey judge was less specific, ordering an adulterer to remove himself to southern California, specifying that he could go anywhere from Santa Barbara to San Diego.[60] Presumably anywhere between those two towns would be sufficiently distant from Monterey. In 1838 the Los Angeles alcalde sent to Monterey a man who had shot a gun at another.[61]

Banishments for minor crimes, particularly adultery or idleness, were not just California phenomena but were common throughout Mexico's northern frontier.[62] The practice reflects the inadequacy of jail facilities and the lack of alternative modern devices, such as probation. More than this, it also demonstrates the localized, community-based notion of criminal justice. A miscreant was a threat to the community and its stability and therefore must be removed. An extremely interesting Santa Barbara case of 1840 neatly illustrates the point. Pablo Cruz was arrested and accused of attempted robbery. The *juez de paz* acquitted Cruz of the charge and concluded the robbery case should be dismissed, but that nevertheless Cruz should be banished. The sub-

[56] A.C. 39:352–58 (1838).
[57] M.A. 3:506–24 (1842).
[58] *Id.,* 6:258 (1836).
[59] *Id.,* 4:1–9, 4:146–47 (1843).
[60] *Id.,* 3:1–2 (1839).
[61] 3 HISTORY OF CALIFORNIA, *supra* note 31, at 638.
[62] Banishments were also ordered by the *jueces de paz* of New Mexico for similar matters, including threats to kill one's wife (1835) and repeated adultery (1829; male banished). *See* Lecompte, *The Independent Women of Hispanic New Mexico, 1821–1846,* 12 W. HIST. Q. 17, 29, 31 (1981).

prefect agreed. But why the banishment if Cruz was innocent? Because the defendant, in the words of the subprefect, is "continually and incorrigibly idle, is a menace to this city. His disgraceful conduct will pervert youth." [63]

Understanding the reasons for banishment as a punishment for minor crimes does not absolve the swapping of offenders between Monterey and Los Angeles. The Anglo-American expatriates were quick to perceive this as ludicrous, and no one expressed their sentiments more forcefully than the American consul, Thomas O. Larkin, in a letter written in 1845:

If for a crime a person is really convicted he is *ordered* [original emphasis] to some other town, and is sure to go when he get ready & returns when he has occation. . . .
Some of the Monterey prisoners are banished to San Diego, those of the latter place to Monterey. Thats fair. If they commit a second offence they may be banished back, and find their own horses on the road, which are easily borrowed with a larzo [lasso]. So the owner of a Monterey Horse who may be stole once near home, and then at San Diego by another Explorer of the Country may see him again, minus some flesh & crooked legs, but then he gets his Horse by giving the man who says he found him at San D a dollar or two. That cheap for bring[i]ng a broken down horse 500 miles. [64]

Economic crime varied in severity of punishment. In 1831 the Monterey alcalde sentenced a horse thief to work two months for his victim, and in 1835 another Monterey judge imposed a sentence of five years in a military prison on another defendant for the same offense. [65] Unquestionably there are factors concerning recidivism and the character of the defendants that do not appear in the surviving judicial notations. Where the records do specifically indicate a concerted criminal activity or a repetition, the sentence was usually heavier. A second offense of stealing brandy

---

[63] L.A.P.R. 1:436B–37B (1840). In the same vein, the judge in Santa Barbara recommended another defendant be ordered out because he was quarrelsome and therefore should be banished until he has corrected his behavior. *Id.*, 1:438 (1840).

[64] 3 THE LARKIN PAPERS: PERSONAL, BUSINESS, AND OFFICIAL CORRESPONDENCE OF THOMAS OLIVER LARKIN, MERCHANT AND UNITED STATES CONSUL IN CALIFORNIA 218–19 (Hammond ed. 1951–1968) (10 vols. & index) [hereinafter cited as LARKIN PAPERS].

[65] 3 HISTORY OF CALIFORNIA, *supra* note 31, at 673 (1831) and 674 (1835).

drew one year in chains in San Diego in 1836.[66] Another San Diegan received a six-month sentence for stealing an ox in 1844,[67] whereas in the previous year a confirmed cattle thief was sent to Mexico by the Monterey judge to serve an eight-year prison term.[68]

The relative severity for cattle theft and the specific segregation of it on the Los Angeles index is understandable. The trade in cattle hides and tallow was the basis of California's economy. Even apparent first-time offenders received one-year sentences in the Santa Barbara presidio.[69] The economic basis of the severe punishment for cattle theft is shown strikingly in a 1838 sentence of two defendants in Monterey for the killing of six cows. They were fined forty pesos and made to give surety for future good behavior,[70] whereas in the same court in 1830 a Californio defendant was ordered to serve one year at public works in a California presidio for the theft of a single cow.[71] Why this apparent disparity in sentencing? Presumably the killing was for food, and the defendants had left behind the truly valuable element of the cattle, the hides, whereas the theft had deprived the owner of the skin.

Assault unaccompanied by serious injury was not considered heinous. One Angelino was simply exiled to Monterey for firing a pistol at another in 1838,[72] while in 1840 another denizen of that community labored for three months at the public works for drawing a knife with murderous intent in the courtroom itself.[73] In 1844 the president of Mexico issued a decree that the crimes of simple robbery, fighting, and carrying weapons illegally would be adjudicated by the trial judges without appeal, but with a maximum punishment of four months of confinement at public works.[74] This reflects the general range of sentencing already practiced for these crimes.

Even the actual infliction of injury was not seriously regarded. A San Diegan was fined five pesos plus damages for wounding an-

[66]*Id.* at 618.
[67]4 HISTORY OF CALIFORNIA, *supra* note 31, at 620.
[68]*Id.* at 654.
[69]M.A. 3:173–200 (1841); *id.,* 3:276–316 (1841).
[70]*Id.,* 3:10–57 (1838).
[71]*Id.,* 1:17–18 (1830).
[72]3 HISTORY OF CALIFORNIA, *supra* note 31, at 638.
[73]*Id.* at 639.
[74]A.C. 43:367 (1844).

other with a knife in 1841,[75] while in the same year a Chilean migrant in Monterey wounded another foreigner and was ordered to pay a fine of twenty-five pesos, to give damages to the victim, and to leave California on a bark then at anchor in the port.[76]

Serious woundings were sometimes treated differently. In 1835 a Kentucky fur trapper, William Day, stabbed a fellow American and Los Angeles merchant, Abel Stearns, in a dispute over the quality of some wine Stearns had sold him. The multiple knife wounds were nearly fatal and left Stearns with an injury to his tongue and a permanent speech impediment.[77] Day was kept in jail for at least a year.[78] An earlier serious wounding in Monterey brought the perpetrator only fifteen days at public works,[79] a sentence so light that the victim's status as an Indian may have been a factor.[80]

In rape cases a significant differentiation was made in punishment for attempt and the act itself. In 1845, Monterey authorities prosecuted two foreigners, one English and the other Italian, for attempted rape. The Englishman received but four months in jail, and part of that was for an earlier jail escape, and the Italian was let off with a warning.[81] On the other hand, for "rape and seduction," as the records indicate, a Monterey defendant was sentenced in 1842 to serve eight years in the armed forces; and, in 1839, a Los Angeles defendant received a five-year term in a mili-

---

[75] 4 HISTORY OF CALIFORNIA, *supra* note 31, at 619.

[76] M.A. 3:260–75 (1841).

[77] WRIGHT, *supra* note 26, at 68–70.

[78] 3 HISTORY OF CALIFORNIA, *supra* note 31, at 631.

[79] M.A. 2:330–57 (n.d.).

[80] Indians within the settled areas were definitely protected by the legal system, and there are many cases in which they were victims of a crime for which a non-Indian was prosecuted. Alternatively, they would be tried as ordinary defendants. These were Indians living in towns or on ranches, not those Indians still in the wild nor the mission Indians. Notwithstanding, Indians were regarded as inferior beings and were treated somewhat more harshly than ordinary defendants. In 1844 the Tribunal Superior rebuked a judge for sentencing an Indian to labor on public works for drunkenness, when such a crime deserved a lesser punishment. A.C. 43:367 (1844). Similarly, there was a tendency to treat the defendants for crimes committed upon even those Indians living within the settled areas with somewhat more leniency.

[81] M.A. 6:1070, 1082 (1845); *id.,* 6:1108 (1845). The latter, that involving the Italian, was simply a private prosecution initiated by the victim's family.

tary prison, which was reduced to two years, for the rape of a young Indian girl that resulted in her death. The sentence was mitigated because of the circumstantial nature of the evidence and the belief that poor medical treatment had caused the girl's death.[82]

Although the judges could be lenient with murderers, they often handed them severe sentences. The particular circumstances of the crime and the parties, as always, played a major role. The range of punishment is impressive. In 1835 a San Diego murderer received only four years in the military prison,[83] whereas in the following year a Monterey counterpart was sent to Mexico to serve ten years, with a woman confederate being confined at a mission for only two years.[84] Prison sentences at a military fortress within this range of time were common. The Indian slayer of another Indian was sentenced to six years in 1841 in Monterey,[85] and three years later in Monterey another murderer, a non-Indian, was ordered to serve five years.[86] Both sentences were to a military presidio, almost certainly in lower Mexico. One suspected slayer of an Irish shoemaker at Monterey was simply banished from California.[87] Presumably there was insufficient evidence to convict.

Punishment for murder could also be capital. In 1842 a Monterey shoemaker from Peru was executed for the murder of an Englishman,[88] and the year before in Los Angeles three Californios were shot for the homicide of a German shopkeeper.[89] Foreigners, as potential victims, were protected by the law of murder, but they were prosecuted as well, as shown by Samuel Taggart's 1842 execution for murder in Los Angeles and the imprisonment of his accomplice, Henry Richards, for ten years in Mexico.[90] Of course, Californios were executed for killing fellow

---

[82] 4 History of California, *supra* note 31, at 653 (1842 case); A.C. 38:397–401; 3 HISTORY OF CALIFORNIA, *supra* note 31, at 638 (1839 case).

[83] 3 HISTORY OF CALIFORNIA, *supra* note 31, at 618.

[84] *Id.*, at 675. Apparently the male defendant was a corporal in the military, and it is not clear why he was tried by a civil court and not by the military.

[85] M.A. 3:591–626; *id.*, 10:933 (1842).

[86] *Id.*, 4:935–1026 (1844).

[87] 4 HISTORY OF CALIFORNIA, *supra* note 31, at 653.

[88] M.A. 3:314–418 (1842).

[89] 4 HISTORY OF CALIFORNIA, *supra* note 31, at 629–30.

[90] A.C. 42:391 (1842); L.A.P.R. 1:686–87 (1842).

natives as well, as occurred following the 1838 slaying of Antonio Aguila by Antonio Valencia in Los Angeles,[91] and in the 1831 execution of Francisco Rubio for the brutal murder of two children in San Francisco.[92]

Murder cases are useful vehicles to study judicial procedures because in most societies they bring out the fullest of available formalities. With that in mind, the relatively short periods between confinement and execution of sentences are revealing. Two examples will suffice. The Peruvian shoemaker mentioned above, Manuel Gonzales, was accused of murdering an Englishman, William Campbell, on February 6, 1842, in San Juan Bautista, a small village within the Monterey court's jurisdiction. He was arrested almost immediately, and the investigation conducted, attorneys appointed, arguments made, all before July 14, 1842, on which date the lower court entered its sentence of the death penalty. Thereafter appeals were made as to the sentence and on July 22, 1842 the Tribunal Superior determined that the crime had been sufficiently proved and that the sentence should be carried out within six days, including the date of its order. The Monterey *juez* then arranged for troops to carry out the sentence by firing squad and on July 27, 1842 entered a certificate of execution into the records.[93] The entire judicial process had taken only about five and one-half months.

On January 23, 1844 there was another murder in San Juan Bautista. Whereas, in 1842, Gonzales had always appeared before

[91] 4 HISTORY OF CALIFORNIA, *supra* note 31, at 632. This incident occurred in 1838, and not the 1842 mentioned in this citation. *See* 3 HISTORY OF CALIFORNIA, *supra* note 31, at 638 and references to the original arrest in A.C. 33:10 (1838).
[92] 2 HISTORY OF CALIFORNIA, *supra* note 31, at 592, 594; 3 HISTORY OF CALIFORNIA, *supra* note 31, at 191–93, 699. This was a military prosecution.
[93] M.A. 3:314–418 (1842) is the *sumaria*. Associated orders are at *id.*, 10: 1005, 1007. Curiously, there was a Court of Second Instance which affirmed the lower court before it was then affirmed by the Tribunal Superior, which would be the Court of Third Instance. There are precious few cases in California where a Court of Second Instance, called the *Segunda Sala,* operated. The only other cases located were from this same period of the summer in 1842, when the Tribunal Superior was first becoming operational. *Id.*, 3:506–24 (1842), and Los Angeles Archives (alcalde records), 2:982–1163 (1842). It seems there was a brief attempt to create the entire panoply of the legislated judicial structure. It has been suggested that the reason for the establishment of the Tribunal Superior in 1842 was to deal with an outbreak of murders. W. HANSEN, THE SEARCH FOR AUTHORITY IN CALIFORNIA 46–47 (1960).

the same *juez,* in 1844 there were two *jueces* in Monterey. Thus the defendant, José Surita, was arraigned before the second *juez* on February 6, 1844 and ordered incarcerated. An investigation ensued and subsequently the second alcalde found Surita *bien preso,* closed the investigation, and passed the file on to the first *juez.* At that point a prosecutor and defense counsel were appointed and written arguments were submitted to the court. On March 26, 1844, just two months from the murder itself, the first alcalde sentenced Surita to five years in a presidio to be selected by the Tribunal Superior. The appellate court then referred the matter to the fiscal, who recommended a confirmation of the sentence and the Acapulco prison as a suitable place of confinement. The Tribunal Superior approved the recommendation and affirmed the sentence on April 15, 1844. The Tribunal Superior sat in Monterey and presumably notified the Monterey alcalde immediately because on the same date as the appeal was decided the first *juez* certified that he had placed the defendant on the bark *California,* then in the harbor and bound for lower Mexico.[94] Here, less than two and one-half months elapsed from arraignment to exhaustion of final appeal and execution of sentence.

As these examples have shown, and with the exception of murder, sentencing was moderate to light. Sanctions in a general sense ranged from banishment from the community for minor crimes, imprisonments of six months to a year for robbery, up to five to ten years, or even execution, for murder. The reasons for this relative leniency are not hard to discover. The most important influence on the California sanctions was the lack of departmental prisons. Although each of the four presidios, or military forts, in San Francisco, Monterey, Santa Barbara, and San Diego, maintained stockades, they were small and not designed for any long-term incarcerations. Furthermore, by the 1830s the presidios were all in varying stages of disrepair with that of San Diego virtually in ruins. Although some use was made of these military prisons, practicality dictated that if long-term confinement were desired, certainly anything beyond a year, a violator would need to be sent to lower Mexico. That itself was difficult because it would mean either waiting for the uncertain arrival of a government bark or, alternatively, that the perpetually insolvent depart-

[94]M.A. 4:935–1026 (1844).

mental government would have to pay a shipper for the convict's passage.

Most localities had a carcel, but these small jails could only serve as temporary holding cells for defendants awaiting sentences or, at best, as places of confinement for short sentences while a defendant served a month or two in labor at local public works. The carcels were inadequate for longer terms because they presented absolutely miserable conditions and because they provided frequent opportunity for escape.

Several writers complained of these jails' poor light, filthy sanitation, and mud floors.[95] Larkin, in his capacity as American consul, had occasion to remind the local authorities that food and humane conditions must be furnished to American prisoners.[96] The judges of the First Instance were required by statute to inspect the jails weekly and to hear prisoner complaints. It is ap-

[95] The Monterey jail was considerably overcrowded by the arrest of more than forty Americans and Britons during the Graham Affair of 1840. Thomas Farnham, an unabashed Mexican hater, described the prison conditions then prevailing:

"Their cells were examined and found destitute of floors! The ground within was so wet that the poor fellows sank into it several inches at every step. On this they stood, sat and slept! From fifty to sixty were crowded into a room eighteen or twenty feet square! They could not all sit at once, even in that vile pool, still less lie down! The cells were so low and tight that the only way of getting air enough to sustain life, was to divide themselves into platoons, each of which in turn stood at the grate awhile to breathe! Most of them had been in prison seven or eight days, with no food except a trifling quantity. . . .

"They looked on damp prison walls, and dragged chains at their wrists and ankles."

T. FARNHAM, TRAVELS IN THE CALIFORNIAS AND SCENES IN THE PACIFIC OCEAN 64–65, 89 (New York, 1844), reprinted as TRAVELS IN CALIFORNIA (1947).

[96] On September 10, 1844, Larkin wrote to the captain of the Port of Monterey in regard to an American, William McGlove, who had apparently been imprisoned by order of the port officer. Why that official was involved is unclear. Larkin represented that he was "obliged to apply to you that he may be provided with the proper food during the time he is imprisoned under your charge.

"[H]e says he has been imprisoned seven days without any provission being given him on part of the government. This appears to me impossible, and I wait with the expectations of hearing that this is not the case. As he has been wanting in his respects to the law its precise that he should be imprisoned but he must not be locked up without food."

Letter, Larkin to Pedro Narváez, Sept. 10, 1844, in 2 LARKIN PAPERS, supra note 64, at 224. On another occasion, Larkin complained to the Monterey juez de paz that some American seamen "have been imprisoned over thirty days without being called to a trial." Letter, Larkin to Juez de Paz, May 8, 1844, in id., 2:116.

parent that the California judges were not fulfilling this portion of their duties, although from the time of its creation the Tribunal Superior made a special effort to insist on adequate judicial supervision of the jails. In June of 1842, the month following its organization, the appellate court personally inspected the jail closest at hand, that of the city wherein it sat. The court issued a blistering report of the treatment of the five prisoners it found in the Monterey jail.

[F]rom the time of their imprisonment they had been given no food; the authorities did not know how they were to subsist. One of them . . . begged . . . until the others at length gave him some food that was brought from their house. Often they asked for water, and were told there was no one to fetch it. . . .

The commission then inspected the calabozo, and were surprised at the picture it presented. It was without any floor but the bare earth, and so wet that a stick would sink some distance into it. The walls were black, and so dark that an object could not be seen more than a yard off. There was neither light nor ventilation, except through two small skylights. . . . [T]hey had to use a barrel as a privy, and the whole place was a sink-hole of filth. The commission severely denounced the condition of the prisoners.[97]

The Tribunal Superior made several orders for the relief of prisoners and continued its inspections throughout 1843 and 1844.[98] It constantly criticized their condition and advised the governor that the jails were uncomfortable, humid, unsanitary, and for the sake of humanity should be improved.[99] The tribunal ordered the judges to remedy the problems,[100] and in October 1844 reminded the judges of their duty of weekly inspections and insisted that they fill out a weekly questionnaire about the conditions they had encountered.[101] These reformist efforts failed, however, because of the indifference and even hostility of most judges and the governor.

Severe overcrowding in the local jails sometimes forced either

[97] BANCROFT, CALIFORNIA PASTORAL, supra note 4, at 609–10 (1888), paraphrasing official report found in A.C. 43:354–57 (1842).

[98] Judges must furnish prisoners one hour of sunshine daily. A.C. 43:358 (1842); medical assistance ordered furnished to specified prisoner. Id., 43:369 (1844).

[99] Id., 42:386 (1843).

[100] Id., 43:364 (1843).

[101] Id., 43:374 (1844).

outright release of prisoners or a leasing out of convicts to private persons.[102] In July 1840, twenty-two prisoners were in Los Angeles. Four were held in the presidio in Santa Barbara, four were confined in the local jail, and the balance were released on bail for want of room and food.[103] The dismal state of local jails is reflected in local governments' frequent calls for volunteers to serve as guards or to furnish food,[104] and in reports of escapes, sometimes of entire jail populations.[105]

What was needed, we would think today, was a prison. That thought did not occur to the American expatriates, probably because the building of penitentiaries in the United States was in its infancy, and the American expatriates would not have had much familiarity with the concept.[106] The Americans lampooned the California jail; in a May 31, 1845 letter to a New York newspaper Larkin complained that:

As some of the gauls [jails] are uncumferable the prisoners were often keepd outside. As the food is bad, they go home to get better. . . . There was one day a complant made to the Alcalde by the Person who lost the property stole, that the theaf was every day out of prison, and every day past his house. The Alcalde said it was very

[102] There are many references scattered throughout the archival records to the leasing of prisoners' labor to private persons. See, e.g., L.A.P.R. 1:137 (1842). In September 1845 the departmental government objected to the practice, apparently because of abuse. 4 HISTORY OF CALIFORNIA, supra note 31, at 634.

[103] A.C. 33:118 (1840); 3 HISTORY OF CALIFORNIA, supra note 31, at 639.

[104] Examples include Los Angeles, 1835: Letter in July from judge to military commandant of San Gabriel complaining of limited security of jails and unreliability of guards, L.A.P.R. A:33–34. A month later the judge made reference to using civilians as guards because all the soldiers were on furlough, id., A: 40–41; San Diego, 1838: no place to keep prisoners in the evening unless someone volunteers the use of a room. Call made for contributions of food. 3 HISTORY OF CALIFORNIA, supra note 31, at 618. Again in 1841, sentences in San Diego could not be executed "for want of food for prisoners." 4 HISTORY OF CALIFORNIA, supra, at 619. An auxiliary force of citizens guarded prisoners in Los Angeles in 1845. Id. at 634.

[105] Local Los Angeles authorities complained to the military commandant at San Gabriel in 1835 that their prisoners had all escaped from jail and requested that he send soldiers because it was difficult to get citizens to serve as guards. L.A.P.R. A:43. Again in August 1839, when five prisoners escaped from the Los Angeles carcel, the juez complained of citizen failure to do guard duty. 3 HISTORY OF CALIFORNIA, supra note 31, at 639.

[106] See L. FRIEDMAN, A HISTORY OF AMERICAN LAW 259–61 (1973); O. LEWIS, THE DEVELOPMENT OF AMERICAN PRISONS AND PRISON CUSTOMS, 1776–1845 (1922).

sorry and in extenuation remarked that he had told the Prisoner to take his fornoon & afternoon pasios [paseos, walks] the other side of the town.[107]

Before evaluating the expatriates' place in the Mexican Californian criminal justice system, it would be well to discuss briefly certain special criminal procedures. Before the Mexican revolution, the Spanish law in New Spain allowed both military and religious personnel to be tried exclusively in their own tribunals.[108] The Mexican Constitution of 1824, the fundamental law throughout this period, provided that the "military and ecclesiastic remain subject to the same laws and tribunals as heretofore."[109] The subsequent judicial law of May 23, 1837 gave broad general jurisdiction to the judges of the First Instance. The power of the first *juez* over criminal cases, however, "of whatever description," was limited by the exception of "cases wherein clergymen and military persons are privileged by the constitutional or other laws in force."[110]

There is no evidence of any ecclesiastic in Mexican California claiming a right to be tried in an ecclesiastical court in order to escape an ordinary criminal prosecution. The claim of military right was common, however, with soldiers.

Naturally the military directly prosecuted soldiers for military crimes, such as desertion.[111] Defendants who were soldiers and were brought before civilian criminal courts for ordinary crimes could claim a privilege to be tried before a military tribunal,[112] and the regular courts would suspend proceedings against mili-

---

[107] Letter, Larkin to Moses Yale Beach, May 31, 1845, 3 LARKIN PAPERS, *supra* note 64, at 218–19.

[108] *See generally* L. MCALISTER, THE "FUERO MILITAR" IN NEW SPAIN 1764–1800 (1957).

[109] Tit. V, Art. 154, § 7. 1 J. WHITE, A NEW COLLECTION OF LAWS, CHARTERS AND LOCAL ORDINANCES OF THE GOVERNMENTS OF GREAT BRITAIN, FRANCE AND SPAIN . . ., 408 (Philadelphia 1839). The Spanish text of the 1824 Mexican constitution may be found in M. GALVÁN, COLECCIÓN DE LOS DECRETOS Y ORDENES DE LAS CORTES DE ESPAÑA, QUE SE REPUTAN VIGENTES EN . . . LOS ESTADOS-UNIDOS MEXICANOS (Mexico City 1829).

[110] Law of May 23, 1837, § 88.

[111] *See, e.g.,* L.A.P.R. 1:648–49A (1842).

[112] *See, e.g.,* 4 HISTORY OF CALIFORNIA, *supra* note 31, at 686 (claim of military privilege before San Jose *juez,* April 1843); L.A.P.R. A:42 (August 1835 claim of privilege).

tary defendants even for such a serious crime as the murder of a civilian victim.[113] Of course, the culprits would not be given free license for their acts but would be tried by military tribunals.

The operation of military courts in New Spain had been characterized by conflict between the military and civilian jurisdictions.[114] This was not the case in Mexican California where cooperation was more common.[115] Military commanders, for example, alerted local authorities to the approach of fleeing military suspects,[116] and military courts frequently requested the civilian courts to order civilians, who would be under the exclusive jurisdiction of the regular courts, to appear as witnesses in military prosecutions.[117] Additionally, commanders advised the civilian authorities when military companies were disbanded, with the result that former members became amenable to the civilian courts.[118]

Anglo-American expatriates had nothing to do with military courts, excepting as occasional witnesses. Nevertheless, they could be as involved as anyone in another special sort of criminal litigation, that of the private prosecution.

A victim could commence a criminal case for relatively minor matters in the same manner as a civil suit. If this were to occur, the matter would proceed in the same way as a civil case. Instead of the incarceration and official investigation, the parties would

---

[113]M.A. 10:1331 (1842). Other examples include A.C. 33:10 (1838) (Los Angeles *juez* declining jurisdiction of military defendant charged with murder and delivering him to military captain); *id.,* 43:361 (1842) (Tribunal Superior orders judge to pass investigation to military commander because a soldier is indicated).
   It may be that in the late years of Mexican California the military exemption was less vigorously applied. In 1844, for example, Governor Micheltorena ordered the ordinary second alcalde of Monterey to investigate and charge a military captain who had beaten a civilian. *Id.,* 43:431 (1844).
   [114]*See generally* MCALISTER, *supra* note 108.
   [115]This is not to say there were no conflicts. In 1839 General Vallejo, the departmental military commander, decided the San Jose alcalde had no right to fine a soldier and that the levy need not be paid. 3 HISTORY OF CALIFORNIA, *supra* note 31, at 731.
   [116]L.A.P.R. 2:463–64 (1842).
   [117]*Id.,* 2:432–33 (1841); *id.,* 1:610–12 (1842). There must have been some friction in this last case, however, because the prefect advised the Los Angeles *juez* that the requested civilian witnesses need not attend the military court unless the military paid their expenses and damages for time lost.
   [118]*Id.,* 1:166–67 (1842).

nominate their representatives, or *hombres buenos,* and a conciliation hearing would be held exactly as in ordinary civil matters. The result might lead to a fine as well as a civil judgment in
favor of the victim.

Section 95 of the judicial law of May 23, 1837 provided that
every sentence in "criminal causes" must be immediately transmitted to the accused and to the complainant, and that either
one of them could appeal. Section 89 extended the required conciliation process generally used in civil suits to a criminal complaint involving "purely personal injuries." The implication of
these two legislative provisions was that criminal matters concerning "purely personal injuries" might be initiated and prosecuted by the victim, who would therefore be entitled to notice
and to rights of appeal but also burdened by the conciliation process. This was merely an extension of older Spanish law.[119] The
majority of private prosecutions in California concerned defamation or injuries to the plaintiff or a member of the plaintiff's family.[120] In Monterey, for example, the conciliation procedure was
used in 1845 to resolve criminal charges of both a lesser offense
of slander and a more serious charge of attempted rape.[121]

The Mexican statute of May 23, 1837 also embodied the sophisticated notion that the criminal process served a societal function that should not be controlled or manipulated solely by the
victim and defendant. It provided that if both the accuser and the
defendant agreed upon a sentence, presumably contemplating a

---

[119] Chapter 3 of the Spanish Cortes Decree of Oct. 9, 1812, referring to the use
of *hombres buenos* and the private initiative in criminal matters, merely confirmed existing practice. Article 5 stated that "in criminal cases of slight faults and
injuries which only require reprimand or light correction . . . the alcaldes, as well
in civil as in criminal matters, will associate good men . . . chosen by each of the
contending parties, and after hearing the plaintiff and defendant, and taking the
opinion of the associates, shall give such a decision before the notary as they
deem just." For more serious crimes, article 8 provided: "The alcaldes, when a
crime has been committed in their towns . . . ought to proceed *ex officio* or at the
request of a party, to institute the first proceedings of the inquest and cause the
criminals to be apprehended." 1 WHITE, *supra* note 109, at 420; GALVAN, *supra*
note 109, at 51.

[120] Robertson, "From Alcalde to Mayor: A History of the Change from the Mexican to the American Local Institutions in California," at 53 (Ph.D. diss., University of California, 1908).

[121] M.A. 6:1116 (1845; Alviso v. Vasquez, slander); *id.,* 6:1108 (1845; Castro v.
Frisconi, attempted rape).

fine as well as compensation to the victim, the trial judge should order the sentence executed, but only if the matter were a trivial crime "for which the law imposes no corporeal punishment." If, however, the cause were one regarding a crime that had such a punishment, then the sentence must be reviewed on appeal, even though both the accuser and the culprit were agreeable thereto.

There were few private prosecutions in Mexican California. One reason for this may have been because the Californio officials clearly recognized the general, social interest in the criminal process. For example, in transmitting a proposed sentence arising out of a private prosecution to the governor, before the establishment of the Tribunal Superior, the prefect remarked that "the decision of this case involves only the government, not only because of its nature and seriousness, but also because it involves criminal incidents."[122] In an ordinary prosecution, not privately conducted, for robbery in 1842, the English victim and the Californio culprit reached an agreement that the victim would suspend the action and the defendant would pay a substantial amount of damages and be released from jail. The Monterey judge passed the proposal along to the Tribunal Superior, which advised the *juez* that because of the public well-being an agreement between victim and defendant was not generally sufficient to suspend an action.[123]

How then did the American and British expatriates fare in the Mexican Californian criminal justice system? First as defendants, it seems clear that the foreigners were hardly victimized by the California criminal process; if anything, they were favored. To be sure, they were denied the Anglo-American "rights" of jury trial, confrontation of witnesses, and sometimes bail. But complain as they might, these losses simply reflect a different legal system and do not indicate that the foreigners were singled out for poorer treatment than that given the Californios themselves.

The American and British immigrants who were the older resi-

---

[122] L.A.P.R. 1:342 (1841).

[123] M.A. 3:829, 878–79, 900–1, 909–11; 4:89–90 (1842–43). Although the Tribunal Superior made this general statement as to the public interest in criminal prosecution, it did order this defendant's release. The appellate order was not based on the agreement but on an insufficiency of proof and the fact that the defendant had been imprisoned many months during the period of investigation. *Id.*, 3:909.

dents, largely seamen and merchants who had arrived in California in the 1820s and 1830s, had little difficulty with the criminal
law with the exception of occasional arrests for smuggling, a
prevalent activity in Mexican California and not regarded as a serious offense. Smuggling was not only widespread, but consumer
demand for smuggled goods generated approval for the practice
by the California populace.[124] Some examples of arrests of Americans for smuggling include Alpheus B. Thompson in 1833 and
William S. Hinckley in 1839, both in San Francisco, while Abel
Stearns was accused of the same activity in Los Angeles in 1835.[125]
These incidents led to inconclusive results: warnings, dismissals,
perhaps secret understandings that a higher proportion of cargo
would be entered "legally" so as to increase the departmental
revenues. With an ad valorem duty of 100 percent, all shippers
engaged in smuggling; it was simply a matter of being discreet.

The newer group of American immigrants, those who arrived in
the late 1830s and in the early 1840s by the overland routes,
were largely farmers and trappers. They tended toward more
criminal activity. Assaults, drunkenness, and insults to authorities were among the most common crimes for this group, and
these tended to be treated lightly. While foreign expatriates occasionally did commit more serious crimes, organized horse theft
or robbery,[126] for example, there is no evidence that suggests they
were treated more harshly than Californios were for equivalent
activities.

There is some evidence, at least in smuggling cases, that foreigners were given preferential treatment as defendants. The for-

---

[124]Dallas, "The Hide and Tallow Trade in Alta California, 1822–1846," at
226–28 (Ph.D. diss., Indiana University, 1955).

[125] 3 HISTORY OF CALIFORNIA, *supra* note 31, at 365–66, 395 (Thompson); A.C.
39:310–42; W. DAVIS, SEVENTY-FIVE YEARS IN CALIFORNIA 176 (1929) (1st ed. as
SIXTY YEARS IN CALIFORNIA (San Francisco 1889) (Hinckley); WRIGHT, *supra* note
26, at 54–58 (Stearns). Smuggling complaints were made against Stearns in
at least the years 1835, 1838, and 1840. Miller, "Henry Delano Fitch: A Yankee
Trader in California, 1826–1849, at 40–41 (Ph.D. diss., University of Southern
California, 1972).

[126] 3 HISTORY OF CALIFORNIA, *supra* note 31, at 722; 4 HISTORY OF CALIFORNIA,
supra, at 113 (James Doyle and his band of horse thieves); 4 HISTORY OF CALIFOR
NIA, *supra*, at 569 (three sailors from American ship *Vandalia* arrested for robbery and released to Larkin after one month's imprisonment); Letter, Josiah
Belden to Larkin, Aug. 7, 1842, 1 LARKIN PAPERS, *supra* note 64, at 262 (Robert
King arrested for stealing Larkin's lumber at Santa Cruz).

eigners alone fulfilled this vital economic function, and had any
Californios been prosecuted for smuggling, probably they also
would have been treated generously. In any event, two Frenchmen, Henry Cambuston and Peter Richards, were caught red-
handed with smuggled goods in 1844. Their defense was that they
had bought the goods from someone they did not know, whose
name they did not remember, and had arranged for this someone
to deliver the goods to the remote location, a favorite of smug-
glers, where they were found with the items. The Monterey alcalde was understandably unimpressed by this feeble defense and
fined then each fifty pesos and sentenced them to serve six
months in the Acapulco prison. The sentence was automatically
appealed to the Tribunal Superior, pursuant to the standard procedure, and that court referred it to its fiscal. That official pointed
out some irregularities in the proceedings and recommended the
punishment be limited to a confiscation of the smuggled goods,
which suggestion the Tribunal Superior adopted.[127] The irregularities were ridiculously weak and consisted of a few papers out
of logical order in the *sumaria* and an absence of a few formal
orders.

American gunboats made recurrent shows of force off the California capital of Monterey. A partial listing includes Commodore
Edmund P. Kennedy in October 1838, with his warship, the *Pea-
cock;* Captain French Forrest with the *Saint Louis* in June 1840;
Commander Hugh N. Page of the *Levant* in October 1845; and
the notable visit of Thomas ap Catesby Jones with two men-of-
war in October 1842. Commodore Jones actually seized Monterey for a few days in the mistaken belief that war had broken
out between the United States and Mexico. All of these American
military men took a keen interest in the treatment given Americans and often American expatriates laid claim of ill treatment
before them.[128] Additionally, the gunboats of England and France

[127] M.A. 4:812–47 (1844). This affair is discussed in Letter, Larkin to Monsieur
Gauden, Apr. 21, 1844, 2 LARKIN PAPERS, *supra* note 64, at 103.

[128] A memorial of Americans resident in Hawaii was addressed to Commodore
Edmund P. Kennedy in 1838 just before his visit to California. They complained of
the California government as follows: "That many serious outrages and unjust
acts have been committed by the governmental authorities of those countries
[California and Mexico] upon American vessels and seamen, and great losses and
damages sustained in consequence."

Then follows a description of two arrests for smuggling, although that word was

were frequent visitors, offering the same interference on behalf of their nationals.

It might be supposed that the lenient treatment afforded the expatriate population was in part influenced by a fear of adverse consequences from the roving military representatives of their governments. But this does not appear to be a significant factor. There is no evidence, moreover, that foreigners from Germany, Italy, Chile, or other nations whose military representatives did not visit California on a regular basis were treated any less favorably or differently than Americans, Englishmen, or Frenchmen. Furthermore, the Californios were a proud people, and when Commodores Kennedy and Jones attempted to interfere with local judicial proceedings in 1836 and 1842, they met an absolutely unyielding opposition by officialdom.[129]

Though treated gently themselves, Anglo-American expatriates found frequent occasion to bemoan the leniency that was extended to everyone else. Most lamented that prosecution of crime was not vigorous enough. William Leidesdorff, an American merchant and vice-consul in San Francisco, felt insulted and threatened by an Englishman, Robert Ridley, in early 1846. He wrote

---

not employed. "We refer to these as instances of grievous embarrassments arbitrarily imposed on our commerce."

"We believe that no vessel of the United States government has, for many years, visited Upper California; and we have great confidence that, were a naval force to appear on that coast, and visit Lower California and Mexico, it would render valuable service to our citizens residing in those countries, would afford needed succor and protection to American vessels, at present employed there, and be attended with results peculiarly advantageous to the general interests of our national commerce."

Following Kennedy's visit to Monterey in October 1838, several American merchants and shippers of Monterey wrote to "return to you their humble and grateful thanks for the lively interest you have been pleased to manifest for our commerce on this coast, and that . . . you have been pleased to enter this port for the protection of our interests. We . . . appreciate . . . the increased security we shall feel by your regard to our welfare."

Quoted in W. RUSCHENBERGER, A VOYAGE ROUND THE WORLD; INCLUDING AN EMBASSY TO MUSCAT AND SIAM IN 1835, 1836, AND 1837 (Philadelphia 1838), reprinted in SKETCHES IN CALIFORNIA 1836, xvi–xviii, 23–24 (1953). The British and American expatriates signed petitions that were presented to other warships as well.

[129] G. Tays, *Commodore Edmund P. Kennedy, U.S.N., Versus Governor Nicholás Gutiérrez: An Incident of 1836*, 12 CAL. HIST. SOC'Y Q. 137 (1933) (Kennedy, 1836); 4 HISTORY OF CALIFORNIA, *supra* note 31, at 39–40 (Jones, 1842).

the alcalde complaining that he had gotten no response to his earlier communications; he wanted to know what charges had been made and told the judge that he had been forced to go forth always armed, that his life and goods were not safe, and "if there is no way to obtain justice in this place, I will write to the office of the Subprefect and the Governor."[130] Larkin noted sardonically in 1845 that "some People dislike prosuting a man for stealing his horse for fear he should be told that the man was only bringig him home by around about road, and demand a dollar for his trouble."[131] George Bellomy, an American shopkeeper in San Jose, colorfully fretted that:

Having had several aggreviances here by robing my shop and othr wise I have asked for redress of the alcaldies her[e] they have refused to give any redress but increased my agriaveances. . . .
They have stolen my effects out of my shop refused to pay me for work the alcaldes has ordered me to give up proprty that I had bough and paid for I have aplied to him again and again for Justice and my patitions has been uterly refused and maglected by the alcaldies here.[132]

This letter was addressed to Larkin as the American consul. Americans frequently asked Larkin to intervene into the machinery of California criminal justice. Following the April 1846 shooting of one American by another, five American settlers wrote Larkin that "in consequence of the well known laxity & want of energy in the laws of the country we are apprehensive that the murderer will go unpunished without your intervention in this affair." They asked that Larkin take any steps he thought "likely to ensure the due execution of justice."[133] In fact, the suspect had already surrendered to Larkin, who turned him over to the authorities. On another occasion, the Swiss proprietor of Sacramento, John Sutter, in his capacity as the local judge, wrote Larkin that an American suspected of attempted rape was on his way to Monterey. Sutter trusted that Larkin would "use every exertion, as far as is consistent with the duties of your office, to

[130] O.D.R.E.S.F. Document 148, *supra* note 15.
[131] Letter, Larkin to Moses Yale Beach, May 31, 1845, 3 LARKIN PAPERS, *supra* note 64, at 218.
[132] Letter, George W. Bellomy to Larkin, May 6, 1845, *id.* at 180.
[133] Letter, John Marsh, et al. to Larkin, April 15, 1846, in 4 LARKIN PAPERS, *supra* note 64, at 288.

bring such base and unprincipled men to a sense of justice by a punctual and rigorous execution of the laws."[134] How Larkin was to do that as American consul was not made clear.

Larkin but infrequently interfered with the criminal justice system by urging prosecution. One of the few times in which he did arose from the wounding of Elliott Libbey, an American sea captain, and Nathan Spear, an American merchant, by a Mexican patrol in San Francisco in October 1845. The patrolmen said they were apprehending deserting sailors and Libbey and Spear had interfered. In any event, Libbey was critically injured, and Larkin personally went to San Francisco and began a vigorous campaign of correspondence with the subprefect and the prefect demanding that prosecution be commenced. Larkin arrived on the American warship *Levant* and the presence of that display of force undoubtedly was an aid. Prosecution was commenced within two weeks; ultimately Libbey's condition improved, and within a few months the defendants had been admitted to bail and the prosecution for all intents and purposes was dropped.[135] This was one of the few prosecutions in which Larkin played any significant role.

The expatriates' complaints about the criminal laws are largely belied by the judicial records. Californio authorities prosecuted criminal activities in which expatriates were victims just as vigorously as all others. Many lesser crimes were not taken seriously in Mexican California, and the worst that can be said is that the expatriate victims were treated equally poorly as the Californio victims.

For serious crimes there was generally vigorous investigation and prosecution. For example, investigations were conducted into the murder of an Englishman, Anthony Campbell, in 1841; into the death of an American, Thomas Smith, in 1842; and into the wounding of another foreigner in 1841.[136] In none of these cases was there a prosecution. There was insufficient evidence in

[134] Letter, Sutter to Larkin, July 23, 1845, 3 LARKIN PAPERS, *supra* note 64, at 285.

[135] R. KELSEY, THE UNITED STATES CONSULATE IN CALIFORNIA, *reprinted in* 1 PUBLICATIONS OF THE ACADEMY OF PACIFIC COAST HISTORY 188–93 (1910). A petition dated Oct. 25, 1844 and signed by several expatriates seeking the protection of the *Levant* was presented to her commander by Larkin. A copy may be found 4 LARKIN PAPERS, *supra* note 64, at 67–68.

[136] M.A. 10:425–29, 567, 587 (1841) (Campbell); *id.,* 10:1106 (1842) (Thomas Smith); *id.,* 3:246–59 (1841) (Miguel Filora, foreigner of unspecified nationality).

the first, an apparently natural death in the second, and no suspect in the third. Even in the absence of a suspect caught in the act, however, investigations were made, looking toward potential prosecution, in these cases where the victim was foreign. It was noted earlier that the murderers of foreign victims were prosecuted and some were executed for their crimes.[137] Foreigners who were victims of woundings and assault were likewise protected by the criminal law, and their attackers were prosecuted. One Frenchman who was badly cut in 1844 in Monterey by Mexican soldiers was even paid a pension by the Mexican government until the time of the American invasion in 1846.[138]

Robbery of foreign expatriates was a frequent source of criminal prosecution. Sometimes foreigners were prosecuted for robbery of fellow expatriates,[139] but more frequently it was native Californios who were charged with the robbery of a foreigner. For example, in 1835 authorities sought two Californios for arrest and prosecution in connection with the assault and theft of an Englishman in Los Angeles.[140] In Monterey another native was prosecuted and jailed for several months for robbery of an Englishman's goods from his home in 1842.[141] A year later another Californio was sentenced to one year at the public works for robbing Larkin's store in Monterey.[142]

Crimes lesser than robbery simply were not punished seriously in Mexican California, no matter by whom committed. There were, however, some occasional prosecutions of defendants who had committed lesser crimes against expatriates.[143]

[137] See *supra* notes 88 and 89 and accompanying text. Of course, expatriates were prosecuted for murder and at least one, Samuel Taggart, was executed. See *supra* note 90 and accompanying text.

[138] 4 HISTORY OF CALIFORNIA, *supra* note 31, at 364 (Pierre Atillan, a Frenchman, given a pension). In another case, a Chileno was fined twenty-five pesos, made to pay damages, and summarily ordered out of California for his wounding of a foreigner by the name of James Gualtern. M.A. 3:260–75 (1841).

[139] James Meadows, Englishman, was prosecuted in 1843 for the theft of twenty-two head of cattle from his employer, John B.R. Cooper, an American. M.A. 3:527–28 and 4:178–243 (1843). The prosecution was ultimately dismissed.

[140] L.A.P.R. A: 32 (1835).

[141] M.A. 3:829, 878–79, 4:89–90 (1842). The defendant was released after several months in jail and the prosecution dismissed, but a factor was the private settlement of damages. *Id.*, 3:900–11.

[142] *Id.*, 4:36–88 (1843).

[143] In 1841 an armed Californio slipped through a window into a Frenchman's home and was sentenced to serve one month at public works. *Id.*, 3:210–25

In short, the Mexican California criminal courts treated the American and the British expatriates fairly and equally. They were not singled out for harsher punishments as defendants, and if victims they were given the same protection as the native Californios. It is true that many more minor crimes went relatively unpunished, but this was owing to a lack of a professionally trained bar, the frequent rotation of lay judges, untrained and specially appointed prosecutors, the absence of prisons, the poor quality of the jails, and a reliance on mere citizen patrols instead of a sheriff or police. That minor crimes escaped punishment was not due to a disproportionate treatment of foreigners. The evidence of many serious crimes against expatriates which were handled adequately must also be considered in reaching this conclusion.

The more generalized expatriate criticisms as to lack of bail, confrontation, and jury trial were founded upon cultural presuppositions they carried with them to California. They failed to recognize that they were in the midst of a completely different legal tradition derived from Roman law and not the common law. In short, by applying the norms of their own tradition, the Anglo-American expatriates saw and described a far gloomier picture of the California criminal justice system, and their relationship to it, than actually existed.

(1841). An Irishman was sentenced to banishment for three years to the northern frontier for adultery with an Englishman's wife. *Id.*, 3:506–24 (1842).

4

Civil Litigation

Civil litigation was commenced by an oral complaint made by the aggrieved party before the local town judge. California followed the procedure of the Judicial Act of May 23, 1837, which specified that the alcalde or justice of the peace should then summon the defendant to a required conciliation hearing, stating in the summons the day, the hour, and the place of the hearing, the object of the complaint, and ordering both parties to bring with them an *hombre bueno,* or "good man."[1]

These *hombres buenos,* chosen by the litigants one apiece, were not advocates. Obviously they were not badly disposed toward the litigants who had selected them for this unpaid service, but their function was not to represent the party. Rather, they were to examine the allegations of the disputants and recommend a just settlement to the alcalde.[2] The *hombres buenos* were taken from all classes of society, although those most otherwise influential in politics or business were more likely to be asked to serve. They never formed a professional class, and no particular names appear with inordinate regularity as *hombres buenos.* Often the records do not reveal any particular relationship between a party and the individual he had asked to serve as his "good man." Thus the institution appears to be much more a community input into the dispute resolution process than advocacy for the parties.

---

[1] Citations to the Spanish text and the English translations of the act of May 23, 1837 may be found in chapter 2, notes 21 & 22.

[2] This function was made clear in a manual for alcaldes published in 1820. J. BARQUERA, A LOS SEÑORES ALCALDES CONSTITUCIONALES (Mexico City 1820), cited in Robertson, "From Alcalde to Mayor: A History of the Change from the Mexican to the American Local Institutions in California," at 52 (Ph.D. dissertation, University of California at Berkeley, 1908).

At the appointed time and place the alcalde or justice of the peace sat down with the parties and their *hombres buenos* and elicited the respective contentions of plaintiff and defendant. The typical conciliation hearing was informal, with no lawyers, no persons acting in the role of lawyers, and no discussion of substantive law other than appeals to rather vaguely described "rights."

The judges usually made an effort to conciliate the parties after their presentations and even before the *hombres buenos* began to discuss the merits of the case.[3] If that failed, pursuant to the mandate of the statute the parties were asked to leave the room, and the *hombres buenos* and judge discussed the matter. After receiving the recommendation of the "good men," the judge had to render a decision within eight days, although it was usually done immediately, that in his opinion would be most likely "to avoid a lawsuit and obtain the agreement of the parties."[4]

The form of the conciliation decision varied. The alcalde's decision was stronger than a recommendation. It was in the form of a judgment (*'providencia'*), though nonbinding unless accepted by the parties. The records of the conciliation process were kept in a separate Book of Conciliations maintained by the judge, and it was often noted that the decision was in agreement with both *hombres buenos* or that the judge and *hombres buenos* jointly made the decision.[5]

Indeed, the rate at which the *hombres buenos* joined together to recommend a particular settlement was overwhelming, notwithstanding that they were selected by opposing parties. A strong impression is that unity among these "good men" in settlement recommendation approached 90 percent, clearly showing their office as conciliators and not partisans. If the *hombres buenos* disagreed, the judge then made a conciliation judgment himself.[6]

The conciliation decision could be conditional and dependent on some official certification of an unclear fact.[7] It could be com-

[3] Some examples include A Prefect Records of Los Angeles, 99–106 (1839) [hereinafter cited as L.A.P.R. in style of L.A.P.R. A:99–106]. These records are on deposit with Henry E. Huntington Library in San Marino, California. Another example may be found in 6 Monterey Archives, at 988–89 (1844) [hereinafter cited as M.A. in style of M.A. 6:988–89]. These records are on file with the Monterey County Historical Society, Salinas, California.

[4] Law of May 23, 1837, § 108.

[5] Examples are M.A. 6:323 (1841), *id.*, 6:1028 (1845).

[6] An example is *id.*, 6:272 (1837).

[7] Examples include *id.*, 6:319 (1841).

plex and detailed, much like a judgment in an English equity court, as for example, the judgment was in the settlement of a dispute between a landowner and a commercial lumber operator.[8] Very few conciliation judgments, whether accepted or not, called for an immediate payment of money. Almost all California judgments called for payments at least partly in goods, usually hides, and most specified installment payments.

In reaching judgment the alcalde could appoint a master to investigate unclear facts,[9] or he could take evidence himself. A charming example of taking evidence in the conciliation hearing is a suit brought in December 1842 by an English carpenter against an American.[10] It was to recover the value of a table ordered by the defendant, five feet long, three feet wide, with one drawer, for the construction of which plaintiff demanded twelve pesos (about $132 in 1987 terms). The judge, a Californio, ordered an appraisal by "one of the profession of the plaintiff that came from the same country," and asked the parties to leave while he questioned him. The expatriate witness started out by asking that his name not be used because he wanted to avoid any animosity, but testified that in his opinion the table was worth only eight pesos. The judge was surprised by this differential and called in still another carpenter, a native. The judge was careful, as he informs us in the Book of Conciliations, not to tell him of the preceding evaluations. The local carpenter also appraised the table at only eight pesos, which is what the *juez* ordered as a conciliation judgment.

It was compulsory to respond to the summons to conciliation, and the statute provided a fine of from two to ten pesos for failure to appear after a second summons.[11] The defendant could avoid conciliation by making an appearance before the alcalde and saying, in the words of the act, that he "renounces the benefit of conciliation."

The conciliation process was popular in California. Access to the local alcalde or justice of the peace was easy, the procedure was fast, and the process was informal. Furthermore, it was inexpensive. Filing fees were generated by the required use of

---

[8]*Id.,* 6:343–44 (1839).
[9]*Id.,* 9:555, 591, 615, 623 (1839).
[10]*Id.,* 6:498 (1842).
[11]Vicente de la Osa was fined three pesos for failure to comply with a summons. L.A.P.R. A:113 (1839).

sealed paper for judicial documents. This specially sealed paper was available in California only about half the time however, and when unavailable there were no costs at all to use the legal machinery. Even if the sealed paper were available its cost was minimal. As of the spring of 1843 it cost only two reales, one-quarter of a peso (now about $2.75), for the issuance of a summons. Even for the filing of a formal lawsuit, a step that could be undertaken only after conciliation, the cost was only a single peso.[12]

The evidence of the conciliations indicates that these were not pro forma, impersonal attempts to settle lawsuits, but were serious efforts to mediate human aggrievements. One example of a small, rather homey dispute illustrates the process and the flavor of a conciliation hearing.[13] The plaintiff was Juan José Abella, commander of a battalion of about two hundred soldiers that Governor Micheltorena had brought with him from Mexico in 1842. Abella was an Indian; he held the rank of captain, and judging from the nature of the lawsuit, dressed well and probably was a bit of a dandy. The defendant was John Romie, an American who had arrived in California in 1843 and was working as a tailor in Monterey. Typical of the "newer arrivals," Romie seems to have been somewhat hard-headed. He had not bothered to learn Spanish after almost a year of residency, and William Hartnell, an Englishman, served as interpreter at the conciliation hearing.

Abella owned a very expensive cape, and in the summer of 1844 it was badly torn by some dogs allegedly owned by Romie's minor son. Abella sued Romie for the value of the cape. Although Abella was a military officer, the case came before the second alcalde of the Monterey civilian court because the defendant was a civilian. Abella brought a fellow military officer of his battalion as his *hombre bueno,* and the defendant selected a Mexican who had been a longtime resident in California. The acting second alcalde was a native Californio. The scales of "presumptive favoritism" are more evenly balanced here than might be imagined since Micheltorena's battalion was composed, to the extent of at least one half, of released convicts, and had acquired in California an unfavorable reputation for petty thefts and lootings.

At the hearing the defendant asserted that the dogs were not

[12] Decree of President Santa Anna circularized by Governor Micheltorena on June 3, 1843. *Id.,* A:123–38 (1843).
[13] M.A. 6:988–89 (1844).

his, to which the plaintiff replied that he would be able to prove
that the dogs were always in the doorway of Romie's house or
with Romie's son. Romie rejoined that while the dogs in question
might have been by his house—apparently everyone knew which
dogs were involved—still it would be unfair to require him to pay
for the cape before it had been repaired and the extent of damages ascertained. At this point the judge suggested that Romie
ought to pay something, to which the defendant responded that
he was only prepared to apologize and ask for Abella's pardon, but
in the name of his son. Apologies and assuagement of honor had a
far greater currency in the society of Mexican California than in
our own, but this clearly was not enough for the captain, and he
refused the offer.

The judge then ordered Abella and Romie to leave so that he
could confer with the *hombres buenos.* After discussion, the
judge suggested to the *hombres buenos* that the captain was only
entitled to the value of the cloth used in the cape, which he felt
was about sixty pesos. While this was a great deal of money for a
coat, it presumably was somewhat less than the value of the cape
itself. After further conference the judge reduced the amount to
fifty pesos, which he ordered Romie to pay as a conciliation
judgment.

When a conciliation judgment was made, the Judicial Act of
1837 required that the parties be informed of it in the presence of
the *hombres buenos,* that it be written down in the Book of Conciliations with an indication of whether the parties accepted it,
and that the entry then be signed by the parties, the alcalde, the
hombres buenos, and the judge's clerk, if there were one. In the
case of *Abella v. Romie,* the conciliation judgment was signed by
the parties but with no indication of agreement or disagreement.

The conciliation process had a huge success rate, and acceptances by the parties of the conciliation judgments appear to have
a rate of about 85 percent. The overwhelming majority of civil
suits in the Mexican California courts terminated in stipulated,
agreed-upon judgments entered in the Book of Conciliations.[14]

If no agreement were reached at the conciliation level, the alcalde or justice of the peace was required upon demand to give
the plaintiff a certificate that conciliation had been attempted.

[14] Robertson, *supra* note 2, at 54, concurs in this judgment.

There are several examples in the California records of certificates of unsuccessful conciliation.[15]

According to the 1837 legislation, the plaintiff's next step was to take the certificate of unsuccessful conciliation to the Court of First Instance and file a formal lawsuit. As noted earlier, however, these courts were not organized in California. What then happened following a failure of conciliation?

The larger cities of Los Angeles and Monterey generally had two justices of the peace or alcaldes from the mid-1830s, and even the smaller cities often had two judges from the early 1840s. The second or junior judge conducted the conciliation hearings and, upon failure, the matter would then be lodged before the first alcalde or first justice of the peace.[16] Of course, viewed with a fine legalistic eye, this other *juez* or alcalde would have jurisdiction in a technical sense in a case involving more than 100 pesos only after the decree of March 2, 1843 allowed California alcaldes and justices of the peace to act as judges of the First Instance. Little importance was attached to jurisdictional restrictions, however, and this decree merely confirmed existing practice. If there was no other judge, or the office was vacant, a formal suit might be filed before the same judge who had attempted conciliation, although this was rare.[17]

The judge who had conducted conciliation could order compliance with the conciliation judgment, even though the parties did not accept it, or he might order judgment notwithstanding disagreement among the *hombres buenos*.[18] This is not as heavy-handed as it seems because the 1837 act did give the alcaldes and justices of the peace a general civil jurisdiction in matters involving less than 100 pesos. In fact, the legislation provided that in

[15]Examples include: M.A. 6:132–33 (1835); *id.*, 6:975 (1844); *id.*, 6:1231 (1846).

[16]An example is *id.*, 6:1000–17, 1084, 8:243, 15:699 (1845).

[17]*Id.*, 6:874, 882–90 (1843).

[18]An example is *id.*, 6:720 (1842). This judgment was clearly binding as the judge specified that execution would follow if defendant did not comply with the judgment. In another matter, a judge ordered a judgment of one heifer and one silver peso in payment of the manufacture of a branding iron after the *hombres buenos* disagreed. *Id.*, 6:272 (1837). The court records are often unclear in regard to these judgments because the conciliation orders were in the *form* of judgments, whether accepted or not, and regardless whether more or less than 100 pesos.

matters of the verbal process, that is, for demands under 100 pesos, the alcalde or *juez de paz* should pronounce a "definitive determination" after conciliation had been attempted and he had "heard" the judgment of the *hombres buenos*. It did not specify that he had to *follow* that judgment. Since the majority of California litigation involved amounts under 100 pesos, the knowledge that a judge could order compliance with the recommended conciliation judgment may well have encouraged litigants to accept the proposed settlements.

If a lawsuit was filed after failure of conciliation, the proceedings became considerably more formal, and written depositions of witness testimony would be taken and a dossier compiled much in the same manner as in criminal cases. Documentary evidence could be obtained by the parties and given to the alcalde as a portion of the file,[19] and certified copies of papers from an official's files might be accessioned directly by the alcalde.[20] Witnesses could be subpoenaed to give testimony before the alcalde.[21] If a witness resided outside of the local judge's jurisdiction, the court in which the suit was pending had to request the alcalde of the town where the witness lived to order the witness to come to the forum court or to give a declaration before his own alcalde.[22] The 1837 legislation provided only for the examination of a witness by the alcalde of the district in which he lived. Of course, there was no jury and a single judge ultimately would render judgment.

Formal proceedings were rare, however, and the stipulated conciliation judgments terminated most litigation, even for claims well over 100 pesos. This success rate can be seen in an inventory

---

[19] Examples include *id.*, 10:1333 (1842) and Official Documents Relating to Early San Francisco. Document 154 (1846) [hereinafter cited as O.D.R.E.S.F.]. These documents are deposited with Bancroft Library. Others are in the Los Angeles Archives, especially vols. 8 and 9.

[20] O.D.R.E.S.F. Document 81 (justice of the peace of San Jose sends documents from subprefect's archives relative to various parties at request of San Francisco alcalde).

[21] M.A. 8:243 (1845) is one example.

[22] Examples are *id.*, 8:151 (1845) (letter from justice of the peace of San Jose to alcalde of Monterey; the witnesses summoned cannot go to Monterey as they are sick); 43 Archives of California, at 351 (1845) [hereinafter cited as A.C. in the style of A.C. 43:351] (justice of the peace of Yerba Buena to alcalde of Monterey, asking the Monterey judge to remit a witness in his jurisdiction). These documents are on deposit with Bancroft Library, University of California, Berkeley, California.

of the Monterey Court of First Instance made on May 1, 1843, upon the occasion of the turnover of the office of the first judge by José Fernández to Teodoro Gonzales. Fernández had been the judge of the First Instance, or first alcalde, since the beginning of 1842 and had kept books and records of cases that had been concluded in the "present year," that is, January to May 1843, and the "past year," 1842.[23] There were five notebooks for 1842 and one for 1843 of closed conciliations. As these records were sometimes as brief as one-half page, this represents a substantial volume, perhaps hundreds of conciliations. For the sixteen months from January 1842 through April 1843, the trial court of California's capital and second largest city had only six concluded formal lawsuits, that is, suits of the written process involving at least 100 pesos. The inventory is not as clear regarding the completed suits as for the conciliations, and some of the six may have been from an earlier period. If so, that would mean that there were even fewer than six formal lawsuits during these sixteen months. There was only one pending lawsuit as of May 1, 1843, and that was suspended by the plaintiff. This dearth of formal litigation does not reflect a lack of contentiousness but rather the success of conciliation.

Most litigants were males, and the status of women as parties to Mexican California lawsuits was ambiguous. Women brought a considerable number of domestic relations suits for separation or relief from spousal harassment. Although parties only infrequently in other litigation, women generally sued through males to whom they gave powers of attorney,[24] the same procedure followed by minor litigants.[25] Women were sued directly as defendants, and it is clear that females were not invariably required to sue through male frontmen.[26] Perhaps much depended on the particular views of individual alcaldes. In 1831, for example, one Paula Garibay filed suit for damages to her residential property.

[23] M.A. 11:301–4 (1843). Fernández may have been absent from his office for two months of this sixteen-month period, but his record books apparently covered the entire time from January 1842 through April 1843.

[24] Examples are in L.A.P.R. A:91–98 (1839) and M.A. 6:276 (1837).

[25] In *Pombert v. Manyarres,* suit was brought by the minor plaintiff's mother through a power of attorney she gave to a male. M.A. 6:1000–17, 8:243, 15:699 (1845).

[26] M.A. 6:457 (1842) (suit for forty pesos for goods bought by female defendant from plaintiff's store).

This plaintiff was not only female but married as well. Yet nothing was made of these facts during the litigation.[27] Suits brought or defended through attorneys-in-fact were common. Yet this practice does not appear to be evidence of a quasi-professional class. Their use reflected frontier conditions generally: the business necessity of travel and frequent absences, a need for collection of debts in distant places, and poor communications. Indeed, powers of attorney were not granted merely for specific litigation but were given generally without reference to a particular lawsuit. They were among the most common of documents recorded by the Californios with the alcaldes. Neither those holding powers of attorney nor those few licensed attorneys present in California appear with any regularity in the judicial records. Indeed, it seems that the licensed lawyers did not practice law beyond their role as asesores, or advisers to the government. Yet occasionally it is clear that a party was present in the city while litigation was being conducted in his name by an attorney-in-fact,[28] and here may have been the early beginnings of a professional body of de facto attorneys.

Among the problems facing any legal system are threshold issues of jurisdiction and remedies—whether the suit is filed in the proper court and against permissible defendants, and whether any prejudgment remedies, such as attachment, are available to aid the plaintiff. The Mexican California legal system used few prejudgment remedies, but it experienced great problems with jurisdiction.

Jurisdictional questions are of two kinds. First is whether a particular court can properly adjudicate a particular kind of controversy (subject matter jurisdiction). A second question is whether a particular court can properly adjudicate a matter against a particular defendant (jurisdiction over the person). Subject matter jurisdiction posed some problems in the area of domestic relations, which will be considered in a separate chapter, but little

---

[27] *Id.,* at 6:347 (1831). The conciliation record indicates on its face that the plaintiff was married. She may have been widowed at the time of the suit, however; she had married twenty-one years earlier in 1810. 1 M. NORTHROP, SPANISH-MEXICAN FAMILIES OF EARLY CALIFORNIA: 1769–1850, at 143 (1976). Women in neighboring New Mexico apparently had considerable freedom in litigation. Lecompte, *The Independent Women of Hispanic New Mexico, 1821–1846,* 12 W. HIST. Q. 17 (1981).

[28] Examples include M.A. 6:1005 (1845) and L.A.P.R. A:155–70 (1845).

difficulty in general litigation regarding the value or type of claim. After March 1843 the alcaldes and justices of the peace in California were expressly authorized to act in the capacities of judges of the First Instance, who constituted, under the 1837 legislation, the trial courts of initial, general, and unlimited jurisdiction. As was discussed in chapter 2, even before March 1843 there was seldom any objection raised by litigant or judge that the 100-peso jurisdiction allotted to the justice of the peace and the alcalde was being exceeded.

There were many problems with jurisdiction over the defendant's person. First was the *fuero* system. Just as in criminal cases, soldiers and priests were entitled in civil litigation to be tried by their own courts. There is no evidence that a California ecclesiastic claimed this right during the Mexican era, but there were a few occasions in which a soldier who found himself a defendant in a civil case raised an initial objection to jurisdiction, claiming that the matter at hand should be dismissed and remanded to a military court.[29]

The most difficult jurisdictional problem was caused by a provision in the May 23, 1837 act that limited the jurisdiction of the judges to the subjects within their judicial districts, meaning the towns in which they sat and the surrounding countryside. This was interpreted to mean that if a creditor resided in Monterey he would be unable to sue a defendant residing in Los Angeles in the Los Angeles court since he, the plaintiff, was not a resident of Los Angeles. It is apparent that this would cause considerable difficulty with litigation other than of an extremely local variety. By the 1840s each small town had its own alcalde and therefore its own judicial district. Some clumsy ways were invented to circumvent the problem.

One method around the difficulty was for the alcalde where the plaintiff lived and had filed suit to formally request that the alcalde where the defendant resided order the defendant to appear

---

[29]M.A. 6:276 (1837); *id.*, 10:1315–19 (1842). Father José María Suárez del Real apparently claimed an exemption from being sued in a civil court during the American military occupation, which claim was denied by the American military governor. *See* 4 Z. ENGELHARDT, THE MISSIONS AND MISSIONARIES OF CALIFORNIA 724 (1908–1916) (4 vols. & index). This may have been an extraordinary occasion because evidence advanced by a modern Franciscan writer suggests that this priest was a scoundrel and dissolute. M. GEIGER, FRANCISCAN MISSIONARIES IN HISPANIC CALIFORNIA 1769–1848, at 249–51 (1969).

in the plaintiff's jurisdiction, first for the conciliation hearing and then, if necessary, for formal suit. In other words, an alcalde who unquestionably had jurisdiction over the defendant could order the defendant to submit to another's jurisdiction. There are many of these alcalde requests in the judicial records, asking that a defendant be ordered to appear in the plaintiff's district.[30] In some cases the defendant's alcalde cooperated and ordered the defendant to respond in the plaintiff's court,[31] and in other cases there was resistance.[32]

Most defendants sued from outside their place of residence had either contracted debts or formerly lived in the plaintiff's town. It was a matter of *returning*. This was not always true, however. Some defendants would be incensed at being sued far from home and complained that only their own alcaldes had jurisdiction over them and questioned how they could be sued outside their own districts.[33]

A second method of dealing with the obstacles to interdistrict

[30] M.A. 11:1101 (first *juez* of San Jose to first alcalde of Monterey); *id.*, 11:443 (1843) (justice of the peace of Branciforte to Monterey *juez*); *id.*, 8:153 (1845); L.A.P.R. 2:424–25 (1841) (San Diego justice of the peace to first justice of the peace of Los Angeles).

[31] L.A.P.R. 1:165 (1842) (request to justice of the peace of Los Angeles from justice of the peace of Santa Barbara; marginal note: "The man in question was sent back."); M.A. 11:349 (1843) (justice of the peace of San Luis Obispo request of first justice of the peace of Monterey; the Monterey judge acknowledges the note and informs San Luis Obispo justice that he has "ordered him [the defendant] to go to your point with the object that he respond to the charges of plaintiff."); O.D.R.E.S.F. Document 70 (1844) (first justice of the peace of San Jose acknowledges request of San Francisco first alcalde and advises that he promptly will take all possible measures to send the defendant to him).

[32] M.A. 11:1405 (1844) (alcalde for Santa Barbara to second Monterey judge: "the defendant you ask to appear in your court has been gone from this place for some time and I am informed he settled with his family in San Luis Obispo"); L.A.P.R. 1:590B–90D (1842) (justice of the peace of San Juan to second justice of the peace of Los Angeles: "the law requires you must specify the purpose of the complaint and hour and place to appear to answer") (i.e., at a conciliation hearing). The San Juan judge was correct as this requirement was in the 1837 legislation. Resistance on the part of the military commandant of Sonoma to return a civil defendant in response to an order of a justice of the peace and a prefect was noted in letter, Larkin to Salvador Vallejo, July 26, 1843, 2 THE LARKIN PAPERS: PERSONAL, BUSINESS AND OFFICIAL CORRESPONDENCE OF THOMAS OLIVER LARKIN, MERCHANT AND UNITED STATES CONSUL IN CALIFORNIA 29 (Hammond ed. 1951–1968) (10 vols. & index) [hereinafter cited as LARKIN PAPERS].

[33] L.A.P.R. 1:415–17 (1840); M.A. 10:1315–19 (1842). See the quote in text accompanying note 34, *infra*.

litigation was for the plaintiff to give a power of attorney, in effect an assignment of the account or obligation, to a resident of the district in which the defendant resided. This technique was especially popular with merchants and tradesmen and helps to account for the large numbers of powers of attorney. Technical distinctions between assignments and powers to sue were not raised.

A third approach to the difficulties of litigation against a resident of a different judicial district was the rare attempt to attach any assets of a nonresident defendant that might be found within the plaintiff's jurisdiction. Seizure of assets might force a defendant into the court in which suit was filed, not through an alcalde's order, but from a desire to defend the attached assets. Today that would be called quasi in rem jurisdiction.

An interesting example of a prejudgment attachment made to obtain jurisdiction over a defendant, and one that reveals much about the limitations of the Mexican California legal system, is a suit brought by José Maldonado against Santiago Argüello. On July 15, 1842, Maldonado presented a petition to the Monterey alcalde reciting that Argüello was a resident of Los Angeles and owed plaintiff, a resident of Monterey, the sum of 220 pesos for goods sold to Argüello in San Pedro—sarapes, bedspreads, sealing wax, and so forth. He alleged further that one Pedro Narváez, a resident of Monterey, owed the defendant more than 600 pesos and asked that the judge order Narváez not to pay these funds until Argüello appeared in Maldonado's lawsuit. On the same day the Monterey *juez* wrote the justice of the peace of Los Angeles that he had been presented with these documents in due form and had ordered Narváez to retain the sums owed defendant pending Argüello's appearance at a conciliation hearing.

The second justice of the peace in Los Angeles summoned Argüello, read the Monterey order to him, and wrote down the defendant's response. Argüello said he was

surprised by the great facility with which that judge [the Monterey judge] attacks me. Is it possible that . . . he has power over me or my interests to make me appear before his court and journey over 190 leagues? [500 miles, although the distance is actually about 325 miles] . . . [H]e has no authority to make me an extortion victim. . . . Is it not clear that the justices of the peace should hear defendants in their respective areas? . . . As a resident here, and such is admitted in the document [the judge's attachment], prevents me from making an appearance before my [local] judge. . . . The justice of the peace of Monterey has no authority or jurisdiction for such an attachment and I protest.[34]

Argüello went on to make various threats to get other authorities involved and to seek damages from all concerned. The response was sent back to Monterey. In late August the Monterey judge acknowledged receipt. The judge, José Fernández, said he regretted the defendant's attitude but noted that the Los Angeles judge had not himself made any objection to the attachment. He found the Argüello's answer offensive and suggested that only officials should be involved in this, not the defendant. He again summoned Argüello "the second and last time so that he or an attorney appear for conciliation."

Time passed with no response. On October 11, Maldonado again petitioned the Monterey judge. He had to leave for the interior on business and wanted an order directing Narváez to deliver the 220 pesos owed by Argüello. The judge granted the request but required the plaintiff to find a surety to guarantee the repayment of the 220 pesos if Argüello might return in the future and prevail. This itself is interesting because it shows that the California judges had no concept of a default, that is, a definite date by which a defendant had to appear or be foreclosed from thereafter being heard on the merits of the lawsuit.

Maldonado v. Argüello was an ordinary lawsuit in its subject matter, yet it is unusual to find a successful use of a prejudgment attachment. Most attempts at prejudgment remedies trailed off into unsuccessful confusion. Such was *Célis v. Sutter*. John Sutter was a large debtor against whom seizures were frequently attempted. He was himself the *juez* of his own district, unlikely to order himself to appear elsewhere, and therefore difficult to sue. He had a boat in which he frequently traveled the river from Sacramento to San Francisco to deliver crops or pick up supplies. There were abortive efforts to attach the boat in 1842,[35] but in 1845 it was actually seized and put into the hands of a neutral keeper by order of the port captain, upon the recommendation of

[34]M.A. 6:525–35, 538–41, 10:1291, 1315–19, 1379 (1842). The note from the Monterey court to the Los Angeles judge may also be found in L.A.P.R. 2:469–70 (1842).

[35]Mariano Vallejo, *Documentos para la historia de California,* (37 vols.) Documents 11:249, 251 (1842). These documents are on deposit with Bancroft Library, University of California, Berkeley, California.

the alcalde. It was for the benefit of a creditor who was a Spanish national, Eulogio Célis. This ignited a complicated controversy in which the Hudson's Bay Company claimed that Sutter had mortgaged the ship to it and therefore the attachment was improper. In addition, the Russian-American Company, a creditor even more substantial than Hudson's, contended that it was entitled to the launch. Although it was clear that the seizure was made only to force Sutter to submit to the San Francisco jurisdiction, and although the mortgage was of dubious validity because it was unrecorded, the governor, to whom Hudson's Bay Company petitioned, dissolved the attachment on the ostensible grounds that the seizure should not have been ordered by an executive official. Apparently the governor erroneously believed that the subprefect had been responsible for the seizure.[36] Political favoritism to Hudson's Bay, then represented by the British consul, was also involved.

The complexities of interdistrict litigation were worse when the objects of the lawsuit were movable, such as horses or cattle. One solution was for the judge to make an initial determination of entitlement and award the movable property accordingly, on condition that the tentatively prevailing litigant obtain a surety or himself assure the court that he would pay any damages if he did not ultimately win the lawsuit.[37]

Interdistrict litigation was also complicated in cases where there were more than two parties who resided in different judicial districts. One example of a suit on a third party beneficiary contract will illustrate.[38] Domínguez, who lived in San Diego, owed a debt to Olivas, who lived in Los Angeles. Domínguez entered into an agreement with Petra, who also lived in Los Angeles, whereby for a consideration from Domínguez to Petra, Petra would pay Olivas. Time passed with no payment. Olivas, the third party creditor beneficiary, sued Petra, the promisor, on the contract

---

[36] This complicated saga is recorded in documents that appear in nonchronological order, in Manuel Castro, *Documentos para la historia de California* (2 vols.) Documents 1:159, 160, 162, 163, 164, 187, 189 and 2:1, 6, 8 and also in Francisco Sánchez, Document dated Oct. 15, 1845 (C–Y/318, free-standing document, not in a collection) (receipt by third-party keeper, Joseph P. Thompson, an American). Both the Castro and Sánchez *Documentos* are on deposit with Bancroft Library, University of California, Berkeley, California.

[37] An example is L.A.P.R. 1:58–60 (1840).

[38] *Id.,* 2:423A–23B (1841).

Petra had made with Domínguez, the promisee. The suit was brought in Los Angeles between two residents. Petra defended on the grounds of failure of consideration in that Domínguez had not performed his part of the Domínguez-Petra contract and therefore no payment was due from him to Olivas. The difficulty was that Domínguez was not a resident of Los Angeles. The justice of the peace in Los Angeles wrote this up as precisely as he could and passed the entire matter to the San Diego judge. We see here not only a sophisticated legal arrangement but a complicated lawsuit, notwithstanding that the consideration from Domínguez to Petra was only a cow and the payment to be made by Petra to Olivas was only six pesos.

What was needed, we would think today, was department-wide power for the summons of any alcalde or justice of the peace, in addition to some clearly defined rules for venue—who could be sued, for what kinds of cases, in which districts. Throughout the Mexican period these problems were never resolved. It is easy to sympathize with the 1843 complaint to the governor from the San Jose *juez* that legal proceedings between citizens of different jurisdictions were "complicated and oppressive."[39]

There was occasional use of other prejudgment remedies, notably the power of arrest to force a defendant into finding a bondsman to stand as surety. In one case a defendant was moving out of the jurisdiction, and the plaintiff asked the court to restrain him until he provided a bond or a mortgage on one of his ranches equal to the 620-peso debt.[40] In another case the Los Angeles judge decided without citation of authority that where a defendant's debts had been contracted against his property he could be jailed and forced to put up a bond.[41] Also in Los Angeles a blacksmith employed on a ship was detained for debt.[42] Prejudgment remedies were unusual, however, whether for interdistrict or intradistrict litigation. The examples related are not paradigmatic of many others and are useful primarily as illuminating the limitations of the Mexican California legal system.

Assuming there were no problems with jurisdiction or prejudg-

[39] 4 H. BANCROFT, HISTORY OF CALIFORNIA 685 (1886) (1884–1890) (7 vols.).

[40] O.D.R.E.S.F. Document 158 (1846) (suit in May 1846 by American against German).

[41] L.A.P.R. 1:44–49, 300 (1840).

[42] *Id.*, 2:441A (1842).

ment remedies, or, if any, they were resolved, the litigation would go on to conciliation or ultimate trial, processes that have already been reviewed. Two questions remain: what sort of judgment could be expected as an ultimate outcome, and how would such a judgment be enforced?

Judgments were often particularized and tailored to the specific abilities of the defendant to pay. If he were a rancher he might be ordered to pay in hides. If appropriate to a defendant's personal situation and source of livelihood, he might be ordered to make payment in soap, wheat, brandy, lumber, or other goods. Some examples are appended.[43] Commodity judgments would be expected in a specie-starved region such as California where hard money was scarce. Judgments especially tailored to a particular defendant also reflect that many disputes were compromised and stipulated through conciliation. In complicated litigation this could result in very specific orders.[44]

One of the most interesting personalized judgments was *Spear v. Angelino,* an 1841 lawsuit of an American versus a Californio. In this San Francisco action for 232 pesos, the defendant admitted the debt but said he had no means for payment. The conciliation recommendation, accepted by the parties, was that the defendant should work for the plaintiff, with half of his salary credited toward the debt and half of his salary given to the defendant's family.[45]

Judgments were often made payable in installments. The order would direct so much to be paid immediately and the balance within a period of time, from six weeks, for example, to two years, or perhaps to be paid in full at the time of the next cattle slaugh-

---

[43] M.A. 6:723 (1842) (judgment of 196 pesos ordered paid half in money, half in goods); *id.,* 6:801 (1843) (defendant given option to pay in money or soap); *id.,* 6:272 (1837) (defendant ordered to pay one heifer and one silver peso to artisan suing for manufacture of branding iron); *id.,* 6:497 (1842) (defendant given option to pay in hides immediately or in money if payment delayed more than eight days); *id.,* 6:802 (1843) (133 pesos to be paid in soap); *id.,* 6:849 (1843) (suit for accounting of work done in partnership; judge recommends payment of 155 pesos in kind). An interesting confessed judgment is found in 2 LARKIN PAPERS, *supra* note 32, at 10–11 ($1,206 in 1843 confession of judgment to be paid one-half in hides and one-half in tallow and grain). Expatriates are well included among both plaintiffs and defendants in these commodity judgments.

[44] M.A. 6:343–44 (1839); *id.,* 15:149 (1835).

[45] O.D.R.E.S.F. Document 54 (1841).

ter. Another variant was monthly installments. An installment style of judgment was a common practice and again some examples are appended.[46]

Another feature of the judgments rendered in the Mexican California courts was that they were modifiable. They were subject to defendants coming back into court with a tale of woe that the crop was bad, the cattle were too thin to slaughter, or some other excuse, and asking that the installment payments be extended.[47] An egregious example of modification was a suit brought by Thomas Larkin against Mariano Castro. It started out with a confession of judgment for $1,206, expressed in dollars, which were used interchangeably with pesos by many persons because of their equal value. The confession of judgment, an agreed judgment without formal suit having been brought, was made in April 1843 and ordered that defendant pay at $200 per month.[48]

Larkin waited eight months during which there were no payments and then applied for an execution sale of defendant's property. The judge gave the defendant more time to comply.[49] In May 1844, Larkin again requested execution. The justice of the peace held a hearing, determined credits for partial payment, and ordered that the balance, $904, be paid partly in seed, soap, and other products in August or September 1844, and partly in hides during the time of the next slaughter, July or August 1844.[50] By November 1844, Larkin still had not been satisfied, and he sent a petition to the Tribunal Superior that ordered immediate execu-

---

[46] M.A. 6:850 (148 peso judgment, 35 pesos now, 75 from hands of third-party debtor of defendant, balance in four months); *id.*, 6:802 (1843) (180 pesos to be paid in August—the next slaughter—in hides at two pesos per hide); *id.*, 6:801 (37 pesos to be paid within six months); *id.*, 6:898 (1843) (defendant ordered to pay 112 pesos in installments); *id.*, 6:823 (1843) (defendant admits debt and wants a few months in which to pay); *id.*, 6:757 (1842) (200-peso judgment, defendant ordered to pay 50 now and 150 in three months). Again, expatriates were as involved as Californios, perhaps more so, with installment judgments, both as plaintiffs and defendants.

[47] L.A.P.R. A:181–83 (1843); M.A. 6:883, 885–86 (1843) are examples. In the Los Angeles example the judgment debtor had petitioned to Governor Micheltorena, alleging that he was an invalid and requesting an extension of time. The governor ordered: "The Judge will arrange between the litigants a reasonable term of time for payment."

[48] Apr. 7, 1843, 2 LARKIN PAPERS, *supra* note 32, at 10–11.

[49] M.A. 11:1611–13 (1844).

[50] *Id.*, 6:930–31 (1844).

tion in December 1844 and which criticized the local judges for their inefficiency.[51]

Excuses began coming in from the various judges involved with the case, and one wrote Larkin that he had urged Castro to deliver his herd to the plaintiff at the annual slaughter (August 1844), but the herd was weak and not enough to cover Larkin's debt. "Of course the fault is not as the Tribunal supposes," but rather the state of the herd. He concluded that "it appears to me that you should wait until the slaughtering time and I think you will be satisfied."[52] The best the judge could suggest to Larkin was further delay, and that is apparently what Larkin received. In September 1845, well after the next slaughter at which the judge was sure Larkin would be paid, Larkin again petitioned for an execution, although acknowledging additional partial payments and a new balance of $621. Castro again sought more time in which to pay.[53]

Payments of judgments could almost be described as voluntary in that enforcement remedies were next to nonexistent. There was clear Mexican law on the procedure of execution on a judgment, but it was not followed in California.[54] There were several requests for seizure of a judgment debtor's property,[55] and there were some judicial threats that execution would soon be carried out if payment were not made.[56] Although there were a very few seizures of the property of judgment debtors in Los Angeles,[57] the closest equivalent in Monterey appears to have been an interesting, but singular, judicial foreclosure of a mortgage, described in a note.[58]

[51] Id., 6:922–23, 925–26 (1844).

[52] Letter, Francisco Díaz to Larkin, Dec. 13, 1844, 2 LARKIN PAPERS, supra note 32, at 327. An excuse of another judge, sent directly to the Tribunal Superior, is in M.A. 6:923–24 (1844).

[53] M.A. 6:916, 1020 (1845).

[54] 3 J. FEBRERO, OBRA COMPLETA DE JURISPRUDENCIA TEÓRICO-PRÁTICA 307–42 (Mexico City 1851) (4 vols.).

[55] M.A. 8:643 (1846); id., 6:882 (1843).

[56] Id., 6:720 (1842); id., 6:337 (1841).

[57] L.A.P.R. A:119–20 (1841); A.C. 38:412–22 (1840).

[58] Howard v. Montenegro, M.A. 8:49, 50, 57 (1845) (American versus Mexican, brought by Mexican, José Abrego, under power of attorney for Howard). This suit was brought in January 1845 to foreclose on a mortgage given by Montenegro to Howard in December 1843 on Montenegro's house in the amount of $1,382. The suit asked for appointment of appraisers, sale of the house, and an order of evic-

The Monterey judicial records for 1835 to 1846 simply fail to reflect a single example of any actual seizure of a judgment debtor's assets. The records do show a few half-hearted attempts by lay judges who did not know what to do. Confronted with petitions for execution, some judges simply forwarded them to the defendants and asked them to answer. The predictable response was often a request for modification.[59] There were other causes of confusion. In *Pombert v. Olivera* (a Canadian versus a Californio, 1842), the auxiliary judge of San Luis Obispo went to the judgment debtor's ranch to seize property pursuant to an order of the judge of the First Instance of Monterey. He did not attach anything because the defendant himself was absent and he heard that he had left to pay his debts.[60] In *Pico v. Amador* (a Californio versus a Californio, 1841) litigation had been carried out so extensively that on appeal to the governor the defendant had been ordered to pay a commodity judgment of 84 fanegas of wheat, or about 146 bushels. Considerable and ludicrous correspondence ensued, summarized in a note, and centering around the problem that the defendant did not have any wheat but only cattle, and no one knew the equivalency of the two and therefore what to seize.[61]

tion directed to the tenants in possession. Subsequently, it appeared that there was another mortgage on the house, in the amount of 950 pesos, granted by Montenegro to José Antonio Aguirre (a Spanish subject) in January of 1844.

The alcalde, Marcelino Escobar, ordered that if there were a sale, Howard must be prepared to pay to Aguirre the balance of his obligation, even though Aguirre's was later in time. Both had been filed shortly after execution, in 1843 and 1844, with the alcalde's office in its notarial function. Escobar appointed three appraisers to ascertain the value, Thomas Larkin (American), David Spence (Scot), and Vicente Molina (Mexican). The appraisers reported the house had a value of 3,000 pesos in hides, and the judge ordered publication for a sale to be held in nine days.

At this point the evidence stops and there is no record of what further developed. One thing is clear: the granting of a mortgage, compared to a simple judgment, did not matter one way or another regarding the judicial boldness exhibited in this case. Stipulated judgments often contained words of mortgage or hypothecation, and that did not seem to make any difference, at least in Monterey, when efforts were made to seek judicial sale of the mortgaged property.

[59] M.A. 6:916, 1020 (1845) is an example.

[60] *Id.*, 10:1295 (1842).

[61] *Id.*, 10:487, 495, 581, 583, 693, 695, 773, 775 (1841). September 25, subprefect to prefect: he will immediately pass on the governor's order to the justice of the peace, although he suggests that the justice is trying to favor the defendant.

What was clearly needed was a well-defined officer authorized to seize a defendant's property and hold a public sale. There was no equivalent to a sheriff's civil division, and the California justice system suffered from its absence.[62] Underlying the legal system as practiced was an assumption that most judgments would be paid voluntarily. The appropriateness of that assumption will be examined in the next chapter.

The civil appellate and supervisory functions were shared by the governor, the prefects and the subprefects, and the Tribunal Superior during the years it operated. The earlier discussion regarding the weakness of the concept of separation of powers and the tradition of the Spanish governor deciding appeals is equally as applicable here as in the criminal arena.

The Tribunal Superior exercised a general superintending authority in civil cases, declaring the local courts incompetent, for example, where one of the local alcaldes was a party to ligitation.[63] In another example, Larkin's suit against Mariano Castro, the tribunal ordered the local judges to proceed to administer postjudgment remedies or inform the tribunal why they were unable to do so.[64] It also granted leaves of absence for the lower court judges.[65] The bulk of this supervisory control was exercised by the prefects, however.

September 25, subprefect to justice of the peace of San Jose: he has gotten nonsense. He wants the justice to work on this and get the defendant to pay. October 2, subprefect to prefect: the justice of the peace told defendant to pay but he has not. How do we proceed? October 9, prefect to subprefect: attach defendant's goods.

October 17, justice of the peace of San Jose to prefect: I asked the subprefect what price I should put on the cattle of the defendant that should be attached. Subprefect answered "that he is not an attorney." With whom should be consult? October 20, prefect to justice of the peace: you should nominate two appraisers, one for plaintiff and another for defendant, to value the cattle in relation to 84 fanegas of wheat [that was the commodity judgment], and in case of disagreement you decide. December 26, subprefect to prefect: today the justice has concluded this, and defendant by agreement has paid the 84 fanegas of wheat at the rate of three pesos per fanega, without having had the attachment.

[62] This point was made by W. HANSEN, THE SEARCH FOR AUTHORITY IN CALIFORNIA 48 (1960).

[63] Albertson, "Jacob P. Leese, Californio," 139–42 (master's thesis, University of California, 1942).

[64] M.A. 6:922–23, 925–26 (1844).

[65] Id., 11:1107 (1844); A.C. 43:369, 370 (1844) are examples. For information on the Tribunal Superior's supervisory functions with regard to criminal litigation, see supra chapter 3, note 37 and accompanying text.

The Tribunal Superior also decided some civil appeals, issuing decrees and reversing lower judgments,[66] but the tribunal was not as active in civil cases as in criminal ones. Furthermore, the court did not meet on a regular basis, and only with great difficulty was it able to accommodate members from both northern and southern California regarding time and place of meeting. Most of the superintending orders and even orders reversing lower decisions were not signed by the entire court but only by the presiding justice and perhaps one associate.

The Tribunal Superior also exercised an original jurisdiction in very large claims brought by foreign companies against John Sutter. It permitted the Russian-American Company to sue Sutter directly in the Tribunal Superior for a claim of 31,559 pesos,[67] approximately $350,000 today and easily the largest lawsuit in the legal history of Mexican California, and allowed the Hudson's Bay Company to sue Sutter in the Tribunal Superior for 6,480 pesos, later amended to 3,323 pesos.[68] These suits never resulted in judgment and apparently meandered aimlessly.

Before the establishment of the Tribunal Superior in 1842, the California governor decided appeals from the alcaldes and justices of the peace, and there are many records of appeals or petitions to the governor for relief from or reversal of a lower court decision.[69] Occasionally petitions would be addressed to the gov-

[66] A.C. 42:399–402 (1844); L.A.P.R. A:155–70 (1843).

[67] O.D.R.E.S.F. Document 117 (1844). A large piece of land litigation may also have been commenced in 1844 in the Tribunal Superior. Osio, *Cartas y documentos,* folder 12, on file with the Bancroft Library, University of California, Berkeley, California (*Berri v. Osio*).

[68] O.D.R.E.S.F. Documents 79, 83, 91 (1844). A letter from Abel Stearns of Los Angeles to Larkin dated Sept. 2, 1845 speaks of presenting a new lawsuit to the "Superior Court." It further says that "the Court is not yet organised and god knows when it will be. The judges have been named, and one of them at least has not accepted." 3 LARKIN PAPERS, *supra* note 32, at 335. The statement regarding lack of organization tends to support the idea that the Tribunal Superior had become inactive by mid-1845. See *supra* chapter 2, note 33 and accompanying text. A suit brought by Nathan Spear against Jacob P. Leese, both Americans, to collect a $3,000 note was probably commenced in the Tribunal Superior in July 1845. A draft of Spear's petition is in Spear, Correspondence and Papers, Box 2, miscellaneous papers, Document 6, on file with the Bancroft Library, University of California, Berkeley, California.

[69] L.A.P.R. 1:262 (1841) (prefect refers to governor's decision); *id.,* 1:12–34 (1838); Manuel Castro, *Correspondence and Papers, 1836–1863,* Box 1, Document 9 (statement by former Governor Alvarado in 1844 regarding his 1839 ap-

ernor even before an alcalde's decision, but these were then passed on to the justice of the peace or alcalde to hear the parties.[70] Similarly, the governor exercised general supervisory authority, ordering alcaldes to suspend judgments pending an investigation, or setting aside from the effect of execution lands granted as a family settlement and not subject to the judgment debtor's control.[71]

One element that seems surprising by our modern lights is the degree of involvement by the governor in the judicial process even after the establishment of the Tribunal Superior. This involvement ranged from simply asking for a report on specific litigation (January 1843),[72] to ordering that a justice of the peace arrange a modification for time of payment by a debtor (May 1843), and even to handling an appeal in a domestic relations suit (November 1843).[73] It is apparent that the tradition of appealing for justice to the governor did not expire with the establishment of the Tribunal Superior. Such were the experiences of neighbor-

---

pellate determination in particular case). Castro's *Correspondence and Papers, 1836–1863* are on deposit with Bancroft Library, University of California, Berkeley, California. Not all governors were willing to act judicially. In 1834, Governor Figueroa refused to consider whether the Los Angeles alcalde should be removed from a case for partiality in a matter involving a dissolution of a partnership of James Johnson (English), Teodoro Salizar (Californio), and José Antonio Aguirre (Spanish). Figueroa said such an action was not within his jurisdiction and referred the petitioner, Johnson, to the appropriate court in lower Mexico. Correspondence between Abel Stearns, attorney in fact for Johnson, Alcalde Pérez, and Governor Figueroa, in Stearns Collection, SG Box 35 (June-August 1834). The Stearns Collection is maintained at the Huntington Library, San Marino, California.

[70]M.A. 11:749 (1843) is an example.

[71]*Archivo de la familia Alviso,* Document 216 (1839?) (letter from Governor Alvarado stating he had ordered the Monterey alcalde to suspend his order pending further discussion). These documents are on file with Bancroft Library, University of California, Berkeley, California. L.A.P.R. A:497E (1841) (governor to prefect regarding Los Angeles justice's seizure of assets of defendant: must not include lands known as San Pedro because that granted as settlement for benefit of his family conjointly and debtor may not transfer or sell that claim).

[72]L.A.P.R. 1:669A–69B (1843).

[73]*Id.,* A:181–83 (1843) (modification of time); M.A. 11:719, 723 (1843) (domestic relations suit). Governor Micheltorena even wrote an order on the margin of a report he received on a probate case. A.C. 33:120 (1844). This resurgence of gubernatorial activity centered around this particular governor, Micheltorena, and to an unknown extent may simply reflect his particular force of personality.

ing New Mexico regarding the governor's role in the administration of justice.[74]

One revealing case involved an appeal to Governor Micheltorena in April 1843. He forwarded the appeal to the acting presiding justice, José Antonio Carrillo. The justice, acting individually, reversed the lower decision for what appear to be substantial procedural errors; the lower judge was related to a party and also permitted a party to testify on his own behalf (a practice not permitted in American courts at this time and allowed in California only in the conciliation proceedings). The presiding justice reported his conclusions to the governor, but at the end of his report added meekly the caveat, "if his Excellency, the Governor, should consider this decision in harmony with the present laws." Micheltorena did not upset the judicial determination and in fact issued an order in conformity, declaring, "I am in complete accord with all the provisions of the foregoing decision."[75] The mere fact that the presiding justice of the Tribunal Superior reported his decision in such an obsequious manner reveals much about the relationship between the governor and the court.

Later in this same year the tribunal attempted to gain some independence for the entire judiciary from the governor and indeed from the prefects. In an August 1843 circular letter to all town judges the court insisted that reports on cases pending in their courts be submitted to the appellate court and any needed consultations be made with the tribunal. A few months later, in October 1843, the court sent another circular to the *jueces,* pointing out the errors that resulted from their sending information to the prefects and insisting that all reports and other communications be sent directly to the Tribunal Superior, not to the governor or the prefects.[76] This effort toward judicial independence was neither strong nor sustained, however; it ran against tradition.

---

[74] A study of the transition from the Mexican to American systems of justice in New Mexico suggests that "the political chief (*jefe político*) or governor was the judge of the alcaldes and served in a measure as an appellate tribunal for the losing party. . . . Many years later native New Mexicans occasionally would still present themselves before the chief executive with their grievances, asking that justice be done," A. POLDERVAART, BLACK-ROBED JUSTICE 16, 19 (1948) (rep. ed. New York, 1976) (emphasis in original).

[75] L.A.P.R. A: 155–70 (1843).

[76] A.C. 43:363 (1843) (August circular); *id.,* 43:365 (1843) (October circular).

Before the formation of the Tribunal Superior the prefects and subprefects had been much closer than the governors to the daily supervision of judges. Prefects acted pursuant to the statutory duty to promote the "prompt and honest administration of justice." Accordingly, the prefects insisted on monthly reports on the status of litigation, appointed special judges or commissions to try cases where the judge had a conflict of interest or was a party to the suit, urged judges to action where they appeared to be dilatory, issued restraining orders against parties from molesting each other, and reprimanded judges for errant behavior, such as becoming a surety for an individual defendant.[77] Supervision was made more important because the judges were all laymen. Of course, not every step needed admonition or supervision from above. An individual judge might recuse himself for impartiality upon challenge without need for appellate order or supervision.[78]

Because of the general confusion as to which office was responsible for exactly which judicial acts, the prefects received a considerable number of original petitions or claims for judicial relief, a very few of which were passed on to an alcalde or justice of the peace with a peremptory order for action.[79] Most were given to the appropriate local judge with an order that the judge investigate and put the parties into their legal rights.[80]

The local town judges were executive officials as well as judicial, and it should not seem strange that the judges thought of the subprefects and prefects as their immediate superiors. In addition to oversight and supervision, the alcaldes and *jueces* both received and solicited advice from the prefects as to the disposi-

[77]Monthly reports: L.A.P.R. 1:261 (1841); *id.,* 1:449B (1840); appointed special judges: *id.,* 1:510D–12 (1841); *id.,* 1:327 (1840); urged action where dilatory: M.A. 10:487, 495 (1841); L.A.P.R. 1:58–60 (1840); issued restraining orders: *id.,* 1:313 (1840); reprimands for errant behavior: *id.,* 1:470 (1840). For information on the prefects' and governors' supervisory functions with regard to criminal litigation, see *supra* chapter 3, notes 31–33 and accompanying text.

[78]L.A.P.R. A:189–94 (1843).

[79]M.A. 10:1351, 1357 (1842); L.A.P.R. 1:506D–7 (1841).

[80]M.A. 8:283 (1845); L.A.P.R. 1:657A–57D (1842); *id.,* 1:354 (1841); *id.,* 1:374 (1841). The vice-governor of the Russian-American Company wrote the prefect of the Northern District in November 1845 and enclosed a list of ten debtors regarding whom he asked help in collection. The prefect replied ambiguously that he would "employ all the measures that are within the orbit of my jurisdiction." Castro, *Documentos, supra* note 36, Documents 1:217, 219, 220 (1845).

tion of cases pending before them, especially before the formation of the Tribunal Superior.[81]

Although it does not appear that the prefects ever actually decided any civil appeals, petitions from litigants in the nature of appeals seeking reversal of a town judge's decision were often lodged with the prefects, a few even after the Tribunal Superior was formed. The typical response of the prefect was to write the judge, either directly or through his subprefect, and demand a justification for the decision,[82] although there is no evidence that any prefect actually changed a judicial decison because of lack of sufficient justification.

Two generalizations may be hazarded regarding the relationship between the executive government and the Mexican California judiciary. First, there was more prefect interference and active control of the judiciary in the Los Angeles District than in Monterey.[83] Second, from 1843 and thereafter there was less prefect involvement with specific lawsuits, particularly in the northern prefecture. Probably this is because the appellate court itself sat in Monterey.

In November 1840 one Los Angeles prefect, defending his refusal to reverse a civil order of the justice of the peace, wrote that "I am not allowed by law to interfere with his functions and judicial actions."[84] In a sense this was self-serving nonsense because the prefects and the governors frequently interfered, at least as today we understand the concept of judicial independence. The concept of separation of powers had not evolved very far in Mexican California. Attitudes were still tied to the Spanish colonial practice where an active executive role in judicial matters was

[81] M.A. 10:933 (1842), 10:977 (1842); L.A.P.R. 1:540–42 (1841).

[82] L.A.P.R. 1:174–77 (December 1842, after formation of Tribunal Superior); M.A. 10:1079 (1842); L.A.P.R. 1:291 (1840); M.A. 9:499 (1839).

[83] It must be remembered, however, that the primary sources for this study were prefect records from Los Angeles, which would naturally tend to emphasize the prefect's activities, and alcalde records from Monterey, where the emphasis would be reversed. The alcalde records, however, include the correspondence from the prefects. It would be convenient if the prefect records for the Northern District were in such tidy shape as those of the Southern District. They are badly scattered, mostly in private papers, such as the Castro *Documentos,* of individuals who served as prefects. Many are destroyed. Despite the limitations of sources, which must be acknowledged, the conclusion still is that stated in the text.

[84] L.A.P.R. 1:340 (1840).

the standard. Of course, another perspective must be kept in mind on the extent of executive activity. Conciliation, it will be recalled, resolved perhaps 85 percent of all lawsuits and of the remaining 15 percent few were appealed.

A statement such as that of the prefect's quoted above, and similar ones emanating from the governors in the context of the criminal law, are not just lies; they do have a meaning. Taken together with the legislative admonition that the prefects were not to meddle in the judges' functions, they demonstrate that Mexican California society was stumbling toward a fuller appreciation of the separation of executive and judicial functions. In truth, however, by the time of the American invasion this evolution was far from complete.

The subject matter of the civil suits brought before the alcaldes—what they were about—varied widely. They could concern issues as sophisticated as whether a transfer of possession of real property was as a mortgage or a sale,[85] or as simple as whether defendant's killing of plaintiff's ox was wrongful,[86] and every degree of complexity in between. Table 7 shows the distribution of civil cases by subject matter in the Monterey court from 1831 through June 1846. It is based on an index made by Alexander S. Taylor and John Ruurd in 1858 of the Monterey records, specifically including 374 lawsuits and conciliations. As is true of so many of the Hispanic California records, the documents from which the index was made are incomplete but are nevertheless representative of the range of litigation, except for land litigation, which was probably slightly higher than the 3.5 percent represented in the table. An explanation of this, together with the methodology of the extrapolation and its limitations, is attached in a note.[87]

---

[85] *Id.*, A:4–12 (1825).

[86] M.A. 6:464 (1842).

[87] The United States government began the collection of the Mexican archives almost immediately after the invasion. In 1858 papers found to be wholly of local interest and value were segregated and returned to their cities of origin. In this manner Monterey reacquired sixteen volumes of Spanish and Mexican archives, which were then indexed by Taylor and Ruurd, except for the five volumes of criminal records, which remain unindexed. It is probable, however, that some records of land litigation that had transpired during the Mexican period were withheld because American litigation concerning the Mexican land grants was still continuing in 1858. Therefore the 3.5 percent represented in the index for

Table 7. Lawsuits Filed in Monterey Court, 1831–June 1846
(374 lawsuits)

Lawsuit	Percent
Debt or money collection	37.7
Recovery of or damages to personal property	27.0
Breach of contract	8.8
Domestic: separation	7.5
custody, bastardy, and other domestic	4.3
Defamation, libel, slander	3.7
Land and other real property	3.5
Assault and battery	2.1
Inheritance litigation, contested probates	1.4
Other	4.0
Total	100.0

What is striking by today's standards is the almost total lack of personal injury lawsuits, except for intentional assault and battery. This reflects more the realities of a preindustrial society with its absence of injury-causing machinery than any peculiarity of Mexican California. The percentage of suits for marital

land litigation is probably slightly lower than the actual percentage it held in the actual litigation of Mexican California, but not by a large factor.

Two caveats are needed for the use of the table. The index entries—a common one might be "suit for an ox"—make it difficult to ascertain whether the suit was for the recovery of the animal itself or for money agreed to be paid for its delivery. Therefore, the relative proportionality of debt as opposed to recovery of personal property is questionable. This could be ascertained more precisely by reading hundreds of conciliation records, but what would be learned does not approximate in value or interest the amount of time necessary.

A second warning is that the records of many lawsuits have been lost, and these figures must be viewed only as an indication of proportionality of the range of litigation types, not of the gross total. For information concerning the confused history and present conditions and locations of the various archives of Mexican California, the best sources are H. BEERS, SPANISH AND MEXICAN RECORDS OF THE AMERICAN SOUTHWEST: A BIBLIOGRAPHICAL GUIDE TO ARCHIVE AND MANUSCRIPT SOURCES (1979) and Bowman, *History of the Provincial Archives of California*, 64 SO. CAL. Q 1 (1982).

separation may seem high for a Catholic country, but many of the filings are repetitive for the same couple and reflect a use of the judicial process to air grievances rather than to procure an actual separation, a technique that will be discussed more thoroughly in the domestic relations chapter. In the United States today, the percentage of defamation suits compared to all filings would be very high. It reflects the Mexican concern for honor of self and family.

One thing the table cannot show is the relatively minor nature of many of the lawsuits. Included under the item of "recovery of or damages to personal property" are such things as suits for possession of a mule, delivery of a mattress, for some woolen clothes, and for taking two horses.[88] Suits concerning injuries, killings, or hire of oxen and horses were especially common. The majority of items under this category are of this kind. Even the debt collection category includes many very minor debts, and suits for debts in the low amounts of twenty to thirty pesos are common and go as low as two pesos.[89] The Taylor and Ruurd index breaks down the peso (or dollar, which then was the same thing) value of 112 suits. Table 8 reveals that an even 50 percent of all these suits sought to recover fifty pesos or less.

Of course, there were much larger suits, for the recovery of 1,382 pesos or 1,206 pesos, for example. There were lawsuits to settle boundaries of lands, entitlement to large ranches, and dissolution of partnerships and accountings in connection therewith.[90] The vast majority of claims presented to the alcaldes and justices of the peace reflect very individual and personal concerns. Perhaps petty in any larger picture, these specific small grievances reveal a paternalistic concept of the role of the village alcalde. There was no suit too small or personal that this village elder could not help resolve.

What can be said of the substantive law, that law which creates

[88]Mule, M.A. 6:952 (1844); id., 6:25 (1831); mattress, id., 6:482 (1842); woolen clothes, id., 6:1217 (1846); two horses, id., 6:55 (1833).

[89]Id., 6:858 (1843) (three pesos); id., 6:455 (1842) (two pesos); id., 6:268 (1837) (three pesos); id., 6:269 (1837) (3½ pesos).

[90]1,382 pesos, id., 8:49 (1845); 1,206 pesos, id., 6:922 (1844); boundaries of land, id., 6:20 (1831); large ranches, id., 11:998–1029, 1205–10, 1223–24 (1844); id., 6:58, 60 (1833); dissolution of partnerships, id., 6:849 (1843); id., 6:215 (1836).

Table 8. Distribution of 112 Lawsuits Filed in Monterey Court
1831–June 1846 by Amount of Recovery Sought
(112 lawsuits)

Lawsuit	Percent
0–50 pesos sought	50.0
51–100 pesos sought	20.5
101–200 pesos sought	16.1
Over 200 pesos sought	13.4
Total	100.0

and defines rights and duties, and how it was applied in the alcalde courts? The expatriates charged that it was virtually nonexistent. This overstated the situation, however, and their critique in reality was an expression of culturally defined legal needs for certainty that will be explored in the next chapter.

There was substantive law in Mexican California, and the appropriate questions are what law was theoretically in force and how well enforced was it in practice. For the important commercial needs the *Ordenanzas de Bilbao,* promulgated by the Spanish for use in Mexico in 1792, continued in force until the first Mexican national commercial code was adopted in 1854.[91] Notwithstanding expatriate denial, there were lawbooks in Mexican California. Several visitors in the postconquest period noted the availability of the multivolume *Recopilación de leyes de las Indias* (*Recompilation of the Laws of the Indies*) and a small book on the organization of the courts and their various powers.[92] Indeed, these books appear in an inventory of the records of the Court of the First Instance in Monterey taken in 1845.[93] In Sonoma, the justice of the peace in 1839 had and used a *Novísima*

[91] Barker & Cormack, *The Mercantile Act: A Study in Mexican Legal Approach,* 6 So. CAL. L. REV. 1, 6–7 (1932); Clagett, *The Sources of the Commercial Law of Mexico,* 18 TUL. L. REV. 437, 438–40 (1944).

[92] E. BRYANT, WHAT I SAW IN CALIFORNIA (New York 1848), (rep. ed. 1936), at 423 (1846 visit); McMurry, *The Beginnings of the Community Property System in California and the Adoption of the Common Law,* 3 CALIF. L. REV. 359, 363 (1915) (quoting a German writer from a 1849 visit).

[93] M.A. 8:5 (1845) (Monterey).

recopilación (1805) and a collection of Mexican statutes and decrees; in Yerba Buena, Francisco de Haro, alcalde in 1835 and again 1838, owned a set of Galvan's *Ordenanzas de tierras y aguas.*[94]

The booklet on judicial organization and powers was either a printing of the judicial law of 1837 or possibly one of two Mexican manuals available on the functions of the alcaldes and justices of the peace.[95] In addition, the repetitive nature of many documents recorded with the alcaldes in their notarial function, especially powers of attorney, indicate the use of some form books. During this period these were usually located at the end of a general practice treatise. Most probably California held a set or two of the 1834 edition of José Febrero's multivolume treatise on Mexican jurisprudence. In July 1848 the first American alcalde of Monterey, Walter Colton, referred to the Febrero volumes as well as another set of treatises by Alverez, although Colton does not clarify whether he found them in California or imported the books.[96]

There was law and there were lawbooks in Mexican California, although not in the sense and the profusion that would satisfy an Anglo-American of the day. For the law that did exist, very little use was made of it, either by litigants or judges. Both relied instead on vague appeals to "rights" or the "law" and seemed satisfied with assertions or denials of "rights" and "laws" that were uninformed by written substantive law that was available to them. Thus justice as actually administered was largely of the curbstone variety. Of course, this disuse of legal materials reflects the untrained lay status of the judges and the lack of professional attorneys as advocates.

The curbstone use of law that was so common reflects that society's awareness of legal standards, and many of these would be based upon statutory materials of which the asserter might be unaware. Beyond this, there was some express and conscious use of law. Occasionally in civil litigation one sees legalistic defenses

---

[94] Bowman, *Libraries in Provincial California,* 43 HIST. SOC'Y SO. CAL.Q. 426, 433 (1961) (Sonoma and Yerba Buena). There were no legal materials in an 1843 inventory of the same Monterey court. M.A. 11:301–304 (1843).

[95] J. BARQUERA, A LOS SEÑORES ALCALDES CONSTITUTIONALES (Mexico City 1820); L. EZETA, MANUAL DE ALCALDES Y JUECES DE PAZ (Mexico City 1845).

[96] W. COLTON, THREE YEARS IN CALIFORNIA (Cincinnati 1850), (rep. ed., 1949), at 249.

such as a defect in a bill of exchange,[97] or a plea of minority as a defense to liability under a contract.[98] The Mexican procedural laws of 1837 were often cited in judicial decisions, pleadings, or official correspondence, but very rarely is there any reference made to a legal treatise[99] or to a substantive statute.[100]

The lack of significant use of substantive law does not mean that the judges' decisions were capricious or that they lacked common sense in the resolution of disputes. The lack of legalism simply reflects a lack of legal training. Although the judges often used the phrase "according to law," as was also true under similar conditions in neighboring New Mexico, the phrase was hardly ever backed by a legal reference.[101]

The Anglo-American expatriates participated in the California judicial process, although in a different manner than the natives themselves. Table 9 presents a compilation of party status, defendant and plaintiff, of the Californios and expatriates, from data derived from the Taylor and Ruurd index of Monterey litigation. Of lawsuits between Californios and expatriates it is striking that so many more were brought by expatriates against Californios, 13 percent, than by Californios against expatriates, only 8.9 percent, notwithstanding that there were far more Californios than expatriates.

The reasons for this difference are not difficult to discover. The

---

[97] M.A. 15:497 (1838).

[98] Id., 6:457 (1842); A.C. 38:412–22 (1840).

[99] L.A.P.R. A:155–70 (1843) is an example.

[100] One example is M.A. 2:143–82 (1835) (plaintiff cites Recopilación de leyes de las Indias in private prosecution for a challenge to a duel).

[101] "The decision of alcaldes and hombres buenos was almost never based on what you would call law. 'According to the law' was a phrase often used in the decision of the juez, but the law referred to is never given citation." (regarding New Mexico). Letter dated 1 January 1982 from Janet Lecompte to author in author's possession. Ms. Lecompte has researched and published on the subject of the alcalde courts of New Mexico.

A similar frontier situation is the earlier Spanish administration of Missouri, where "the laws were never published and an official was forced to consult a voluminous digest if he wanted to determine what the law was. So in civil cases, the subordinant [sic] officers of the territory, who were not near to the capital, decided cases according to their own conceptions of equity or the written instructions of their superiors which generally contained useful hints derived from the civil law or the code of the Indies." Knaup, The Transition from Spanish Civil Law to English Common Law in Missouri, 16 St. L. U. L.J. 218, 220 (1971).

Table 9. Category of Parties, Monterey Lawsuits, 1831–June 1846
(374 lawsuits)

Parties to Suits	Percent
Californios versus Californios	69.4
Californios versus Expatriates	8.9
Expatriates versus Californios	13.0
Expatriates versus Expatriates	8.7
Total	100.0

expatriates predominated as the merchants and traders of Mexican California. Commercial trade in California, particularly in the important hide-and-tallow trade, depended upon extensions of unsecured credit by merchants and traders.[102] Therefore, the expatriates were in a position within the economic structure to make it more likely that they would be suing Californios than the other way round. Of the categories of suit delineated in Table 7, litigation brought by expatriates against Californios was concentrated 87.5 percent in the three commercial categories combined, debt or money collection, recovery of or damages to personal property, and breach of contract. As shown in Table 7, for all litigation regardless of party, these categories accounted for 73.5 percent. Suits in the single category of debt collection amounted to 45.8 percent of expatriate versus Californio litigation, as distinct from the 37.7 percent of all litigation without regard to party relationship.

Interestingly, 72.9 percent of all Monterey litigation by expatriates against Californios was brought by six individual plaintiffs of four nationalities. All were involved in commercial activities, and half of them were major merchants and traders or their representatives.[103] The primary use of the legal system by expatriates

[102] Dallas, "The Hide and Tallow Trade in Alta California, 1822–1846," 66 (Ph.D. diss., Indiana University, 1955; Ogden, *New England Traders in Spanish and Mexican California,* in GREATER AMERICA: ESSAYS IN HONOR OF HERBERT EUGENE BOLTON 402 (1945).

[103] Dodero, Nicolas (Italian); Garner, William (English); Juan (or John), Ricardo (French); Larkin, Thomas O. (American); McKinley, James (Scot); Stokes, James (English).

suing Californios was that of debt collection and related commercial litigation. The same can be said of suits by Californios against expatriates, where 81.8 percent fell within the three commercial categories. The limitations of this data explained in the note accompanying Table 7 must be borne in mind, but the broad generalizations suggested seem sound. The nature of the lawsuits brought between expatriates as both plaintiff and defendant will be analyzed in the chapter dealing with dispute resolution between expatriates.

The qualitative experience of expatriate litigants, plaintiff or defendant, appears to have been about the same as that of the Californios. The foreigners were treated the same as the locals. As both plaintiffs and defendants, the expatriates tended to use Californio *hombres buenos*. Expatriates in either position had no particular hesitancy in refusing the recommendations of the judges and *hombres buenos*.[104] There is no sense that the expatriates were intimidated.

Neither judges nor Californio *hombres buenos* were reluctant to issue conciliation judgments in favor of expatriates against Californio defendants.[105] The same is true of formal litigation following a failure of conciliation, although the total number of these cases is too small for satisfactory analysis. Nor did Californio defendants display any greater tendency to refuse conciliation suggestions where the plaintiff was expatriate.

It is clear that postjudgment remedies were weak. Within their limitations, however, the California judges threatened defendants with execution and made actual efforts to seize property with as much vigor when expatriates were plaintiffs as when Californios were.[106] In fact, there seems to have been more effort exerted by the judiciary to seize debtors' assets on behalf of expatriates. Probably this was because of a greater insistence by the expatriates that this remedy be pursued.

---

[104]Examples include M.A. 6:988–89 (1844) (American defendant refused judge's settlement suggestion); *id.*, 6:132–33 (1835) (English defendant refused conciliation judgment of judge and *hombres buenos*); In M.A. 6:848 (1843) a Scot plaintiff refused a settlement offer at a conciliation hearing.

[105]*Id.*, 6:1028 (1845); *id.*, 6:802 (1843); *id.*, 6:757 (1842), are examples. Interestingly, in the last two matters there were no *hombres buenos*.

[106]*Id.*, 6:923, 925–26; *id.*, 11:1313 (1844); *id.*, 10:1295 (1842), are examples of judicial exertions to seize property on behalf of expatriates.

Whatever the weaknesses of the Mexican California legal system, the expatriates were treated as equals in the civil process. What was not at all equal was the reaction of the expatriates to these perceived weaknesses in the system. From Californios came an occasional trickle of criticism; a virtual torrent of complaint issued from the expatriates. This difference resulted from differing expectations of what the legal system ought to accomplish, which in turn reflected great contrasts in underlying cultural values that a legal system should ideally serve.

The Anglo-Americans insisted that a legal system enforce predictable "rights" defined by positive law, but the Californios asked for something else. The Californios called upon their legal system to grant equitable and personalized solutions to economic and social problems as they arose. They were far less interested in defining abstract "rights." The two expectations of what a legal system should do are in direct conflict, and it is to this topic that the next chapter is addressed.

5

Legal Values in Collision

The popularity and effectiveness of conciliation as a means of resolving Mexican California disputes, disposing of nearly 85 percent of civil litigation, have been explored. To understand this
phenomenon and the hostility of the expatriates toward this system, the legal historian must probe behind the procedures themselves to extrapolate the cultural values that the system represented. The difficulty is that such cultural norms are usually
unstated, and the proof of social function of the Mexican California legal system must therefore rest primarily upon inference and
seldom upon a direct statement of purpose. Nevertheless, it has
been aptly said that the historian of the law "must make explicit
convictions that were often unspoken, for if left unspoken we
cannot understand the actions of the men who held them."[1]

The thesis here is that the primary social function of the Mexican process of civil litigation was to heal the breach in the community and between the parties caused by the dispute. Resolving
the lawsuit itself, in the sense of determining disputed facts, declaring who was right and who wrong, or compensating victims
for harms suffered, all this was secondary. Conciliation was an
effort to utilize a paternalistic process that involved *hombres
buenos* and especially alcaldes as "father-figures" to assert gentle
pressures upon the disputants to reconcile themselves and accept a face-saving settlement without the necessity of formal adjudication. This form of dispute resolution, it was believed, would
heal the breach in society and in the community through the rap-
prochement of its disputacious members. The thesis implies,
then, that the primary function of the Mexican California courts

[1]Hay, *Property, Authority and the Criminal Law,* in ALBION'S FATAL TREE 53
(Hay ed. 1975).

was to prevent litigation, a startling reversal of our normal expectations of the judicial process.[2]

What evidence can be adduced to support this conclusion? The first is historical because a legal system necessarily reflects the cultural evolution of the people who have formed it.[3] There was a Spanish tradition of compromise as early as the late Middle Ages. Although Castile was reasonably litigious, its communities emphasized the need for rapid and amicable resolution of disputes. Compromise was the ideal, and a settlement arbitrated within the community was the preferred method of dispute resolution. Lawsuits, on the other hand, were regarded as disruptive of the community's functions.[4]

The alcalde system had its origin in the Moorish institutions transmitted to the Spanish villages in the Middle Ages. The paternalistic nature of this village elder was well understood and overwhelmingly approved in the Spanish colonies. Indeed, the conciliation procedure and the use of *hombres buenos* selected by the parties was Spanish in concept, although carried on enthusiastically by Mexico after its revolution. Even the Mexican Constitution of 1824 mandated the use of conciliation, although it did not set forth specific procedures.[5]

Aside from the historical, there is other evidence, contempo-

---

[2] The point that the alcalde courts were designed to prevent litigation was made in W. HANSEN, THE SEARCH FOR AUTHORITY IN CALIFORNIA 46 (1960).

[3] Kuhn, *The Function of the Comparative Method in Legal History and Philosophy*, 13 TUL. L. REV. 350, 351 (1939).

[4] R. KAGAN, LAWSUITS AND LITIGANTS IN CASTILE, 1500–1700, at 18 (1981).

[5] Article 155 of the 1824 Mexican constitution provided: "No suit can be instituted, either for civil or criminal injury, without previous demand in conciliation." 1 J. WHITE, A NEW COLLECTION OF LAWS, CHARTERS AND LOCAL ORDINANCES . . . 408 (Philadelphia 1839) (2 vols.). "The Spanish principle was to shun litigation and to make the costs of securing a reconcilment as low as possible." Robertson, "From Alcalde to Mayor: A History of the Change from the Mexican to the American Local Institutions in California," at 51 (Ph.D. dissertation, University of California at Berkeley, 1908). The Spanish Cortes, or Parliament, codified the use of *hombres buenos* and the conciliation process in a decree of October 9, 1812, although the procedures were older. English translations of this portion of the decree may be found in THE COMING OF JUSTICE TO CALIFORNIA 75–76 (Galvin ed. 1963) and also in 1 WHITE, *supra* at 419–20. The Spanish text is in M. GALVAN, COLECCIÓN DE LOS DECRETOS Y ORDENES DE LAS CORTES DE ESPAÑA, QUE SE REPUTAN VIGENTES EN LA REPÚBLICA DE LOS ESTADOS-UNITOS MEXICANOS 50–51 (Mexico City 1829).

rary to the mid-nineteenth century, that indicates Mexican society believed litigation was to be avoided—almost at all costs—and that the alcaldes and *hombres buenos* were to play a paternalistic role in the reconciliation of the parties. José Febrero was the leading Mexican jurist of the period. What he wrote concerning the function of conciliation was not in an arcane journal, where theoretical discussions would be most likely, but in a practical treatise of Mexican jurisprudence. His remarks are therefore more likely to reflect broadly based cultural attitudes:

The evils that lawsuits cause society, diminishing the fortunes of families and promoting private disputes and interminable discussions, are deterred through our laws by the beneficial object of securing their prevention in their origin. Thus it is that it has been prudently prescribed as a required procedure to initiate lawsuits, that an act be performed through which means authority interposes its office and attempts with discreet observations to conciliate the spirits of the litigants, proposing to them some means of agreement and exhorting them to amiably compromise their differences.[6]

In 1820 a Mexican lawyer, Juan M. Barquera, wrote a manual of procedures and law for the guidance of alcaldes, almost none of whom had formal legal training. This again was an immensely practical, semipopular work that makes Barquera's descriptions of alcaldes, *hombres buenos,* and conciliation even more significant as expressions of the culture. Alcaldes, he said, are "citizens chosen as fathers of the country," and "true fathers of the pueblos." They should "work assiduously for the interior harmony of society" and be an "organ of the peace of the families and of the public tranquility." The *hombres buenos* should have the "natural fairness of an honest heart, impartial and loving the peace of their fellow citizens," and it is for this that they are called good men. The process of conciliation itself, he wrote, was to avoid the "odious procedures" of a formal trial.[7]

These quotations illustrate the Mexican concept of the function of law—the application of a paternalistic process to heal the

[6]3 J. Febrero, Obra completa de jurisprudencia teórico-prática 134 (Mexico City 1851) (4 vols.).

[7]J. Barquera, A los señores alcaldes constitucionales (Mexico City 1820), quoted in Robertson, *supra* note 5, at 42 n.1 (alcaldes), 52 n.2 (*hombres buenos*), and 51 (conciliation).

breach in community caused by a dispute. The healing, reconciliatory process can also be seen in actual decisions of the California alcaldes. In an 1835 slander suit the alcalde decided that
not only should the defendant make a public apology, but that he,
the judge, would give the plaintiff a certificate of good reputation.[8] In an 1841 suit for breach of contract the *juez de paz*
explained in his conciliation judgment that the *hombres buenos* had made their recommendation "in order to avoid ruinous
litigation."[9]

The paternalistic expectations of the California populace were
present in the nature of the disputes presented by Californios to
Walter Colton, the American alcalde who served in Monterey immediately after the American invasion. He was asked to resolve a
family's complaint that the rivalry of two suitors for the hand of
their daughter disturbed their tranquility, a charge of a mother
that her adult son had struck her, and a grievance of a washer
woman that another washer woman had invaded her territorial rights on the bank of a local stream. Colton noted that the
California alcalde was the "guardian of the public peace, and is
charged with the maintenance of law and order, whenever and
wherever threatened. . . . His prerogatives and official duties extend over all the multiplied interests and concerns of his department, and reach to every grievance and crime."[10]

---

[8] 6 Monterey Archives, 174 (1835) [hereinafter cited as M.A. in style of M.A.
6:174]. These records are on deposit with the Monterey County Historical Society, Salinas, California.

[9] M.A. 6:323 (1841).

[10] W. COLTON, THREE YEARS IN CALIFORNIA (Cincinnati 1850), (rep. ed. 1949), at
34, 192, 112–13 (examples), 230–31 (quotation). Perhaps Colton was exercising
a bit of literary license. The preconquest disputes brought to the alcaldes on occasion involved extremely small sums of money, but very few of the rather petty
personal matters Colton described. Perhaps Colton was regarded as so personally
trustworthy that the Californios simply extended the tendencies of alcalde paternalism further than they had previously by bringing to Colton even the most
minor matters. In this regard it should be pointed out that Thomas O. Larkin
wrote in a letter to James Buchanan, secretary of state, on Aug. 22, 1846, that
"many [Californios] are contented, and are making application for justice in
many petty domestic cases, that from their own Alcaldis they never thought of
obtaining. This speaks volumes of their opinion of the political change of the
Country." 5 THE LARKIN PAPERS: PERSONAL, BUSINESS, AND OFFICIAL CORRESPON-
DENCE OF THOMAS OLIVER LARKIN, MERCHANT AND UNITED STATES CONSUL IN CALI-
FORNIA 213 (Hammond ed. 1951–1968) (10 vols. & index) [hereinafter cited as
LARKIN PAPERS].

An excellent example of the reconciliatory, communal, and paternalistic nature of much California litigation is in an 1841 lawsuit, which is of a sort that would not readily occur to the Anglo-American imagination. A widow and her son sued a distant relative who was building a house on neighboring land—because it was too close, or a nuisance? No, in fact, the opposite. The prefect observed, apparently on an appeal:

[T]he house started by citizen R. Orduno is detrimental to the interests of the widow María Ygnacia Verdugo; and as the widow and her son José Antonio only wish to avoid such prejudice from being done and not to hinder Orduno in establishing his farm there, they request him to build near their home for mutual aid and harmony, which they should extend to each other. Therefore, the judge will order citizen Ramón Orduno to build his house near that of the widow, and so prevent in this manner any disagreement between families related by blood.[11]

For all the talk about healing breaches, community, and paternalism, it still remains difficult for the modern Western mind to understand how a legal system could function with virtually no substantive standards or formal law. Or how it could operate with no enforcement mechanism, an equivalent of a sheriff, to levy against assets, or to have that possibility realistically available so as to induce compliance with judicial judgments. How could the system work and what do its workings inform us about the society in which it functioned?

It must be recognized that it did not always work. Some defendants simply thumbed their noses at judicial decrees. The system usually did work, however, and that itself is significant and reason for us to inquire why. First, the form of the judgments themselves were such as to make it as easy as possible for a defendant to comply. They were individualized, payable in the goods or products most likely for the defendant to possess; they were payable in installments, often timed to the annual cattle slaughters; and finally, anticipating a change in the circumstances of the defendant, the judgments were modifiable.

Second, that the overwhelming majority of judgments were reached through the consensual process of conciliation also ren-

---

[11] 1 Prefect Records of Los Angeles, 349 (1841). These records are on deposit with Henry E. Huntington Library in San Marino, California.

dered more likely compliance without coercion. The closest modern equivalent to most Mexican California litigation is the modern small claims court, which offers the parties an opportunity to litigate claims without the intervention of lawyers, in amounts of up to $1,500. This would be about the same as the limits of the verbal process, or 100 pesos.

Recent studies of small claims courts suggest that defendants are much more likely to comply voluntarily with mediated settlements to which they have agreed than those imposed by a judge. One particular study of mediation in small claims courts in the state of Maine demonstrated that defendants are almost twice as likely to comply fully with mediated outcomes as with judgments imposed by the court after trial. The work concluded that "consensual processes lead to social psychological pressures for compliance that are not associated with authoritative judgments," and that the consent involved in a mediated judgment greatly promoted defendants' actual compliance.[12]

The rate of compliance in a homogeneous society, such as Mexican California, would be even higher. Voluntary compliance depended on a sense of honor, a precious value in the Hispanic scheme of things. The defendant had not only agreed to a judgment, but in the process had involved someone else whom he respected and had selected and requested to serve as his *hombre bueno,* and who in almost all cases had joined with the *juez* and opponent's *hombre bueno* in recommending settlement.

Furthermore, these disputes and judgments were public and probably known about by a large portion of the defendant's community. The typical California town was small, with only a few hundred inhabitants, and the population of each of California's largest communities, Monterey and Los Angeles, was only slightly over one thousand. In these tiny villages everyone belonged to the same church and knew everybody else; many were related to one another, and all shared the same fiestas, bucolic outlook, and general orientation. Community pressures on a defendant to perform as he had agreed and as the much-respected alcalde had ordered, doubtless were great.

Law has often been equated with the force of a sovereign com-

---

[12]McEwen & Maiman, *Mediation in Small Claims Court: Achieving Compliance Through Consent,* 18 LAW & SOC'Y. REV. 11 (1984).

mand, meaning that law simply cannot exist unless governmental force or the threat of force stands behind it. This positivist view has been challenged by studies suggesting that adequate systems of order can be more dependent on societal consensus than force, and that a cohesive and consistent legal system may be developed without code or precedent.[13] To draw from an American example, the enforcement machinery for arbitration was very weak in seventeenth-century Connecticut. Yet entirely voluntary compliance was high because of the trusting nature of the small towns and their strong community identities.[14]

The argument has been made that the reason why Mexican California did not require an elaborate judiciary or enforcement mechanism was because of Spanish traditions of obedience to authority, of submission to directives from above, and authority's regulation of the minute affairs of daily life.[15] This explanation is not adequate, although the Californio's greater disposition to obey authority than that of the more rambunctious American may have been one factor in rendering enforcement mechanisms unnecessary. Granted that the alcaldes were respected figures, both historically and in California they were much more community representatives than authority figures from "above." In Mexi-

[13] *See* J. AUERBACH, JUSTICE WITHOUT LAW? (1983); M. BARKUN, LAW WITHOUT SANCTIONS: ORDER IN PRIMITIVE SOCITIES AND THE WORLD COMMUNITY (1968); L. FALLERS, LAW WITHOUT PRECEDENT: LEGAL IDEAS IN ACTION IN THE COURTS OF COLONIAL BUSOGA (1969); and W. NELSON, DISPUTE AND CONFLICT RESOLUTION IN PLYMOUTH COLONY, MASSACHUSETTS, 1725–1825 (1981).

[14] Mann, *The Formalization of Informal Law: Arbitration Before the American Revolution,* 59 N.Y.U. L. REV. 443, 448–52 (1984).

[15] HANSEN, *supra* note 2, at 45, 47: "[T]he Californian's conception of his place in society had roots that remained deeply imbedded in the feudal past of Spain and New Spain. For example Spanish colonial administration had infused the expectation that minute vice-regal regulations would control the affairs of daily life. . . . In Alta California, the conception of order as something achieved by obedience to directives from some source of authority above persisted long after a new conception had taken root in Spain. . . .

"Alta California, with its sparse, scattered population did not require an elaborate judicial system exercising authority in the manner that citizens of the United States and England had known it. And it did not require such a system for at least two reasons. In the first place, order in Alta California had traditionally been associated with recognition of and submission to directives from above. Secondly, California society, even after the appearance of the institution of private property, remained a status society: The ranchero was substituted for the missionary and the merchant prince for the military officer."

can California the alcaldes and *jueces* seldom held office for more than a year or two, and many asked to be relieved after only a few months. They were not professional jurists and almost always adjudged cases in conformity with both *hombres buenos,* over the selection of whom the authorities had absolutely no control. That the alcaldes had little real power aside from functioning as community conduits is seen from the fact that so many of those selected to serve tried so hard to get out of the job.

As representatives of the closely knit California communities, the alcaldes and *jueces de paz* had little need of either enforcement powers or well-defined substantive law. That the alcaldes often knew little formal law and had access to relatively few law books does not mean that they did not accomplish substantial justice. That they made decisions according to their own judgment of what was right, and inevitably reflected community mores, was exactly what they were supposed to do; it was the system's greatest merit.[16]

In the last analysis, the Mexican California legal system reflected the values that history and culture had given to its people. Therefore, the Californios respected the legal system, and because of its perceived legitimacy, most Californios obeyed the system's decrees. On the other hand, the Mexican California legal system did not reflect the values that their different history and culture had given the Anglo-Americans. The expatriates did not respect the legal system; they believed it lacked legitimacy and they severely criticized it.

One Anglo-American value was the certainty and predictability in the law that was demanded of the Anglo courts. The rise of the new commercial and industrial order associated with the Industrial Revolution required that fixed legal rules be known in advance. Several legal historians have noted the judicial and commercial emphasis on certainty in the early nineteenth century.

One of the commercial community's greatest needs was for certainty and predictability in the law. The courts recognized that if the rules of law were "unknown and uncertain among those concerned

---

[16]Robertson, *supra* note 5, at 54. Equity, discretion, and the common good were significant factors in the adjudication of water rights as well. *See* M. MEYER, WATER IN THE HISPANIC SOUTHWEST: A SOCIAL AND LEGAL HISTORY 1550–1850, at 156–64 (1984).

in . . . [a] branch of commerce, . . . the effects of that uncertainty could not fail to be embarrassing and mischievous" [citing cases]. A businessman had to know the rules applicable to his business, for "his calculations depend[ed] not infrequently on [such] a knowledge [citing a case]."[17]

Heavy capital investment and rational planning required that property rights be exact. The law of contracts was just as much in need of certainty because businessmen needed to know at the time of contracting, long before breach or dispute, precisely how their agreements would be interpreted. As the California Supreme Court said in 1858:

Men knowing how the law has been generally received and repeatedly adjudged, govern themselves and are advised by their counsel accordingly; but if Courts establish new rules whenever they are dissatisfied with the reasons upon which the old ones rest, the standards of commercial transactions would be destroyed, and commercial business regulated by a mere guess at what the opinion of Judges for the time might be, and not by a knowledge of what the doctrines of recognized works of authority and the precedents of the Courts are.[18]

If these requirements were not critical in relaxed, preindustrial Mexican California, they had been in the East and in England. They were part of the cultural expectations the expatriates brought with them because the ideals that a legal system is intended to effectuate are carried with a man wherever he goes.[19]

---

[17] W. Nelson, Americanization of the Common Law: The Impact of Legal Change on Massachusetts Society, 1760–1830, at 154 (1975). *See also* M. Hindus, Prison and Plantation: Crime, Justice, and Authority in Massachusetts and South Carolina, 1767–1878, at 86 (1980): "It is almost a cliche to associate predictability and certainty with the commercial-industrial order of the modern world, yet these were, nevertheless, paramount values. Large-scale enterprise of every sort required some form of guarantee of stability, some assurance that certain basic entitlements—such as the sanctity of private property—would not be upset. Promoters of such enterprises frequently turned to the legal system for protection." As to this point of demand for certainty, see also G. Bakken, the Development of Law in Frontier California: Civil Law and society, 1850–1890, at 7 (1985) and M. Horwitz, The Transformation of American Law, 1780–1860, at 160 (1977).

[18] Aud v. Magruder, 10 Cal. 282, 291 (1858).

[19] Young, *The Law as an Expression of Community Ideals and the Lawmaking Functions of Courts,* 27 Yale L.J. 1, 13 (1917).

In this Anglo-American legal expectation there was every demand for settled substantive law firmly applied, and no room at all for a quixotic judge varying the rules to achieve justice in a particular case. The California practices of installment judgments and modification deeply offended that principle. So also did the absence of a well-defined substantive law and the highly particularistic manner in which justice was meted out to individual litigants.

There is no doubt that most Americans of this generation sincerely believed that the common law promoted and facilitated commerce, while the civil law retarded it. As a new state, California faced the question of whether to adopt the common law or retain its Hispanic civil law heritage. In choosing the common law, the state Senate Judiciary Committee opined in 1850 that in common law countries "you perceive the activity, the throng, the tumult of business life . . . [and] the boldness, the impetuosity . . . of advancing knowledge and civilization." In nations embracing the civil law, however, one can see only "the stagnation of an inconsiderable and waning trade . . . feebleness of intellect [and] timidity of spirit." It suggested that the "free principles and exact justice" of the common law was an influence "in developing the sturdy, sagacious, and self-relying spirit of the English and American people."[20]

This commercially desirable "boldness" and "tumult" was related by the committee to the principle of certainty.

[W]hen a trade is fairly consumated . . . the rights of the parties are fixed, and it becomes too late for retraction. In other words, the Common Law allows parties to make their own bargains, and when they are made, holds them to a strict compliance; whilst the Civil Law looks upon man as incapable of judging for himself, assumes the guardianship over him, and interpolates into a contract that which the parties never agreed to.[21]

Of course, this is hardly a sophisticated interpretation of the two systems. There is irony in the Anglo-American demand for certainty because the civil law tradition has placed at least as much emphasis, if not more, on the need for certainty in the law

[20] CALIFORNIA SENATE COMMITTEE ON THE JUDICIARY, REPORT ON CIVIL AND COMMON LAW (1850) *reprinted in* Appendix, 1 Cal. 588, 598.

[21] *Id.,* at 595.

than has the common law.[22] In any event, however, the committee's remarks cast valuable light on American perceptions of California practices that had been in place only four years earlier.

The committee's statement also demonstrates the relationship of certainty to the Anglo-American penchant for individualism, another distinct legal value at fever pitch during this period. This too was probably related to the quickening pace of life and the acquisitiveness associated with commercialism and the Industrial Revolution. Many observers, both contemporaries and retrospective historians, have recognized the individualistic qualities in the common law of this period. Dean Roscoe Pound wrote of "the individualistic spirit of the common law" and that "from the beginning the main reliance of our common law system has been individual initiative."[23] Other historians have noted that "the heyday of nineteenth-century legal individualism was the mid-nineteenth century" period that is the focus here;[24] that in the first half of the nineteenth century American commercial law had "a certain Adam Smith severity, a certain flavor of the rugged individual";[25] and that the middle-class public of Jeffersonian America, cherishing the ideals of competition, utilitarianism, and self-advancement, found itself unwilling to forego the advantages of an individualistic legal system in favor of significant reform.[26]

Still another scholar has noted that in the late American colonial period and beyond, the emergent values of individualism and acquisitiveness became the necessary context for a growth of litigation. This litigation, which "encouraged the clash of individual differences amid constant jostling for private advantage," largely eclipsed the earlier reliance on mediation and arbitration, which had "tended to express the needs of those who were mutually bound in continuing cooperative relationships."[27]

This is a portrait of a culture in sharp relief with that of Mexi-

---

[22] J. MERRYMAN, THE CIVIL LAW TRADITION: AN INTRODUCTION TO THE LEGAL SYSTEMS OF WESTERN EUROPE AND LATIN AMERICA 48–50 (2d ed. 1985).

[23] Pound, *The Causes of Popular Dissatisfaction with the Administration of Justice*, 29 A.B.A. REPORTS 395, 403 (1906).

[24] P. STEIN & J. SHAND, LEGAL VALUES IN WESTERN SOCIETY 119 (1974).

[25] L. FRIEDMAN, A HISTORY OF AMERICAN LAW 233 (1973).

[26] *See generally* R. ELLIS, THE JEFFERSONIAN CRISIS: COURTS AND POLITICS IN THE YOUNG REPUBLIC (1971).

[27] AUERBACH, *supra* note 13, at 34.

can California. In contrast to the Californios, who respected community-based sanctions and paternal authority, the American individualists, according to de Tocqueville's classic 1835 account, "owe nothing to any man, they expect nothing from any man; they acquire the habit of always considering themselves as standing alone, and they are apt to imagine that their whole destiny is in their own hands."[28]

What does individualism imply for a legal system, the absence of which could be criticized by the expatriates? First is "the decision to define a disputant as an adversary, and to struggle until there is a clear winner and loser; [instead of attempts] to resolve conflict in a way that will preserve, rather than destroy, a relationship."[29] The harsh common law judgment accomplishes this adversarial definition by reducing a controversy to a clearly defined winner.

The typical common law judgment is simply a judicial declaration that "plaintiff have and recover from defendant the sum of $xx dollars." It is clear and clean, with no gray areas, although it leaves the collection entirely to the plaintiff. On the other hand, it is rigid in form in that it is payable immediately, only in dollars or pounds, and it has no provision for modification. All of these features are in contrast with the Mexican California judgments, which were often payable in goods, in installments over time, and were modifiable.

Second, legal individualism implied that a trial should be conducted by the classic common law procedures to effectuate the "struggle until there is a clear winner." Each litigant should look out for his own interests, conduct a vigorous examination of the witnesses, and the judge's role ought be limited to that of an umpire. The adversary system

means that each party presents his side, legally and factually, of the controversy in what he regards as its best light to the court. The latter, without independently investigating the matter, decides the case on the basis of what the parties have presented. Thus the plaintiff, or at least his lawyer, decides whether to use all available legal arguments, and if not all are to be used, which to advance, and how best to press them. He also determines what factual information to put before the tribunal and, within the rules of evidence, how to do

[28] A. DeTocqueville, Democracy in America 368 (World's Classics ed. 1946).
[29] Auerbach, *supra* note 13, at 8.

that. The defendant, in turn, does the same thing. The court, otherwise uninformed as to the facts at least, makes no effort to go beyond the parties' exposition of the problem. Rather it is reactive; its judgment responds to their presentation.[30]

But this "contentious procedure" of the common law, Dean Pound points out, is not a "fundamental fact of jurisprudence, it is peculiar to Anglo-American law. . . . [W]e take it as a matter of course that a judge should be a mere umpire, to pass upon objections and hold counsel to the rules of the game, and that the parties should fight out their own game in their own way without judicial interference."[31] In contrast, Mexican California, in criminal cases and for the small number of civil cases passing beyond conciliation, loosely followed the Continental model of trial. Judges took a much more active role because Latin American justice is basically inquisitorial. The judge tightly controls the trial, and it is the judge, not the counsel of the parties, who orders the production of evidence, interrogates the witnesses, and directs the case from beginning to end.[32] The open adversarial trial, controlled by the parties, with confrontation and cross-examination of witnesses, so vital to the common law and beloved of the common law lawyers, was simply never held in Mexican California, and judgment followed the completion of the judge's own investigation.

Despite the expatriates' dislike of conciliation, it had a history in nineteenth-century America. By mid-nineteenth century New York and a few other states had constitutional provisions authorizing their legislatures to create conciliation courts, but they were never successfully utilized in New York or elsewhere.[33] An opponent of conciliation at the New York Constitutional Convention in 1846 charged that "such courts belonged only to a despotic government, where the people were ignorant, and had a superior class over them, and not for our free Yankee population; who consider they are competent to judge for themselves in such matters."[34]

[30] J. McCoid, Civil Procedure: Cases and Materials 24 (1974).
[31] Pound, *supra* note 23, at 405.
[32] A. Golbert & Y. Nun, Latin American Laws and Institutions 20 (1982).
[33] Steele, *The Historical Context of Small Claims Courts,* 1981 A.B. Found. Research J. 293, 306–8.
[34] W. Bishop & W. Attree, Report of the Debates and Proceedings of the

An 1866 law journal article opined that conciliation would only be effective where litigants "look up to the opinion and advice of the judge as only an ignorant and dependent people can look up . . . to one whom they personally revere as higher than them-selves." This would never do for the stubborn independence and self-reliance typical of even "the least elevated and educated Yankee."[35] Given this climate of opinion, it is hardly surprising that in 1850 the California Supreme Court during its very first term rejected conciliation as a required procedure. Conciliation may have been suitable for the Mexicans, the court noted, but "amongst American people it can be looked upon in no other light than as a useless and dilatory formality."[36] It is ironic that in recent years the hierarchy of the American judiciary has be-come so concerned with "alternative" methods of dispute reso-lution that, in 1985, the chief justice of the United States Su-preme Court urged American lawyers to become peacemakers and conciliators.

Thus we see the embodiment into law of individualism, en-shrined as a norm by the Anglo-Americans, in conflict with the paternalism, communalism, and spirit of conciliation embodied into law by the Mexican Californians.[37] The conflict in California was between "the cohesive Spanish ideal, and the loose indepen-dent, individualistic American ideal. These two could not coexist. The new settlers brought with them the spirit of individualism, which is characteristic of pioneer America, and the common law tradition which embodies it."[38]

Another legal institution held so dear by the Anglo-Americans

---

CONVENTION FOR THE REVISION OF THE CONSTITUTION OF THE STATE OF NEW YORK, 1846, at 588 (Albany, New York 1846), quoted in Steele, *supra* note 33, at 307.

[35] *Courts of Conciliation,* 102 N. AM. REV. 135, 144 (1866), quoted in Steele, *supra* note 33, at 307–8.

[36] Von Schmidt v. Huntington, 1 Cal. 55, 65 (1850).

[37] "The friction that ensued was an inevitable conflict between the two types of civilization, the extreme individualism of the western part of the United States and the paternalism of the Spanish colony." Robertson, *supra* note 5, at 90.

[38] Yankwich, *Social Attitudes as Reflected in Early California Law,* 10 HAST-INGS L.J. 250, 252 (1959): "California's early American settlers personified cer-tain characteristics. Among these were intrepidity, individualism, and a tolerance for human weakness. . . . In addition to this they considered human life cheap. California's legal history reflects the qualities and defects of this ideology. The older ideology of the Spanish gave way to this spirit."

of this period that it became an independent legal value in itself was the jury. Popular enthusiasm for the jury ran particularly high in the late eighteenth century and first half of the nineteenth. Indeed, the "United States entered the nineteenth century with a burst of popular enthusiasm for the jury."[39] Alexander Hamilton in *Federalist #83* wrote that the only dispute in the Constitutional Convention concerning the jury was between those who regarded the institution as "a valuable safeguard to liberty" and others who saw the jury as "the very palladium of free government."[40] In other words, the high regard was unanimous. Even the United States Supreme Court had occasion to observe in 1830 that "trial by jury is justly dear to the American people. It has always been an object of deep interest and solicitude, and every encroachment upon it has been watched with great jealousy."[41]

Of course, there was no jury in the Roman civil law, to which system Mexico and Mexican California were heirs through Spain. The tradition of the Latin American civil law system holds that the judge is better qualified to decide legal matters than are private citizens, who lack legal training and are possibly susceptible to emotional appeals by attorneys.[42] The lack of juries gave the Anglo-American expatriates still another cause for dissatisfaction. That the *hombres buenos* and frequent rotation of judges also allowed community input into the adjudication process was ignored, probably because of the nearly reverential attitude toward the form of the common law jury.

Upon their invasion in 1846 the Americans immediately instituted the jury. A navy chaplain, Walter Colton, was appointed the municipal judge for Monterey, with the office still being called alcalde. He presided over California's first jury trial, a civil case, in September 1846. Consciously aware that this was the first jury ever summoned in California, Colton was moved to remark in his diary at the conclusion of the case that "if there is anything on earth besides religion for which I would die, it is the right of trial by jury."[43] It is interesting, however, that after the arrival in Mon-

---

[39] L. MOORE, THE JURY: TOOL OF KINGS, PALLADIUM OF LIBERTY 143 (1973).
[40] THE FEDERALIST NO. 83, at 543 (A. Hamilton) (Modern Library ed.).
[41] Parsons v. Bedford, 28 U.S. (3 Pet.) 433, 446 (1830).
[42] GOLBERT & NUN, *supra* note 32, at 20.
[43] COLTON, *supra* note 10, at 48.

terey of American attorneys, Colton, although permitting their participation in the examination of witnesses, used the civil law as a shield to prevent these lawyers from summing up or arguing to the juries in his court.[44]

With this evident collision of Mexican Californian and Anglo-American expectations of law, it is not surprising that the ex-patriates sharply criticized the California legal system. Even Anglo-American visitors carped. The most famous of the American visitors, Richard Henry Dana, Jr., remarked in *Two Years Before the Mast* that California had "no common law, and no judiciary. . . . As for justice, they know no law but will and fear."[45] James Douglas, an official of the Hudson's Bay Company, visited California in 1840 and wrote in his diary that "the Judicial authority is that of Alcalde or Justice of the Peace, an office seldom adequately filled by persons of education or a competent knowledge of the existing laws."[46] Another Englishman, putting things more bluntly, remarked in 1841 that the California "judicial system is rotten to the core."[47]

The foreign residents criticized as well. It is common in the correspondence of the traders of the hide-and-tallow trade to find complaints of law enforcement in California, and Americans, in particular, made much of a supposed superiority of United States or Massachusetts justice.[48] One American trader referred to the alcaldes' "rascality," deeming them "superlatively the worst" in

---

[44]"We have at this time [June 19, 1847] three young lawyers in Monterey. . . . Mexican statutes, which prevail here, permit lawyers as counsel, but preclude their pleas. They may examine witnesses, sift evidence, but not build arguments. This spoils the whole business, and every effort has been made to have the impediment removed, and the floodgate of eloquence lifted. . . . I should never get through with the business pressing on my hands. . . . I tell them after the evidence has been submitted, the verdict or decision must follow, and then if any in the courtroom desire to hear the arguments, they can adjourn to another apartment, and plead as long as they like." COLTON, *supra* note 10, at 199–200.

[45]1 R. DANA, TWO YEARS BEFORE THE MAST (New York 1840), (Kemble ed. 1964) (2 vols.), at 169.

[46]Douglas, *From the Columbia to California in 1840: From the Journal of Sir James Douglas*, 8 CAL. HIST. Q. 97, 103 (1929).

[47]G. SIMPSON, NARRATIVE OF A JOURNEY ROUND THE WORLD, DURING THE YEARS 1841 AND 1842 (London 1847), reprinted as NARRATIVE OF A VOYAGE TO CALIFORNIA PORTS IN 1841–42, at 75 (1930).

[48]Dallas, "The Hide and Tallow Trade in Alta California, 1822–1846," at 282 (Ph.D. diss., Indiana University, 1955).

that quality among a list of other great rascals: "Horses, Whores, Women, Men and Alcaldes." Another American expatriate expressed a subjective judgment of poor treatment, writing in 1844 that "I have but little hope of getting justice for I am told that a foreigner cannot get justice done him in this country." Still a third American complained that "was it not that the Jugado [*juzgado,* court] has no force I would sue the whole bunch of them."[49] The English expatriates complained too. James Alexander Forbes, the British vice-consul, wrote the California governor in October 1845 that "in the present state of this District it is very difficult to collect any debt when the debtor himself does not voluntarily pay."[50]

At least one of the foreign residents had good to say of the legal system. A most eloquent defense was written years later by an American merchant, William Heath Davis, Jr.:

These alcaldes as a class were men of good, strong common sense, and many of them had a fair education. As a rule they were honest in their administration of justice and sought to give every man his dues. I had occasion to appear before them frequently in my business transactions, with reference to hides that were not branded according to law, and other matters. I always found them ready upon a proper representation of the case to do what was just to all concerned.[51]

Hubert Howe Bancroft, the preeminent historian of Hispanic California, noted of Davis that "the value of his historical testimony is somewhat impaired by a tendency to eulogize everybody."[52] In any event, Davis stands virtually alone among the Anglo-American expatriates. What he said in his memoirs written long after the American conquest may have been accurate

[49] F. ATHERTON, THE CALIFORNIA DIARY OF FAXON DEAN ATHERTON 14 (Nunis ed. 1964) ("Horses, Whores, . . . Alcaldes"); Letter, William L. Wiggins to Larkin, Apr. 23, 1844, 2 LARKIN PAPERS, *supra* note 10, at 107 ("a foreigner cannot get justice"); Letter, John H. Everett to Larkin, July 26, 1844, 2 LARKIN PAPERS, *supra* at 179 ("the Jugado has no force.").

[50] Letter, Forbes to Secretary of Governor, Oct. 3, 1945, in Manuel Castro, *Documentos para la historia de California,* Document # 189. These documents are on file with the Bancroft Library, University of California, Berkeley, California.

[51] W. DAVIS, SEVENTY-FIVE YEARS IN CALIFORNIA 86 (1929).

[52] 2 H. BANCROFT, HISTORY OF CALIFORNIA 777 (1886) (1884–1890) (7 vols.).

enough. The contemporary remarks of Anglo-Americans, however, penned while still under Mexican administration, are much more indicative of true feelings, even if not more objectively truthful. Far more typical of contemporary expatriate comments are the complaint of Josiah Belden in 1842 that "there is no forc in the law here to do any thing,"[53] and the regret of John B. R. Cooper in 1838 that he lived in a "country where there [is] neither law or justice."[54]

In many of the expatriate complaints, one can see a reflection of the legal values of certainty and predictability and the concern for their perceived lack in the California courts. Larkin wrote in 1845:

To make a thousand dollar obligation good it necessary to purchase from govt a Eight dollar stamp paper, & I have never seen an Alcalde inforce the payment of the debt, altho Eight doll was paid to make it legal. Sometime the debtor pleads to much rain for his crop. At other time the season is to dry—or he is too busy to attend.[55]

Behind these words one glimpses Larkin's own unsatisfactory courtroom experiences with obligations or judgments, absolute in the Anglo-American manner of thinking, but in Mexican California legal thought still susceptible to modification and payment by installment. A wonderful example of criticism founded on a misconception of differing legal values is a story that the Englishman James Douglas wrote into his diary in 1840:

As an instance of the way civil cases are disposed of in the strangest of all strange places, I may cite the example of a Mr. Stokes, who summoned a farmer before the Alcalde, to compel payment of a debt which had been 2 years outstanding, contrary to the previous stipulation between the parties.

The Justice instead of meeting the case referred it to arbitration. The case was going against the farmer who entreated for a further indulgence, as if compelled to pay at that moment, he would be compelled to sell his cattle at a heavy sacrifice. Well, says the Justice,

---

[53] Letter, Belden to Larkin, Aug. 7, 1842, 1 LARKIN PAPERS, *supra* note 10, at 263.

[54] Letter, Cooper to Kriruff & Blake, Mar. 26, 1838, 29 Vallejo, *Documentos para la historia de California,* Document 215 (37 vols.). These documents are on file with the Bancroft Library, University of California, Berkeley, California.

[55] Letter, Larkin to Beach, May 31, 1845, 3 LARKIN PAPERS, *supra* note 10, at 218.

how long do you ask? Why, says the farmer, I promise to make the first instalment in 12 months hence.

Very well, replied the Justice with the utmost indifference, that will do, and the case was dismissed without further proceedings.[56]

Douglas obviously received this story secondhand, and undoubtedly the "instead of meeting the case referred it to arbitration" had reference simply to the usual conciliation procedures. The alcalde in all probability did not dismiss the case "without further proceedings," but entered into the Book of Conciliations the parties' acquiesence in the conciliation judgment. The judge's conciliation recommendation, it will be recalled, was in the form of an order—the "very well . . . that will do" of the story. And the "further indulgence" because of a reluctance to "sell his cattle at a heavy sacrifice" is nothing more than a request for an installment judgment, a normal part of California practice. To Douglas, accustomed to the sternness and tidiness of an immediately due common law judgment, rendered after adversarial clash of trial, all this was merely an example of the "strangest of all strange places."

Still other Anglo-American visitors wrote stories, second or third hand, of experiences in the alcalde courts. They are either terribly inaccurate, as in William Ruschenberger's 1836 fable, which makes out the alcalde as an absolute fool,[57] or they are both inaccurate and deliberately vicious, as in Lansford Hastings's account of the importance of swearing and bribery in the presentation of a case before the alcalde.[58] Without question, stupidity and bribery existed on some occasions.[59] More balanced,

[56] Douglas, *supra* note 46, at 109–10.

[57] W. RUSCHENBERGER, A VOYAGE ROUND THE WORLD; INCLUDING AN EMBASSY TO MUSCAT AND SIAM IN 1835, 1836, AND 1837 (Philadelphia 1838), *reprinted in* SKETCHES IN CALIFORNIA 1836, at 12–14 (1953).

[58] L. HASTINGS, THE EMIGRANTS' GUIDE TO OREGON AND CALIFORNIA (Cincinnati 1845), (rep. ed. 1969, at 127–28).

[59] John Parrott, an American trader with considerable experience trading with California, wrote Larkin regarding a proposed lawsuit against another trader and added that "if it should come to the pinch you will give the judge who takes charge of the affair a Small gratification in order to induce him to take up the affair with spirit." Parrott also recommended an attachment be made of the defendant's vessel. An attachment was no small matter in Mexican California, so perhaps Parrott, writing from Mazatlán, was simply reflecting the use of bribes there rather than in California. Parrott spent little time actually in California. Letter, Parrott & Co. to Larkin, May 2, 1845, 3 LARKIN PAPERS, *supra* note 10, at 163–64.

however, was the conclusion of Bancroft that these reports of foreigners, "who knew little or nothing of what they were saying, were to a great extent exaggerated and false. Justice then was plain and crude, but it differed not so much after all from justice now."[60]

Another area of Anglo-American complaint, also related to certainty and predictability, was the lack of specific substantive law. This was equated in the expatriates' minds with written statutes. Edwin Bryant, an observant immigrant who arrived immediately after the American invasion, said that "there is no written statute law in the country" and that "the principles of natural right and justice" are the "foundation of California jurisprudence."[61] Another American settler who had been a resident since 1841 noted many years later that "printed codes were practically unknown. Officers, civil and military, there were: their decisions and commands were seemingly always accepted as law without reference to book or authority. . . . There was not to my knowledge in all California a lawyer or law book."[62]

After the invasion in July 1846, the complaints of lack of statutory law increased in volume.[63] "What laws are we to be governed by?" asked the editor of the *California Star* in its inaugural issue of January 9, 1847.[64] " 'Tis said, and some believe the story," wrote Larkin in June 1847, although he knew better, "that Mexico had laws in C.[alifornia] but they cannot be found and the oldest residents have no remembrance of them either in theory or practice. We must live on as formerly in lawless blessedness."[65]

All this was an exaggeration. As noted earlier, there was substantive law and there were at least a few law books, some basic Spanish treatises, Mexican texts, and copies of the essential Mexican procedural statutes.[66] For a homogeneous people who

[60] H. BANCROFT, CALIFORNIA PASTORAL 606 (1888).

[61] E. BRYANT, WHAT I SAW IN CALIFORNIA (New York 1848), reprint ed. 423 (1936).

[62] Letter, John Bidwell to Hunt, Apr. 3, 1895, quoted in R. HUNT, JOHN BIDWELL, PRINCE OF CALIFORNIA PIONEERS 446 (1942).

[63] *See* Hunt, *Legal Status of California, 1846–1849,* 12 ANNALS AM. ACAD. POL. SOC. SCI. 387, 391, 394 (1898).

[64] Quoted in N. HARLOW, CALIFORNIA CONQUERED: WAR AND PEACE ON THE PACIFIC, 1846–1850, at 333 (1982).

[65] Letter, Larkin to Bennett, June 1, 1847, in 6 LARKIN PAPERS, *supra* note 10, at 187. That Larkin knew better is shown in his letter of Feb. 1, 1846, to a justice of the peace and concerning the Mexican law relative to release on bail. *Id.,* at 4:189.

[66] See the discussion in chapter 4, *supra,* accompanying notes 91–100.

relied on a shared community consensus and a common culture that favored conciliation as the bases for dispute resolution, this was enough. But for the individualistic, competitive, noncommunally oriented Anglo-Americans, much more was necessary. Extensive, specific, statutory law, readily available, was needed to provide the certainty and predictability upon which the success of contractual and commercial arrangements were felt to depend. The great fault of Mexican California law was that it "failed to exert a guiding authority upon the lives of Americans who conceived of life as a great competition in the acquisition of property and who relied only upon contracts to bring order into their lives."[67]

Although the foreign residents in California were free to criticize the local legal system, they were not free to ignore it. There was within them their own cultural pressure toward legal regularity and compliance with local authority. John Reid has demonstrated that the overland pioneers, many of whom were bound for California, were both law-knowledgeable and law-abiding to the extent that legal notions had become a part of their common cultural stock. He concluded that "the habits, actions, and values of nineteenth-century American society were formed by a behaviorism based on law."[68] This helps to explain the depth of the Anglo-American critique of the Mexican California legal system, but it also created a dilemma. The cultural suppositions that caused the expatriates to be repelled by the California courts also required them to pay them heed. They felt compelled to play within the local rules, to the extent they could, in order to legitimate their conduct.

The next four chapters describe the expatriates' legal activities in the areas of contract formation, credit creation and debt collection, dispute resolution, and domestic relations. One theme will be how the Anglo-Americans attempted to regularize their conduct within an official legal system they thought inadequate. Certainly, if one were to return to Monterey in the late 1830s and ask an American merchant if his legal life was different in Mexican California from what he would have in Massachusetts, he would have replied that it was greatly different, and he would have attributed all differences to California's inadequate legal system.

[67] HANSEN, *supra* note 2, at 50.

[68] J. REID, LAW FOR THE ELEPHANT: PROPERTY AND SOCIAL BEHAVIOR ON THE OVERLAND TRAIL 11 (1980).

Throughout these next four chapters the reader will also see conduct that was as much adaptive to the geographic and economic realities of a frontier region as to a weak legal system. Therefore, the legal relationships and conduct described for these specified areas should be read as a reaction to vast distances, poor transportation, and the lack of a banking system, as much as a reaction to a despised legal system, with the caveat that the Anglo-American expatriates themselves would not have viewed their conduct in this light.

Illustrations

Cuartel House, Monterey, California. 1875

El Cuartel, a barracks and general government office building, photographed in 1875. It was built in 1839 under the administration of Governor Juan Bautista Alvarado. It housed the Monterey alcalde courts as well as the Tribunal Superior. Courtesy The Bancroft Library.

Ruins of the Mexican carcel, or jail, in Monterey, photographed in 1875. Courtesy The Bancroft Library.

José Antonio Ezequiel Carrillo, 1796–1862, Associate Justice of the California Tribunal Superior. Photograph of oil portrait. Courtesy The Bancroft Library.

Thomas O. Larkin, surrounded by friends and commercial companions, c. 1850. Their energy and grim determination is obvious. *Seated, left to right:* Jacob P. Leese, Larkin, and William D. M. Howard. *Standing, left to right:* Talbot H. Green(?) (perhaps Samuel J. Hensley) and Sam Brannan. Courtesy The Bancroft Library.

Record of conciliation hearing between two American expatriates, Isaac Graham and John Williams, May 2, 1846. See chapter 8 for translation and discussion. Courtesy Monterey County Historical Society.

173

dos hermanos sean rebajados de los
doscientos cinco pesos que D. Isaac Graham le reclama, y que D. Juan Williams pague a D. Isaac Graham
los ciento setenta y siete pesos res-
tantes en plata ó esquilmos á su
ser de plata. Lo que firmaron
con migo y los SS. hombres buenos. = entre renglones falle bale = roso
do Williams. Vive=roso=los=
Juan Dion

Teodoro Gonzalez

Jorje Allen   Isaac Graham

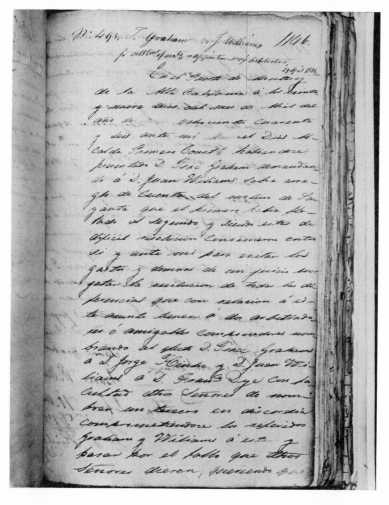

Agreement to arbitrate between Isaac Graham and John Williams, April 29, 1846, and referral by the alcalde to an arbitration panel. See chapter 8 for translation and discussion. Courtesy Monterey County Historical Society.

los Juece á quiene Compete los ob[...]
guen y compelan al cumplimient[o]
del referido fallo como sentencia
pasada en autoridad de cosa juz-
gada, debiendo resarcir con l[as]
costas daños y perjuicios aquel
que recuse dar cumplimien[to] al [pa-]
go de estos acreditadores, y decla-
rando á mas ser nula y de ningu[n]
valor y efecto la obligacion que en
Sta Cruz firmaron obligandose á [sa-]
tis[...] por lo que falleen en este mismo
asunto los Sõs Thomas Gonzalez por [no]
haber tenido efecto dicho juicio. Y pa[ra]
el cumplim[to] de todo lo referido firmaron con migo y los hombres buenos que lo eran por la actora D Jorge [...]
lcy y por la demandada D Franc[...]
Dye   Isaac Graham
   Marcos Dias   Isaac Williams
                John Williams
        Ior John Frances Dye
             Jorge Richar[d]

Isaac Graham. Photograph of oil portrait.
Courtesy California State Library.

6

Contract Formation

This chapter concerns the Californio and expatriate formation of commercial transactions such as wholesale sales of retail goods, sale or leasing of trade or real property, service contracts for the management of ranches and stores, cutting of timber, and a wide variety of similar commercial activities. All such contracts, except for the minority calling for immediate payment in goods or cash, necessarily involved the creation of credit through the use of contract debt, bills of exchange, or promissory notes. It is more convenient, however, to discuss the credit aspects of contract formation in the following chapter, immediately alongside its eternal companion of debt collection.

The Mexican procedure for forming a contract was derived from a broader civil law tradition involving the office of the notary public. The notary, then as now, had three critical functions in the making of a contract. First, the notary is often the actual draftsman of the contract, a function that is well-expressed in the Spanish word for notary public, *escribano público,* or literally, public clerk. Second, in the civil law tradition the notary serves as a public record office for contracts, as well as for other documents. Private contracts thereby become public records. The notary retains the original of the document he has written and furnishes authenticated copies upon request. Third, the notary's authentication of the document gives it special evidentiary effect in any subsequent litigation concerning the subject matter of the contract. The document is taken as genuine and accurate in its recitation of what the contracting parties said before the notary and what the notary saw and heard. Contrary evidence, for example, a denial by one party that he had agreed to a particular provision, is inadmissable.[1]

[1] J. MERRYMAN, THE CIVIL LAW TRADITION: AN INTRODUCTION TO THE LEGAL SYSTEM OF WESTERN EUROPE AND LATIN AMERICA 106 (2d ed. 1985).

The civil law tradition does not invalidate the common law variety of contract, that is, an agreement that is not undertaken before a notary and not a matter of public record. Nevertheless, in the civil law an agreement lacking notarial authority requires additional substantiation for use in litigation, and a court may either refuse to accept the validity of such a private instrument or refuse to give it substantial evidentiary weight.[2]

Mexico added another requirement to contract formation—the use of officially sealed paper, which had to be purchased. Sealed paper was blank sheets of paper bearing a government seal or stamp of varying denominations on which contracts were required to be written. The necessity of using this special paper was obviously a revenue measure, and the expense to the consumer was not great. In 1842 contracts with values of between 500 and 2,000 pesos (approximately $5,500 to $22,000 in current American dollars) were required to be written on paper costing four pesos (now about $44). Paper for contracts of less value cost a single peso and for greater value, eight pesos. The sale of sealed paper to register land titles and wills carried the same fees, based on the value of the underlying assets. If a contract was written on other than officially sealed paper, the obligor, in theory, had twice the time in which to meet his obligation, and no lawsuit could be brought until the fees were paid. Furthermore, the parties to an unsealed contract were subject, again in theory, to a fine of three times the value of the paper that should have been used.[3]

These traditions and requirements for contract formation were followed by the Californios in Mexican California with two significant exceptions. First, there were no notaries public in California, and their functions were undertaken by the alcaldes and justices of the peace. When alcaldes or justices of the peace drafted a contract, the document would recite that the parties appeared before the judge and two witnesses, who acted in the absence of a notary. Thereafter, to serve the recordation function of the no-

---

[2] A. GOLBERT & Y. NUN, LATIN AMERICAN LAWS AND INSTITUTIONS 20, 25–27 (1982).
[3] Decree of President Santa Anna (1842) circulated by Governor Micheltorena on June 3, 1843. A Prefect Records of Los Angeles, 123–38 (1843) [hereinafter cited as L.A.P.R. in style of L.A.P.R. A.:123–38]. These records are on deposit with Henry E. Huntington Library in San Marino, California.

tary, the judge would simply keep the document among his official papers, separate and apart from the judicial papers.

The second exception was the frequent unavailability of the government sealed paper. For a brief time in the mid-1830s a small amount of stamped paper was printed locally in California, but the bulk of the supply was dependent upon unreliable shipments from mainland Mexico. The Californios generally used the official paper when it was available, but countless documents recite that they are written on ordinary paper because of the unavailability of sealed paper.

The practice of the alcaldes to draft contracts was of great utility to Mexican California. Many Californios were illiterate, and the alcaldes would read the instruments aloud to ascertain that those who could not read had assented to the agreement.[4] In the early period of Mexican California the alcalde-drafted documents tended to be long and complex. For example, the 1829 sale of Rancho Bolsa de Potrero by José Joaquín de la Torre was conducted before an alcalde. The document not only recited the background of the seller's own acquisition, but it also went into the seller's use of the property, his motives for selling (poor health), the joinder and consent of the seller's sons to the transfer and their renunciation of any rights of inheritance, a reserved right of the seller to graze certain cattle on the ranch—all of this in addition to a detailed description of the property, a recital of lack of encumbrances, an assurance of quiet title, and a statement of the consideration for the transfer, 2,000 pesos (now about $22,000). Curiously, the manner of the payment of the price was not specified but simply referred to as "the terms in which both parties agreed before signing the document."[5]

As the tempo of commercial activity increased in the 1830s

[4]Robertson, "From Alcalde to Mayor: A History of the Change from the Mexican to the American Local Institutions in California," at 58 (Ph.D. diss., University of California at Berkeley, 1908). Occasionally, the alcalde would recite that one or both of the parties to an undertaking or contract understood the document. For example, Arias and Orozco, 15 Monterey Archives, 687 (1845) [hereinafter cited as M.A. in style of M.A. 15:687]. These records are on deposit with the Monterey County Historical Society, Salinas, California.

[5]Manuel Castro, *Documentos para la historia de California,* Document 1:10 (Oct. 2, 1829) (2 vols.). The Castro *Documentos* are on deposit with Bancroft Library, University of California, Berkeley, California.

and 1840s, the alcalde-written documents became considerably shorter. They were taken from form books and not drafted from scratch for the particular parties before the judge. The Californios would occasionally enter into transactions in writing outside of the presence of the alcalde, and then bring the document to the judge for recordation. In 1835, for example, José Espinosa made an extrajudicial sale of a house to José Arana and only thereafter was the sale recorded.[6] This practice was much more common among the Anglo-Americans than the local populace, however.

The Californios were more prone to follow the traditional method of allowing the notary, or town judge in California, to draft their agreements. Thus their transfers of ranches and houses were made before the *juez de paz;* mortgages were created, leases granted, debts acknowledged, and wills written.[7] All of these thereby became public documents.

One extremely common instrument entered into by the Californios and recorded before the town judge was the power of attorney. Probably the frequent use of this device was caused by the vast distances and slowness of transportation in Mexican California, and the consequent need for long periods of absence from home for any business trip. The most common power of attorney used by the Californios conferred general powers, but there were also powers granted for the specific purposes of collecting debts,[8] to buy or sell real property,[9] and other specific purposes. Interest-

---

[6] M.A. 15:169 (1835).

[7] Examples include: ranches, Armento to Abrego, *id.,* 11:1399 (1844); Chávez to Soberanes, *id.,* 8:207 (1845); houses, Arias to Eschevaria, *id.,* 15:737 (1838); Casarín to Gómez, *id.,* 15:139 (1835); mortgages; Montenegro to Aguirre, *id.,* 11:990 (1844); leases, Abrego to Díaz, *id.,* 15:575 (1839); Díaz to Pacheco, *id.,* 9:723 (1839); debts, Ruiz to Sepúlveda, L.A.P.R. A:108 (1839); wills, Espinosa, Salvador, M.A. 8:441 (January 1846); Amesquito, Juan, *id.,* 15:577 (1840); Félix, Diego, *id.,* 15:539 (Apr. 7, 1840; interesting as he was a murderer awaiting execution). These are only examples, and it is fair to say there were more Californio and Mexican wills recorded than the other classes of instruments with the exception of powers of attorney.

[8] For example, Aguirre to Amesti (Spanish Basque), *id.,* 15:573 (1840); Estate of Quijano to Díaz, *id.,* 11:849 (1843).

[9] For example, Abrego to Abrego, *id.,* 15:645 (1841); Castro to Castro, *id.,* 11:571 (1844).

ingly, a few of these powers of attorney were given by husbands to their wives.[10]

The Californios were a preindustrial people and it would hardly be expected that they would make as many commercial contracts among themselves as the Anglo-Americans, who were from cultures that had experienced the quickening pace of life associated with the Industrial Revolution. The Monterey records reveal the recordation of only a very few commercial contracts of the local population.[11] As we shall see, the Californios entered into more contracts with Anglo-Americans than with each other. Nevertheless, there are a handful of commercial agreements recorded in the Monterey records involving Californios only, for services,[12] the sale of goods,[13] and other matters.

The Anglo-American expatriates did not generally engage the alcaldes to draft their contracts, nor did they generally employ stamped paper, even though they tended to enter into contractual relations with fair regularity. In part this refusal to use the official mode of contract formation reflects the individualistic, anti-authoritarian bent of the expatriates. It also reflects the greater use by Anglo-Americans of oral contracts and especially contracts formed by letter, neither of which would involve judicial participation in their creation.

Although oral contracts were made by the expatriates, their diaries and journals do not suggest there were any great number. This may be misleading, however, as oral contracts, even if commercial or wholesale, which called for immediate performance would not likely be discussed in a merchant's correspondence or diary, for the same reasons that the dozens of daily retail transactions of a merchant—technically oral contracts—would hardly

---

[10] The Abrego power of attorney cited in the preceding footnote was from José Abrego to his wife, Josefa Abrego.

[11] W. HANSEN, THE SEARCH FOR AUTHORITY IN CALIFORNIA 45 (1960), notes that the Californios used relatively few contracts among themselves, but appears to attribute this to obedience to authority and social betters as organizing principles of Mexican California, rather than to the more simple explanation of a preindustrial economy.

[12] For example, Arias and González, M.A. 9:743 (1839); González and de la Torre, *id.*, 11:917 (1844; for raising horses).

[13] For example, Romero and Amesti (Spanish Basque), *id.*, 11:1119 (1844; sale of a crop of wheat); Esquir and Rangel, *id.*, 8:1062 (May 1846; a horse).

merit his discussion. Taken individually they were not important enough for comment.

Some employment contracts between expatriates doubtlessly were oral. For example, the American Cyrus Alexander had a relatively detailed verbal agreement with fellow American Henry Delano Fitch to manage Fitch's Rancho Sotoyome.[14] But this was unusual. Ranch management contracts were the subject of a great many formal written contracts. Even much more casual employment agreements between Anglo-Americans were usually reduced to writing. When, in February 1846, Thomas O. Larkin hired an Englishman, William Anderson, to work for one year as an unskilled worker at Larkin's soap factory, their agreement was expressed in a signed, witnessed writing.[15]

The expatriates were almost fastidious in reducing agreements to writing. In 1839 an English sawyer in the Santa Cruz Mountains found he needed a helper. He wrote to Larkin that he had "hired a man for a year made out an agreement in writing got him to sign it and likewise signed by S. Thompson as witness."[16] In 1839, Faxon Dean Atherton, an American merchant based in Valparaiso but with years of experience in California, agreed with Henry Paty, an American merchant in Hawaii likewise with considerable California experience, to establish a saw mill in California. Unfortunately, Atherton left Hawaii before the agreement could be signed, and the document could only be signed for Henry Paty on shipboard by his brother William, who was not himself financially interested in the mill. Atherton protested this irregularity, at least to his diary:

I signed an agreement this day with W Paty relative to the procurement of a steam engine. W P is mentioned in the agreement though

---

[14] Miller, "Henry Delano Fitch: A Yankee Trader in California: 1826–1849," at 193 (Ph.D. dissertation, University of Southern California, 1972).

[15] 4 THE LARKIN PAPERS: PERSONAL, BUSINESS, AND OFFICIAL CORRESPONDENCE OF THOMAS OLIVER LARKIN, MERCHANT AND UNITED STATES CONSUL IN CALIFORNIA 204–5 (Hammond ed. 1951–1968) (10 vols. & index) [hereinafter cited as LARKIN PAPERS]. The contract does not specify exactly what Anderson was to do, but in all probability it was unskilled labor. Larkin had already entered into a joint venture agreement for a Californio to manage the factory and Anderson's compensation was only $400 for the entire year, with a forefeiture of one-half if he left before its expiration.

[16] Letter, William R. Garner to Larkin, July 7, 1839, 1 LARKIN PAPERS, *supra* note 15, at 16.

the verbal agreement in Oahu was with Henry Paty. . . . But as I left Oahu in such haste that I had no time to make out a document and agreed verbally with H P to make one out during the voyage, and that William should sign, but . . . William has no power to sign for H P individually. . . . This manner of proceeding appears to me to be very wrong as I ought to have urged the making of the proper document before leaving Oahu.[17]

A second class of expatriate contracts that by their nature could not be written before a notary or alcalde were the many letter contracts. Typically, these were letters between foreign merchants, asking for goods for which the requesting merchant had a market, or accompanying goods sent from one merchant to another on consignment and specifying the terms at which the goods could be offered for sale at the recipient merchant's market. This kind of letter was almost always sent over considerable distance from one port to another, and they offered the formation of a class of contract that lawyers call unilateral.

What was desired by the writers of these letters was not a promise by the recipient merchant but performance, that is, the shipment of requested goods or the sale of consigned items. If merchant *A* wrote merchant *B* that he would like to buy 100 widgets (say) at $20 apiece, the contract between the two would be *formed* by merchant *B*'s shipment of the 100 widgets. There would be no need or expectation that merchant *B* would write merchant *A* any letter promising shipment nor enter into any agreement to ship. Merchant *B* would accept *A*'s offer, making the contract, by his performance of the offer, that is, by the shipment. This is to be distinguished from the more usual type of contract, called bilateral, in which both parties to the contract promise something, usually one promising the future performance of an act or the delivery of goods, and the other, the payment of money.

The substance of these letter contracts will be discussed later in conjunction with the substance of the formal written contracts. Clearly, a contract of this kind did not involve anything that could be written by or recorded before an alcalde. An example of a typical letter contract is the following 1845 letter sent by Larkin to a Hawaiian mercantile firm, E. & H. Grimes, in

---

[17]F. ATHERTON, THE CALIFORNIA DIARY OF FAXON DEAN ATHERTON, 1836–1839, at 140 (Nunis ed. 1964) (entry for May 22, 1839).

which the following run-on sentence appears: "I will take ten
or twenty try pots at twenty five dollars each put on board the
Fama in good order new pots or those a little used providing they
are good payable in cash Six months after you ship them intrest
after that time If I do not meet with an oppertunity of sending
the money."[18]

The contract here would be performed and completed by E. &
H. Grimes's shipment of the try pots—metallic pots used to render
whale blubber. Larkin is not asking for a return letter or a formal
agreement promising to supply the pots. If an offer like this, quite
common among merchants on the California coast, reached
fruition by the shipment of goods (or in the case of consignment,
a sale of the goods by the consignee merchant), there was no formal writing at all, and all that remained was a duty to pay. Hence,
an entire and major category of expatriate contracts was simply
not susceptible of the usual California procedure for contract
formation.

The Anglo-American expatriates also entered into a great number of formal, written agreements. These, of course, could have
been written on stamped paper, written by a judge acting as a notary, or both. If a contract was written by a judge it would have
been on officially stamped paper, unless sealed paper were unavailable. Most of the written contracts of foreigners were not
formed in this official manner, although some were made before
the alcalde. For example, Kentuckian Job Dye entered into a five-
year contract to manage a ranch for fellow expatriate John B. R.
Cooper in 1843;[19] two Irishmen bought and sold a Monterey
blacksmith shop, one to the other, in 1842;[20] and in 1839 the Russian manager of the Russian-American Company rented half of
Englishman William Richardson's house in Yerba Buena to store
grain.[21] These were exceptions to the general practice of the
Anglo-Americans to make agreements among themselves and on
ordinary unstamped paper.

[18] Letter, Larkin to E. & H. Grimes, Jan. 24, 1845, 3 LARKIN PAPERS, *supra*
note 15, at 21–22.

[19] Cooper and Dye, M.A. 11:399 (1843; contract to manage Rancho El Sur).

[20] McAllister and Durick, *id.*, 10:871 (1842). See also *id.*, 15:711 (1842; apparently same transaction).

[21] Rotchef and Richardson, Official Documents Relating to Early San Francisco.
Document 23 (1839) [hereinafter cited as O.D.R.E.S.F.]. These documents are deposited with Bancroft Library, University of California, Berkeley, California.

Under two circumstances only were contracts to which the expatriates were parties generally written by an alcalde or justice of the peace. The first was when the other party to the agreement was a Californio. These mixed contracts between Californios and foreigners, whether involving a conveyance of property and the conditions of payment,[22] or a contract for manufacturing services,[23] usually conformed to the local official practice of alcalde draftsmanship. So also for mixed contracts for sales of goods.[24] Again, there were some exceptions, and one can find a few mixed contracts formed in the expatriate style, rather than through the local customs.[25]

The other circumstance in which it was common for the foreign community to make contracts before the alcalde was for the undertaking of a debt obligation. This was a flexible procedure in California and similar to a common law recognizance. If money were owed by one person to another, either because of a loan or a settlement of outstanding accounts and transactions, the two could go before the alcalde; the debtor would acknowledge the debt and the terms of payment; both would sign the short docu-

[22] For example, de la Torre to Cooper, Castro *Documentos, supra* note 5, Document 1 : 10 (1829); Figueroa to Stearns, Book B of Deeds, Los Angeles County Records, 71–74 (1842).

[23] For example, Larkin and Cano, M.A. 15 : 147 (1835) (Cano to furnish Larkin with 10,000 adobe bricks, Larkin supplying all necessary tools and paying Cano 15 pesos per 1,000, half in cash, half in goods); Larkin and Sánchez, 3 Larkin Papers, *supra* note 15, at 152–53 (1845; joint venture agreement to manufacture soap). The last document, the Larkin-Sánchez contract, is curious in that it was a hybrid, being written on stamped paper but not drafted by a judge or recorded. A similar document is a lease made by Larkin on behalf of and under power of attorney for a Californio, José María Carrasco, whereby he leased Carrasco's house for use as a store by a foreigner, Milton Little. The lease was on stamped paper, probably a concession to the sensitivities of the Mexican lessor. But it was neither alcalde-drafted nor recorded, although written in Spanish. Lease, Dec. 31, 1845, 4 Larkin Papers, *supra* note 15, at 136–37 (1845).

[24] For example, Elizalde and Williams, 34 Archives of California, 219 (1836); agreement for future delivery of 150 gallons of liquor). These documents are on deposit with Bancroft Library, University of California, Berkeley, California.

[25] For example, when Juan José Abeya left California for mainland Mexico, in connection with the expulsion of Governor Micheltorena, in March 1845, he delivered all his personal goods and endorsed his personal accounts receivable to Larkin for recovery of credits and payment of his debts. This was done in a private document with no alcalde or stamped paper. 3 Larkin Papers, *supra* note 15, at 98–102 (1845). Another example of a document involving a Californio and a foreigner and not prepared before an alcalde is given in note 23, *supra.*

ment the judge drew up; and it would become part of the official records. This device was frequently used by the expatriates with respect to debts owed them by Californios.[26] The expatriate community also employed the procedure for debts among themselves, and it was not an infrequent occurrence for two foreigners to appear before an alcalde and one acknowledge a debt to the other.[27]

An interesting aspect of the foreign community's process of contract formation was its use of the alcalde in his role as the notarial recording office. It should not be particularly surprising that the expatriates might record with a governmental official such documents as dispositive instruments transferring property, powers of attorney, or wills, even where the documents were wholly between and involving foreigners. These are the kinds of papers, excluding wills, that were frequently recorded or otherwise made public in the Anglo-American legal culture. Wills traditionally were private until the time of death, but there were few expatriate wills recorded in California.[28]

Today it seems strange to observe the relative frequency with which other agreements not written by the alcaldes or justices of

[26] For example, Mariano Soberanes acknowledged a 260-peso obligation to James Stokes, written by the justice of the peace, on Jan. 20, 1842. M.A. 10:875 (1842); Montenegro to Howard, *id.,* 11:873 (1843; $1,382, mortgage also granted). Of course, foreigners acknowledged debts to Californios as well, as the Frenchman Ricardo Juan did to Manuel Díaz, *id.,* 11:1693 (1844; 270 pesos with mortgage).

[27] For example, Dye to Grant, *id.,* 6:806 (1843; 24 pesos, 4 reales, to be paid 12 in first month and 12 in second month); Meadows, James (English) to Larkin, *id.,* 15:495 (1838; $17); Stokes to McKinley (English and Scot), *id.,* 10:1363–70 (1842; prior private contract, not recorded, for mercantile expedition liquidated by debt of 2,089 pesos, half to be paid in finished wood delivered to the beach at Santa Cruz within fourteen days and half in hides, cattle, and tallow in June and July of 1843).

[28] Property: Houlster to McIntosh, *id.,* 7:467 (1829; sale of house and lot); Hinckley to Richardson, *id.,* 15:87 (1833; transfer of ship; alcalde-drafted); wills: McIntosh, Edward Manuel (Scot), *id.,* 11:569 (1842); Watson, José María (probably Englishman James Watson), *id.,* 15:627 (1841); powers of attorney: Larkin to Faxon, William (both American), *id.,* 15:683 (1845; before alcalde, probably copied from Mexican form book); Jones, John to Spence, David (American, Scottish), *id.,* 15:393 (1836; document written in English). There were far more recorded powers of attorney among the Californios than among the expatriates. There was a Mexican procedure to create a secret will, so cumbersome that the California Supreme Court opined that it was proabably never used. Panaud v. Jones, 1 Cal. 488, 502 (1851).

the peace, but entirely prepared by foreigners themselves, were then brought to the judge to cause them to become recorded public documents. For example, it is not traditional in the Anglo-American legal culture for promissory notes to be recorded. The use of promissory notes in credit was frequent among the expatriates in Mexican California, and this was in addition to the practice previously discussed whereby the parties would personally appear before the alcalde and one acknowledge a debt to the other.

Sometimes foreign merchants would record these promissory notes with the town judge, in circumstances where the document makes it clear that it was drafted outside of court and not by the alcalde.[29] In the last few years of Mexican California, Larkin used printed forms of promissory notes, with himself as payee, and with the debtor simply signing the form out of court. He then recorded some of these notes.[30]

Occasionally foreigners would prepare a complete contract among themselves and then take it to the judge for recordation. The majority of expatriate contracts, however, were written directly by the parties involved and never made public by recordation. The circumstance under which it appears that most extrajudicial contracts were subsequently recorded was when the parties to the contract, both foreigners, were themselves of different nationalities.[31] An outstanding example of this was the 1841 sale of the Russian settlements at Ross and Bodega by the Russian-American Company to the Swiss-born John Sutter, for the huge sum of $30,000.[32]

It would be tempting to view the recordation of promissory notes and contracts as one effort to resolve the expatriate dilemma sketched in the preceding chapter. It could be seen as a method whereby the expatriates essentially operated outside the official system, which involved the alcalde actually writing the

---

[29] For example, Garner, William R. (English) to Larkin, M.A. 6:920 (1843). This is the actual note, not an alcalde recitation of the indebtedness. No due date is specified.

[30] For example, two notes both dated Jan. 1, 1845, from Californio Gil Sánchez to Larkin, M.A. 8:782 (1845) and id., 8:784 (1845). Both are for fifty pesos payable in six months, one in hides and the other in produce.

[31] For example, the 1842 partnership agreement of Juan, Ricardo (French) and Moz, François (Canadian) was written by the parties and only then recorded. Id., 15:719 (1842).

[32] Castro, *Documentos, supra* note 5, Documents 1:57, 59, 63 (1841).

agreement, and yet also preserved a veneer of conformity with the local legal system by the recordation of the nonconforming documents.

It is certain that lodging the agreements and promissory notes with the alcalde created no advantage in their enforcement. If subsequent litigation became necessary, the conciliation hearings were quite informal and the extrajudicial or nonrecorded agreements were not treated any differently by the *jueces de paz* and *hombres buenos* than were the properly drafted and recorded instruments. The real effect of recording a contract written by the parties outside of the courthouse was apparently some subjective feeling it gave to the party so recording it. Therefore, it is tempting indeed to theorize that its function was to give a sense of participation to the expatriates, a sense of satisfaction that at least on one level they were in compliance with the official system. Unfortunately, there is not enough evidence either to sustain or to dismiss this speculation.

What can be said of the substance of the contracts the Anglo-Americans made among themselves? What was their subject matter; what did they concern? The contracts made through merchants' letters, an example of which is Larkin's request to buy try pots, were almost always concerned with mercantile trade. They were primarily of two kinds. The first requested the recipient to supply goods or to obtain goods from a third party supplier. Another example is the October 1845 request of an American merchant of San Francisco, Henry Mellus, addressed to James Watson, an English trader at Monterey:

I wish you would purchase for me, payable next season or in the spring, three bales of sugar, of Malarín, if he will let you have it, at six dollars the arroba. And if not, see if Don Manuel Díaz will let you have it at that price or less. Get two bales at any price you can, if you cannot get it at the price named, and deliver one to the *Advance* when she arrives in Monterey, and send the other one or two, as may be, to San Francisco.[33]

The second variety of merchant letter-contract was that which accompanied goods sent by one merchant or trader to another for sale on consignment. Typical of these letters is that from John

---

[33] H. Bancroft, California Pastoral 478 (1888).

Ebbets, an American supercargo or shipper's business agent. It was sent in May 1833 to fellow American Abel Stearns, a merchant in Los Angeles:

Herewith I hand you an Invoice of goods, which you will please sell as you may consider most to my advantage, taking in payment Tallow at twelve riales the arra. [arroba] and merchantable Hides at two Dollars each. . . . I agree to pay the freight of the goods from the port to the Pueblo, also to allow you ten per cent on what goods you may dispose of at private sale, and five per cent on what goods may be sold at Auction. . . . I flatter myself that you will be able to close the Sales within three or four mos. at the farthest.[34]

The business correspondence of the leading expatriate merchants, especially Larkin and Stearns, contains many examples of this kind of letter-contract. They are unilateral in nature, bargaining for some kind of performance, rather than a return promise. Therefore, they rarely resulted in any more formal agreement than the letters themselves, or perhaps, some follow-up correspondence confirming the results. It should also be noted that the letter-contract usually created an express agency relationship, that is, it authorized one merchant to act on behalf of the other.

In an 1842 letter to a fellow American merchant who traded between California and Hawaii, Larkin wrote: "I wish you would purchase in Oahu for me the following articles [detailed listing of items and quantities but not prices] and I will pay you the cost and fifty pr cent on the same, I paying here also all duties you may pay."[35] This offer would only affect the legal relations between the two merchants. Another letter offer between the same pair of merchants, however, would involve legal relationships with third parties as well. John Paty wrote Larkin from San Francisco on August 3, 1842: "If you wish me to deliver lumber to any person here on your account I will do it (provide I have it) at $5 M. advance on cost."[36] Suppose Larkin, based in Monterey, owed delivery of any lumber to one of his customers in San Francisco, or perhaps was in a position whereby he could quickly

[34] D. Wright, A Yankee in Mexican California: Abel Stearns, 1798–1848, at 65 (1977).

[35] Letter, Larkin to John Paty, Apr. 22, 1842, 1 Larkin Papers, *supra* note 15, at 207.

[36] Letter, John Paty to Larkin, Aug. 3, 1842, *id.*, at 259.

arrange a sale of lumber to a customer in San Francisco. Paty was offering for the consideration mentioned to satisfy Larkin's obligation by himself delivering the lumber to Larkin's customers, and thereby discharging Larkin's obligation to this third party.

If the offer were accepted, this arrangement would become what is called a third party beneficiary contract, to be examined more closely later in this chapter. It is interesting to note that in both of these letter offers neither Larkin nor Paty found it necessary to specify exact prices in their offers. This reflects considerable price stability and a shared expectation of the approximate costs of the articles concerning which their offers were made and that they would not materially change.

The expatriates sometimes created elaborate arrangements in their formal written contracts. Some of the simpler expatriate contracts were alcalde-drafted, such as the 1842 sale of a blacksmith shop from one Irishman to another, or an 1839 carpentry apprenticeship agreement between two Americans.[37] Other, more complex documents were almost always created without the assistance of the alcalde by the foreigners themselves. In judging the diversity and extent of these contracts, it must be recalled that there were no attorneys among the Anglo-Americans and that these instruments represent laymen's recollections from their pasts of the appropriate forms of contractual undertakings.

A common subject of these expatriate contracts were arrangements whereby one expatriate agreed to manage another's ranch. The owner generally agreed to put a specified number of horses or cattle on the ranch; the managing party agreed to exert his best efforts; and a compensation was agreed to be paid the manager, usually one third to one half of the profits. For example, in a June 1834 agreement between John B. R. Cooper and Job Dye, both Americans, for the management of Cooper's El Sur rancho, the parties agreed to operate the ranch as a mule-raising venture and Dye was to be compensated by one half of the increase. Additionally, Cooper agreed to leave the existing mares on the ranch, to compensate Dye for costs of obtaining additional stock on a varying scale, and to supply Dye with provisions. Dye was to "guard and take proper care of [the animals] for the purpose of

---

[37]McVicker and Hathaway, M.A. 15:507 (1839) (apprenticeship). For sale of blacksmith shop, see note 20, *supra*.

raising their young . . . [and] to follow while taking care of said mares no other business that will interfere with his business of taking care of said mares."

Dye was also obligated to erect a "well built log house with shingled roof . . . to be at least fifteen yards long and five and a half yards wide." The duration of the arrangement was left open, Dye agreeing to stay at least one year, to a maximum of five years. Apparently it did not work out; Dye later recalled that because it became unprofitable he abandoned the stock business after two years.[38]

Willard Buzzell's 1845 agreement to manage William Leides-dorff's ranch on the Sacramento River is another example of a ranch management contract. This was a more typical California operation, devoted primarily to cattle, but with a variety of other stock and grain. Leidesdorff agreed to furnish 300 head of meat cattle, 30 mares and a stud, 12 tame horses, 200 sheep, and to provide necessary tools. Buzzell agreed to exert his best efforts exclusively to the management of the ranch, to keep account of all goods needed for its operation and of all "payments made to Indians, or other servants employed in said farm, noting the prices thereof as acostumed in the adjacent farms," and to deliver all produce to Leidesdorff, without trading with others. For his efforts Buzzell was to receive a third part of all increase in cattle, horses, other stock, and produce. Apparently this arrangement did not work out well either, as Buzzell abandoned the ranch the following year.[39]

Neither of these two ranch management agreements was writ-

[38] The 1834 agreement can be found in 31 Vallejo, *Documentos para la historia de California*, 338–40 (37 vols.). These documents are on deposit with the Bancroft Library, University of California, Berkeley, California. That it became unprofitable is based on a statement by Job Dye himself in an article, "Recollections of a Pioneer of California," Santa Cruz Sentinel, May 15, 1869: "I entered into a contract with Capt. John B.R. Cooper, of Monterey, to take 217 brood mares and convey them to his ranch, on the Coast, 'El Sur,' and go into a general stock-raising business. It was designed to raise mules, in the main, and I commenced business in October, 1833, [undoubtedly confused for 1834] and continued it until the fall of '35, when finding it unprofitable, abandoned the stock business and opened a distillery." Apparently there were no bad feelings since in 1843 Cooper hired Dye once again to manage El Sur. M.A. 11:399 (1843).

[39] Manning, "William A. Leidesdorff's Career in California," at 96A–100 (M.A. thesis, University of California at Berkeley, 1942). On the abandonment, see *id.*, at 61–63.

ten by an alcalde but by the parties themselves. Both were witnessed, although neither was recorded. The Leidesdorff-Buzzell document is reproduced in its entirety as Appendix A, preceding the bibliography.

A second common variety of Anglo-American contract, although more varied in nature than the ranch arrangements, was the partnership agreement. By their nature they varied, depending on the objects of the partnerships, ranging, for example, from a mercantile business or a grist mill to a large-scale overseas trading venture.[40] Foreigners of other nationalities also entered into partnerships, and these were often alcalde-written or recorded.[41] The Anglo-American partnerships typically were neither, although it was common for them to be in writing and witnessed.

Because of the wide diversity of partnership purposes, it is difficult to generalize on their provisions. A typical mercantile partnership agreement is Appendix B. It is an 1836 contract between Nathan Spear, William Hinckley, and Jacob Leese, all Americans, to establish and operate a retail store in San Francisco.[42] This partnership was soon to dissolve and generate significant controversy between the erstwhile partners, a development discussed in the chapter on dispute resolution.

The single most common type of written contract that the Anglo-Americans entered into among themselves was the service agreement. The ranch management agreements were merely a

---

[40] Examples include mercantile business, the German Charles Weber and American William Gulnac had a mercantile partnership in San Jose in 1842–43 and thereafter amicably dissolved it by written agreement. G. HAMMOND, THE WEBER ERA IN STOCKTON HISTORY 28–30 (1982); grist mill, ATHERTON, *supra*, note 17, at 123, 127, 140; large-scale trading company, a formal contract concerning the trading expedition of a ship, the *Nymph,* was entered into on May 22, 1841 by Abel Stearns, John Temple, James McKinley, and Henry Fitch, all Americans except James McKinley who was Scots. Although the mother tongue of all concerned was English, the document was written in Spanish. This reflects a high degree of assimilation and acculturation. Fitch, *Documentos para la historia de California,* Document 156. These documents are deposited with the Bancroft Library, University of California, Berkeley, California.

[41] An 1842 partnership between Ricardo Juan, French, and François Moz, Canadian, was not alcalde-drafted but was recorded. M.A. 15:719 (1842). An 1844 partnership agreement in Los Angeles, involving several French expatriates, was not written before a judge but probably was recorded. L.A.P.R. 2:617–19 (1844).

[42] Spear, *Correspondence,* Box II, Miscellaneous Papers, Item 2. These papers are on file with the Bancroft Library, University of California, Berkeley, California.

particularly common subspecies of this variety, with the rest of the service contracts varying considerably in their nature. The great variety that Larkin alone made demonstrates this diversity. In September 1845, Nicholas Gordon was hired by Larkin to work in his blacksmith shop. The pay was $600 in cash per year plus board and lodging, Larkin to furnish the shop and a helper. The "year" was specified as three hundred days, and Gordon could keep half of the value of any work he performed beyond the three hundred days or at night.[43] This is a hybrid arrangement, a cross between straight employment and a partnership. Apparently it did not suit the parties well in that form since at the beginning of the following year Larkin leased the blacksmith shop outright to Gordon.[44]

Other examples of Larkin's contractual undertakings include the hiring of an English laborer for his soap factory,[45] hiring an Englishman and a Scot to cut timber,[46] and employing an American, Talbot Green, to manage his retail store. There are several examples of written intra-expatriate contracts to manage retail stores and warehouses. In May 1843, Larkin agreed that Talbot Green would manage his Monterey retail store and warehouse for an annual compensation of $400 and 5 percent of the profits.[47] At the beginning of 1846 the parties altered their understandings by a partnership agreement whereby Green received a third of the profits, and Larkin agreed to provide a capital stock of goods and provisions valued at $10,000 at cost prices.[48]

In Los Angeles the American merchant Abel Stearns engaged in a number of employment contracts, most concerning the management of his public warehouse in San Pablo. For example, in July 1840, Stearns agreed with John Forster, an Englishman, that Forster would manage the warehouse for 400 pesos annually, half

---

[43] 3 LARKIN PAPERS, *supra* note 15, at 345–46.

[44] 4 LARKIN PAPERS, *supra* note 15, at 146.

[45] Larkin and Anderson, *id.* at 204–5.

[46] Larkin, Trevethan, and Brander, 1 LARKIN PAPERS, *supra* note 15, at 99.

[47] Larkin and Green, 2 LARKIN PAPERS, *supra* note 15, at 15. There is an interesting story in connection with Talbot Green. In 1851, after eleven successful years in California, and while a prominent candidate for mayor of San Francisco, he was exposed to be an imposter who was actually a Paul Geddes, an embezzling bank clerk who had fled Pennsylvania leaving behind a wife and children.

[48] 4 LARKIN PAPERS, *supra* note 15, at 145–46.

in goods and half in the "currency of the country," meaning cattle hides. Stearns promised to stock the warehouse with goods for retail sale, and Forster was to receive half of the net proceeds of retail sales, either from the sale of Stearns's goods or from other merchandise consigned by third parties for retail sale.[49]

None of these service contracts mentioned was alcalde-drafted, and none was recorded. All but the 1843 Larkin-Green agreement were also signed by a third party as a witness. The 1843 Larkin-Green document is reproduced as Appendix C as a specimen of this kind of contract.

There are at least three remarkable aspects to these expatriate contracts. The first is their sophistication in the legal relationships created. The second is the sophistication of the expatriate merchants in their interpretations of the legal effect of their contracts. The third and most remarkable aspect of these agreements—the nature of law itself—is deferred. It can best be appreciated after the first two features have been studied.

The contractual provisions of these Anglo-Americans obviously cannot compare to the polished documents drawn by attorneys in Boston or solicitors in London. The expatriate contracts were drafted by laymen, with no lawyers to guide them; they were thousands of miles from their homelands and in the middle of societies quite different from their own. Given these facts, the legal sophistication of these contractual provisions is impressive.

The variety of these provisions makes their listing read much like a table of contents of a contracts treatise. The expatriates sold goods by sample,[50] utilized conditions subsequent,[51] applied liquidated damages and contractual forfeitures,[52] and insisted in

[49] WRIGHT, *supra* note 34, at 41–42.

[50] Letter, William Hartnell to Larkin, May 8, 1839, 1 LARKIN PAPERS, *supra* note 15, at 10 (offer of sale of flour; one barrel offered as sample); letter, Larkin to Parrott & Co., Jan. 12, 1842, *id.* at 150 ("You showd me some on a shelf—but I did not receve Hffs. [handkerchiefs] of the same quality"). At least one Californio also sold by sample. Letter, Talbot Green to Larkin, Sept. 26, 1842, *id.* at 292 ("Quinten Ortega sends you 5 potatoes as a sample. . . . The Sample is only for quality not for size.")

[51] Letter, Josiah Belden to Larkin, July 20, 1842, *id.* at 251 ("I told him I would take a few things that I was in need of on condition that if you objected to it he should take them back").

[52] Letter, Nicholas Den to Larkin, Mar. 21, 1842, *id.* at 178 ("I feel much disappointment [that Larkin cannot ship any lumber] owing to an agreement of contract which I entered into with two Carpenters here [Santa Barbara] which binds

their contracts that delivered goods be "merchantable," a technical legal term referring to quality.[53] In their leases they recognized the general principle that at the end of the lease term any improvements made by the tenant and attached to the building or land will belong to the landlord. They also drew the fine distinction that this principle does not apply to trade fixtures put into a building by a commercial tenant, such as a shopkeeper. This 1845 store lease in Monterey illustrates the point:

> Milton Little will be able to make all the improvements that he wishes in the house at his own expense, but at the end of the stipulated time, all the improvements that may have been made, will remain to the benefit of the property, with the sole exception of the counter and shelves of the store, which will be recognized always as the property of Milton Little, who will be able to remove them when he may make the surrender of the house.[54]

The foreigners also entered into third party beneficiary contracts. This is an arrangement whereby one party to a contract agrees to render performance, usually the payment of money, to a creditor of the party with whom he contracts. It is a sophisticated concept. A relatively straightforward example is Abel Stearns's purchase of Los Alamitos ranch from Francisco Figueroa in 1842. Figueroa owed several large debts, and in the conveyance of the ranch to Stearns it was specified that Stearns was to pay these debts, in installments, to the creditors directly, paying only the net balance to Figueroa.[55]

Third party beneficiary contracts could be considerably more complicated, however. In January 1843, Salvador Vallejo owed Thomas O. Larkin $200. At the same time Larkin owed Henry Fitch the delivery of fifty young cows, which had a value of $4

---

in a penalty if the Lumber is not at hand before the middle of next month.''); Larkin and Anderson, 4 LARKIN PAPERS, *supra,* at 204–5 (labor agreement; forfeiture of one-half of wages if laborer fails to complete a full year of employment).

[53] Letter, John Ebbets to Abel Stearns, May 4, 1833, quoted from WRIGHT, *supra* note 34, at 65; letter, Alpheus B. Thompson to Fitch, Jan. 19, 1843, Fitch *Documentos, supra* note 40, Document 242 ("I examined them [skins] and found several small, and others damaged . . . and I could not pass more than eighty, for merchantable.").

[54] Carrasco (by Larkin through power of attorney) and Little, Dec. 31, 1845, in 4 LARKIN PAPERS, *supra* note 15, at 136–37.

[55] Figueroa to Stearns, Book B of Deeds, Los Angeles County Records, 71–74 (1842). This transaction is discussed in WRIGHT, *supra* note 34, at 98–101.

apiece, or $200. The parties arranged to liquidate these accounts by the delivery of fifty young cows from Vallejo directly to Fitch, thereby satisfying both debts, even though there was no debt owed by Vallejo to Fitch.[56]

The delivery by Vallejo to Fitch was exactly the same as though Vallejo had delivered the cows to Larkin, satisfying the first debt, and then Larkin had immediately given these same cows to Fitch, satisfying the second debt, it also being understood that prices were so constant that cows would be acceptable at $4 apiece to pay the $200. There is one very big difference, however. In a region of vast distances and primitive transportation, the use of third party beneficiary arrangements such as this could be of great advantage. The parties could line up their respective debtors and creditors so that a single delivery needed to satisfy two debts could be made between persons in the same location.

One aspect of the expatriate use of third party beneficiary contracts is especially interesting. The period 1835 to 1846 is before the American and English courts generally had begun to enforce this kind of contract. Therefore, the expatriate use is an example of business practice preceding legal recognition of a trade usage.

In addition to the sophistication of the contractual provisions, the expatriates were expert and precise in their interpretations of these clauses. For some matters of interpretation the foreign merchants appealed to local California trade usages. Thus custom indicated the allowable discounts on drafts and bills of exchange[57] and the limits of allowable waste in the storage of liquids.[58] It was contended that there was a California trade practice that older debts were to be paid before newer obligations,[59] and that no in-

[56] Letter, Larkin to Salvador Vallejo, Jan. 11, 1843, 2 LARKIN PAPERS, *supra* note 15, at 3. Apparently this particular transaction did not end up well as there were subsequent disagreements as to the quality of the cows. Miller, *supra* note 14, at 195–96. The Californios also made a few less elaborate third party beneficiary contracts. See text accompanying footnote 38 of chapter 4. See also Arias and Richards, M.A. 15:687 (1845) (alcalde recites that Francisco Arias understands a document in which he promises to pay the debt of Pierre Richards (Frenchman) to José María Orozco in January of 1846).

[57] Bills of exchange will be discussed in the following chapter dealing with credit formation and debt collection.

[58] Tariff (regarding Stearns's warehouse at San Pedro), in WRIGHT, *supra* note 34, at 40–41.

[59] Letter, Alpheus B. Thompson to Larkin, Nov. 1, 1844, 2 LARKIN PAPERS, *supra* note 15, at 269 ("agreeable to law and usage here the Oldest debts are to be discharged first").

terest was allowable on trade debts arising from the wholesale purchase of goods but only on cash lent, and that payment of trade obligations within eighteen months was timely. As Larkin pithily wrote to a merchant in Mazatlán: "Payment in full in California in 12 to 18 months is considered by us good, and we obtain no interest only on Cash lent."[60]

The expatriates, at least the merchants among them, had sophisticated legal understanding, and they often used legalistic concepts in their interpretations of contractual arrangements. They frequently asserted technical legal rights in their correspondence with one another. In these letters they sought rescission of contracts on the grounds of mistake, made charge-backs on accounts for short weight or damaged goods, recognized that they were relieved of the duty of contractually required performance because of the other party's own breach of contract, and granted rights of first refusal.[61] They drew a proper distinction between the sale of rotten goods and a knowing sale thereof,[62] and recognized that a tangled background to the signing of a note did not matter if the note were in negotiable form because prior rights would now be extinguished.[63] They also knew that the revocation of an offer was not possible if the offeree had accepted the offer by substantial performance. "If you have not purchased or sent the two horses we wrote for sometime since," a firm in Honolulu wrote

[60] Letter, Larkin to Copmann and Lomer, May 25, 1845, 3 LARKIN PAPERS, *supra* note 15 at 196. For similar expression by Larkin, see *id.* 200, 213 and letter, Larkin to Alfred Robinson, May 6, 1845, *id.* at 177 ("Its just, its common, all debts pay it interest . . . not cargo at 50 pr ct profet.").

[61] Rescission, Letter, John C. Jones to Larkin, Nov. 20, 1841, 1 LARKIN PAPERS, *supra* note 15, at 135 ("It appears however to have been otherwise, and now let me cancell the obligation."); charge-backs, Letter, Eliab Grimes to Larkin, Aug. 6, 1844, 2 LARKIN PAPERS, at 184; Letter, Marshall and Johnson to Larkin, May 26, 1842, 1 LARKIN PAPERS, *supra* at 223; relieved of duty of performance, Letter Henry D. Fitch to Larkin, Dec. 4, 1842, in *id.* at 331 ("I am sorry that you did not send the money by Capt. Arther as was agreed upon. I do not consider myself now bound to pay you for the lumber on account of Mackinlay."); rights of first refusal, Letter, John C. Jones to Larkin, July 21, 1841, *id.* at 98 ("You shall however have the refusal should I conclude to sell them.").

[62] Letter, Hiram Teal to Larkin, Sept. 7, 1841, 1 LARKIN PAPERS, *supra* note 15, at 117.

[63] Letter, Larkin to Peirce and Brewer, Dec. 19, 1842, *id.* at 345 (long, tangled story of background for a note followed by "This Note of 500$ being negociatble does not require the long story above"). Chapter 7 contains a more extended discussion of negotiability.

Larkin, "you will please consider the order countermanded."[64] These merchants also knew that partners were individually responsible for the debts of a partnership. A Mazatlán trader matter-of-factly mentioned this to Larkin: "[W]hen Mr. Thompson made his purchase from us, we considered that he was in partnership with Mr. Jno. C. Jones, and we now understand said partnership has been dissolved. Even if this be the fact, both parties are liable for debts contracted during the partnership."[65]

This degree of sophistication was not typical of all Anglo-Americans in California. Though this discussion concerns merchants, they were not exclusively California merchants. Several of the examples have been drawn from Mazatlán and Oahu traders writing to their California equivalents. The letters from outside California necessarily reflect an anticipated level of sophistication on the part of the Anglo-American recipients in California. Taken as a whole, the level of legal sophistication on the part of these California expatriate merchants is remarkably high.

The single most remarkable thing about these expatriate contracts is what they say about the nature of law itself. There is one view of law that sees the concrete results of enforcement—the power of coercion—as law itself. For this school of thought, a defect of remedy, a lack of adequate enforcement power, means that a claimed right simply does not exist. The only real law is that which can be seen in its enforcement. This can be contrasted with an alternative and older view of law as Platonic in reality. This school of thought contends that law exists, that is to say legal rights and legal wrongs exist, quite apart from an ability to enforce those rights or punish the wrongs.

The "realistic" notion of law, that it exists only so far as some government official will enforce a claimed right, has a long intellectual heritage. In the United States it reached its judicial height in Supreme Court Justice Oliver Wendell Holmes, Jr. Holmes asked "the fundamental question, what constitutes the law?" and suggested that the answer was "prophecies of what the courts will do in fact, and nothing more pretentious."[66] An eminent legal

[64] Letter, Marshall and Johnson to Larkin, Mar. 16, 1842, 1 LARKIN PAPERS, *supra* note 15, at 177.

[65] Letter, Mott Talbot & Co. to Larkin, May 2, 1845, 3 LARKIN PAPERS, *supra* note 15, at 167.

[66] Holmes, *The Path of the Law,* 10 HARV. L. REV. 457, 460–61 (1897).

scholar of the 1930s, Karl Llewellyn, wrote that "judges or sher-
iffs or clerks or jailers or lawyers, are officials of the law. What
these officials do about disputes is, to my mind, the law itself. . . .
[A]bsence of remedy is absence of right. Defect of remedy is
defect of right. A right is as big, precisely, as what the courts
will do."[67]

Americans of the mid-nineteenth century articulated the view
that enforcement was essential to make law, but acted to the contrary. We speak now of the great mass, the law-followers, and not
the tiny minority of law-makers, judges and legislators. John P.
Reid studied the contractual obligations incurred by emigrants
while on the overland trail bound for California and Oregon.
These emigrants were contemporaries of the Anglo-American
merchants whose formal contracts have been reviewed. Reid
found many instances of contractual undertakings in the diaries
and other records of the overlanders.

Most emigrants . . . said there was no law on the overland trail, yet
their actions contradicted their beliefs. Daily behavior was premised
on expectations that there was law on the overland trail and that enforcement machinery—courts, advocates, process servers—were
not necessary to have and to obey a body of "law." . . . If such agreements surprise us, it is because we are thinking of enforceability, an
issue that apparently gave the overland emigrants little concern. . . .
They were relying on a tradition of shared legal notions: expecting
that the other party shared the same values they did, understood a
contract in the same sense they did and believed that promises mutually exchanged created obligations for the same reason they did.[68]

The same is true of the Anglo-American merchants in Mexican
California. Recall that they had absolutely no confidence in the
ability of the local Mexican courts to enforce their agreements or
collect their debts. If enforcement or the coercive power of government is the essence of law, why would these men enter into
these elaborate arrangements? Even more to the point, why
would they have bothered to send each other letters claiming

[67] K. LLEWELLYN, THE BRAMBLE BUSH: ON OUR LAW AND ITS STUDY 12, 83–84
(1975). Neither Holmes nor Llewellyn were as cynical as their statements super-
ficially suggest. The discussion of their thought would take us far afield from the
topic at hand.
[68] Reid, *Binding the Elephant: Contracts and Legal Obligations on the Overland Trail,* 21 AM. J. LEGAL HIST. 285, 288, 300, 314 (1977).

rights and asserting legalistic contentions in respect to the contracts they had made and their proper interpretations? What would be the point if they had equated law with enforcement?

The evidence from Mexican California suggests that these Anglo-Americans entered into contractual relationships in reliance and in expectation of mutual performance, not because of the presence of lawyers or confidence in judicial remedies in the event of breach. The men from Massachusetts, Kentucky, England, and Scotland shared a common mercantile culture. To a significant extent that culture included law. The law was a reality they believed in. It was for that reason that in the face of potential breakdown of contractual relations, these men could make technical legal claims of one another, claims of which they had no subjective hope of enforcement in the local courts, but with every hope that they could convince their opponent of the rightfulness of their positions.

The expatriates may have bleated loudly about living in a land without law. This meant a lack of confidence in the alcalde courts. But they had such strongly internalized understandings of the common law that they had brought with them to California that they constantly acted in reliance on that law in their dealings with one another.

7

Credit Formation and Debt Collection

The extension of credit and the collection of debt varied considerably in their complexity between the hide-and-tallow trade, on the one hand, and intramerchant transactions, on the other. In general the transactions arising out of the hide-and-tallow trade were retail in nature, consumers were the debtors, and these debtors were the local Californios. The intramerchant transactions giving rise to credit were usually wholesale, with the debts arising in the course of business, and the debtors were foreigners.

Reality was not this neatly divided. Some expatriates were ranchers and incurred consumer debts. Some Californios were merchants, or even as ranchers incurred debt for capital improvements and not merely for consumption. The differences in the ways credit transactions were conducted are so striking that it is helpful, albeit artificial, to divide the transactions into these two groups.

The retail sales arising out of the hide-and-tallow trade are far simpler to explain than the intramerchant debts, although no less troublesome to the merchants themselves. Hides and tallows were sold for consumer goods (and the few capital goods involved as well) in three ways.

The first was amidst the somewhat carnival atmosphere that prevailed when the hide ships arrived on the California coast. Once docked, the ships became retail trade bazaars, filled with the consumer goods of the world. The Californios would flock to the ships to shop, making a social occasion of the event. The second method of trade was through the ships' business agents, the supercargoes, who would often travel into the interior with sample books, selling goods on order to more isolated ranchers.

The third method was through the local, fixed merchants, such as Larkin in Monterey, Stearns in Los Angeles, and Fitch in San

Diego. These major merchants had a large retail trade and also conducted wholesale operations, particularly Larkin and Stearns, with smaller merchants in more remote locations. The more remote and smaller storekeepers, "country merchants" as they were called, were either employees of the larger merchants or had a loose agency relationship with the wholesale dealers. The major fixed merchants were independent in that they either arranged for direct shipments of goods, from Mexico, Hawaii, or elsewhere, or themselves bought goods from the hide ships at wholesale prices. They were neither employees nor agents of the Boston shipping concerns that financed the major hide-and-tallow voyages.

A common feature of all three levels of trade was the extension of credit with payment for consumer goods to be made in the future and usually in hides or tallow. The customers were generally ranchers, or managers of the ranchos, the mayordomos, or others who themselves had trade or contact with the ranchos. Although some trade was conducted in silver coin or with such products as soap or grain, the bulk of California trade called for payment in hides and secondarily tallow. These were the products that had a large and dependable external market. This form of payment itself made credit inevitable because the hides were taken and tallow rendered from fat most efficiently at the annual roundups and slaughters known as *matanzas*.

Thus unsecured credit extension was a regular and expected feature of the hide-and-tallow trade,[1] and generally payment was extended over twelve to twenty-four months.[2] The reason for the lengthy wait for payment was because, as noted by a British official of the Hudson's Bay Company, "a farmer after greatly involving himself in dealing with one vessel, will often forget his liabilities and sell elsewhere the produce he intended for his creditors, who may have to wait another year, before he receives payment."[3] Nor

---

[1] Ogden, *New England Traders in Spanish and Mexican California,* in GREATER AMERICA: ESSAYS IN HONOR OF HERBERT EUGENE BOLTON 402 (1945); Ogden, *Boston Hide Droughers Along California Shores,* 8 CAL. HIST. SOC'Y Q. 289, 302 (1929).

[2] Dallas, "The Hide and Tallow Trade in Alta California, 1822–1846," at 66 (Ph.D. diss., Indiana University, 1955).

[3] Douglas, *From the Columbia to California in 1840: From the Journal of Sir James Douglas,* 8 CAL. HIST. SOC'Y Q. 97, 107 (1929).

was this a singular observation. Both a French visitor in 1840, Joseph de Rosamel,[4] and a resident American merchant, William H. Davis,[5] recorded their impressions that the ranchers frequently paid their debts in no more rational an order than whichever creditor called on them first.

The result of this was that there was a considerable amount of debt dunning of the ranchers by the merchants. Some of it was by appeal to pride. "This is the third person who has refused to take the word of D. Salvador Vallejo at his own request for a small debt," Larkin once informed the same Salvador Vallejo.[6] Most of the collection efforts were "by persistent efforts and persuasion,"[7] as Davis put it, and involved wearying journeys up and down the coast calling on ranchers. Henry Fitch wrote to business associate James McKinley from Los Angeles in August 1842:

We shall touch at Sta. Barbara, Sn. Luis and at Monterrey, and I shall try and make all the collections that I can on my way up. I wish you could arrange it to meet me in Monterrey with Horses . . . and you could procede down the coast. It is absolutely necessary that you should come down this way, as I make but a poor fist of collecting from the People which you trusted last March and April. I am tired of running after them. I have been out to William's, Bandini's, Palomares and about there. They all promise to pay but God knows when. I shall leave a note here who pays. I cannot conceive how you came to trust so many vagabonds. There are upwards to 40, and some of them such as Leonardo Cota and others I think will never pay. Williams as yet has paid nothing. I saw him again yesterday. He says that he has commenced his Matanza and intends to pay us up, but I doubt it very much.[8]

---

[4]Rosamel, *California Prior to Conquest: A Frenchman's Views* (Shepard, trans.), 37 CAL. HIST. Q. 63, 69 (1958).

[5]W. DAVIS, SEVENTY-FIVE YEARS IN CALIFORNIA 246 (1929).

[6]Letter, Larkin to Salvador Vallejo, Jan. 11, 1843, 2 THE LARKIN PAPERS: PERSONAL, BUSINESS, AND OFFICIAL CORRESPONDENCE OF THOMAS OLIVER LARKIN, MERCHANT AND UNITED STATES CONSUL IN CALIFORNIA 3 (Hammond ed. 1951–1968) (10 vols & index) [hereinafter cited as LARKIN PAPERS]. Another good example is Letter, Larkin to William S. Hinckley, Oct. 1845 (no date specified), in 4 LARKIN PAPERS, at 15–16.

[7]DAVIS, *supra* note 5, at 246.

[8]Letter, Henry D. Fitch to James McKinley, Aug. 21, 1842, 1 LARKIN PAPERS, *supra* note 6, at 275.

One method the merchants attempted in an effort to avoid collection problems with the ranchers, and which they used with even greater frequency in intramerchant dealings, was to exchange current credit information with one another. For example, Talbot Green wrote fellow American trader William T. Faxon in August 1842 about a Monterey rancher, warning that "if a man by the name of Philippe Aguala [Felipe Aguila] should want any credit dont trust him."[9] Likewise, Scotsman Hugo Reid confided in American merchant Abel Stearns that "if Silvestro Portillo [Silvestre Portilla, a grantee of a rancho in present-day San Diego County] owes you any money, you had better send on powers [i.e., powers of attorney for a lawsuit] before he squanders away all he has, as I am pretty certain he never intends returning to California. This I tell you in *confianza*."[10]

Although a foreigner and not a local Californio, the Swiss-born John Sutter was also closely watched by the merchants. He was a large debtor, for capital items as well as consumer goods, and the fluctuations of his enormous enterprise were the subject of many reports. "The salmon fishery fail'd at the Sacramento this year," Larkin was informed in July 1842, "but the crop is said to come of tolerably well; Sutter has harvested . . . about $4000 fanegas wheat."[11] Only two weeks later, however, another informant, the Hudson's Bay Company representative, wrote that "Sutter is due me $3400 and I am of opinion neither of us will get a farthing from him this year."[12]

The effect of this credit watch showed on Sutter, as it must have on other ranchers. He complained to Larkin of creditors who "do their best to ruin my Credit,"[13] and was eager to advise Larkin of favorable credit information such as the present ability to pay certain debts.[14]

[9]Letter, Green to Faxon, Aug. 1, 1842, *id.* at 257.

[10]S. DAKIN, A SCOTCH PAISANO IN OLD LOS ANGELES: HUGO REID'S LIFE IN CALIFORNIA, 1832–1852, DERIVED FROM HIS CORRESPONDENCE 38 (1939) (rep. ed. 1978).

[11]Letter, Rufus Titcomb to Larkin, July 20, 1842, 1 LARKIN PAPERS, *supra* note 6, at 252.

[12]Letter, William Glen Rae to Larkin, Aug. 3, 1842, *id.,* at 260.

[13]Letter, John Augustus Sutter to Larkin, July 22, 1845, 3 LARKIN PAPERS, *supra* note 6, at 282.

[14]There were several such letters. One example is letter, Sutter to Larkin, Sept. 11, 1845, *id.* at 347.

Notwithstanding these collection efforts, a number of the ranchers were simply slow pays. Almost every merchant's correspondence has a good number of letters from retail customers making excuses for the present and promising payment in the future. If all else failed, the merchant could bring suit in the alcalde courts, and many did, as noted in chapter 4. There were far more suits brought by expatriates against Californios filed in Monterey from 1831 to 1846 than the reverse, and almost half of the claims foreigners brought against Californios were for debt collection. The number of these suits is far less than the number of bad debts, however, because of the expatriates' distrust of the local courts and their reluctance to use them.

Even with credit information, collection efforts, and some litigation, the foreign merchants were often burdened with a goodly amount of bad debts. The California branch of Hudson's Bay Company opened in San Francisco in 1841 and in just four years, by 1845, was in serious financial difficulties, in large part because of the inability to collect bad debts. It was liquidated in the following year.[15] No one described the traders' difficulties more vividly than John C. Jones in writing Larkin from Santa Barbara in October 1842:

[E]very thing is going wrong in this miserable corner of the world. What miserable business, some of us are doing, what gloomy prospects ahead. The Fama obliged to return to the Islands with a paltry Cargo of Lumber, instead of thirty thusnd hides, which she ought to have had, had there been any honesty amongst the people of California. As for myself, for the schoones cargo, I have received One hundred hides, and no more, tho' at this moment thaer is due, over three thousnd, solmenly pledged to have been paid this year; I am quite discoraged; gods! What wuld tempt me to bring an other cargo this miserable land of rogues and cheats; nothing short of a security for eternal salvation.[16]

The system of credit used between the foreign merchants themselves was much more complex. There was a considerable trade between Oahu and Mazatlán merchants and the hide-and-tallow

---

[15] See 4 H. BANCROFT, HISTORY OF CALIFORNIA 593–94 (1886) (7 vols.) (1884–1890) and references therein.

[16] Letter, John Coffin Jones to Larkin, Oct. 22, 1842, 1 LARKIN PAPERS, *supra* note 6, at 300.

ships, on the one hand, and the expatriate California merchants on the other. In addition, the California traders frequently sent goods back and forth to each other, sometimes on consignment for sale and sometimes in response to a request for goods desired by one merchant to meet a local scarcity.

Some of these transactions were represented by running open accounts between the merchants involved, but most were settled, as indeed even the open accounts were ultimately settled, by credit instruments. It was essential to use credit instruments because of the scarcity of hard money, or specie. Merchants paid for goods by the issuance of promissory notes or bills of exchange, or by the negotiation and delivery of instruments of these kinds that had been originally issued by third parties.

The promissory note is familiar; it is an unconditional promise by one person to pay a second party. That second party can sign the note, technically endorse it, and use it himself, just as money is used, to pay his own debts by delivering it to a third party. After presentation of the note, the first party becomes liable to the third party.

Promissory notes were used in California. Indeed, Larkin had preprinted forms of promissory notes payable to him. Much more common in Mexican California among the merchants, and generally more common in the first half of the nineteenth century, however, was the other form of negotiable instrument, the bill of exchange. The bill of exchange is an old commercial device.[17] It is a written order by one person, the drawer, addressed to another person, the drawee, ordering the drawee to pay a specified sum of money at a specified time to a third person, the payee. The paper is usually given to the payee, who may then either present it to the drawee and demand payment, or endorse it and, as in the case of a promissory note, deliver it to a second person, or taker (and there later may be a third, a fourth, and so on), in payment of an obligation of the first holder.

This is not as complicated as it may appear. Today there is only

---

[17] The early history of the law of negotiable instruments is ably discussed in Read, *The Origin, Early History, and Later Development of Bills of Exchange and Certain Other Negotiable Instruments,* 4 CANADIAN B. REV. 440 & 665 (1926). *See also* Beutel, *The Development of Negotiable Instruments in Early English Law,* 51 HARV. L. REV. 813 (1938); Beutel, *Colonial Sources of the Negotiable Instruments Law of the United States,* 34 ILL. L. REV. 137 (1939); Weinberg, *Commercial Paper in Economic Theory and Legal History,* 70 KY. L.J. 567 (1982).

one truly common bill of exchange, but that form is used almost daily by most persons. The ordinary check is a negotiable bill of exchange wherein a bank is the drawee. In writing a check, our bank is ordered to pay money to a third person, called the payee. That holder can go to the bank on which the check was written and demand cash, but in fact usually endorses it to a third party, generally his or her own bank as a collection agent, but occasionally to another nonbank holder.

Bills of exchange were extremely important to trade in Mexican California because there were no banks and very little coin. These merchant-issued bills became a kind of currency in themselves and were traded back and forth in mercantile transactions. In California the parties on whom the bills were drawn (the drawees) were usually other merchants with whom the issuing merchants had credit balances. In other words, the drawer wrote an order on someone who owed him money, perhaps, as one example, because of a sale of goods which had been held on consignment. The issuing-drawer would give the bill of exchange to the payee in payment of some obligation, and typically then write the drawee informing him informally that he had drawn on him. "I have given Capt Blin an Order [a term frequently used by the merchants for the more legalistic bill of exchange] on you for the amt. du us," Henry Paty & Company advised Larkin in April 1839.[18]

The letter sent Larkin by Henry Paty & Company was merely an informal courtesy and not the bill of exchange itself. The bills themselves were given to the payee, although they were usually in the form of a letter. The bills were usually nothing like our modern printed checks, but appeared to be just what they were, letters from one merchant to another directing the other to pay a third party.[19]

The informal letters concerning drafts or orders, both common

---

[18] Letter, Henry Paty & Co. to Larkin, Apr. 19, 1839, 1 LARKIN PAPERS, *supra* note 6, at 8; letter, John Temple to Larkin, June 9, 1840, *id.* at 44 ("I shall probably draw on you in favor of Mr. McKinley for the ballanc due on the aguarte [*aguardiente,* or liquor] & expences on the flour which is 202.1").

[19] Typical is letter, Henry D. Fitch to Miguel de Pedrorena (Spanish supercargo), Dec. 22, 1838, ordering Pedrorena to deliver 530 hides to José Antonio Aguirre (Spanish trader), with notation by Aguirre that he has received the hides, in Henry D. Fitch, *Documentos para la historia de California,* Document 47 [hereinafter cited as Fitch *Documentos*]. The Fitch *Documentos* are on deposit with the Bancroft Library, University of California, Berkeley, California.

nineteenth-century terms for bills of exchange, were even more common than the negotiable instruments themselves. Courtesy letters were often written by one merchant to another acknowledging that a bill had been paid. Abel Stearns wrote Larkin in September 1840 that "your order in favour of Mr. A. Robinson for fifty Dolls. has been paid."[20] Larkin then knew that this particular liability he had created was satisfied and no longer floating about as currency. Another courtesy was advice as to the availability of a credit balance on which another merchant could draw. "Your Lumber is sold at Last," Isaac Sparks advised Larkin from Santa Barbara in September 1840; "you can draw on me for the Proceeds as soon as you wish."[21] This lumber had apparently been held on consignment.

An alternative method of credit formation was the situation where one merchant drew on another even though the first had no credit balance with the drawee. This would amount to a pure extension of credit, that is, a loan. John Paty wrote Henry D. Fitch in February 1844, informing him that he had drawn on him in favor of Thomas Jones in the amount of $100. "I will return you the money with interest—or—pay it unto your order," promised Paty.[22]

Of course, Fitch could have refused to pay Jones when the bill was presented for payment. The drawer could not force the drawee to pay out money to the payee if there were no credit balance due the drawer. If the drawee refused to pay, the bill of exchange would be said to be dishonored.

Another alternative for the drawee was to indicate to the holder that he would honor the drawer's order, but not now; he would pay at some definite time in the future.[23] Without becoming too technical, it should be noted that this procedure would be improper with certain kinds of bills of exchange, especially those

[20] Letter, Abel Stearns to Larkin, Sept. 5, 1840, 1 LARKIN PAPERS, *supra* note 6, at 55.
[21] Letter, Isaac J. Sparks to Larkin, Sept. 5, 1840, *id.* at 54.
[22] Letter, John Paty to Fitch, Feb. 5, 1844, in Fitch *Documentos, supra* note 19, Document 289.
[23] Typical of this kind of acceptance is Letter, José Abrego to Fitch, June 19, 1840, requesting Fitch to place at the disposal of Larkin, 1,611 pesos, 1,311 in coin and 300 in merchandise, with note by Fitch that he would pay within three months, and note of receipt by Larkin, in Fitch *Documentos, supra* note 19, Document 125.

payable at sight or on demand. The precise distinctions between these kinds of bills and methods of treatment are not important for our purposes except to note that they were all utilized by the expatriate merchants in Mexican California.

The common law rule was that a negotiable bill must call for payment in money. In the American colonies chattel notes were used frequently, specifying payment in produce or animals. Tobacco notes, for example, were ubiquitous in Maryland and Virginia.[24] Later in the republican period, many American frontier jurisdictions, such as Alabama, Georgia, Mississippi, and others, legalized chattel notes by statute.[25] The frontier practices of bills payable in goods reflected the scarcity of coin. This lack of specie was true in Mexican California as well, and bills of exchange were commonly payable, in whole or in part, in merchandise or in hides.[26]

The feature that gave special utility to these letter-orders from one merchant to another was the concept of negotiability. The idea of negotiability in turn depended on two legal notions, both of which had been fully developed only in the first quarter of the nineteenth century.

The first important legal development was the principle that affected a "taker" of negotiable paper, that is, a new holder to whom the document is endorsed by the original payee. If the bill of exchange or note is in proper form and on its face free from suspicion, and if the new taker is in good faith and pays value for the instrument, he then takes it free of prior claims or equities of the original parties. Phrased another way, the holder in "due course," paying value and taking in good faith, cuts off prior claims and defenses. Suppose a draft were given in consumption of a commercial sale of goods that turned out to be defective. The buyer might be able to make a successful claim against the seller. But if the buyer had issued a bill of exchange and that order had

[24] L. FRIEDMAN, HISTORY OF AMERICAN LAW 69 (1973).

[25] For a discussion of American chattel bills in the nineteenth century, see Culp, *Negotiability of Promissory Notes Payable in Specifics,* 9 MISS. L.J. 277 (1937).

[26] For example, Letter, José Abrego to Fitch, June 20, 1840, in Fitch *Documentos, supra* note 19, Document 128 (place 854 pesos in silver and 1,021 pesos in goods at disposal of José Rafael González); Letter, Fitch to Miguel de Pedrorena, Dec. 22, 1838, *id.,* Document 47 (deliver 530 hides to José Antonio Aguirre).

passed into the hands of a subsequent taker, or new holder, in due course who had paid value for the instrument, the liability became absolute. The buyer (drawer) would still have to pay his note, and the drawee would still have to honor the bill (assuming there was a credit balance) regardless of the buyer's (drawer's) claims. Thus strangers to a transaction who acquired the paper arising out of it would always be protected.

The second important legal development was the evolution of a doctrine of merger. The underlying debt arising out of a commercial transaction and for which a bill of exchange, or note, was issued was not merely represented by the negotiable instrument. The bill or note became the debt itself and therefore would ordinarily be required for physical presentation upon payment. If taking free from prior defenses to a transaction benefited subsequent takers of the note or bill, as explained above, merger protected the original drawer and drawee by making it impossible to become liable to multiple claimants arising out of fraudulent and duplicate assignments by the payee. The drawee can protect all concerned by paying whoever physically presents the note or bill because that is in itself the obligation.

The effect of these two rules, and they are more complicated than suggested here, made bills and promissory notes negotiable, as the term is understood today. In turn, this meant that bills and notes became a kind of currency in trading regions, such as California, with a scarcity of hard money and an absence of banks. Bills drawn by a reputable merchant upon an equally reputable merchant as drawee, or bills drawn by a responsible party upon an eastern bank, or bills drawn by a foreign naval captain officially visiting California upon a fiscally responsible government would all be received as the equivalent of money in the settlement of accounts. Indeed, they had advantages over gold or hides in that a safe bill of exchange was more secure against robbery. It would do a thief no good until endorsed (assuming a restrictive endorsement), and it was more compact than gold or hides and therefore easier to transport and deliver.

The California expatriate merchants used negotiable paper frequently and creatively. They endorsed each others' notes and drafts and used them as currency to pay debts and settle accounts. As an alternative to physical endorsement, and probably because of the vast physical distances, they also sometimes wrote letters directing the delivery of goods or money to another party. For example, if Merchant *A* draws on Merchant *B* for the payment of money to Merchant *C*, the signature of *C* is required in legal theory to endorse the document in order for Merchant *B* to be liable to pay a fourth party, Merchant *D*. California practice permitted Merchant *C* simply to write Merchant *B* and direct him by letter to pay *D*.[27]

The foreigners also frequently swapped debts, represented by bills and notes, of third parties, and bought and sold these credit instruments. Larkin, particularly, was as much financier as merchant. He expressed interest in buying drafts drawn on eastern firms,[28] and he purchased drafts on the British government issued by the officers of English warships,[29] Larkin's purchases being at a discount from the face value of the bill.

Larkin was even more deeply involved as a financier than merely as a purchaser of bills and notes. He often loaned money to the California departmental government, both by permitting the government to draw upon himself,[30] and by an actual delivery of money in exchange for orders from the governor against the Custom House for sums payable when the next ship to arrive paid its duties.[31]

Larkin acted as a collection agent for many merchants, collecting from local debtors on behalf of more remotely located creditors. He charged a collection fee and made the net balance collected available to be drawn upon by the referring merchant.[32]

---

[27] For example, Letter, Alpheus B. Thompson to Pio Pico, Nov. 2, 1844, requesting him to give Henry D. Fitch 145 pesos, with note from Fitch to pay the money to the order of John Temple, and note written for John Temple by F.P. Temple acknowledging receipt of the money, in Pio Pico, *Documentos para la historia de California*, Calendar Item 7. The Pico *Documentos* are on deposit with the Bancroft Library, University of California, Berkeley, California.

[28] An example is Letter, Larkin to Thomas W. Waldron (American naval officer), Sept. 1, 1841, 1 LARKIN PAPERS, *supra* note 6, at 116 ("I want to purchase bills on home. Please inform me if you will have to sell Bills and at what discount.").

[29] Letter, Larkin to Uhde and Pini, Dec. 10, 1844, 2 LARKIN PAPERS, *supra* note 6, at 316 (trading English drafts he had acquired).

[30] *See* Letter, Larkin to Manuel Micheltorena (governor of California), Apr. 20, 1843, *id.* at 12; Letter, Micheltorena to Larkin, May 25, 1844, *id.* at 129.

[31] Letter, Larkin to Talbot H. Green, May 25, 1843, *id.* at 16 (authorizing negotiations with the governor toward this end). Larkin subsequently became heavily involved with the financing of Micheltorena's government.

[32] For example, Letter, John Temple to Larkin, Aug. 23, 1839, 1 LARKIN PAPERS,

Sometimes even when there was no collection problem, a merchant might deliver a bill or note to Larkin and ask that he hold the sums received from the instruments subject to a later draw.[33] In this case Larkin acted as a bank.

It is relatively simple to describe this system of credit formation, but for the merchants to implement it was considerably more complicated. The accounting practices of the day were imprecise, and personal accounts and firm or partnership accounts were frequently commingled. In addition, poor communications made obtaining accurate information a slow process. The mercantile correspondence illustrates a great stumbling with these accounts and the painful process of resolving the amount of the credit accounts on which they could draw.[34]

Intramerchant credit was formed through their own notes and bills of exchange, but the problem of credit collection still remained. Debtors did not escape liability for the purchase of goods or the repayment of a loan by the mere issuance of a bill of exchange in payment. If the draft were dishonored and not paid by the drawee, the issuing drawer was still responsible for the debt instrument in the same manner that the drawer of a returned bank check is liable.

Debt collection was the focus of two efforts. First, the expatriate community employed techniques of credit control in an effort to avoid the creation of doubtful accounts. Second were the actual collection efforts for debts that had become delinquent. The methods used to avoid delinquent accounts included both the exchange of current credit information about fellow foreigners and also the active monitoring of executory contracts, those not yet performed, to prevent potential breaches.

The expatriate merchants had a steady correspondence with

---

supra note 6, at 26 ("I enclose you a note on Jose Z. Fernández for $15.4 rs. which I wish you to collect & hold it subject to my order.")

[33] Letter, John Paty to Larkin, Aug. 14, 1845, 3 LARKIN PAPERS, *supra* note 6, at 311 ("I have inclosed a draft on Mr Parrott for $1719.43 and have endorsed it in your favor. I wish you to recieve the Same and hold it Subject to my order. . . . I do not expect that you will charge me any commissions on this transaction, as I shall always be ready to do you the same favor.") The expectation of no commission probably indicates that no collection problem, and no need for active dunning, was anticipated. Larkin's role was then to be solely a holder of funds subject to order; in other words, he was to perform a banking function.

[34] Some examples are Letter, Nathan Spear to Larkin, Aug. 15, 1840, in 1

each other on such topics as market information, supply and demand, current prices at various ports, and political news. They also constantly exchanged credit information. Employees, such as Josiah Belden who managed Larkin's Santa Cruz branch store, quite naturally sent credit reports on his customers to his boss. "Peter Collins wishes me to write to you," Belden mentioned in a July 1842 letter, "and I think you can trust him to a small amount with safety. What I have trusted him with here he has always paid verry well. . . . He is owing me now about 25 dollars."[35] Business associates likewise exchanged such news. "Do not trust the Missions any more," Henry Fitch wrote partner James McKinley in June 1842, "but get what you can from them as I expect there will be a change when the new Govr. arrives."[36]

Of course, merchants requesting collection help from another merchant would pass along pertinent credit information.[37] The most serious appraisals of a debtor's prospects were usually made in conjunction with collection efforts. Larkin undertook some collections for Mott Talbot & Company, a Mazatlán trading company. In July 1845 he replied to a credit inquiry concerning Alpheus B. Thompson, sending the referring firm a detailed account of who Thompson owed, the extent of the obligations, what debts were owing Thompson, and an analysis of Thompson's past conduct and future prospects.[38] Larkin received equally detailed advice from his collectors. At the end of 1845, William Faxon wrote him from Santa Barbara:

Doct Den has a prospect of paying next year better than he has had heretofore, as in march next he has to receive 800 head of cattle

LARKIN PAPERS, *supra* note 6, at 49; Letter, Larkin to Henry A. Peirce, Mar. 12, 1842, *id.* at 174.

[35] Letter, Josiah Belden to Larkin, July 31, 1842, *id.* at 255; Letter, Belden to Larkin, July 29, 1842, *id.* at 253 ("Mr. Wilson wishes . . . you to send him out a pit saw. . . . He generally attends to his work and seems willing to do the best he can. He has the most of his debt paid off to me and I think will soon pay it all.").

[36] Letter, Henry D. Fitch to James McKinley, June 9, 1842, *id.* at 238.

[37] For example, Letter, John Parrott to Larkin, May 2, 1845, in 3 LARKIN PAPERS, *supra* note 6, at 165 ("in regard to Mr. Thompson allow me to repeat to you . . . the request you will not loose sight of the affair or suffer yourself to be decieved by him as I understand that it is a custom with him to pay nobody if he can avoid it.")

[38] Letter, Larkin to Mott Talbot & Co., July 8, 1845, *id.* at 262–63 ("I can not say that the situation of Mr. A.B. Thompson's business in California is so critical as to cause you any fear of losing the debt.")

which are the proceeds of some which he placed out for the increase and they become due at that time. Consequently he can pay then if has the disposition.[39]

These are all examples of credit exchanges among expatriates who had some special relationship with each other, as employees, partners, or collection agents. Additionally, however, American and British merchants in Mazatlán, Oahu, and California would pass along information on a network basis and without any immediate need or economic relationship between those exchanging the information. It was shop gossip, but of a very vital kind, since the entire structure of trade depended on credit and the creditworthiness of the privately created notes and bills of exchange used for currency.

Some of the correspondence merely requested information. "Capt. Hinkly's prospects are tho't to have met a reverse. What is your opinion?" asked Stephen Reynolds of Larkin in June 1840 from Oahu. "Will Capt. Hinkly recover, or will he get deeper into the Ditch?"[40] Some of the gossip was comprised merely of growling complaints, as when William Leidesdorff wrote Talbot Green in early 1846 that he had "not received that small ballance of Ridleys, nor do I ever exspect to, for he never intends paying his debts."[41] And, of course, much of the credit watch consisted of straightforward warnings as in "keep a good look out for Old Smith & do not let him get too deep in your books,"[42] and "have nothing more to do with the dfts [drafts] of the Governor of this Custom House, as none of them will henceforward be paid."[43]

In addition to the exchange of financial information, the expatriates closely watched open contracts that had not been fully performed in an effort to prevent breach and avoid the resulting bad debts. In the summer of 1842, Scotsman John Gilroy and Englishman Jack Matthews owed Larkin considerable sums of money which they had promised to liquidate shortly through the deliv-

---

[39] Letter, William T. Faxon to Larkin, Dec. 9, 1845, 4 LARKIN PAPERS, *supra* note 6, at 117.

[40] Letter, Stephen Reynolds to Larkin, June 6, 1840, 1 LARKIN PAPERS, *supra* note 6, at 41.

[41] William A. Leidesdorff to Talbot H. Green, Jan. 6, 1846, 4 LARKIN PAPERS, *supra* note 6, at 159.

[42] Letter, Samuel J. Hastings to Larkin, Nov. 9, 1845, *id.* at 93.

[43] Letter, John Parrott to Larkin, June 29, 1844, in 2 LARKIN PAPERS, *supra* note 6, at 155.

ery of soap they were making. The manufacturing was taking place in the Santa Clara valley, not too far distant from Monterey, and Larkin monitored the situation both by personal visits and through reports from his agent, Talbot H. Green.

In August things appeared to be going well with Gilroy and at least not too badly with Matthews. Green reported that: "Mr Gilroy is getting on very well at present with his soap. . . . My opinion is he will pay from 1300$ to 1800$ of his accont. . . . Jack Mathews is not a going to make any great exertions to pay you. . . . about ⅓ of the soap he had on hand when you was here is gone."[44]

By September 10 an unsettling development had occurred. A shortage of soap in San Francisco had led to a rise in price and greater competition for Gilroy's and Matthews' output.

They are out of soap at St Francisco and have been writing down & sending for soap but if the people here pay there debts they will have none to sell. I dont no what to think of Jack Mathews. . . . I overherd him say to mr Ridley mr Spears clerk [a San Francisco merchant] when he was here a few days ago to let him know if mr Spear would trade aguadent [liquor] for soap. If so he would trade with him.[45]

The morning after writing this letter Green added an ominous postscript:

Mr Gilroy told me this mornig that Jack Mathews told him that he was a going to take his soap up to St Francisco & trade for rum. Gilroy asked him if he did not owe you the soap. He said yes but that was nothing. Gilroy dont want his name mentioned that he said any thing about it.[46]

Gilroy apparently remained steadfast in his willingness to honor his contract even in the face of a rising market. Even so, Green advised Larkin that he had "best urge him hard about the other soap. I know it is his intention to pay & his wish but he wants urgeing."[47]

The available evidence is that both the credit network and contract performance monitoring had positive effects. The credit talk certainly stung many debtors. Alpheus B. Thompson was a man

---

[44]Letter, Talbot H. Green to Larkin, Aug. 26, 1842, 1 LARKIN PAPERS, *supra* note 6, at 278–79.

[45]Letter, Green to Larkin, Sept. 10, 1842, *id.* at 286.

[46]*Id.* at 286–87.

[47]Letter, Green to Larkin, Sept. 27, 1842, *id.* at 293.

of whom many credit queries and aspersions were made. Larkin once said, amidst the general laxity of California ways, that Thompson was "not noted for punctuaty even in C."[48] The gossip affected even such a man as Thompson, who complained once of a supercargo that he had been "determined to injure . . . as far as talk goes."[49] The network of credit reporting undoubtedly spurred some otherwise bad accounts into payment and prevented still other accounts from becoming delinquent. This is somewhat ironic. The Anglo-Americans were here relying on group pressures to enforce the payment of debts in much the same manner the Californios relied on group pressures from the community to enforce the alcaldes' judgments. The major difference is that these are two different kinds of communities. The expatriate community was one of interest, specifically mutual mercantile concerns. The Californio concept of community was geographic, although the homogeneity of population meant a large base of common concerns as well.

The contract compliance monitoring had the same effect. There was an interesting conclusion to Matthews's attempt to evade his promise to pay Larkin with soap by selling or trading it in San Francisco. Larkin shrewdly told others, whom he knew would be in contact with his debtor, that Matthews *had already* broken his word and by so doing he apparently shamed or embarrassed Matthews into *keeping* it. The threat to breach the contract was reported to Larkin on September 10, 1845. By the end of the same month Green was able to advise Larkin more happily:

> M M Castro was here last night & told Jack Mathewes that you told him how he had taken a load of soap to St Francisco & was not going to pay you a real. He told me this morning that by the middel of october he will deliver you your soap. I now think he will send you some. Howeve I shall watch him close & see that he dose not take it any place else.[50]

Assume that a merchant had made reasonable efforts to ascertain an expatriate customer's creditworthiness and had done

---

[48] Letter, Larkin to Mott Talbot & Co., July 8, 1845, 3 LARKIN PAPERS, *supra* note 6, at 263.

[49] Letter, Alpheus B. Thompson to Larkin, Feb. 16, 1846, 4 LARKIN PAPERS, *supra* note 6, at 203.

[50] Letter, Green to Larkin, Sept. 28, 1842, 1 LARKIN PAPERS, *supra* note 6, at 293.

whatever was reasonable to monitor his outstanding accounts and contracts. Nonetheless, a badly delinquent debt has arisen. How could the merchant collect it while operating in California, in whose courts he had very little confidence?

It is but another testament to the Anglo-Americans' internalization of legal understandings and sense of legal obligation that the problem was not far worse. Rights derived from the various credit instruments and their usages were recognized. The majority of Anglo-American debts were paid, albeit sometimes slowly. Still, there is no question that debt repudiation and collection problems were major difficulties facing the expatriate merchants.[51] The traders frequently complained of their collection problems.[52]

The first step in any collection effort was to make demands, and the mercantile correspondence is replete with requests and demands, in various shadings, for payment. "I know . . . *you can* pay the debt if you choose," Larkin emphasized to one expatriate debtor in October 1845; "with pain I say it but . . . I can not believe all you have seen fit to write to me respectig my demands. . . . Your excuses have not only been too numerous, but so badly made out in one following the other."[53]

The expatriate traders in California, and in Oahu and Mazatlán respecting California accounts, frequently assigned delinquent accounts back and forth. If a merchant in San Jose had a debtor in Los Angeles who would not pay, it made sense to refer it to a Los Angeles trader who could more easily and frequently remind the offending debtor. Larkin played a large role in assignments for collection. Many merchants in Oahu and Mazatlán, some of whom have been mentioned already, sent doubtful accounts of delinquent California-based expatriates to Larkin.[54]

[51] Dallas, *supra* note 2, at 187, 256, 290.

[52] For example, Letter, Rufus Titcomb to Larkin, July 20, 1842, 1 LARKIN PAPERS, *supra* note 6, at 252 ("Mr Teal is . . . colecting or trying to colect; he appears to be immensely disgusted with the business of the country, & the vast toil & trabajo [work] attending it risque & bad debts &c."); Letter, Larkin to Joseph O. Carter, Nov. 18, 1842, *id.* at 323 ("the payments of debts are horrible. It appears if every one had come to a conclusion that it was not necessary to pay old debts.").

[53] Letter, Larkin to William S. Hinckley, Oct. 1845 (no date specified), 4 LARKIN PAPERS, *supra* note 6, at 15.

[54] In May 1845, Larkin was attempting to collect $2,284.14 (or about $25,000

Within California, Larkin also received mercantile collection requests, such as Nathan Spears's referral of George Allen's debt,[55] and John Everett's assignment of Job Dye's obligation.[56] In turn, other merchants collected Larkin's expatriate debts outside Monterey. For example, James Weekes attempted to collect Isaac Graham's debt, and the accounts of several other foreigners, in Santa Cruz,[57] and William Leidesdorff received $86 on Larkin's behalf in San Francisco from a Captain Barnums.[58]

Although a chief participant, Larkin was hardly the hub of all California intra-expatriate collections. For example, Henry Fitch made collections in San Diego for Los Angeles merchant Abel Stearns,[59] and William Leidesdorff was appointed an agent of the Russian-American Company to attempt collection of its huge debt owing from Sutter.[60] Some of these intramerchant assignments were actual sales of accounts at discounts, but most—in the case of Larkin, definitely the most—were not sales but simply arrangements for collection as agent and for a commission.[61]

---

in 1987 dollars) from Alpheus B. Thompson on behalf of Mott Talbot & Co. of Mazatlán; Letter, Mott Talbot & Co. to Larkin, May 2, 1845, 3 LARKIN PAPERS, *supra* note 6, at 167. At the same time Larkin was also trying to recover $5,371.59 from the same Thompson on the account of Parrott & Co. of Oahu. Letter, Parrott & Co. to Larkin, Feb. 13, 1845, *id.* at 43, and Letter, John Parrott to Larkin, May 2, 1845, *id.* at 165. These constitute an example of only one large debtor, and Larkin held commissions to collect from many more of lesser scale.

[55] Letter, Nathan Spear to Larkin, June 1, 1844, 2 LARKIN PAPERS, *supra* note 6, at 135 ($25).

[56] Letter, John H. Everett to Larkin, July 13, 1844, *id.* at 166–67 ($531.25).

[57] Letter, James W. Weekes to Larkin, May 1844 (no date specified), *id.* at 133–34.

[58] Letter, William A. Leidesdorff to Larkin, Jan. 3, 1845 (1846), 4 LARKIN PAPERS, *supra* note 6, at 150.

[59] Miller, "Henry Delano Fitch: A Yankee Trader in California: 1826–1849," at 83–84 (Ph.D. diss., University of Southern California, 1972).

[60] Manning, "William A. Leidesdorff's Career in California," at 31 (master's thesis, University of California, 1942).

[61] Dallas, *supra* note 2, at 195–97, discusses the two methods of assignment and makes the interesting point that most of the mercantile correspondence regarding assignments, and it was substantial, did not specify a collection commission. Perhaps a specific percentage was a general trade practice, so well known that it need not have been expressed. Perhaps fees were largely discretionary and based on efforts expended and not a percentage. If this had been the case, however, we would expect arguments about the charges, and there were none. It is certain that the merchants did not undertake collections as a mere accommodation. Two of the few specific pieces of information on this point are helpful. One is Larkin's 1845 offer to collect debts owed by the departmental government in Mon-

This widespread system of collection assignments is related to the credit network discussed earlier. A man's debts would not remain hidden, although geographically remote in origin, when they were assigned to a merchant in the very community in which he was doing business. If a trader in San Diego left a debt due in Monterey, it would be an embarrassment to his business to be dunned by a fellow San Diego expatriate merchant. The potential effectiveness of a referral to another merchant can be seen in a debtor's complaint respecting one of Larkin's assignments, a debt owed by American merchant William Hinckley, which was referred to Scotsman William Rae, the manager of the Hudson's Bay Company store in San Francisco:

Your letter to Mr Rae was shown me by the kindness of that gentleman. . . . I did not imagine that you would think it necessary to write so dunning, and through another person, and I am inclined to think that it is not absolutely necessary to have a person on the spot as you express.[62]

One recourse for a creditor merchant at his wit's end in exasperation with a troublesome account was to shun the debtor and have no further commercial intercourse with him. "In conclusion," William G. Rae, the Hudson's Bay Company representative, summed up a diatribe directed at Larkin, "I shall not in future wish the favor of any more mercantile transactions with you or desire the honor of further correspondence."[63] Business being business, these were inevitably idle threats. It was far more likely that an offender would merely be shut off from further credit, as when in the spring of 1846 hunters working for Alpheus B. Thompson discovered they could not obtain supplies in Monterey on Thompson's credit,[64] or when Faxon Dean Atherton

terey at a 5 percent commission, Letter, Larkin to Abel Stearns and John Temple, July 20, 1845, in T. LARKIN, FIRST AND LAST CONSUL: THOMAS OLIVER LARKIN AND THE AMERICANIZATION OF CALIFORNIA 30 (Hawgood ed.) (2d ed. 1970). The other is John Paty's letter of August 14, 1845 in which he asks Larkin to receive funds from a third party without commission, implying that Larkin usually charged a collection fee. See note 33, *supra*.

[62] Letter, William S. Hinckley to Larkin, Aug. 6, 1842, 1 LARKIN PAPERS, *supra* note 6, at 261.

[63] Letter, William G. Rae to Larkin, Sept. 2, 1844, 2 LARKIN PAPERS, *supra* note 6, at 214.

[64] G. NIDEVER, THE LIFE AND ADVENTURES OF GEORGE NIDEVER 61 (Ellison ed. 1937).

tersely noted in his diary for February 24, 1838, in regard to a Californio, "'old Sanchez' came to purchase but told him 'cash or no trade'."[65]

One of the most ingenious tools the expatriate merchants employed to collect debts was through the maneuvering of accounts so as to create setoffs. A setoff is created when two people each owe the other money. Either party may regard their debts as paid, that is, set off against each other, to the extent of the lesser obligation.

Suppose Merchant *A* was owed money by Merchant *B*, who would not pay. Merchant *A* could contact another merchant, most probably Larkin, to see if Larkin owed *B* money. If Larkin were indebted to Merchant *B*, then *A* could trade his note, account, or draft from *B* to Larkin in exchange for goods. Now Merchant *A* had goods that he could sell, instead of an uncollectable account, note, or bill of exchange from *B*. Larkin has sold goods at a favorable rate; he is content. Larkin also has *B*'s note or order, which he can then set off against his own obligation to *B* and cancel both to the extent of the lesser amount. The transaction between *A* and Larkin thereby had the effect of collecting the debt owed by Merchant *B* to Merchant *A*.

"I wish to ask you whether you have business with Capt. Hinkly, so that you could off sett in any way—to amount of two thousand dollars—or any part thereof?"[66] Stephen Reynolds asked Larkin in June 1840. Since Reynolds was in Oahu, and it might not be readily convenient or efficient in cost for Larkin to actually ship goods to Oahu, as opposed to the illustration between merchants *A* and *B*, Reynolds had a different variant of the setoff in mind. He had written earlier that "if you have dealings with him [Hinckley], I should like you to give an order, to him, (not him an order) on me—but let this be between you & me."[67]

In effect Reynolds was offering to become a creditor of Larkin, under the assumption that would be surer debt than Hinckley's. He was asking Larkin that if he had dealings with Hinckley so that he owed Hinckley money, to pay off his debt with a bill of ex-

---

[65] F. ATHERTON, THE CALIFORNIA DIARY OF FAXON DEAN ATHERTON, 1836–1839, at 88 (Nunis ed. 1964).

[66] Letter, Stephen Reynolds to Larkin, June 6, 1840, 1 LARKIN PAPERS, *supra* note 6, at 41.

[67] Letter, Stephen Reynolds to Larkin, Jan. 21, 1840, *id.* at 33.

change "to him" but drawn "on me," that is, with Reynolds as drawee. It would be as though, when Hinckley came to collect from Reynolds on Larkin's bill of exchange, Reynolds could say: "here is your money, but I'm taking it back and setting it off against what you already owe me, so I will pay you by cancelling your debt to me." Of course, they did not have to go through this ceremony, and Reynolds could accomplish the purpose of the set-off by simple notification to Hinckley. If Reynolds had already owed Larkin money—assume the same amount for simplicity—then everyone would be even. If Reynolds and Larkin had already been even, then Reynolds's honoring of Larkin's order would be an extension of credit to Larkin. From Reynolds's viewpoint, Larkin would now be his debtor and not the problematic Hinckley. From Larkin's vantage, he would owe Reynolds money and no longer owe Hinckley.

Setoffs were a handy way of collecting debts in other circumstances as well. If a shipping firm was owed money by a shipper, it might simply seize further shipments in partial payment.[68] Analogously, if hides were put into a second party's hands for delivery to a third person, the second party could simply refuse to deliver them if owed money by the first party.[69] Josiah Belden, as manager of Larkin's branch store in Santa Cruz, had charge of letting contracts for the hauling of lumber to the beach to be made ready for shipment by boat. He gave preference in these contracts to those already indebted to the store.[70] If Larkin had to incur an obligation to have his lumber hauled, what better person to owe than someone who already owed him. No cash outlay would be required, and the resulting setoff would collect by cancellation what might have been a doubtful account.

It should also be observed that the creation of setoffs was not merely of benefit to creditors. From a debtor's position, it might be a convenient method of paying a bill. In January of 1846, Abel

[68] Letter, Nicholas A. Den to Larkin, Feb. 10, 1846, 4 LARKIN PAPERS, *supra* note 6, at 192 ("I even once send you five Barrils of aguardiente in part payment, but found to my great surprise that the Ship who took it gave me credit for it in my act with them, as I was also owning the concern").

[69] Letter, John Temple to Larkin, Oct. 9, 1839, 1 LARKIN PAPERS, *supra* note 6, at 29 ("Wm. Warren's account is correct as I gave it to you. I never rec'd any hides from him, as Dn. Luis would not deliver them as he said that he owed him").

[70] Letter, Josiah Belden to Larkin, July 31, 1842, *id.* at 255.

Stearns referred from Los Angeles a note drawn on the departmental government to Larkin for collection. He endorsed it in Larkin's favor and asked that after collection Larkin remit the proceeds by a bill of exchange drawn on the ship *Moscow*. Why?

As the Moscow belongs to the same owners as the ship Sterling & as we have accounts with Mr. Park I wish an order on the Moscow for the amount, and you will leave it to me to settle with the Supercargo by my reciving the amt. of him or pasing it in acct. with the Sterling.[71]

Mr. Park was the supercargo of the *Sterling* and Stearns owed that ship money. Since the *Moscow* and the *Sterling* had the same owners, Stearns reasoned he could conveniently pay his account by the presentation of the bill drawn on the *Moscow*. A setoff could be created if Stearns wished to treat the cross-obligations in this manner. If he used the setoff by "pasing it in acct. with the Sterling," it would be a convenient way for him to pay his bill, far easier, given the difficulties of transportation, than a physical delivery of hides or tallow.

If no setoffs could be obtained and dunning, directly or through an assignee, failed to produce a collection, the expatriate creditor could sue the foreign debtor. In a very few circumstances debts arising in California were litigated in American courts in the East. Larkin assigned the debts of an absconding American carpenter, Humphrey Hathaway, for collection in the United States.[72] A lawsuit was actually brought in the Massachusetts courts to collect a claim of Larkin and his half brother, John B. R. Cooper, both in California, in respect to the sale in California of the cargo of the ship *Rover*. It was ultimately settled for the substantial sum of $2,000.[73]

Yet it would be a very unusual circumstance in which California debts could be collected by litigation in the United States. The only usual recourse in the face of an obdurate debtor was to file suit in the local California courts. The expatriates occasion-

[71] Letter, Abel Stearns to Larkin, Jan. 22, 1846, 4 LARKIN PAPERS, *supra* note 6, at 175–76.

[72] Letter, Larkin to Thomas A. Norton, Aug. 10, 1844, 2 LARKIN PAPERS, *supra* note 6, at 190–91.

[73] Letter, William M. Rogers to John B.R. Cooper, July 9, 1841, 1 LARKIN PAPERS, *supra* note 6, at 92–93; Letter, William M. Rogers to John B.R. Cooper, Feb. 14, 1842, *id.* at 166–67; Letter, James Hunnewell to John B.R. Cooper, Nov. 4, 1843, 2 LARKIN PAPERS, *supra* at 54.

ally threatened to do just that in their efforts to collect debts from fellow foreigners,[74] and in fact did file suit against one another.[75]

A California lawsuit was not a popular remedy, however, probably because of the poor regard in which the alcalde courts were held by the expatriates. The local courts were seldom used by the Anglo-American expatriates for collecting debts from fellow expatriates. The most striking evidence of this is that from 1831 through June 1846, Larkin, the chief merchant of Monterey and the largest creditor in California, filed only two lawsuits against Anglo-Americans in the Monterey courts.[76]

[74] For example, Letter, William T. Faxon to Nicholas Den, Sept. 10, 1845, 3 LARKIN PAPERS, *supra* note 6, at 345 ("as your act. with Mr Larkin has been a long time standing, and . . . as you have not condescended even to answer his letters to you on the subject, I have sent an abstract of your act. to Capt Robbins with instructions for him to sue you for the amt. If you think the measure harsh you have only to blame yourself . . . and it is still in your power to avoid it by arranging with Capt Robbins").

[75] For example, Scotsman James McKinley sued Irishman James Murphy in 1840 to collect a debt of $515. 6 Monterey Archives, 339 (1840) [hereinafter cited as M.A. in style of M.A. 6:339]. These records are on deposit with the Monterey County Historical Society, Salinas, California. As another example, in 1843, Englishman James Meadows sued a fellow Englishman, William Anderson, for $148. *Id.*, 6:850 (1843).

[76] These were not for significant sums, being brought against Englishman James Stokes for 21 hides, or $42, *id.*, 6:497 (1842), and against A.D. Forbes (undetermined nationality) for $37, *id.*, 6:801 (1843). Larkin gave William Faxon power of attorney to sue for debts in September 1845, *id.*, 15:683 (1845), but there is no record of Faxon's use of that power in any Monterey litigation. Talbot H. Green filed only one lawsuit in Monterey, *id.*, 6:753 (1842), and this was before he became manager of Larkin's store. Thus the two lawsuits filed by Larkin probably represent the total of his efforts to judicially collect debts from fellow expatriates in the Monterey courts.

8

Dispute Resolution

This chapter will discuss the process by which the Anglo-Americans in Mexican California resolved their commercial disputes. The term "commercial disputes" as used here embraces arguments about the quality of goods, shortages in delivery, the propriety of expenses charged by one partner to a partnership—in short, all of the conflicting positions taken on business questions with the exception of the collection of liquidated, amount-certain debts, discussed in chapter 7.

The level of bickering and invective in the California commercial correspondence was high.[1] An example from the letters of Henry D. Fitch will illustrate. In 1844 he was embroiled in a squabble, the details of which are unimportant, with Henry Peirce, who for years had been with the Hawaii firm of Peirce and Brewer in Oahu. Peirce had apparently complained that "there seems to be a great want of moral principle" among the expatriate traders in California, thereby specifically including Fitch. A lack of ethics was a charge often made in respect to the foreign businessmen in California.[2]

---

[1] Dallas, "The Hide and Tallow Trade in Alta California, 1822–1846," at 195 (Ph.D. diss., Indiana University, 1955).

[2] Letter, Fitch to Henry Peirce, June 30, 1844 (quoting Peirce), in Henry D. Fitch, *Documentos para la historia de California* Document 304 [hereinafter cited as Fitch *Documentos*]. The Fitch *Documentos* are on deposit with the Bancroft Library, University of California, Berkeley, California. Letter, John C. Jones to Larkin, Sept. 4, 1844, 2 THE LARKIN PAPERS: PERSONAL, BUSINESS, AND OFFICIAL CORRESPONDENCE OF THOMAS OLIVER LARKIN, MERCHANT AND UNITED STATES CONSUL IN CALIFORNIA 216 (Hammond ed. 1951–1968) (10 vols. & index) [hereinafter cited as LARKIN PAPERS] ("Nature appears to be changing here altogether. What may we expect next, possibly that some of the Californians [referring to expatriate traders] will turn honest men. That indeed would be a miricle."); Letter, Hawaiian merchant Stephen Reynolds to Larkin, June 6, 1840,

Fitch hotly replied that "when Californians . . . can cope with Sandwich Island [Hawaiian] merchants in down right roguery and piracy then the great work will have been accomplished—all men will be equal to see each other face to face."[3] He suggested that perhaps Peirce was ashamed of having lived among men of such few moral principles. Peirce was then home in Massachusetts, and Fitch charged that now, "after getting back to where honest men live," Peirce was ashamed of his former life and acting like "a common street walker who on marrying becomes the heroine of all that's virtuous & lashes her former associates to pieces."[4]

These insults and harpings were largely mere posturing. Yet they were common, as also shown in the number of complaints about insulting remarks in the commercial correspondence.[5] Whether posturing or not, the frequency of snide bickering, coupled with the reluctance of the expatriates to use the local courts, would not seem to bode well for the settlement of business disputes of any complexity.

Some commercial disputes were not resolved except through the power of economic pressure or geographic position. An example is a wholesale transfer of twenty-seven barrels of liquor in

1 LARKIN PAPERS, *supra* at 41 ("Thompson had no right [alleging a commercial wrongdoing] . . . and if we were in old Massachusetts, he should soon be taught it. You Californians are strange *critturs!*).

[3] Letter, Fitch to Henry Peirce, June 30, 1844, in Fitch *Documentos, supra* note 2, Document 304.

[4] *Id.*

[5] Letter, James A. Forbes to Larkin, Apr. 1, 1845, 3 LARKIN PAPERS, *supra* note 2, at 113 ("you heap upon me a torrent of invectives as if you had received an injury from me, entering into a long argument upon topics that have been most grossly misrepresented to you."); Letter, Alfred Robinson to Larkin, Jan. 16, 1846, 4 LARKIN PAPERS, *supra* at 165–66:

"I . . . am even charged with cheating you in the purchases for your consular outfit. I can only reply to this *gross* and *ungrateful* imputation, by assuring you on the word of an honest heart, which has *never* as yet been false to *any one* in any *negotiation,* that *all* and *everything* was obtained at the lowest *cash* prices. . . . if you ever belive me incapable of conducting as you have published to the world, why you must promulgate that opinion ere I can *again* have any more to do with a *slanderer.*"

Letter, Fitch to Henry Peirce, June 30, 1844, in Fitch *Documentos, supra* note 2, Document 304 ("use less abrasive expressions, *others* can feel as well as *you* can . . . thief, blackguard swindler &c. are dealt out in double allowances without necessity").

1839 by John Temple of Los Angeles to Thomas Larkin in Monterey. Temple shipped the liquor to Larkin, indicating a price of $60 per barrel, payable in hides, which Larkin had previously indicated he would pay on any of the liquor he would take on his own account.[6] One problem was that Larkin shipped flour in payment, which Temple claimed he could not sell at the price at which Larkin asked to be credited because the current market for flour in Los Angeles was poor.[7] Other problems surfaced when Larkin claimed that only twenty-five barrels, not twenty-seven, had been received and insisted that he would only pay $50 per barrel, contending that was the current market price, but a rate far below that agreed upon originally.[8] Temple protested, suggesting that Larkin inquire of the supercargo of the ship that had transported the liquor as to the shortage and where it might have gone. Temple also pointed out he had a letter with Larkin's signature as to the price.[9]

Larkin's response to the protest demonstrates the maximum use of geographic and economic leverage. Recall that Larkin was already the largest merchant in California, with much more trade than Temple. As for an inquiry of the shipping firm, Larkin cavalierly wrote that "*I* shall not put myself to that trouble; if *you* wish for prove, I will enquire for you." Concerning the lower price for the liquor and the payment by flour, "you need not *repeat,* that you have my signature for payment of 60$ Etc. I also know you have. I thought you would be willing to take good flour at a fair price, in order to continue trade between us. . . . It seams not!"[10]

In the event, this dispute was settled almost entirely by economic and geographic pressures. Larkin's flour was in a third party's warehouse in San Pedro near Los Angeles, hundreds of miles from his immediate control, and accumulating storage charges. He sold it to another person in Los Angeles.[11] Temple's

[6] Letter, Temple to Larkin, May 5, 1839, 1 LARKIN PAPERS, *supra* note 2, at 9.

[7] Letter, Temple to Larkin, May 23, 1839, *id.* at 11.

[8] Letter, Larkin to Temple, June 4, 1839, *id.* at 12. The transaction and resulting difficulties are somewhat more complicated than indicated, but the major points are all included. Apparently the price of liquor had dropped in Monterey because of the arrival of a ship from Massachusetts, which not only brought greater supply but superior quality.

[9] Letter, Temple to Larkin, June 20, 1839, *id.* at 13–14.

[10] Letter, Larkin to Temple, July 22, 1839, *id.* at 17–18.

[11] *Id.* Larkin had offered it for sale to the third party as early as June 22. Letter,

liquor was in Monterey, in Larkin's hands, and Temple settled for the lower price, reciting economic necessity, and for the reduced amount Larkin acknowledged having received.[12]

Not all California commercial disputes were settled in this manner. True, there was considerable internecine bickering among the merchants, and they were certainly disinclined to use the local courts. Furthermore, California's vast distances and poor transportation facilities offered many opportunities to apply economic and geographic leverage to force favorable settlements. Notwithstanding these factors and temptations, many mercantile disputes in Mexican California were resolved through a more rational procedure. That alternative process of dispute resolution was, in a word, arbitration.

Arbitration is an old method of resolving disputes, with a lineage dating back to ancient Greece.[13] The period of legal incubation, where the Anglo-American expatriates formed their impressions of law, was of course the early nineteenth century. By this time the law was clear that when the parties to a controversy had voluntarily submitted their dispute to arbitrators, and a decision had been rendered, the arbitral award was final and could be judicially enforced.[14] There was, however, still considerable judicial hostility to agreements to arbitrate future disputes, and contractual provisions to arbitrate disagreements arising in the future were generally unenforceable, in the sense that either party could revoke the agreement to arbitrate and sue in a law court.[15]

Isaac Williams to Larkin, July 13, 1839, *id.* at 17. It turned out that the flour was of poor quality. Letter, Isaac Williams to Larkin, Aug. 9, 1839, *id.* at 23 ("Mr. Tempell has delevred the fower over it is in a bad State to leaf it is full of weavell.").

[12] Letter, Temple to Larkin, Aug. 23, 1839, *id.* at 26 ("the aguardiente I wish to close, as I am in want of funds . . . you may take it at your offer of June 4th that is at 50$ bbl in hides for the 25 bbls you acknowledge to have rec'd . . . and I will try to make Mr. Park [ship's supercargo] pay the other two bbls as he has charg'd me freight on 27 bbls.").

[13] Some good historical discussions of arbitration include Jones, *Three Centuries of Commercial Arbitration in New York: A Brief Survey,* 1956 WASH. U. L.Q. 193; Sayre, *Development of Commercial Arbitration Law,* 37 YALE L.J. 595 (1928); Wolaver, *The Historical Background of Commercial Arbitration,* 83 U. PA. L. REV. 132 (1934).

[14] For example, Tevis v. Tevis, 20 Ky. (4 T.B. Mon.) 46 (1826); Hodges v. Hodges, 46 Mass. (5 Met.) 205 (1842). See also historical articles in note 13, *supra.*

[15] One of the clearest expressions of judicial hostility was written by Justice

Notwithstanding the difficulty of assuring that future mercantile disputes would be arbitrated, American and British merchants regularly employed arbitration to resolve commercial questions once they had arisen. Indeed, it has been suggested that "in the nineteenth century arbitration in one form or another became the most important form of mercantile dispute settlement both in the United States and in Britain,"[16] This popularity extended to the Anglo-American merchants in Mexican California.

It is difficult to judge with precision how frequently arbitration was used in Mexican California in the period 1835 to 1846, although it is clear that it was popular. Many of the arbitrations left no trace in the judicial records, although some did. Often no records were kept after an arbitration was complete. References and what records were retained of many arbitrations exist only in scattered mercantile papers and the finding of them is largely a matter of serendipity. Nonetheless, the Larkin Papers, through spring 1846, contain references to two actual arbitrations involving Larkin[17] and two additional offers to arbitrate disputes.[18] Abel Stearns, whose mercantile standing in Los Angeles matched Larkin's in Monterey, was involved in at least two arbitrations, to neither of which was Larkin a party.[19] Isaac Graham was not a

---

Story, who stated the prevailing rule precisely, in Tobey v. County of Bristol, 23 F. Cas. 1313, 1321 (C.C.D. Mass. 1845) (No. 14,065): "It is certainly the policy of the common law, not to compel men to submit their rights and interests to arbitration, or to enforce agreements for such a purpose. . . . even if a submission has been made to arbitrators . . . with an express stipulation, that the submission shall be irrevocable, it still is revocable and countermandable, by either party, before the award is actually made, although not afterwards"). *See also, e.g.,* Frink v. Ryan, 4 Ill. (3 Scam.) 322 (1841), and the historical articles in note 13, *supra.* One of the best historical studies of the revocability of agreements to arbitrate is in Kulukundis Shipping Co. v. Amtorg Trading Corp., 126 F.2d 978, 982–85 (2d Cir. 1942) (Frank, J.).

[16] Jones, *An Inquiry into the History of the Adjudication of Mercantile Disputes in Great Britain and the United States,* 25 U. CHI. L. REV. 445, 461–62 (1958).

[17] Letter, Larkin to Charles Brewer, June 3, 1848, 7 LARKIN PAPERS, *supra* note 2, at 293 (1845 arbitration between Larkin and the partners Peirce and Brewer); Letter, Larkin to Robert Thomas Ridley, Dec. 28, 1844, 2 LARKIN PAPERS, *supra* note 2, at 339 (1844 arbitration between Larkin and William Glen Rae as manager of Hudson's Bay Company).

[18] Letter, John Paty to Larkin, Dec. 21, 1840, 1 LARKIN PAPERS, *supra* note 2, at 66; Letter, Isaac Williams to Larkin, Oct. 17, 1840, *id.* at 61–62.

[19] 1841 arbitration between Stearns, Peirce and Brewer, in Miller, "Henry Del-

merchant but an American fur trapper who established a sawmill in the Santa Cruz Mountains in 1841. In his capacity as a businessman he was involved in at least two pre-1846 arbitrations.[20]

Although they were unenforceable, the Anglo-Americans often wrote arbitration clauses into their contracts. It is another example of an expectation that agreements would be honored even in the absence of coercion. In an 1845 contract to manage a ranch, the two expatriate parties provided that "in case of any misunderstanding or disagreement, it is mutually agreed that any question which may arise shall be settled by the usual mode of arbitration without recourse to law."[21] A partnership agreement for a major commercial venture, involving the expedition of a hide ship, formed in California between three Americans and a Scotsman, likewise had an arbitration clause.[22]

If arbitration was popular among the Anglo-Americans in Mexican California, it must nevertheless be viewed in perspective. It was not simply a convenient alternative to the ill-regarded alcalde courts, although it was that as well. The expatriate practices were rooted more basically in the general popularity of commercial arbitration in the nineteenth century. The Californios themselves arbitrated some disputes. Sometimes these arbitrations involved a foreigner as one party. In 1843, for example, Mission Santa Barbara arbitrated with Irishman Nicholas Den concerning the boundary line between mission property and Den's ranch; and in 1827 the former governor, Luis Antonio Argüello, settled a dispute by arbitration with American John B. R. Cooper

ano Fitch: A Yankee Trader in California: 1826–1849," at 110 (Ph.D. diss., University of Southern California, 1972); 1845 arbitration between Stearns and Henry D. Fitch, James McKinley, and John Temple regarding the expedition of the *Nymph,* in Fitch *Documentos, supra* note 2, Documents 349–57. A systematic examination of the Abel Stearns Collection, approximately 12,500 documents, in the Huntington Library, San Marino, California, would undoubtedly reveal additional arbitrations involving Stearns.

[20] April 1846 arbitration between Graham and John Williams, 6 Monterey Archives, 1146–47 (1846) [hereinafter cited as M.A. in style of M.A. 6:1146–47]. These records are on deposit with the Monterey County Historical Society, Salinas, California. 1837 arbitration between Graham and Henry Naile against the Estate of John Price, *id.,* 7:1470–71 (1837).

[21] Manning, "William A. Leidesdorff's Career in California," at 100 (master's thesis, University of California, 1942).

[22] Agreement, May 22, 1841, between Abel Stearns, John Temple, Henry D. Fitch, and James McKinley regarding the voyage of the ship *Nymph,* in Fitch *Documentos, supra* note 2, Document 156 (paragraph 6).

relative to the sale of a ship to the California territorial government.[23] Sometimes the Californios arbitrated solely among themselves.[24] Mexican law provided for arbitration, and the 1824 constitution guaranteed a right to use the procedure.[25] This was completely apart from the conciliation process that was a standard feature of ordinary litigation. After the American invasion most of the local Californio alcaldes resigned and were replaced by Americans. Even with Americans as judges and far more efficient methods of enforcement of judicial decrees, during the military occupation in California, 1846 to 1849, foreigners in California continued to arbitrate many commercial disputes. The Monterey records reflect four arbitrations involving foreigners in 1847 alone.[26]

The available evidence of the Anglo-American arbitrations, although there are not as many records of California arbitrations as one would wish, does suggest certain procedural patterns. The arbitrators were usually two in number, one chosen by each party, with the two arbitrators empowered to select a third who would

[23] 1843 arbitration between Irishman Nicholas Den and the Mission Santa Barbara relative to boundary lines of Den's Dos Pueblos Rancho, in 4 H. BANCROFT, HISTORY OF CALIFORNIA 642 n.22 (1886) (1884–1890) (7 vols.); 1827 arbitration between American John B.R. Cooper and former Governor Luis Antonio Argüello relative to the sale of the ship *Rover* to the California territorial government, in J. WOOLFENDEN & A. ELKINTON, COOPER: JUAN BAUTISTA ROGERS COOPER, SEA CAPTAIN, ADVENTURER, RANCHERO, AND EARLY CALIFORNIA PIONEER, 1791–1872, 31 (1983); A. OGDEN, THE CALIFORNIA SEA OTTER TRADE, 1784–1848, at 207 n.19 (1941).

[24] A Prefect Records of Los Angeles, 115–17 (1840): An 1840 arbitration in an estate proceeding involving Californios, seeking appointment of an arbitrator "to mediate in any disagreements that might arise between the heirs and the administrator," no dispute apparently then existing. The Prefect Records are on deposit with Henry E. Huntington Library in San Marino, California. *See also* an 1845 arbitration between Californios, Abel Stearns as arbitrator, in Los Angeles Archives, 8 : 58–107.

[25] *See* 3 J. FEBRERO, OBRA COMPLETA DE JURISPRUDENCIA TEÓRICO-PRÁCTICA 34–39 (Mexico City 1851) (4 vols.). Article 156 of the 1824 constitution provided: "No one can be deprived of the right of terminating his differences before arbitrators chosen by each party, in every stage of the cause." 1 J. WHITE, A NEW COLLECTION OF LAWS, CHARTERS AND LOCAL ORDINANCES . . . , 408 (Philadelphia 1839) (2 vols.).

[26] The ship *Sterling* and James McKinley (Scot), M.A. 12 : 197 and 14 : 29; Alberto Tresconi (Italian) and Zephyrin Rochon (nationality unknown), M.A. 13 : 1379; Victor Prudon (French) and Jacob P. Leese (American), *id.,* 13 : 259; M. Clurg & Co. and J.D. Taber (American), *id.,* 13 : 467, 535, 539.

decide the case in the event of disagreement among the original two. There were arbitrations where three arbitrators were initially chosen, but this was not usual.[27] Normally the two-man panel would render a unanimous written decision, and it was highly unusual for the panel to call on the services of a third to decide the case.

One of the exceptions was an 1845 arbitration between Eulogio Célis, a Spanish national and trader in California, and James Alexander Forbes, a Scot and the British consul in California. Célis had permitted Forbes to use his boat, the *Sarmiento,* in the San Francisco Bay, although the exact nature of the permission, as an agent or as a renter, was in sharp dispute. The boat ran aground at Coyote Point, near present-day San Mateo, and was damaged. There were clashing contentions as to whether the damages were attributable to preexisting conditions of the boat, or whether the boat had run aground because of improper management by Forbes in hiring an insufficient and incompetent crew. Last, there were legal issues in dispute regarding an alleged absolute responsibility of the owner as, under Forbes's theory of the case, he was earning freight for Célis at the time of the accident.

It was the kind of complicated commercial matter that the expatriates typically arbitrated. Célis chose an American sea captain, John Paty, as his arbitrator; Forbes selected a Scot shipmaster. The two sea captains could not agree and even reached the level of demanding the answers to written interrogatories from each other. Although the proceeding was conducted in San Francisco, the arbitrators ultimately sent the matter for final decision to Pedro Narváez, a well-respected Mexican naval lieutenant who was the port captain of Monterey.[28]

This *Sarmiento* arbitration was unusual in another respect beyond the need for a third arbitrator. The American and British

---

[27] Two examples are the 1838 arbitration between John C. Jones and Alpheus B. Thompson against Eliab Grimes. *See* F. ATHERTON, THE CALIFORNIA DIARY OF FAXON DEAN ATHERTON, 1836–1839, at 111–12, 117–18 (Nunis ed. 1964) (Francis J. Greenway, British; William French and Stephen Reynolds, American); and 1847 arbitration between Alberto Tresconi and Zephyrin Rochon, M.A. 13:1379 (1847) (Milton Little, American; José Abrego, Mexican; and William Longley, nationality unknown).

[28] Rafael Pinto, 2 *Documentos para la historia de California,* 139–99 (2 vols.). The Pinto *Documentos* are on deposit with the Bancroft Library, University of California, Berkeley, California.

residents in California usually chose only Americans, English-men, or Scotsmen to serve as arbitrators. This was probably not due so much to any feeling of discrimination as simply a desire to select arbitrators familiar with the mercantile or seafaring activity involved in the dispute. The Anglo-Americans asked a German, Charles W. Flügge, who reputedly had some legal training, to serve as an arbitrator,[29] and in one commercial arbitration a Mexican trader, José Abrego, was included in the panel.[30] The selection of Americans and British expatriates who had some commercial experience, although some had very little, was more common.[31]

Many California controversies involved Hawaiian merchants or Hawaii-based sea captains. Often these were arbitrated in Honolulu, which was much more sophisticated in mercantile matters and had a group of merchants who quite regularly served as arbitrators. One of these, an American retail merchant named Stephen Reynolds, was a correspondent with Larkin; he had considerable self-training in law and arbitrated several California disputes.[32]

Arbitration is an informal proceeding, usually without a formal record, so there is little evidence of the manner in which they were conducted. Some things may be inferred from the existing evidence, however. Witnesses were sometimes sworn, but not always, and when sworn their testimony was often reduced to a set

[29] Fitch *Documentos, supra* note 2, Documents 349–57.

[30] M.A. 13:1379 (1847).

[31] For example, Scotsman George Kinlock and Kentuckian Job Francis Dye, arbitrators between John Williams and Isaac Graham in April 1846, were only minor retail tradesmen. *Id.,* 6:1146–47 (1846). Some of the other Americans who served as arbitrators were involved in trade only in a minor manner, such as Jacob Snyder, surveyor, *id.,* 6:1146–47 (1846) (first panel of arbitrators) and John Marsh, rancher and physician, *id.,* 7:1470–71 (1837). Biographical information from H. BANCROFT, CALIFORNIA PIONEER REGISTER AND INDEX, 1542–1848 (1964) (extracted from HISTORY OF CALIFORNIA (1884–1890)).

[32] One was an 1838 dispute between John C. Jones, Alpheus B. Thompson, and Eliab Grimes, in ATHERTON, *supra* note 27, at 111–12, 117–18. Another was an 1845 arbitration between Larkin and Peirce and Brewer. Letter, Larkin to Charles Brewer, June 3, 1848, 7 LARKIN PAPERS, *supra* note 2, at 293. Reynolds's many letters to Larkin are filled with comments on legal news, court cases, arbitrations, new statutes, and legal personalities of Hawaii. In his diary Reynolds frequently mentioned various law books he was reading, solid things such as Kent's *Commentaries,* and the litigation in which he was acting as attorney or arbitrator. His diary is on deposit with the Peabody Museum, Salem, Massachusetts.

of written questions and answers.[33] The parties to a dispute frequently submitted lengthy briefs with representations of facts, legal arguments, and comments on the credibility of the witnesses.[34] The disputing parties were not themselves usually allowed to be sworn and testify.[35] The common law regarded parties to a lawsuit as so interested in the outcome, and therefore likely to lie or distort, that they were rendered incompetent and disqualified from giving sworn testimony. The earliest American statute to remove interest as a general disqualification and thereby permit plaintiffs and defendants to freely testify was enacted by Michigan in 1846.[36] The instances in California and Hawaii where the arbitrators did not permit the disputing parties to testify undoubtedly reflected their awareness of this interesting detail of American and English law.

Accountings and other documents were freely considered as evidence.[37] One kind of document of considerable importance to the resolution of commercial disputes in California was the merchant's certificate of condition. It was an adaptation of an old admiralty idea that when a ship or cargo arrived in a damaged or questioned condition, a committee of local sea captains or merchants would be called to survey, as it was called, the extent of

---

[33] Sworn witness testimony was reduced to a written form in Graham and Naile versus Estate of Price, M.A. 7:1470–71 (1837) and in the *Sarmiento* arbitration, 2 Pinto *Documentos, supra* note 28, at 151–52, 166–73, 178–79, 199. In the matter of Jones and Thompson versus Grimes, arbitrated in Honolulu in 1838, the witnesses were apparently not sworn since a party requested at midpoint in the arbitration that "he desired that the oaths of all witnesses might be taken," ATHERTON, *supra* note 27, at 118.

[34] For example, in the *Nymph* arbitration, Fitch *Documentos, supra* note 2, Documents 354–57; and in the *Sarmiento* arbitration, 2 Pinto *Documentos, supra* note 28, at 146, 150, 153–56, 189–95.

[35] The testimony of the plaintiffs was not taken in Graham and Naile versus Estate of Price, M.A. 7:1470–71 (1837), nor in Jones and Thompson versus Grimes, ATHERTON, *supra* note 27, at 117–18.

[36] 1 J. WIGMORE, A TREATISE ON THE ANGLO-AMERICAN SYSTEM OF EVIDENCE 996–1004 (2d ed. 1923) (5 vols.).

[37] For example, the *Nymph* arbitration, Fitch *Documentos, supra* note 2, Documents 349–57, and Peirce and Brewer versus Stearns, Miller, *supra* note 19, at 110, both involved reliance on documentary evidence, as did other arbitrations as well, including the *Sarmiento,* in 2 Pinto, *Documentos, supra* note 28, at 139–99. The Jones and Thompson versus Grimes arbitration in ATHERTON, *supra* note 27, at 117–18, used evidence by sample of goods as well as sales memorandum books.

the condition or damage. A neutral survey could then be an important piece of evidence used in a dispute between shipper, consignee, ship owner, and insurer.

Vast distances and slow communications necessitated these surveys, and the expatriate merchants in California, and elsewhere, used the technique broadly and not just in reference to admiralty matters.[38] Among the mercantile papers there is an occasional certificate whose vitality as evidence in a subsequent dispute is manifest:

Monterey Upper California. Nov. 30 1841
We David Spence & James Watson, principal Merchants of this Port. Having this day been called on by Thomas O. Larkin to examine some pieces of Cotten Hffs—that he brought in a Box marked T O L #55 from Mazatlan in June last—in the Government Schooner California John R. Cooper Master do hereby certify that we have examined the same, and find that they are rotten and unfit for sale. Therefore consider they are not worth nothing pr peice in this market.[39]

Although two of the most frequent arbitrators, Charles Flügge and Stephen Reynolds, had some amount of legal training, taken as a group the arbitrators showed no particular inclination to follow or to understand legal doctrines. For example, in an 1837 case brought on a promissory note against the estate of the maker, the note apparently had been lost but there was some confused evidence of its existence. The arbitrators concluded that "there is not sufficient evidence before them to come to any final settlement of the case."[40] Such a conclusion would amuse a lawyer, who would think without much reflection that insufficient evi-

---

[38] For example, Certificate of John J. Halstead, Mar. 22, 1842, 1 LARKIN PAPERS, *supra* note 2, at 179 ("I do hereby certify that the just & true Measurement of 45 logs of Red Wood landed at this port, from the Schr California by Capt. Cooper, is Five Thousand one hundred and Seventy one feet, say 5171 ft."); Letter, Isaac Williams to Larkin, Oct. 17, 1840, *id.* at 61 ("I Caled Mr Requano Mr Poyo & Mr Worne to Exame the State of the flowr whin I Recvd it."). In the *Sarmiento* arbitration a survey of the damaged boat was introduced before the final, third arbitrator. Letter, James Alexander Forbes to Pedro Narváez, Sept. 27, 1845, 2 Pinto *Documentos, supra* note 28, at 189–95 (survey by three ship captains and three carpenters).
[39] Drafts of Affidavits, David Spence and James Watson, Nov. 30, 1841, 1 LARKIN PAPERS, *supra* note 2, at 138.
[40] M.A. 7:1471 (1837).

dence to decide requires a decision against the party bringing the case since that person has the burden of persuasion. The arbitrators in charge of the case probably were unaware of who, in law, would have the burden of proof.

It probably would not be desirable for arbitrators to possess much legal sophistication. Commercial arbitration is a practical remedy for merchants and tradesmen who have a sense of community with each other sufficient for them to desire to resolve disputes among themselves without outside interference.[41] Because of this, far more emphasis is properly placed on commercial practice and usage than on technical legal doctrine. An interesting illustration of this is in the 1845 arbitration between Abel Stearns, James McKinley, Henry D. Fitch, and John Temple. Abel Stearns had submitted a brief to the arbitrators containing a number of references to the *Ordenanzas de Bilbao,* which were in fact the substantive commercial laws applicable to Mexican California. The reply brief of James McKinley and Henry D. Fitch brushed this legalism aside:

> We are for our part entirely ignorant of such laws as those stated as being "Ordenanzas de Bilboa," except in reason; and rather feel surprised at such copious quotation from them to adjust differences which common sense coupled together with a commercial knowledge & love of justice is sufficient to decide. In the same contract referred to by him, mention is merely made of leaving our differences to the decision of Arbitrators, no mention being made of Ordinanzas de Bilbao, which almost makes us feel assured that Mr. Stearns at that time was as little versed in them as we ourselves are at present. Such being the case we shall take no more notice of them.[42]

Typical of commercial arbitration of Mexican California, the expatriate arbitrators apparently did not think much of the *Ordenanzas* either. In rendering a lengthy written judgment against Stearns they did not refer to them at all.[43]

An interesting feature of the expatriate arbitrations in Mexican California is the high instance in which the Anglo-Americans caused the arbitration decision to become a judgment of the local

---

[41] For further discussion of this point, see J. AUERBACH, JUSTICE WITHOUT LAW? 43–44 (1983) and Jones, *Three Centuries of Commercial Arbitration in New York: A Brief Survey, supra* note 13, at 219.

[42] Fitch *Documentos, supra* note 2, Documents 354–57.

[43] *Id.,* Documents 349–51.

alcalde court. For example, in an 1837 matter involving a lost note and claim against the decedent's estate, the arbitrators recited in their decision that they had been "called on by the magistrate of this place," which was San Jose, to decide on the claim.[44] In the *Sarmiento* arbitration of 1845 between Eulogio Célis and James Alexander Forbes to determine the liability for damages to a boat, the arbitrators were appointed at the request and nomination of the parties by an order of the captain of the port of San Francisco,[45] an official who apparently had assumed an ill-defined, quasi-judicial authority over nautical claims. In an April 1846 arbitration between two Americans the parties appeared before Manual Díaz, the alcalde of Monterey, and agreed to submit their dispute to two specified arbitrators, agreeing further that the arbitral decision would have the effect of "a judgment entered by authority of the court."[46]

This Anglo-American proclivity to make private arbitration decisions take on the force of a Mexican judgment is all the more striking when it is recalled that they strongly believed that the local court orders had no force. The expatriates had repeatedly criticized these same tribunals, and many had fruitlessly sought execution sales against the property of nonpaying judgment debtors. They certainly had no reason for confidence that collectability would be enhanced by the transformation of a private arbitration decision into a Mexican judgment.

One way to view this use of the Mexican courts is as a response to the expatriates' internalized needs for legal regularity. The Anglo-Americans had a need for playing within the local legal rules, even though these rules might themselves be regarded with contempt. The use of a local process to refer a dispute to their own privately selected arbitrators could be a solution to their dilemma. On the one hand, they could avoid the courts they disparaged and the procedures they despised, conciliation, for example. On the other hand, they would legitimate their activities in their own minds by the arbitral decisions taking on the color and patina of official authority.

Probably arbitration did fill this function for many of the foreigners. Yet it cannot be said that this was the only reason for the

[44]M.A. 7:1470 (1837).
[45]2 Pinto *Documentos, supra* note 28, at 142–43, 146–48.
[46]M.A. 6:1146–47 (1846).

use of courts to appoint arbitrators. The procedure has an older history. The technique of petitioning a court and requesting that the court order arbitration and appoint the arbitrators chosen by the parties goes back to eighteenth-century practice.

By the early 1600s English case law had decided that an agreement to arbitrate could be revoked and canceled by either party.[47] Arbitration was a popular commercial institution, though, and at the end of the 1600s, Parliament initiated a series of enactments,[48] the thrust of which was to make a submission to arbitrate irrevocable if it was done by court order or, as it was said, "rule of court." The idea was that arbitration could be commenced by a referral from a court to a panel of referees, who today would be called arbitrators. It was somewhat akin to the modern judicial appointment of masters, except that the referees were expected to decide the case, and not, as in the case of modern-day masters, simply report facts back to the court for the court's approval.

By the end of the eighteenth century it was the usual practice of English and American arbitration to use merchant referees from a judicial referral commenced by litigation,[49] the purpose of which was to make the arbitration submission irrevocable.[50] Mexican California presented a different situation, of course, since irrevocability of an agreement to arbitrate would mean less to the expatriates for whom the local court system was not a satisfactory alternative in any event. Reflecting the nineteenth-century movement away from arbitration initiated by court action, there were some expatriate arbitrations begun and com-

---

[47] The idea may have originated in dictum expressed in Vynior's Case, 8 Coke Rep. 80a and 81B (1609), and was in any event solidified by the time of Kill v. Hollister, 1 Wils. 129, 95 Eng. Rep. 532 (1746).

[48] This first arbitration statute was 9 Will. III, ch. 15 (1698).

[49] Jones, *An Inquiry into the History of the Adjudication of Mercantile Disputes, supra* note 16, at 459–60, 463–64. In Connecticut there was an increasing use of rule of court and variations thereon, as a means of initiating arbitration, from 1750 on. Mann, *The Formalization of Informal Law: Arbitration Before the American Revolution,* 59 N.Y.U. L. REV. 443, 473–74 (1984). The first Virginia arbitration statute, that of 1759, provided for parties "to agree, that their submission [to arbitration] should be made a rule of any court of record which the parties shall chuse." *Early American Arbitration: II. In Old Virginia,* 1 ARB. J. (n.s.) 174 (1946).

[50] Sayre, *supra* note 13, at 605.

pleted in California without any judicial involvement, although these were in the minority.[51]

A major reason for the initiation of Anglo-American arbitrations through the alcalde courts must have been the simple feeling that this was the proper way to do things and not a specific desire to tie private arbitrations with Mexican law. Nonetheless, the notion that an alcalde court's referral would legitimize private dispute resolutions, unarticulated and perhaps not even consciously held, undoubtedly was present as well. Indeed, the judicial record of one arbitration between foreigners specifically recites that the arbitrators were appointed pursuant to Mexican law.[52]

The Anglo-Americans in Mexican California did not have a wide variety of choice in dispute resolution techniques. If a dispute could not be settled between the parties, a claimant had either to forego the claim or seek outside aid. In seeking outside assistance he was limited to arbitration or the often ineffectual litigation in the alcalde courts which was a form of conciliation. Since arbitration required the consent of the defendant, and the only alternative was a drawn-out and weak remedy, that arbitration occurred at all indicates a dedication on the part of most merchants and tradesmen to an amicable resolution of disputes despite the detriment to a defendant's interest in delay. A defendant must have perceived his greater interest to lie in the procedure and not the outcome of a particular case. As with the credit network, the Anglo-Americans relied on a community of interest, here to support an inducement to arbitrate and a willingness to comply with the results, in much the same sense that the Californios relied on a homogeneous, geographic community to enforce judicial decrees.

As noted earlier, 8.7 percent of the lawsuits filed in the Monterey courts between 1831 and 1846 involved one foreigner suing

[51] For example, the 1845 *Nymph* arbitration between Abel Stearns, Henry D. Fitch, James McKinley, and John Temple in Fitch *Documentos, supra* note 2, Documents 349–57. This involved rather complicated accounts of considerable size. Another example is the 1838 arbitration between John C. Jones, Alpheus B. Thompson, and Eliab Grimes, mentioned in ATHERTON, *supra* note 27, at 111–12, 117–18.

[52] M.A. 13:259 (1847). In addition, the arbitrations conducted entirely between Californios, referred to in note 24 *supra,* both proceeded through judicial reference.

another. Although this represents only thirty-two lawsuits, small in absolute terms, it is without doubt far more than the arbitrations conducted in Monterey during the same period, and perhaps more than all the expatriate arbitrations in California for the same period. It raises the question of which kinds of conflicts did the expatriates take to the local courts, and which kinds of controversies did they arbitrate.

Where a dispute was relatively simple, the foreigners freely used the Mexican courts. In simple debt collections for a set, liquidated sum, or, alternatively, for a breach of contract where the damages were in dispute and not fixed but the issues simple or the dollar amount not large, the Anglo-Americans used the local alcalde courts to sue one another.[53] Where a dispute involved either a complex issue or an uncertain but potentially large amount of damages, the Anglo-Americans tended to resolve their commercial disputes through arbitration conducted by fellow commercial men, usually other expatriates.

Of course, there were exceptions. Some complex matters between expatriates were not resolved by arbitration,[54] and, on a level of impression and not statistics, this seems more true when either the claimant or the defendant was a foreigner but neither British nor American.[55] Generally speaking, two conditions prompted arbitration: first, the expatriate status, especially

[53] Some representative suits brought by American plaintiffs against American defendants include Faxon v. Hathaway, *id.*, 6:437 (1842) ($150); Meek v. Dye, *id.*, 6:942 (1844) ($127, counterclaim of $132); Smith v. Larkin, *id.*, 6:267 (1837) (suit for value of rifle left on bailment, value $50). Some representative suits brought by British plaintiffs include Stokes v. Anderson, *id.*, 6:490 (1842) (English defendant, $190); McIntosh v. Discont, *id.*, 6:175 (1835) (probably Dixon, American, for recovery of a rifle).

[54] Jacob P. Leese, Nathan Spear, and William S. Hinckley, Americans all, had formed a partnership for a store in San Francisco which they dissolved amid considerable bitterness in 1838. They enlisted the aid of the local alcalde and the governor of California in resolving their dispute involving their accounts, but did not attempt arbitration. Albertson, "Jacob P. Leese, Californio," at 67–73 (M.A. thesis, University of California, 1947).

[55] For example, a relatively complicated matter concerning a contract to repair a mill was litigated in Dodero v. Kinlock, M.A. 9:555, 591, 615, 623 (1839) (contract recorded at *id.*, 15:493) between an Italian plaintiff and Scot defendant. Danish-American William A. Leidesdorff sued German Andrew Hoeppner for the moderately substantial sum of 620 pesos in May 1846. *Official Documents Relating to Early San Francisco, 1835–1857,* Document 158. These documents are on deposit with Bancroft Library, University of California, Berkeley, California.

Anglo-American, of both plaintiff and defendant, and second, the complexity of the issues in dispute, especially when coupled with a high monetary stake.

Examples of the kinds of issues submitted to arbitration by British and Americans as both claimants and defendants include the validity of a claim against a deceased American's estate based upon a lost promissory note allegedly executed in New Mexico,[56] and a breach of a wholesale contract based on nonconformance of goods delivered to the quality represented where the damages alleged exceeded $5,000 (about $55,000 in today's dollar).[57] Also arbitrated among Anglo-Americans was a complex dispute concerning the voyage of the ship *Nymph*. This was a settlement of accounts of a commercial trading partnership formed to conduct a trading voyage of several month's duration. There were difficult issues of commissions payable to individual partners, expenses of certain of the partners who participated in the voyage, and the prices at which the partners should be charged for partnership goods taken by them individually on their own accounts.[58]

One particular dispute with Americans on both sides well illustrates the kinds of matters arbitrated and those dealt with in the alcalde courts. It is illustrative of these differences because the controversy had two facets, one of which was taken to the local courts and one of which went to arbitration.

On one hand it involved Isaac Graham, the mountain man from Kentucky. He had been expelled from California in 1840 but was back within a year. Graham then turned his hand to the operation of a sawmill that he called "Zayante," which was located in the coastal mountains near Santa Cruz. On the other side were John Williams and his two brothers, James and Isaac Williams. The Williams brothers, all in their twenties, were overland immigrants from the United States who had arrived in 1843. They had experience in lumbering, tanning, and blacksmithing.[59]

At some point in 1845, the exact date is unclear, Graham leased his sawmill to John Williams and his two brothers. The lease was for six months and had a rental of a flat rate of 400 lum-

[56] M.A. 7:1470–71 (1837).

[57] ATHERTON, *supra* note 27, at 111–12, 117–18.

[58] Fitch *Documentos, supra* note 2, Documents 349–57.

[59] This and subsequent biographical information is from BANCROFT, CALIFORNIA PIONEER REGISTER AND INDEX, 1542–1848, *supra* note 31.

bered feet of wood per day, at an equivalent price of $35 per 1,000 feet. Thus the total rental obligation was about $2,100, or in current dollars about $23,000.[60]

Two problems developed. First and most important was that the mill was in disrepair and could not be operated at the start of the lease period. Second, Graham furnished food to the Williams brothers and rendered some other minor services that had not been provided for in the lease. John Williams claimed $1,000 damages for Graham's failure to repair the mill before commencement of the lease,[61] and Graham claimed $205 compensation for the food and other services provided.[62] There may have been other aspects to the dispute, but these were the major items.

Printed below is a translation of the alcalde's notes of a hearing between Graham and Williams held on May 2, 1846.[63] This is the record of a conciliation hearing of an ordinary lawsuit, and it is typical of the documentation for the hearings that terminated approximately 85 percent of the civil cases in Mexican California. A photograph of the original document is included in the illustrations section.

In the Port of Monterey, Upper California, on May 2, 1846, before me, Manuel Dias, First Constitutional Alcalde of this jurisdiction and in charge of the Court of the First Instance, were present Messrs. Isaac Graham, with his good man Mr. Teodoro Gonzalez, and John Williams with his, Mr. George Allen, the first demanding of the third [i.e., *Graham v. Williams*], the payment of 205 pesos for food and damages to some tools of the mill that he [Williams] had in his charge, to which the defendant answered that there must be reduced from that account labor of 14 days that was done to repair said mill, and after the various allegations of both parties I ordered them to withdraw, and in conformity with the opinion of the good men I rendered a verdict as a route of conciliation that the 28 pesos that the 14 days of labor of Mr. John Williams and his brothers amounts to, be deducted from the 205 pesos that Mr. Isaac Graham demands

---

[60] This information is from a table of accounts, dated Apr. 28, 1846, between Graham and Williams, obviously prepared on behalf of Williams, probably for some phase of the arbitration, but likely to be accurate in these particular regards. It is located at M.A. 8:572.

[61] *Id.*

[62] This information is from an undated account apparently prepared on behalf of Graham and probably for the arbitration. It may be found at *id.*, 12:417.

[63] *Id.*, 6 :1150–51 (1846).

from him and that Mr. John Williams pay to Mr. Isaac Graham the resulting 177 pesos in money or produce at money's worth. Thus the messrs. good men sign with me—the interlining "I rendered a verdict" is valid—Williams is not signing because he does not know how to—

Manl Dias

Jorge Allen

Teodoro Gonzales

Isaac Graham

This record, personally prepared by the judge, recites the presence of the plaintiff, Graham, together with his *hombre bueno,* Teodoro González. González was a Mexican who had arrived in California in 1825. He was a solid citizen, had served in several government offices, including a year or two as a judge, and was the grantee of two ranchos. Graham's association with González is curious and inexplicable. John Williams appeared with his good man, George Allen. Allen was Irish and had come to California in 1822. He had held a number of minor governmental positions and was considerably older than the Williams brothers, being fifty years of age in 1846. Again, there does not appear to be any particular reason for the choice. Neither of these *hombres buenos* appear in the records with significant regularity as good men. Although only John Williams is named as defendant, all three brothers were involved in the lease, and although only Graham is named as plaintiff, he had a partner in the ownership of the mill, Henry Naile. Specificity of parties plaintiff or defendant was not a strong point of California practice.

In the conciliation record the judge states that Graham was demanding $205 for food and some damages. Note that Williams was not denying liability but merely alleged that from the $205 "there must be reduced . . . labor of 14 days that was done to repair said mill." In other words, all Williams wanted was a small setoff. Thus the entire piece of litigation devolved into the single issue of what was the value of fourteen days of labor for three men. This was the kind of simple issue with low economic stakes for which it was typical that the expatriates would litigate in the California courts.

The judge ordered the parties to withdraw and arrived at a recommendation "in conformity with the opinion of the good men." This is the typical unanimity of judge and both good men. The value of the labor was set at twenty-eight pesos. Williams was ordered to pay the balance after setoff in money or, again very typically, in produce.

Printed below is a translation of the record of another proceeding held by the same two men before the same judge, a few days earlier on April 29, 1846.[64] It is an agreement to arbitrate and a judicial referral to an arbitration panel. A photograph of the original is included in the illustrations section.

In the Port of Monterey, Upper California, on April 29, 1846, before me, Manuel Dias, First Constitutional Alcalde, being present Mr. Isaac Graham demanding of Mr. John Williams, a settlement of accounts concerning a mill, Zayante, that the first had rented to the second, and it being of difficult resolution, they agreed amongst themselves and before me that in order to avoid the expenses and delays of a trial to submit the resolution of all of the differences that have relation to this point to two arbitrators or friendly compromisers, Mr. Isaac Graham naming for this purpose Mr. George Kinlock and Mr. John Williams [naming] Mr. Francis Dye, with the power in these men to nominate a third in discord [a neutral arbitrator if they disagreed], the referenced Graham and Williams binding themselves to this and to go forward with the judgment that the stated gentlemen may give, desiring that they might judge among them [and] they might completely obligate and compel the performance of the referenced decision as a judgment entered by authority of the court, encumbering with the costs, damages and prejudices whoever might decline to perform the judgment of the stated arbitrators, declaring moreover to be null and of no value or effect the undertaking they signed in Santa Cruz obligating themselves to be bound by the verdict [which] may be rendered by Messrs. Hames [and] Snyder on this same matter for the stated judgment not having had effect. And for the completion of all that is referred to they sign with me and the good men that were, for the plaintiff, Mr. George Kinlock and for the defendant Mr. Francis Dye.

Manl Dias		Isaac Graham
		Isaac Williams
	for	John Williams
		Francis Dye
		George Kinlock

In this document Graham and Williams agreed to arbitrate the accounts for the mill rental, reciting that they were "of difficult

[64] *Id.*, 6:1146–47.

resolution." The major aspect of the dispute was Williams's demand for $1,000 damages ($11,000 today), for the delay caused by the mill's disrepair at the beginning of the lease. That, of course, is a much larger sum than was involved in Graham's counter demand. In addition, the issue in Williams's claim is more complex because the question of his actual losses would involve consideration of what business he had arranged for the commencement of the lease and had lost because of a brief delay. This is, therefore, a relatively complex issue with unfixed and unsettled but potentially large damages, and with all parties, plaintiff and defendant, being expatriates. It was a typical matter for arbitration.

Graham's nominee as arbitrator was George Kinlock, a Scotsman, in California since 1830, who worked as a carpenter and minor trader in Monterey. He was forty-nine years old in 1846. Williams's choice was Francis Dye, also sometimes referred to as Job Francis Dye, a Kentuckian who had entered California in 1832. He had a number of occupations and at various times in California had a store, a mill, and a distillery. By the mid-1840s he operated as a small trader in Monterey and was also engaged in running, at long distance, a ranch he had been granted in the northern central valley. Dye was forty-one years old in 1846.

The arbitration agreement recorded by the judge also contained a provision that the arbitral decision, of which there is no record, would be the equivalent of a court judgment, as was commonly done. The only thing atypical of this arbitration submission is the parties' mutual rescission of an earlier written arbitration agreement signed in Santa Cruz. That arbitration was before John Hames and Jacob Snyder. Hames was a foreigner, probably American, who had arrived in 1844. Snyder was an 1845 arrival, a native of Pennsylvania, and a surveyor.

The previous arbitrators fit within the general pattern as they were themselves foreigners. Then why were they removed from the case? The answer offers a dramatic ending to this chapter, although it was highly unusual. At a hearing before the two previous arbitrators there had been a violent exchange of words between one of the defendants, James Williams, a brother of John Williams, and Henry Naile, Graham's partner. One thing led to another, and James Williams killed Naile in the presence of the two arbitrators.[65]

[65] Letter, Isaac Graham to Abel Stearns, Apr. 24, 1846, in 2 Manuel Castro,

Probably Hames and Snyder simply refused to proceed further. By the date of these documents, April 29 and May 2, 1846, James had been jailed in Monterey on a murder charge.[66] Truly remarkable was the commitment of the remaining defendants and the remaining plaintiff to an orderly resolution of their disputes.

Documentos para la historia de California, Document 68 (2 vols.). The Castro *Documentos* are on deposit with the Bancroft Library, University of California, Berkeley, California. The killing is also discussed, and the arbitrators indicated as witnesses, in 5 BANCROFT, *supra* note 23, at 641 (1886).

[66] Letter, Larkin to William A. Leidesdorff, Apr. 13, 1846, in 4 LARKIN PAPERS, *supra* note 2, at 284–85.

9

Domestic Relations

In approaching the topic of domestic relations law, the Mexican California law and procedures will be discussed first, and after that will be a review of the Anglo-American adaptations. The legal procedures of marriage, which were few, will be followed by the law regarding marital separations, which was considerable. Last will come the miscellaneous aspects of domestic relations law, such as bastardy, child support, and guardianship. Discussion of the expatriates will parallel this, with a review of the immigrants' search for proper authorities to perform non-Catholic marriages and discussion of the difficulty of arranging divorces in a society that did not recognize their legitimacy.

There is no evidence the Anglo-Americans experienced significant difficulty with the miscellaneous aspects of domestic relations law, such as child support or guardianship, during the Mexican period. To the limited extent they did, their problems were resolved in the same manner as those of the Californios, through the regular judicial procedures. Foreign plaintiffs and defendants are identified as such in the discussion of the California legal system's handling of these matters. The chapter concludes with a case study of the Bennett women, whose marital problems are in many ways paradigmatic of the legal difficulties of domestic relations encountered by the expatriates in Mexican California. It should be recalled that most of the older expatriate residents, arriving by sea and before 1841, became assimilated into Mexican California. Most became at least nominal Catholics and married California women. They tended not to experience the domestic relations difficulties that faced the less assimilated newer arrivals. The primary focus of this chapter will therefore be on the overland immigrants arriving in 1841 and thereafter.

In the legal system of Catholic Mexican California, civilian authorities had little involvement with marriage. Neither alcaldes nor *jueces de paz* had any authority to perform marriages. As Governor Juan B. Alvarado (1836 to 1842) explained: "The prerogative of performing marriages belonged solely to the ministers of the church and the laws called for the severe punishment of soldiers and civilians who tried to infringe on this prerogative of Catholic priests and friars."[1] Nevertheless, there was a significant bureaucratic procedure because the missionary friars conducted a detailed premarital investigation. They took testimony, reduced to written form, not only from bride and groom but also from other witnesses as to the motives for the marriage, the character and relationship of the parties, possible impediments, and similar matters.[2] These matrimonial investigation tribunals, the *Diligencias Matrimoniales,* became less thorough, according to a longtime English resident, after the Spanish padres were replaced by Mexican priests, a process which began in 1835.[3]

This investigation was entirely under ecclesiastical control, and the only role played by the civilian authorities in the entire matrimonial process was the necessity of the prefect's consent to marriage of a minor. These consents in the form of letters to the officiating priests appear occasionally in the governmental records, as well, of course, as in the ecclesiastical archives.[4]

Divorce as modernly conceived was unknown to Catholic California. There were, however, two forms of marital separation. The first was an annulment, which attacked the validity of the marriage itself, if, for example, the parties were within the prohibited

[1] 4 Alvarado, *Historia de California,* ch. 38, on file with the Bancroft Library, University of California, Berkeley, California.

[2] *See* Miranda, *Gente de Razón Marriage Patterns in Spanish and Mexican California: A Case Study of Santa Barbara and Los Angeles,* 63 S. Cal. Q. 1, 11–13 (1981). A detailed discussion of a matrimonial investigation for an 1841 marriage between an American expatriate and California woman is in D. Wright, A Yankee in Mexican California: Abel Stearns, 1798–1848, at 85–90 (1977).

[3] W. Garner, Letters from California 1846–1847, at 170 (Craig ed. 1970).

[4] An example of a prefect's consent is Letter, prefect to Padre Real, Jan. 9, 1841, in 10 Monterey Archives, 48 (1841) [hereinafter cited as M.A. in style of M.A. 10:48]. The Monterey Archives are deposited with the Monterey County Historical Society, Salinas, California. Another example is *id.,* 10:361 (1841) (prefect to Padre Mercado). For information about the various California ecclesiastical archives, which were not used for this study because of their tangential nature, see H. Beers, Spanish and Mexican Records of the American Southwest 282–305 (1979).

degrees of consanguinity. Such a procedure restored the putative spouses to the status of single persons who were then free to marry again. A second kind of marital separation was a separation from bed and board, *a mensa et thoro* in the common law expression. Such a legal decree would separate the spouses temporarily or permanently and might include orders protecting the parties from each other's interference or abuse; it might provide for an award of support, but it would not alter the married status of the spouses nor permit them to remarry.

Annulments were under the exclusive jurisdiction of the ecclesiastical authorities, and before 1842 various of the Franciscan missionary padres assumed sporadic roles as ecclesiastical courts. The first bishop sent to California, Francisco García Diego y Moreno, arrived at the end of December 1841. Among his other duties, he functioned rather systematically as an ecclesiastical tribunal. The alcalde and justice of the peace courts had jurisdiction over temporary separations not involving an attack on the validity or continuation of the marriage itself, and also had jurisdiction over all forms of protective and support orders. As for permanent separations, they were virtually nonexistent in Mexican California.

Although it seems in retrospect that the division line in the two jurisdictions is clear, it was not so evident to the contemporaries. Bishop García Diego maintained a steady correspondence with priests, alcaldes, *jueces de paz,* and other officials concerning specific marital disputes.[5] In his letters he was given to overbroad claims of jurisdiction, irrelevant to the specific facts before him, much in the nature of dicta. On other occasions he would deny ecclesiastical jurisdiction and remand matters to the alcaldes in a somewhat irritated manner.[6]

The situation was sufficiently confused that many alcaldes and justices of the peace routinely referred domestic matters to the bishop for his resolution of the jurisdictional question. Sometimes the prefect or even the governor would order the trial court

[5]Much, but not all, of this correspondence may be found in F. García Diego, The Writings of Francisco García Diego y Moreno, Obispo de Ambas Californias (Weber ed. 1976).

[6]The bishop's statements and correspondence are analyzed in Langum, *Expatriate Domestic Relations Law in Mexican California,* 7 Pepperdine L. Rev. 41, 51–52 n.27 (1979).

to clarify the jurisdictional issue with the bishop.[7] The acceptances and denials of jurisdiction, as well as the ultimate resolution of cases for which jurisdiction was taken, were, of course, communicated by the bishop to the civil authorities.[8]

When the civil courts adjudicated domestic matters they would proceed along the regular pattern of litigation. A complaint would be made, usually but not invariably by the wife. Most suits asked for a separation, but some merely sought orders directing the other spouse to refrain from specified conduct. Then there would be a conciliation hearing with the usual *hombres buenos*. If a reconciliation was not achieved at the hearing, or occasionally if emergency compelled it even earlier, as the first procedural step the judge would order the wife placed in an honorable home other than that of her husband. This deposit into a "safe house," as they were called, was designed to protect the wife from abuse and to prevent the possible scandal of an unchaperoned female in the community. It was also a step that would assuage Latin male suspiciousness and sense of honor and therefore promote subsequent reconciliation. Generally wives were placed in the home of their father or other adult male relative, such as an uncle or a married brother.[9] They were sometimes placed with their *hombre bueno*,[10] however, or with other figures above reproach in the community, such as Thomas O. Larkin and his wife.[11] This procedure was not unique to California and was followed elsewhere in Mexico.[12]

---

[7] In 1844, concerning a triangle involving Teodoro Robles, his wife, and a young lady, the governor ordered the Monterey justice of the peace to inquire whether the bishop had jurisdiction. García Diego replied that he did not. GARCÍA DIEGO, *supra* note 5, at 167–68; M.A. 11:1111 (1844). Another example is the 1843 separation of the Hernández couple, M.A. 11:681 (1843) (governor orders reference from justice of the peace to bishop).

[8] For example, GARCÍA DIEGO, *supra* note 5, at 144–46; M.A. 11:1587 (1844) (declaring marriage null and void on account of lack of dispensation from impediment of third degree of affinity); Letter, Padre Real to justice of the peace, June 3, 1842, *id.*, 10:1231 (1842) (communicating account of ecclesiastical jurisdiction).

[9] For example, in the 1842 Castañares separation action, the wife was ordered to live with her father. GARNER, *supra* note 3, at 30 n.39 (introduction by editor).

[10] For example, M.A. 6:730 (1842).

[11] *Id.*, 6:908 (1844).

[12] For example, in New Mexico, "like California, alcaldes sent women to 'safe and honorable' houses to be kept 'in deposito' until a case was settled." Letter,

With the wife secured in a safe house, the alcalde turned to setting a level of support for the wife. This was usually modest. In 1842, Englishman Edward Watson was ordered to pay his wife twelve pesos monthly for her support and that of their son.[13] In 1835 the alcalde ordered Bonifacio Madariaga to pay fifteen pesos monthly for his wife's maintenance and also to provide a cook.[14]

The court made other protective orders at this time. They ranged from a simple order that the husband behave himself,[15] to jailing the husband because of domestic violence.[16] The alcaldes' decrees at times were creative, as in one order on behalf of a husband that his mother-in-law should desist from hiding her daughter,[17] or another order on behalf of a wife that her husband should take her clothes out of pawn.[18]

The conciliation process of ordinary litigation was designed to achieve harmony, and it worked even more effectively than its usual high rate in the cases of marital separations. The alcaldes would frequently exhort spouses to attend to the obligations owed each other and to forget resentments.[19] The rate of reconciliation was extremely high. In case after case one finds a notation or subsequent order indicating reconciliation, sometimes as early as the initial conciliation hearing,[20] or within a short period thereafter and with the help of the parties' *hombres buenos*.[21] At times there was a much longer period of separation, sometimes many months, before reconciliation.[22]

Regardless of the period of separation, the significant fact is that there were so many reconciliations, approaching, although not reaching, all of the suits filed for separation. Indeed, the Mon-

Janet Lecompte to David J. Langum, Jan. 1, 1982, on file with author. Ms. Lecompte is an authority on the Hispanic period legal history of New Mexico and has researched and published in this area.

[13] M.A. 6:730 (1842).

[14] *Id.*, 6:161 (1835).

[15] *Id.*, 6:130 (1835).

[16] *Id.*, 8:283 (1845) (Hernández); *id.*, 11:719, 723 (1843) (Andrew Watson, Englishman).

[17] 1 Prefect Records of Los Angeles 337 (1840) [hereinafter cited as L.A.P.R. in style of L.A.P.R. 1:337]. These documents are on deposit with the Huntington Library, San Marino, California.

[18] M.A. 6:130 (1835).

[19] For example, *id.* at 45 (1833) and *id.* at 870 (1843).

[20] *Id.* at 746 (1842).

[21] GARNER, *supra* note 3, at 30 (introduction by editor); M.A. 6:750 (1842).

[22] M.A. 6:727, 756 (1842).

terey Archives do not appear to contain any judicial orders that resemble a *final* support order or separation decree. They are all temporary in apparent expectation of a later reconciliation. These archives also appear to include only one written separation agreement between spouses, providing for a permanent separation and property division.[23]

The extremely high rate of reconciliation strongly suggests that the judicial lawsuit for marital separation served a social function other than the separation of spouses. As with the cultural values underlying the entire structure of civil litigation examined in chapter 5, the social function of marital litigation was not clearly articulated. It must be found by inference from the evidence.

It appears that the actual purpose served by these lawsuits was to allow parties to air grievances in order to reform spousal behavior. Several pieces of evidence lead to that conclusion. First, these lawsuits were filed within extremely small communities where most persons knew each other. The exact nature of the complaints suggests that there was a specific feature of the other spouse's conduct that the complainant wanted changed. In one suit the wife alleged that her husband wanted to marry another and so had threatened to kill her;[24] another wife complained that her husband called her a bad woman and a *puta,* or whore. The husband admitted that he did so when he was angry, but that it really was not true.[25] One husband complained that his wife would not have sexual relations with him;[26] another husband alleged that he had gone out one Sunday morning for milk and returned to find his servant in bed with his wife. She said the servant forced his attentions.[27]

The specificity of complaint seems calculated to embarrass the other spouse. They appear designed to put the other party in a position of public exposure and disgrace, remembering again the small-town, local nature of this litigation. It can be assumed that many private threats to file preceded most such lawsuits in an

---

[23] *Id.,* 11:899 (1844) (Juan Romero gives permission to his wife, Juana, to live separate from him, and turns over to her specified property, cattle and other animals, for her maintenance and that of their children).

[24] *Id.,* 6:45 (1833).

[25] *Id.,* 6:908 (1844).

[26] *Id.,* 9:1178 (1840).

[27] *Id.,* 8:283 (1845).

effort to make a fear of public exposure of grievances modify the offending spouse's behavior.

For many couples involved in marital litigation, the filing of a lawsuit must have represented a statement that "this time you, wife or husband, have really gone too far." Many consumers of the alcaldes' marital services were repeat customers, filing repetitive complaints. Juan Rangel and spouse were before the alcalde for separation in 1836, were reconciled, and filed again in 1843. Again they reconciled.[28] Bonifacio Madariaga and wife were in such a suit in January 1833, reconciled, and then only two months later the wife brought another complaint. Apparently this too resulted in a reconciliation as there was a third complaint in early 1835.[29] Another repetitive twosome was the Hernández couple who litigated in both 1843 and 1845.[30]

Thus a complaint to the alcalde concerning one's spouse, whether expressly seeking a judicial separation or not, in reality sought to air grievances, obtain counseling, and modify spousal behavior. Just as in neighboring New Mexico, "in the absence of lawyers and marriage counselors, alcalde courts served as the first resort in marital difficulties. Many married couples appeared in the courts seeking reconciliation, looking to the *juez* and *hombres buenos* for advice and guidance as well as legal means of assuring better treatment from their spouses."[31] It is an interesting question, although beyond the scope of this study, why this function was not fulfilled by the priests.

Two interesting judicial orders confirm the behavioral and conciliatory nature of the alcaldes' services in matrimonial matters. On the evening of February 4, 1841, Francis Westgate, an expatriate, apparently struck his California wife, María. The next day she complained to the alcalde. The judge immediately ordered the parties reunited but under the penalty of punishment for Francis should he ever hit his wife again.[32] In 1837 there was a curious petition before the Monterey court. Demetrio Mendoza

---

[28] *Id.*, 6:216 (1836); *id.* at 845 (1843).

[29] *Id.*, 6:90 (January 1833); *id.*, 6:45 (March 1833); *id.*, 6:130 (January 1835).

[30] *Id.*, 6:870 (1843); *id.*, 8:283 (1845).

[31] Lecompte, *The Independent Women of Hispanic New Mexico, 1821–1846,* 12 W. Hist. Q. 17, 29 (1981).

[32] *Official Documents Relating to Early San Francisco,* Document 54 (1841). These documents are on deposit with the Bancroft Library, University of California, Berkeley, California.

asked the alcalde for a reunion with his wife, who apparently had been judicially separated. The judge ordered that Mendoza could obtain a reunion, but only upon proof of a change in his conduct. Demetrio had not shown enough improvement and therefore would have to do without his wife while he tried harder to reform.[33]

Since there was very little permanent marital separation in Mexican California, there was a corresponding dearth of litigation between spouses concerning child support or custody, although there was some.[34] These issues also often arose in connection with bastardy proceedings.

Illegitimacy tended to follow class lines. The upper economic classes had carefully sheltered courtships, and young women were not permitted in the company of suitors without the presence of their *dueñas,* or chaperons.[35] Among the lower classes, however, there was a Spanish folk practice that tolerated informal unions of single persons who were without any impediment to marriage,[36] and this attitude, not shared by church or officialdom, may have carried to California. The perceptions of foreign male visitors to Mexican California certainly suggest a sharp differentiation in the standards of morality between upper-class women and their lower-class counterparts.[37] Quite apart from casual observations and speculation, the judicial records reveal a considerable instance of bastardy.

There was litigation for the support of illegitimate children, but it tended not to be direct suits of the mother against the putative father. Rather, the support issues often arose indirectly, as in a suit for support of an illegitimate minor brought against the widow of the alleged father,[38] or in a claim for inheritance as-

[33] M.A. 6:268 (1837). Good-behavior bonds were also used.
[34] *Id.,* 16:356 (1841) (children divided on temporary basis, some to mother, some to father; father ordered to support those with mother); *id.,* 12:44 (1839) (petition by mother for custody of legitimate child). *Compare id.,* 6:985 (1844), wherein deceased wife had left children in charge of her sister. The father later sought them and defendant-sister claimed father could not care for their education or training. At the conciliation hearing the father agreed that the children should remain with their aunt.
[35] Miranda, *supra* note 2, at 10.
[36] Borah & Cook, *Marriage and Legitimacy in Mexican Culture: Mexico and California,* 54 Calif. L. Rev. 946, 949–52, 960–62 (1966).
[37] Langum, *Californio Women and the Image of Virtue,* 59 S. Cal. Q. 245 (1977).
[38] M.A. 6:975 (1844).

serted on behalf of an illegitimate child against the estate of the alleged father, an American expatriate, John Price.[39]

Surprisingly by modern standards, there was a considerable amount of litigation over the custody of illegitimate children. The father was preferred, even as to bastards, over the mother. An investigation would be made and the preference was not always honored. Some litigation was directly between mother and father with no other parties.[40] Often the suit for custody was brought by a man alleging paternity against another male having custody of the child. In 1835, for example, Mariano Domínguez alleged paternity of an eleven-year-old and sought custody from a godfather who had reared him.[41]

Another variation of a paternity claim brought by one male against another involved married couples where an outside male alleged he was the father of an illegitimate child of the wife, presumptively the legitimate issue of the husband. Two interesting lawsuits illustrate the operation of the presumption of legitimacy. In an 1840 Los Angeles case a male expatriate alleged that he was the natural father of certain children born of an Indian woman married to an Indian male. The foreigner claimed the children were in bad circumstances, and the *juez de paz* awarded him the children's custody. The Indian couple appealed to the prefect, who reversed the decision. The principle of legitimacy of issue of a marriage controlled, and the prefect ordered the justice of the peace to return the children to the married couple.[42]

In a February 1846 Monterey case, the putative father, a Californio, alleged that the mother of the child was pregnant by him before her marriage. The mother and her husband claimed legitimacy because the child was born after the marriage. At a conciliation hearing the judge and the *hombres buenos* recommended that the child be put in the custody of a third party, at the cost of the plaintiff, with visitation rights to the mother. They reasoned that the plaintiff had a greater financial capacity to provide an

[39] *Id.*, 7:916, 10:168–69, and 10:196–97 (1839).

[40] *Id.*, 11:767–71 (1843); *id.*, 9:21 (1839) (suit for possession of a child, apparently between mother and father).

[41] 34 Archives of California, 196 (1835) [hereinafter cited as A.C. in the style of A.C. 34:196]. These archives are on deposit with the Bancroft Library, University of California, Berkeley, California.

[42] L.A.P.R. 1:61–62, 64–66 (1840).

education and maintenance for the child. The mother and her husband flatly refused the settlement suggestion, asserting that "in no manner and in no case would they agree to the delivery of the girl."[43] There is no indication of any further trial.

The alcalde courts were also kept busy with guardianship problems. These arose in many ways. At one level, in his notarial function, the alcalde recorded agreements creating guardianships of minors. These included documents whereby the mother of an illegitimate child renounced her maternal rights to another woman or couple in what were, in effect, private adoptions,[44] and a very few apprenticeship agreements, in which a father gave paternal rights over a son for the purpose of training in a trade.[45]

Guardianships were at times created upon the request of the minor.[46] Additionally, rights of emancipation from parental control were granted upon request and good cause, as in the case of Dolores Vásquez who wanted to leave the paternal roof in 1835 because her father beat her. Her petition was granted.[47] On the other hand, errant youths were ordered delivered to their parents.[48]

Alcaldes also created guardianships involuntarily, as with the Indian Josefa, who had begun a "career of laziness" through the neglect of her parents,[49] and in the case of a young woman of Los Ángeles who confessed that she had been leading an evil life.[50] Since these involuntary guardianships usually meant the removal

[43] M.A. 6:1237 (February 1846).

[44] For example, Galinda and Gonzales, *id.*, 7:503 (February 1846) (Ana Gonzales promising she will educate and care for the child); *id.*, 15:487 (1838).

[45] For example, Osio and Still, *id.*, 15:491 (1838) (apprenticeship agreement of five years and six months' duration, with Captain Joseph Still to teach Antonio Osio's 14-year-old son the trade of carpentry. The son was a signatory to the agreement).

[46] L.A.P.R. 1:632A–32B (1842) (according to the prefect, the minor girl having reached the age of puberty, she may appoint her own guardian, near relatives being preferred).

[47] M.A. 6:166 (1835).

[48] For example, *id.*, 10:228 (1841) (prefect orders justice of the peace at Branciforte to deliver a youth to her parents).

[49] A.C. 42:189 (1845). A foreigner, Louis Jordan, was named as her guardian.

[50] L.A.P.R. 1:621 (1842) (prefect orders her placed in custody of cousin). *Compare id.*, 1:522B (1841) (decedent father left care of children to two men, not the mother; prefect advises that judge should take charge of their care and education and appoint official guardian).

of minor children from their parents, the judicial authorities also had to deal with parental petitions to regain custody. The records disclose several of these,[51] as well as petitions asserting a favored position to a guardianship over another who had been appointed.[52]

A final duty of all those who had an official duty respecting law enforcement, *jueces de paz*, prefects, and even the governors, was to read complaints from the California clergy respecting the morals of their flocks and to deal with their demands for official action. An example is Padre Durán's complaint to the prefect of the Southern District in June 1840 about the scandal of María Pegui, single and living in concubinage with an Irishman, Santiago Bore (James W. Burke), who was married to Josefa Boronda. According to Durán, María followed her Irishman around wherever he went, and the priest asked the prefect to put a stop to this and expel María from Santa Barbara.[53] Another example is the letter Bishop García Diego wrote Governor Pio Pico on October 2, 1845, complaining of the

scandalous concubinage in which José de Jesús Vallejo and Soledad Sánchez have lived at Mission San Jose. . . . I hereby ask Your Excellency to take whatever means might be necessary to correct this scandal. . . . I am confident that your Christian zeal will not allow you to refuse this plea, for otherwise this evil and other similar ones will bring upon you the divine wrath.[54]

The older expatriates who arrived before 1841 tended to become thoroughly assimilated into Californio society, and this included marrying local women. The Anglo-Americans were required to become Catholic, at least nominally, and in the very

[51] *Id.*, 1:353 (1841) (widow petitions prefect requesting custody of minor children separated from her by the court); A.C. 38:402 (1841) (petition to governor from father seeking return of daughter placed in third party "safe house" by prefect and *juez de paz* in light of allegations by the mother of incest. Governor orders justice of the peace to investigate and to take deposition of the mother).

[52] L.A.P.R. A:213–30, 955A (1845). The parents of this minor boy were apparently deceased and his grandmother had given a guardianship to Louis Bouchet, a French expatriate and nonrelative. The petitioner urged his priority of guardianship because he was a relative. The grandmother resisted on the grounds that petitioner had "criminal tendencies" and had seduced her daughter-in-law. After an investigation, the petitioner's request for a transfer of guardianship was denied.

[53] *Id.*, 1:451B–52A (1840). On the first of July 1840, the justice of the peace of Santa Barbara ordered María's expulsion. *Id.*, 1:447B (1840).

[54] García Diego, *supra* note 5, at 181.

early days there was some Californio resistence to these mixed marriages. For example, an early marriage of an expatriate to a California woman was that of Henry Fitch and Josefa Carrillo in 1829. That romance produced bitter feelings, an elopement to South America, and an ecclesiastical trial upon the couple's return.[55] Nevertheless, by the mid-1830s ambitious Anglo-Americans were welcomed into unions with the upper-class daughters of California.[56]

The overland migration that commenced in 1841 brought a much different class of pioneer: crude, many already with families, most were agriculturally inclined and eager to settle but not to assimilate. The great majority of these later arrivals were Protestant. In fact, many immigrants entered into marriages along the overland trails, most of which were solemnized by Protestant ministers.[57] These ministers were bound for Oregon and did not continue on to California. Until 1846 there were no Protestant religious officials in California.[58]

The usual desires of these expatriates could not be suspended simply on account of their arrival in California. Some wished to cohabit and to legitimize that cohabitation by marriage, and others desired to separate from their spouses. Both were difficult for Protestant expatriates to achieve in a Catholic country. The resolution of the conflict between the immigrants' needs and the lack of legal forms through which to accomplish them often led to confusion. Yet the attempted resolutions reveal that these lay pioneers had both a reasonably good understanding of the current law of domestic relations and great skill in adapting these norms to the situation in which they found themselves.

If there were no Protestant ministers in California, there were certainly Roman Catholic priests. In accordance with Mexican

[55] Miller, *A California Romance in Perspective; The Elopement, Marriage, and Ecclesiastical Trial of Henry D. Fitch and Josefa Carrillo,* 19 J. SAN DIEGO HIST. 1 (1973).

[56] Miranda, *supra* note 2, at 8.

[57] Several examples are given in M. MATTES, THE GREAT PLATTE RIVER ROAD: THE COVERED WAGON MAINLINE VIA FORT KEARNY TO FORT LARAMIE 63 (1969).

[58] 4 Z. ENGELHARDT, THE MISSIONS AND MISSIONARIES OF CALIFORNIA 415 n.7 (1915) (4 vols. & index). Apparently the first to arrive, in late 1846, was Adna A. Hecox, who, although he engaged in numerous secular occupations, was licensed by the Methodist Episcopal church. M. HECOX, CALIFORNIA CARAVAN: THE 1846 OVERLAND TRAIL MEMOIR OF MARGARET M. HECOX 12–13, 17 (Dillon ed. 1966).

law, however, the priests refused to officiate at any marriage in which both parties were not Catholic.[59] None of the Mexican civil authorities in California had authority to perform marriages. Even after the American invasion, the multipurpose alcaldes were prohibited from performing marriages when either party was Catholic.[60] This prohibition of secular participation in mixed

[59] Priests in Mexican Texas likewise refused to perform marriages if one party was non-Catholic. Baade, *The Form of Marriage in Spanish North America,* 61 CORNELL L. REV. 1, 55–57 (1975). In Texas, as in California, the immigrants were required to become at least nominal Catholics to obtain the priests' services. Unlike California, however, Texas had too few priests to serve the largely expatriate communities. A practice developed whereby couples cohabited and put up a surety bond that their marriage would be solemnized as soon as a priest was available or passed through the area. This "marriage by bond," as it was called, occasioned much litigation, legislation, and other legal difficulties. *Id.* at 5–19.

[60] After the American conquest, in 1847, a local priest and the administrator of the Diocese of California filed complaints with Colonel Mason, then military governor, that John Burton, an American alcalde of San Jose, had united in marriage an American and a Catholic Mexican woman. Mason, anxious as a military occupier to preserve the status quo and not give the civilian population unnecessary offense, issued a circular order to all alcaldes and other civil authorities under date of August 23, 1847, prohibiting them from performing any marriage when one of the parties was "a member of the Catholic Church in California," a phrase that was ambiguous regarding a union of two Americans one of whom might be Catholic. Neither of the complainants objected to the alcalde marriage of two Protestants and implicity condoned the practice. The priest, Fr. José Real, originally made his complaint directly to Burton by letter of June 8, 1847, so that it may be inferred that alcalde and presumably others had assumed matrimonial powers before that date. 4 Z. ENGELHARDT, *supra* note 58, at 597–603. For example, the American alcalde, William Ide, married John S. Williams to Maria Louisa Gordon on June 17, 1847. 4 H. BANCROFT, HISTORY OF CALIFORNIA 689 (1886) (1884–1890) (7 vols.); 5 H. BANCROFT, HISTORY OF CALIFORNIA 776 (1886).

After California was ceded to the United States, the military government, continuing on in default of any other government authorized by Congress, declined to enforce the previous order, thereby permitting civil authorities to marry anyone. This position was clarified in an official letter of H. W. Halleck, secretary of state, for Governor and Brigadier-General Bennett Riley of Aug. 13, 1849:

"The order of Governor Mason above referred to was one issued under the laws of war, and before California became a part of the territory of the United States, and it ceased to have any force on the ratification of the treaty of peace. Indeed, it was evidently intended to be only of a temporary character, and to continue only during the military occupation of the country. Neither Governor Mason, nor Governor Riley, has claimed authority to make any new laws for California since the war, that power being vested in Congress alone; and even Congress is prohibited in the Constitution from making any laws respecting an establishment of religion, or prohibiting the free exercise thereof. The Governor has, therefore, no power

marriages continued until the formal cession of California to the United States in 1848 through the Treaty of Guadalupe-Hidalgo. Thus, until the American invasion of July 1846, for a significant number of immigrants, there was no authorized Mexican official, religious or civil, to whom they could turn to solemnize their marriages.

Some of the newer arrivals turned to common law marriages. The union of Isaac Graham and Tillatha Catherine Bennett, one of the Bennett women in the later case study, is an example. Thomas Larkin, in an official letter as consul, reported to the secretary of state in January 1846 that many marriages had occurred in California between United States citizens. "Some of them have taken place by private written contracts (so said)."[61]

The term "common law marriage" does not denote an informal liaison without any pretense of a marital relationship, although there were several of such casual cohabitations of American bachelors with Indian women that are not considered herein. With the disestablishment of churches in the early nineteenth century, marriage in the United States theoretically had become a civil contract. A common law marriage existed where there was an agreement, however informal, between a man and a woman to live together and regard themselves as husband and wife. These contractual marriages were frequent in early nineteenth-century America, and most state jurisdictions recognized their validity.[62] Their legitimization was of recent origin and the employment of

---

either to enforce or to renew the order of Colonel Mason above referred to." Letter, H.W. Halleck to Fr. González Rubio, Aug. 13, 1849, in 4 ENGELHARDT, *supra*, at 604–5.

[61] Letter, Larkin to Secretary of State, Jan. 6, 1846, 4 THE LARKIN PAPERS: PERSONAL, BUSINESS, AND OFFICIAL CORRESPONDENCE OF THOMAS OLIVER LARKIN, MERCHANT AND UNITED STATES CONSUL IN CALIFORNIA 158 (Hammond ed. 1951–1968) (10 vols. & index) [hereinafter cited as LARKIN PAPERS].

[62] O. KOEGEL, COMMON LAW MARRIAGE AND ITS DEVELOPMENT IN THE UNITED STATES 79–104 (1922); M. BLOOMFIELD, AMERICAN LAWYERS IN A CHANGING SOCIETY, 1776–1876, at 106–8 (1976); L. FRIEDMAN, A HISTORY OF AMERICAN LAW 179–81 (1973). For contemporary expressions of legal approval, see e.g., Fenton v. Reed, 4 Johns. (N.Y.) 52 (1809); Hantz v. Sealy, 6 Binn. (Pa.) 405 (1814) (dictum); 2 J. KENT, COMMENTARIES ON AMERICAN LAW 87 (2d ed. 1832). Not all jurisdictions treated informal, consensual marriages as valid. For example, in Grisham v. State, 10 Tenn. 589 (1831), the court held the legislatively prescribed modes of marriage to be repugnant to and therefore invalidating of what the court presumed to be common law, and informal, marriage.

this device by the expatriates in California demonstrates a familiarity with recent developments in American law.

Marriage retained significant religious overtones notwithstanding its conversion from sacrament to contract.[63] The American overland immigrants, both those destined for California and those for Oregon, were largely devout.[64] It was probably for these reasons that most of the California expatriates did not choose common law marriage but searched instead for a legitimizing ceremony conducted before someone having at least color of authority, whether of the local jurisdiction or not.

When Thomas O. Larkin was initially appointed as United States consul in 1843, he anticipated the probability that an increasing number of American immigrants would call upon him to perform marriages. At the same time, he entertained serious doubt as to his authority to perform the rite. Accordingly he wrote the secretary of state on April 11, 1844 for clarification:

There have arrived in California several Citizens of the United States by land with their Families. I expect the number to increase yearly. . . . I look for application from some of these new Settlers to proform the ceremony of matrimony between them, and beg leave to ask from you if I can preform it legally.

Correct and prompt information on this subject is of the most importance to many young Americans who may come to California to settle and want to marry on their arrival. I speak were [where] both parties are Americans.[65]

Time passed but no instructions arrived and on August 18, 1844, Larkin again requested instructions. He analogized his situation to that of an American consul on shipboard, wherein he

[63] Chancellor Kent allowed that although the "consent of the parties is all that is required" for a valid marriage, nevertheless the participation of a clergyman is a "very becoming practice." 2 KENT, *supra* note 62, at 86–87.

[64] A leading historian of the overland trail writes that "religion played a large role in the Great Migration, for the majority of pilgrims were devout churchgoers. . . . Whether to observe the Sabbath or not was a perennial issue among the emigrants. . . . The Sabbath was observed widely on the Plains, but in most cases not with the rigidity expected by those who took the Bible literally." MATTES, *supra* note 57, at 74–75.

[65] Letter, Larkin to Secretary of State, Apr. 11, 1844, 2 LARKIN PAPERS, *supra* note 61, at 92–93.

believed a consul could validly perform marriages.[66] A full year passed with no response when Larkin, no doubt yielding to the pressures of an extreme case, married one couple from Missouri on August 24, 1845.[67] His defensiveness over his authority is revealed by his tardiness in informing the State Department of his action, doing so more than four months later by a letter in which he mentioned that during the nuptial rites he had flown the American flag outside the consular house, doubtless for an aura of greater solemnity. For good measure, he reminded the secretary that he had "repeatedly asked for information from the Department on these subjects."[68]

The eventual reply by the secretary of state to Larkin's queries must have been a double surprise, first that it came at all, by letter dated July 14, 1846, more than two years from the original request, and second in its content. Relying on the writings of the great American legal commentator, Chancellor Kent, the secretary informed Larkin that there "is no law in existence which authorises Consuls of the United States to perform the marriage ceremony. The contract of matrimony is local in its nature and the manner in which it shall be entered into is regulated by the laws of the place."[69] Larkin had requested information about his

[66] Letter, Larkin to Secretary of State, Aug. 18, 1844, *id.* at 206: "The undersigned would again call the attention of his Government to the marriages that are taking place among American and English emigrants in California who have come here by land from the U.S. . . . As our countrymen are flocking into California from home more of these marriages may take place which among families of property in the future generations may cause perplexities before unknown to our laws. It has been allowed that consuls can perform the ceremony of marriage between their countrymen in any port of the world if on board an American ship, as the ship in the harbour is as much under the jurisdiction of the U.S. as the City of Washington. It is therefore of much importance to many Americans in California and will be of more to their children to know if they can be married in their consular house."

[67] Letter, Larkin to Moses Yale Beach, Sept. 30, 1845, 3 LARKIN PAPERS, *supra* note 61, at 372.

[68] Letter, Larkin to Secretary of State, Jan. 6, 1846, 4 LARKIN PAPERS, *supra* note 61, at 158.

[69] Letter, Secretary of State to Larkin, July 14, 1846, 5 LARKIN PAPERS, *supra* note 61, at 135. American consuls were empowered to perform marriages by Act of June 22, 1860, Pub. L. No. 36–179, § 31, 12 Stat. 72. Under church law applicable to Mexico, consular marriages were invalid. Baade, *supra* note 59, at 61–62, 84.

authority to act inside the consular house and had assumed that a consul on an American ship would have matrimonial powers. The response, going beyond what was sought, to the effect that consuls had no authority to perform marriages, with no exceptions indicated, must have startled Larkin. His own marriage in 1833 was performed by John Coffin Jones, consular agent to the Sandwich Islands (Hawaii) on board an American ship within the roadstead of Santa Barbara, California.[70]

Larkin's counterpart, James Alexander Forbes, the British vice-consul, was also solemnizing at least a few marriages. By uniting Protestants and Catholics, however, he invoked the ire of the California bishop, García Diego, who vigorously protested to Governor Pio Pico, that consular authorities

cannot, without violating ecclesiastical and civil laws, authorize marriages between a Catholic and a Protestant. Even if the Catholic party be a non-resident, he remains bound by church law. . . . For this reason, I strongly urge you to take action so that in the future, none of the consuls or vice-consuls in this area will dare to perform a marriage between . . . a Protestant and a Catholic. . . .

Although two Protestants may validly marry before the consul of their nation, and though such a union can be authorized aboard one of his ships even that should be done privately.[71]

Although the native Californio alcaldes would not perform marriages, one alcalde, simply by force of will, enlarged his jurisdiction and assumed such powers. John Sutter founded his nearly feudal fiefdom in the interior valley in 1839 and, without any apparent thought or concern over its legality, began to marry those who requested his services.[72] His establishment, an armed fort surrounded by various ranching, farming, and other economic

[70] 4 BANCROFT, HISTORY OF CALIFORNIA *supra* note 60, at 706.

[71] Letter, Bishop García Diego to Governor Pio Pico, Jan. 9, 1846, GARCÍA DIEGO, *supra* note 5, at 183–84.

[72] Sutter dictated his reminiscences for the historian Hubert Howe Bancroft in 1876. He said he was performing marriages as early as 1842. Portions of his reminiscences are quoted in the introduction to the published *New Helvetia Diary*, a diary of occurrences at Sutter's Fort, September 1845–December 1846 and May 1847–May 1848. For the portion of Sutter's reminiscences relevant to marriage, see J. SUTTER, NEW HELVETIA DIARY xi (1939). A contemporary American observer confirmed that Sutter was performing marriages as early as 1841. C. WILKES, NARRATIVE OF THE UNITED STATES EXPLORING EXPEDITION DURING THE YEARS 1838, 1839, 1840, 1841, 1842, at 178 (1856).

operations, was in the direct path of the overland trail from the East. His matrimonial offices were eagerly sought by incoming immigrants, as well as by Americans already in the employ of his various enterprises. For example, during the four months from December 1845 through March 1846, an active period, a total of seven marriages were performed at Sutter's Fort, apparently all involving Americans.[73]

In many letters written by the American consul to the State Department, Larkin reported Sutter's activities involving the marriage of Americans and gave his opinion that such marriages were invalid because violative of Mexican law, which he understood permitted only priests to validly perform marriages.[74] Larkin was increasingly disturbed by Sutter's actions because some of the couples he had united thereafter separated and were casting doubts on the validity of the marriages. Further, he was concerned about future disputes between a putative spouse or children of such marriages and persons who would otherwise be heirs of a decedent. Larkin wrote directly to Sutter on January 20, 1846, outlining his views and the difficulties the marriages might entail.[75] Sutter, however, was not moved by pressure from either the American consul or California authorities. As a native of Switzerland and a naturalized citizen of Mexico, his armaments, together with his considerable distance from the settled areas of California, gave him virtual immunity from local governmental control. He continued marrying all who presented themselves.

More controversy developed when he began marrying couples of which one party was Catholic. Bishop García Diego learned of these developments at the end of 1845. Padre Real had separated two such couples, married by Sutter, who had moved to the Santa Clara area; they were eventually required to remarry in the church. The bishop requested the governor to "reprimand and punish severely the insolence of Sutter, who as a subject of the Mexican Republic and within her territory, exercises only that authority derived from governmental or military sources."[76] The reply from Governor Pio Pico is interesting in that it expresses

<hr>

[73] SUTTER, *supra* note 72.

[74] See *supra* notes 65, 66, and 68, and accompanying text.

[75] Letter, Larkin to Sutter, Jan. 20, 1846, 4 LARKIN PAPERS, *supra* note 61, at 168.

[76] Letter, Bishop García Diego to Governor Pio Pico, Jan. 9, 1846, GARCÍA

surprise at the illegal marriages of "persons of a different religion."[77] No objection was made by the governor regarding Sutter's lack of authority as alcalde or justice of the peace to perform marriages at all.

On the eve of the American conquest, a pattern was beginning to emerge regarding marriages of American expatriates. Some simply engaged in consensual common law marriages, a practice that was generally a valid alternative to formal ceremonial marriage in the communities from which they came. Most, however, favored a stronger, more legitimizing ceremony, and in the absence of Protestant ministers a few sought the services of the American consul. Yet most were content with the alcalde. The only clearly articulated objection of the government was centered around the church's concern for its exclusive authority where either party was Catholic. Even before the American invasion several older American and British residents had become local alcaldes. A two-tier pattern, alcaldes having authority to marry where both parties were non-Catholics and the church having exclusive jurisdiction where either party was Catholic, was forming in Mexican California before the American conquest established it as official policy.[78]

The procedures for judicial separation in Mexican California had little attraction for American women who desired to separate from their husbands. Not only was the process slow and cumbersome, but American women took umbrage at being ordered about summarily by the alcaldes and being confined in a safe house. One young American immigrant, Susan Biggerton, was abandoned by her stepfather upon their arrival in California. She mar-

---

DIEGO, *supra* note 5, at 183. The justice of the peace in Sonoma also complained to the prefect of the Northern District that Sutter's matrimonial activities were "against the institutes of our religion and against the articles of the laws of the Mexican nation," 1 Manuel Castro, *Documentos para la historia de California,* Document nos. 225–26 (2 vols.). The Castro *Documentos* are on file with the Bancroft Library, University of California, Berkeley, California.

[77] Letter, Governor Pio Pico to Bishop García Diego, Feb. 13, 1846, quoted in 4 ENGELHARDT, *supra* note 58, at 415–16 n. 9.

[78] Former Governor Juan Bautista Alvarado (1836 to 1842) later criticized Sutter's activities on the basis that he was performing marriages at all, not just that he was marrying mixed couples. 4 Alvarado, *Historia de California,* ch. 38, on file with the Bancroft Library, University of California, Berkeley, California. For a discussion of the alcaldes' role after the American conquest, see note 60, *supra* .

ried William Lewis, an Englishman, at Sutter's Fort, apparently in reliance upon her suitor's representations that he was wealthy and had a good farm and many cattle in Yerba Buena (San Francisco). After a short while the couple traveled to Yerba Buena, where she discovered that he was in fact impoverished and that his inducements were all false. She immediately left him and stayed temporarily with an American couple.

Unfortunately, Lewis was not willing to give her up and enlisted the aid of the local alcalde to institute proceedings to compel her return. Following customary California procedure, the alcalde sought to place the wife in a safe house pending his investigation into the status of the marriage. In a manner that was obviously resented by the young woman, the alcalde and another man, an Englishman and owner of the house where the husband was boarding, "came and told me I must leave the house I am now in and go to one they may think fit to find me, and if I do not go to morrow they will take me by force."[79] Writing to William Leidesdorff, the American vice-consul stationed in Yerba Buena, she begged to

ask your interference, and wish to know what I have committed that I am to reside where those people think fit to Send me, and being a perfect Stranger in this place and having a great dislike to the idea of living in a Spanish house as a Prisoner I hope you will advise me and assist me with your Protection.[80]

[79] Letter, Susan Biggerton to Larkin, Dec. 31, 1845, 4 LARKIN PAPERS, *supra* note 61, at 136.

[80] *Id.* Apparently they had been married by Sutter on December 21, 1845, just some seven or eight days before the separation. An entry in the *New Helvetia Diary* for that date records: "Wm Lewis and Miss [no name indicated] were married." SUTTER, *supra* note 72. It is not clear how the matter was resolved. But see note 87 *infra.* The vice-consul immediately wrote the alcalde's administrative supervisor, the prefect, pointing out the circumstances, suggesting that the young lady would be more comfortable staying with Americans since she spoke no Spanish, and offering to be responsible for her appearance at any court proceedings. The prefect responded the next day, somewhat officiously stating that everyone in California ought to be aware of and respect the local laws. The close of the letter was "God and the Law," rather than the usual Mexican valediction, "God and Liberty." Letters, Leidesdorff to Francisco Guerrero y Palomares, and Guerrero y Palomares to Leidesdorff, Jan. 1, 1846 (misdated 1845 in MS) and Jan. 2, 1846, 4 LARKIN PAPERS, *supra* note 61, at 148–49. The consul himself offered no help. Larkin merely bemoaned still another example of the evil consequences of Sutter's nuptial activities and cautioned his subordinate Leidesdorff that he could "be

Because American women would not willingly follow the California procedure, separations of Americans were generally informal, with requests for intervention from the local authorities being limited to protection from harassment and breach of the peace. Not all expatriate couples desiring to separate had that alone in mind. Some wished to marry other partners and sought a divorce absolute. As yet, divorce laws had not formed a clear pattern in the United States. Although there was a trend toward judicially granted divorces under general statutes requiring findings of fault or grounds, a number of states still limited divorce to legislative bills, rarely passed, and then only on an individual basis.[81] A desire for divorce absolute presented a real problem to the American and British expatriates because neither the legislative body nor the courts of Catholic California could grant such a decree. Indeed, even after the American invasion, the alcaldes, still operating under Mexican law, could not grant actual divorces, although they began doing so in the period following the formal cession of California in 1848 and before the institution of state government.[82]

---

at no Government expence in regard to the Woman who you have boarded out." Letter, Larkin to Leidesdorff, Jan. 20, 1846, *id.*, at 170–71.

[81] FRIEDMAN, *supra* note 62, at 181–84.

[82] Before the 1848 cession of California, on December 8, 1847, the military governor, Colonel Mason, wrote that neither he nor the alcaldes had power to grant a divorce. Letter, Mason to Hetty C. Brown, Dec. 8, 1847, H. BANCROFT, CALIFORNIA PASTORAL 314 (1888); 6 BANCROFT, HISTORY OF CALIFORNIA, *supra* note 60, at 268 n.31 (1888). The California Constitution of 1849, adopted in October 1849, provided that "no contract of marriage, if otherwise duly made, shall be invalidated for want of conformity to the requirements of any religious sect." CAL. CONST. art. XI, § 12 (1849). Although an early act of the First Legislature declared marriage a civil contract (Laws 1850, c. 140, effective Apr. 22, 1850), no statute of divorce was enacted until the following year (Laws 1851, c. 20, effective Mar. 25, 1851). The alcaldes, acting as courts of the first instance, had begun granting divorces, while operating under Mexican law, but apparently after the formal cession of California in 1848 by the Treaty of Guadalupe-Hidalgo. This practice was subsequently approved by the California Supreme Court:

"By the Mexican law . . . marriage lawfully contracted in the face of the Catholic church . . . is elevated to the rank of a sacrament and cannot be dissolved by the civil tribunals. On the other hand, the union of a man and woman, in the character of husband and wife, without the sanction of the church, when both of them belong to the class of the *unfaithful,* is considered as a *mere civil contract.* . . .

"There is nothing in this case showing that either of the parties belonged to the privileged class of the *faithful,* or that their nuptials were celebrated with the rites

Larkin declined to grant divorces. In the fall of 1844 a young immigrant wife, Rebecca Fowler, separated from her husband, William. The husband wrote Larkin a long letter asking for his help, declaring he had done nothing to harm his wife, that she had been enticed away by an evil sister, and that he desired a reconciliation. Larkin wrote kind letters to both, urging each to be circumspect in their conduct and to treat the other with kindness and affection.[83] It was to no avail. The husband next wrote Larkin on February 12, 1845, asking whether as consul he could grant a divorce, and if so, to please do so as he wished to return to the United States in the spring. Undoubtedly aware of the growing requirement of grounds for divorce, Fowler again emphasized his own good behavior, asserting that it was solely his wife's conduct that had led to the separation. Larkin responded that he could be of no assistance. Divorce, he explained, was within the province of the separate states, each of which had different procedures and different grounds. From the correspondence "and from hearsay" he doubted there were grounds sufficient for any jurisdiction, but he suggested that Mrs. Fowler might prepare a detailed affidavit as to why the divorce was needed. If the husband were to return to the East, perhaps he could obtain a divorce with the aid of such an affidavit.[84]

Therefore, in Mexican California there was no agency of the Mexican government nor any official of the American government from whom the immigrants could obtain an absolute divorce that would permit them to remarry. Consistent with the prevailing American viewpoint of marriage as a civil contract,[85]

of the Catholic church. Their union, therefore, not having attained the sanctity of a sacrament, should be regarded as a civil contract, and as such, like other contracts, it comes within the legitimate sphere of the ordinary jurisdiction of courts of First Instance."
Harman v. Harman, 1 Cal. 215, 215–16 (1850) (emphasis in original).

[83] Letters, William Fowler to Larkin, Dec. 4, 1844; Larkin to William Fowler, Dec. 24, 1844; Larkin to Rebecca Fowler, Dec. 24, 1844, 2 LARKIN PAPERS, *supra* note 61, at 305–6, 334–36.

[84] Letters, William Fowler to Larkin, Feb. 12, 1845; Larkin to William Fowler, Mar. 16, 1845, 3 LARKIN PAPERS, *supra* note 61, at 39–40,68–69.

[85] "It [marriage] is a mere civil contract. . . . Its form and execution are subjects of civil laws and usages; and religion has no legitimate concern with it, except to prescribe and enforce its duties," Londonderry v. Chester, 2 N.H. 268, 278 (1820). Many cases throughout the early nineteenth century referred to marriages as contracts. *See, e.g.,* Putnam v. Putnam, 25 Mass. (8 Pick.) 433 (1829);

the immigrants might have formed groups of arbitrators, appointed among themselves, to determine and declare marital dissolution and division of property. Expatriates on occasion did do this when local courts were nonexistent or inadequate,[86] but there is no evidence the Anglo-Americans took this step in California. An alternative course of action was available to the courageous among the expatriates. Again consistent with their transplanted notions of marriage as a civil contract, they could simply *rescind* that contract, a step they could not have taken in their own jurisdictions but which is naively consistent with an understanding that marriage is a contract. Some American expatriates did take this step, and several examples are appended in a note,[87] illustrat-

---

Inhabitants of West Cambridge v. Inhabitants of Lexington, 18 Mass. (1 Pick.) 506 (1823); Burtis v. Burtis, 1 Hopk. Ch. (N.Y.) 557 (1825).

[86] An American traveler noted this interesting phenomenon in Tahiti in his diary entry of February 12, 1839: "Yesterday there was a meeting of a number of the foreigners here who constituted themselves judges in a case of crim con, and they decided that the proof against the wife was good and sufficient and consequently that Capt. Wm. Henry should be considered as divorced." F. ATHERTON, THE CALIFORNIA DIARY OF FAXON DEAN ATHERTON, 1836–1839, at 130 (1964). "Crim con" refers to criminal conversation, the tortious aspect of adultery.

Another occurrence failed to materialize. Apparently Sutter did not grant any divorces, or at least there is no record of such an occurrence. In fact, his diary notes only one separation, that of Sebastian Keyser, which lasted from July 25, 1847 to September 6, 1847. SUTTER, *supra* note 72. Probably Sutter would have regarded divorce as beyond his powers as a Mexican alcalde. The Fowler couple who so much desired a divorce, *supra* notes 83 and 84 and accompanying text, resided at Sutter's Fort (New Helvetia) while they wrote Larkin for his aid. They are not mentioned in Sutter's diary as requesting a divorce. Perhaps the couple had informally asked Sutter for a divorce and were turned down.

[87] The Fowler couple, referred to *supra* notes 83, 84, and 86 and accompanying text, considered themselves divorced after learning that Larkin could not aid them. With his letter to Larkin of February 12, 1845, Fowler had enclosed a certificate of his wife, of same date, in part as follows: "This is to certify that I Rebecca Fowler, the lawful wife of William Fowler, have by my own free act left his "bed and board", and do not consider myself longer under his care and protection and do not longer acknowledge his control over me as a husband." Although the certificate went on to recite a consent to a "legal divorce" to dissolve "the contract of Marriage which at this time exists between us," the couple later acted as though the certificate was sufficient. Letter, Rebecca Fowler to Larkin, Feb. 12, 1845, 3 LARKIN PAPERS, *supra* note 61, at 40–41. Rebecca took her maiden name of Kelsey and on December 28, 1845 was married by Sutter to another immigrant, Grove C. Cook. SUTTER, *supra* note 72; H. BANCROFT, CALIFORNIA PIONEER REGISTER AND INDEX, 1542–1848, at 206 (extracted from HISTORY OF CALIFORNIA) (1964). In December 1846, John H. Brown, an Englishman, married Hetty C. Pell.

ing the capacity of these immigrants creatively to apply, albeit erroneously, the concepts of law remembered from home.

Many of these generalizations concerning expatriate domestic relations law may be illustrated by a detailed examination of two American women, Mary Bennett and her daughter, Tillatha, usually referred to by her middle name of Catherine. The Bennett family had been living in Yerba Buena, soon to be renamed San Francisco, for a little more than two years when, in June of 1845, Mary Bennett separated from her husband, Vardamon, taking her large flock of children with her.[88]

The doing of this required considerable courage. Illiterate in her native English tongue, there is no evidence that Mary had even a speaking command of Spanish. She was an alien living in a foreign land, separated from her own family in Georgia by thousands of miles in distance and months of time in travel, and living in a society and culture that condemned not only divorce and separation in particular, but feminine independence in general. With her were four children who were still young: Samantha, five; Julia, seven; Mansel, nine; and Mary Ann or Amanda, fourteen. One older son, Winston, had already gone out on his own, but three other children remained at home who were old enough to be of real help: Catherine, twenty-one; Dennis, twenty; and Jack, eighteen.[89]

They soon separated, and in April 1847 he advertised the fact of her leaving in a San Francisco newspaper. Regarding this as sufficient, he remarried. *Id.* at 72–73. She desired the divorce as well and, in fact, was the woman to whom Governor Mason had written that he had no power to grant divorces, *supra* note 82. Apparently she also quickly remarried. *Id.* at 279. Susan Biggerton has been discussed before as the young lady who was fraudulently induced to marry William Lewis. *See supra* notes 79 and 80 and accompanying text. Apparently she decided the fraud was sufficient that she could unilaterally rescind the marriage contract, as she was probably the same Mrs. Lewis who was married by Sutter to Perry McCoon on February 5, 1846, just one month following her difficulty with the alcalde of Yerba Buena. SUTTER, *supra* note 72. Unfortunately, she died four months later. Identification of Mrs. Lewis as the former Susan Biggerton is not certain, but is the most probable after examination of other candidates. *See* BANCROFT, CALIFORNIA PIONEER REGISTER . . . , *supra,* at 220–21.

[88] The Bennett family moved from Arkansas to Oregon in 1842 and in the following year moved to Sutter's fort. Later, in December of 1843, they moved to Yerba Buena. San Jose Pioneer, May 26, 1877, at 1. These are memoirs written by the eldest son of the Bennett family, Winston, and continued in a second installment, published June 2, 1877.

[89] Ages are approximated, and for the younger children are based on ages re-

As was usual with American expatriates in marital trouble, Mary Bennett declined to seek the aid of the local alcalde to formalize her separation or to seek a support order. Instead, she looked about for a realistic means of supporting herself, selecting the area surrounding the former Mission Santa Clara as a suitable location. She made inquiry of the priest in charge to see if she and her family might be allowed to live in one of the mission buildings and if he might be disposed to recommend to the government that she be granted a parcel of land out of the mission's former holdings. In this approach she was aided by a Californio woman, Silvelia Pacheco de Cole, who was sympathetic to Mary's plight. She simply "went to the priest—the curate of the mission, and told him that Mrs. Bennett wanted a piece of land there, and he told me that he would give her a piece of land anywhere that she wanted it."[90] This simple request began the procedures that led to an eventual formal land grant. It was the usual practice that land grants were made to males, but other women did on occasion receive land in their own names from the Mexican government in California.[91]

Armed with this promise from the priest, Mrs. Bennett was now ready to formalize her desire for separation. She traveled to the capital, Monterey, and appeared before the American consul. She presented the following petition, undoubtedly drafted by Larkin himself after his conference with her. Dated June 6, 1845 it was signed by her mark and declared:

Your Petitioner Mary Bennett a native of Georgia in the United States of America would represent to you as Consul of her country

----

ported in the 1850 United States Census. A. BOWMAN, INDEX TO THE 1850 CENSUS OF THE STATE OF CALIFORNIA 438 (1972). For Dennis and Jack, ages are based upon the San Francisco *padrón*, or census, of 1844, cited in 2 BANCROFT, *supra* note 60, at 716. For Catherine's 1824 birthdate *see* Santa Cruz Riptide, Oct. 19, 1950, at 42, cols. 1–2.

[90] Deposition of Silvelia Pacheco de Cole. Records (N.D. Cal.), Land Case No. 361, Mary S. Bennett, Claimant, on file with the Bancroft Library, University of California, Berkeley, California.

[91] Women even received grants of ranchos. There were approximately seven hundred Mexican private land grants. A cursory look at a list of grantees indicates approximately thirty feminine names. R. COWAN, RANCHOS OF CALIFORNIA: A LIST OF SPANISH CONCESSIONS 1775–1822 AND MEXICAN GRANTS 1822–1846, at 115–23 (1977). Of course, all married women would have a community property interest in their husbands' grants but without rights of management.

that she has for one year or more been living in California with a family of eight children and that her Husband Vardamon Bennett the Father of said children has entirely neglected her and Family, refuses to support and maintain them, and takes from them by force their daily earnings and even their clothes leaving her and said children destitute of living.

Your petitioner therefore begs of you to take some measures, that she may be protected from her husband in her person and the persons of her children that she may be enabled to live separate from said Vardamon Bennett and support herself and family free from molestation on his part relieving her said Husband from all care charge or protection hereafter of herself and children.

Your petitioner requests further of you that you would represent her case to the Alcalde of the Pueblo of Sn. Jose and Santa Clara that he may take the proper measures for her protection from he[r] Husband as she is in fear of her person and life from words and threats that he continually uses toward her.[92]

It is difficult to speculate about Mary's real motives for the separation. It was not, however, her husband's improvidence or rough treatment, and certainly not that she was "in fear of her person and life." Mary Bennett was six feet in height and grossly obese. She was described by one observer who saw her in 1846 as having "amazonian proportions."[93] Mary thoroughly enjoyed a fracas and engaged in many physical fights.[94] An American merchant re-

[92] Petition of Mary Bennett, June 6, 1845, 3 LARKIN PAPERS, *supra* note 61, at 223–24.

[93] E. BRYANT, WHAT I SAW IN CALIFORNIA 298 (1936) (1st ed. Philadelphia 1848).

[94] Three examples include: (a) She was the instigator of a nearly riotous water fight in Yerba Buena in 1843. W. DAVIS, SEVENTY-FIVE YEARS IN CALIFORNIA 197 (1929) (1st ed. as SIXTY YEARS IN CALIFORNIA (San Francisco 1889)); (b) There was a minor skirmish outside the Santa Clara Mission during a brief insurrection that followed the American invasion in 1846. On that occasion Mary Bennett was closely observed by a female American immigrant and seemed anxious to take part in the fight: "She waltzed back and forth in front of the Mission yelling orders to the men at the top of her voice. Growing more excited she ran forward and grabbing up a large bone lying in the yard, rushed up to a man who had refused to fight, saying that he had no gun. Stopping squarely in front of the startled fellow, she thrust the bone into his hands and shouted "take that, you puppy, and go out there and bat the brains out of some Mexican or I'll use it on you." HECOX, *supra* note 58, at 54; and (c) On another earlier occasion, in 1842, Mrs. Bennett personally participated in repelling an Indian raid on the group with which the family traveled to California from Oregon. Her son noticed his mother "in the thickest of the fight. She said she couldn't stand it to be under shelter while her boys were out liable to be killed." Bennett (Winston), *supra* note 88.

siding in Yerba Buena contemporaneously with the Bennetts knew the family and succinctly described Mary as "unmistakably the head of the family,—a large, powerful woman, uncultivated, but well-meaning and very industrious. Her word was law, and her husband stood in becoming awe of her."[95] It cannot be that the earnings and clothes of such a woman were stolen by such a husband.

If the petition were counterfactual, these baseless allegations should be seen as Larkin's ideas (or perhaps Mary Bennett's) of "grounds" for a separation or divorce. As such it reflected an awareness of the then-growing trend in American law of divorce legislation of general applicability based on fault, or legally recognized grounds, a trend that was a compromise between conflicting positions favoring either sparsely granted legislative bills of divorce, or, alternatively, freely available divorce based on mere consent.[96] The allegations of fault in the petition were also a means of legitimizing her status as separated, as well as a practical device that would allow Larkin to request protection on her behalf from the local authorities.

That same day Larkin wrote the alcalde of San Jose, whose jurisdiction included the Santa Clara Mission, only a few miles distant.[97] He recited the allegation that Vardamon Bennett had refused to support his family for more than a year and advised that Mrs. Bennett wished to separate and live within the alcalde's jurisdiction in order that "she may be enabled to maintain herself and children, which she says she can not do while her Husband is allowed to molist and deprive her of her earnings." He closed with a request for the alcalde's cooperation, anticipating the possibility that the husband might harass the wife or cause a disturbance. Officially invoking the protection of local authorities for American citizens, Larkin asked that if necessary, the judge might "see that Justice is administated towards the parties."[98]

[95] DAVIS, *supra* note 94, at 195.

[96] FRIEDMAN, *supra* note 62, at 184.

[97] Of course, the alcalde had no jurisdiction over the church activities or property. After the missions were secularized in the mid-1830s and stripped of most of their lands, small settlements grew up around the missions. The civil authorities had full jurisdiction over these small towns.

[98] Letter, Larkin to Antonio María Pico, June 6, 1845, 3 LARKIN PAPERS, *supra* note 61, at 225–26.

The separation was not to be peaceable. Acting in a manner familiar to every divorce attorney, both Vardamon and Mary immediately attempted to lay hands on all liquid or moveable assets and to harass the other through the manipulation of their children. In one particular instance, Vardamon precipitously took seven horses that were in the care of the emancipated 23-year-old son, Winston. When Mary sought out Larkin, she brought Winston with her for the purpose of filing his own petition alleging the theft by force of his horses by his own father. On the same date of Mary's petition, June 6, 1845, Larkin wrote to the alcalde of Yerba Buena asking the judge to investigate and adjudicate the alleged theft of the horses.[99] The results of the investigation, as well as what is known of Mary's character, clearly show the overreaching nature of her representations to Larkin.

When the Yerba Buena alcalde summoned both father and son together, Winston testified that the horses had been given to him by his father but admitted that the purpose was for the "service and common benefit of the family." The alcalde determined and reported to Larkin that not only was the violent stealing of the horses falsely imputed to Vardamon, but so also "the rest that is asserted in your writing with respect to his ignoring of his obligations to his family." Reasoning that since the gift of the horses was for the maintenance of the family, the alcalde determined that Vardamon had the right to revoke and invalidate the gift in light of the scandalous gossip and "in view of the reproachable conduct with which his wife and children have conducted themselves (as is public and notorious) and as his ungrateful sons have abandoned him." Referring to the entire Bennett matter as one of the most scandalous happenings of Yerba Buena, the alcalde concluded that Vardamon Bennett's reclamation of the horses was proper and that "they remain taken by right."[100] As a whole, the decision reflects a blend of an overstatement of facts by Mary and Winston, mixed with a cultural reaction to Mary's antics and forcefulness.

That Winston, on reflection, must have felt himself his mother's pawn in the parental battle is suggested by the total silence of his

[99] Letter, Larkin to Alcalde of Yerba Buena, June 6, 1845, *id.* at 226.
[100] Letter, Second Alcalde of Yerba Buena to Larkin, May 12, 1845 (error in MS, probably June 12, 1845), *id.* at 182–83.

memoirs concerning this affair.[101] Vardamon soon made a coun-
terattack upon Mary through his efforts to obtain custody of the
children, a process initiated by his own application to the American consul. Larkin once again wrote the Yerba Buena alcalde, in
an apparent oversight of the earlier events and his own letters
of the same month. His letter accurately reflected the general
American law of the early nineteenth century, which recognized
fathers as the primary custodians of minor legitimate children.[102]
On June 25, 1845 he wrote the Yerba Buena judge that:

> Mr. Bennet[t] a Citizen of the United States has applyed to me for
> advice respecting his taking charge of his own children in preference
> to their being with their Mother.
> I have only to say, that by the Laws of the United States, I consider
> that the Father of minor children should have the care of them when
> there is no dispute, but he is willing and able to provide for them in a
> proper manner.[103]

At this remove one can only imagine the threats and inducements being offered by both Mary and Vardamon to their children
and of the slurs made upon the other party. Children often react
strongly to such pressures and by midsummer of 1845 the oldest
girl, Catherine, was alienated from both her mother and father.
To escape from her parents she was to enter into a relationship
with Isaac Graham, the obstreperous mountain man described
earlier. In 1845 he was long-returned from his exile to mainland Mexico and was living on his ranch in the mountains near
Santa Cruz.

Within five years Catherine's relationship with Graham was to

---

[101] Bennett (Winston), *supra* note 88.

[102] Of course, the father's rights were not regarded as absolute. A fair statement
of the generally prevailing law is that "in the absence of any positive disqualification on the part of the father, for the proper discharge of his parental duties, and
when there is no other special reason, touching the welfare of the children, for
preferring the mother, the father has a paramount right to the custody, which no
court is at liberty to disregard." Mercein v. People *ex rel.* Barry, 25 Wend. (N.Y.)
64, 73 (1840). *Accord,* United States v. Green, 26 F. Cas. 30 (C.C.D.R.I. 1824)
(No. 15,256). For a more detailed analysis of the American law regarding child
custody in the nineteenth century, see Zainaldin, *The Emergence of a Modern
American Family Law: Child Custody, Adoption, and the Courts, 1796–1851,*
73 NW. U. L. REV. 1038 (1979).

[103] Letter, Larkin to Alcalde of Yerba Buena, June 25, 1845, 3 LARKIN PAPERS,
supra note 61, at 248.

end in tragedy. Its beginnings, however, can be seen in a mid-July letter to Larkin from an American overland immigrant, Julius Martin, who was living with his family in Santa Cruz:

> I have one of old man Bennetts daughters aliving with me and I shall go back to Gilroys Ranch Ranch [sic] next weeke and have no house sutable for company and she wishes to come to Montarey and live with your wife for a short time as she is determined never to live with her Farther nor mother any more. You will find her a very industrious girle for bisness. If she can come let me know by letter the first oppotunity and I will come in with her and if not I must looch out a place for her unttill I moove on the other side of the Bay or become more settled some wheare. I remain yours Ob.[104]

There is no evidence of a reply. Perhaps Larkin feared a crossfire from the Bennetts, or perhaps events with Catherine simply unfolded too fast for Larkin's good offices. Perhaps also she did live temporarily with the Larkins.[105] In any event, Catherine was disgusted with her parents, restless, twenty-one, and ready to make her move. Undoubtedly she was in contact with her older brother Winston, the one Bennett child who was emancipated and living apart from both parents. Since early 1845, Winston had been employed on Graham's Zayante Rancho near Felton, California, in the Santa Cruz Mountains and not far from where Catherine was temporarily staying with the Martin couple. Winston was to remain at Zayante until the fall, sowing and harvesting a crop of grain,[106] and it was probably in late July 1845 that he introduced his sister Catherine to his employer, Isaac Graham.

The beginnings of the Graham romance can be dated rather accurately since the July 11 letter from Martin to Larkin recited Catherine's desire to live with the Larkins in Monterey. Obviously she was not yet involved with Graham. Only three weeks later she was.[107] By September, Catherine and Graham were living to-

---

[104] Letter, Julius Martin to Larkin, July 11, 1845, *id.* at 268.

[105] Catherine Bennett was one of the witnesses to the wedding Larkin performed on August 24, 1845. There is no indication of where she was living, but obviously on that date she was in Monterey and with Larkin. Consular Records of Thomas Oliver Larkin, at 12. These records were formerly on deposit with the Monterey County Recorder's Office, Salinas, California, and are believed to be among those transferred to the Monterey County Historical Society, Salinas, California.

[106] Bennett (Winston), *supra* note 88.

[107] On August 2 and 3, 1845, Graham had a house guest named James Clyman,

gether in a common law marriage. In doing so they were following a pattern of marriage then common to Americans back east in the United States. Interestingly, they did not simply enter into a consensual relationship by agreement but attempted to solemnize their status by a reading of the marriage ceremony, the essential facts of which were then recited by the following simple document, witnessed by two loggers and ranchmen of the Santa Cruz Mountains:

> Marriage in the year 1845. Isaac Graham, of Santa Cruz, and Catharine Bennet[t], of San Francisco, were married at Lyant [Zayante], by banns, this 26th day of September, in the year of 1845, by one who was requested to read the ceremony, Henry Ford. This marriage was solemnized between us, Isaac Graham, Catharine Bennet[t]. In the presence of William Wern, Henry Ford.[108]

The news was soon to reach Catherine's mother Mary, and anger at Vardamon was at least partially replaced with outrage at such an improper affair. Again, the long-suffering American consul was pressed into service, and by November Larkin had written to the Santa Cruz justice of the peace, José Antonio Bolcoff.

---

an old fur trapper and mountain man who had recently guided a party from Oregon. Clyman, one of the few mountain men who was literate, kept a daily diary. For those two days he recorded, in a style reminiscent of James Fenimore Cooper, that "if report be correct the hardy vetrian is fast softning down and he is about to cast away the deathly rifle and the unerring tomahawk for the soft smiles of a female companion to nurrish him in his old age." J. CLYMAN, JOURNAL OF A MOUNTAIN MAN 205 (1984). This is the most recent edition, but the Clyman diaries have appeared in other editions as well. Clyman's comment may have been self-consciously imitative of Cooper. Clyman was a remarkable man and was everything most mountain men were not—educated, literate, and with a refined mind.

[108]Quoted in Graham v. Bennet[t], 2 Cal. 503 (1852). This case is but one of the many lawsuits to subsequently arise between Isaac and Catherine. See *infra* notes 113 and 114 and accompanying text. In this case Catherine sought damages from Graham for assault and the abduction of their children, following her own previous removal of them to Oregon. This placed in issue the question of whether the children were legitimate. The court held that they were, even though the marriage itself was void because Graham had a wife still living in Tennessee. In dicta the court suggested that had there been no such disability, the marriage would have been valid. See *infra* note 110. Non-Catholic Americans in Spanish Florida also contracted marriages by asking friends and neighbors to act as witnesses to informal ceremonies. Curley, *Church and State in the Spanish Floridas (1783–1822),* 30 CATH. HIST. STUDIES 224 (1940).

Again Larkin's letter is interesting as a reflection of his layman's understanding of law. Although as a young man he had briefly served as a justice of the peace, he had received no formal legal training and his most extensive practical experience in legal matters was as a merchant dealing with commercial law and in his role as consul. Even in that latter role, however, Larkin's consular activity primarily involved seamen and admiralty matters and his experience in domestic matters was limited.[109] Yet he grasped the sophisticated legal point that the validity of the Graham marriage was not to be judged by whether a common law marriage would be valid if contracted in the United States. Rather, its invalidity in the United States would result because of its invalidity under the Mexican law of California, the place where it was performed.[110] In other words, American law would look to the law of the place where the marriage was celebrated in order to determine the marriage's validity. Larkin wrote the Santa Cruz judge:

I am informed that Mr Isaac Graham and Catherine Bennett both citizens of the United States of North America are living together as married people, without being legally married, and as this cannot be

[109] For an examination of Larkin's consular practice, see Kelsey, *The United States Consulate in California,* 1 PUBLICATIONS OF THE ACADEMY OF PACIFIC COAST HISTORY 161 (1910). Originally from Massachusetts, Larkin had lived for several years in North Carolina. There, he was appointed to serve as a local justice of the peace. Nonetheless, it does not appear he had received any legal training or had handled problems of choice of law. *See generally* T. LARKIN, CHAPTERS IN THE EARLY LIFE OF THOMAS OLIVER LARKIN (Parker ed. 1939).

[110] This is not inconsistent with Larkin's hope that he might be authorized to marry Americans within the consulate house, because his rationale for authority for those marriages was that the consular house was an extraterritorial extension of American soil. See *supra* note 66 and accompanying text. The California Supreme Court later suggested in dicta that this common law marriage would have been valid but for Graham's first wife being still alive. It did so with no discussion of that fact that it was contracted before the American invasion, long before the Mexican cession, and while California was indisputably under Mexican law:

"Marriage is regarded as a civil contract, and no form is necessary for its solemnization. If it takes place between parties able to contract, an open avowal of the intention, and an assumption of the relative duties which it imposes on each other, is sufficient to render it valid and binding.

"The ceremony, therefore, which took place between the plaintiff and defendant, as shown by the complaint, was sufficient to constitute them man and wife, if there had been no legal disability."
Graham v. Bennet[t], 2 Cal. 503, 506 (1852).

permitted according to the laws of this country [i.e., California] and their children . . . are illegitimate according to the laws of thier country [i.e., United States], unless their parents are married by a competent authority, you will confer a favor on the undersigned by causing an immediate seperation of these two people without any excuse from either party, and in case that Mr Graham cannot on account of sickness, present himself with Catherine Bennett at this consulate, do me the favour to remove her from the house of Mr Graham, and send her to her parents or place her in some respectable family for the present.[111]

Bolcoff, recalling the violent character of Graham and the frustrations of dealing with him, did little more than interview Graham, not having the heart to tangle with him further. His report to Larkin was prompt and delivered in early December 1845:

Graham said that they were well married and that he would not separate from the side of Bennett, that he would lose a thousand lives before he would give her up, and that Mr. Parrott and other Gentlemen having approved of his Marriage, that nobody could force a separation from Bennett, and that he could not present himself before you account of his infirmities.

You well know the character of Graham. He never likes to obey any authority; I leave it to your judgement. I would have taken from his side Bennett, but to avoid scandal, and I tell you that he talks much against whoever it may be.[112]

Consequently, as far as Larkin was concerned, the matter died. Before many months had passed, even Mary Bennett became reconciled to the marriage. Perhaps the birth of a baby girl, Matilda Jane, helped. As the first child of American parents in the Santa Cruz area, born appropriately on July 4, 1846,[113] her birth gave Mary Bennett her first grandchild. Unfortunately, this child was soon to be the center of the first contested child custody proceedings before the California Supreme Court. In 1850, Graham's son by his previous Tennessee marriage came out to visit. He brought the startling news that Graham's former wife was still alive and that Graham had not been widowed as he had represented. In other words, he was still married at the time of his purported

---

[111]Letter, Larkin to José Antonio Bolcoff, Nov. 19, 1845, 4 LARKIN PAPERS, *supra* note 61, at 101–2.

[112]Letter, Bolcoff to Larkin, Dec. 4, 1845, *id.* at 115–16.

[113]D. NUNIS, THE TRIALS OF ISAAC GRAHAM 64 (1967).

marriage to Bennett. Catherine departed with the child and a significant amount of gold, then returned, allegedly by Graham's forceful abduction. A massive amount of litigation ensued. During the bitterness, Dennis Bennett, one of Mary's sons, was killed by one of Graham's sons. A resulting charge of murder was not settled until 1888.[114]

By the time of Catherine's marriage it was clear that Mary and Vardamon would manage their separation without further disturbance or breach of the peace. Nevertheless, both faced significant legal problems regarding future acquisitions of property. Their response suggests a working familiarity with the common law rules regarding property owned or acquired during marriage. They conducted their subsequent property transactions, as best they could, on the assumption they were operating within the common law, the only legal system they knew. In 1847, for example, Vardamon decided to purchase some lots in the newly founded town of Benicia. As he was still married to Mary, she would have acquired dower rights in that property. He did the only thing reasonably practicable under the circumstances, hiding the asset by taking title in the name of an agent.[115]

Mary Bennett had even more to concern herself with. If she acquired real property, not only would her spouse again gain rights of curtesy, a life estate following her death, but more important, Vardamon could have claimed common law rights to manage and control his wife's property while she was alive during the existence of the marriage.[116] How then could Mary use the land that

[114] *See id.,* for materials on this entire maelstrom of discord.

[115] When purchasing his Benicia property in 1847, Vardamon dealt with Josiah Belden, one of Larkin's agents. The ubiquitous Larkin was a principal in the development. Belden advised Larkin that "Mr. Bennet[t] does not want the lots placed to his name, but says he is going to Benicia to select others." Larkin obliged in his reply: "As Mr. Bennett goes to Benicia and will probably select lots for himself I have made out the deed of the lot formerly in his name in that of yours and which you will find enclosed." Letters, Josiah Belden to Larkin, Larkin to Belden, Sept. 2 and Sept. 9, 1847, 6 LARKIN PAPERS, *supra* note 61, at 306, 327. This correspondence is not absolutely clear. It could be read that Bennett simply decided not to buy certain lots in which he had originally expressed interest, and that Belden decided to buy them for himself. It could also be inferred that Vardamon asked Belden to do him the favor of taking title in his name.

[116] A succinct statement of the then applicable law, with allowance for some minor exceptions, was given by Chief Justice Zephaniah Swift of Connecticut in 1818: "The husband, by marriage, acquires a right to the use of the real estate of

the local priest in Santa Clara·would recommend that the Mexican government grant her with assurance that Vardamon would not show up and demand its control? In her efforts to hide this asset, Mary also demonstrated her familiarity with the remembered common law rules of the eastern states.

At first she applied for her land grant in her maiden name, and then, thinking better of that, she forged her son Winston's name to naturalization and land grant petitions and submitted them to the Californio authorities, all in Winston's absence and apparently without consultation with him. Title to the grant was taken in his name, but Mary throughout was the real beneficial owner.[117] The problem of title to the land grant was raised by Larkin himself in a letter to Padre Real, the local priest at Santa Clara. He thanked the padre for his generosity and assistance in helping Mary and her children settle near the mission, but as to the proposed land grant, he advised,

---

his wife, during her life; and if they have a child born alive, then, if he survives, during his life, as tenant by the curtesey. He acquires an absolute right to her chattels real, and may dispose of them. . . . He acquires an absolute property in her chattels personal in possession. . . . As to the property of the wife accruing during coverture, the same rule is applicable." Griswold v. Penniman, 2 Conn. 564, 565–66 (1818).

[117] See generally Records (N.D. Cal.), Land Case No. 361, Mary S. Bennett, Claimant, on file with the Bancroft Library, University of California, Berkeley, California. The petitions for naturalization and for the land grant itself were dated September 4, 1845. At that time Winston was working for Isaac Graham at Zayante, near Felton, in the Santa Cruz Mountains, and probably did not sign any petition in San Jose, which is the place of execution shown on the petitions. A resident of Santa Clara in 1845 later testified in the land-claims litigation that Mrs. Bennett had procured Winston's naturalization without his knowledge or consent and that he had heard Winston so say. Deposition of George W. Bolling, Land Case No. 361, Mary S. Bennett, Claimant, supra. In his own memoirs Winston says nothing about his naturalization as a Mexican nor about any land grant. San Jose Pioneer, May 26, 1877 and June 2, 1877, at 1 (both editions). On April 22, 1854, during the time of the proceedings before the Land Claims Commission, a deed was recorded in the Recorder's Office of Santa Clara County from Winston Bennett (under the Hispanicized form of Narciso in which the petitions had been made) to his mother, Mary Bennett. The deed described the lands received under the grants (two separate parcels), recited a nominal consideration, and acknowledged that the lands to which title was being transferred, "have been heretofore in the use and occupancy of my mother the said party of the second part." Book G of Deeds, pages 310 et seq., Official Records of Santa Clara County. There was no reason under California practice why a land grant could not be made to a woman. See supra note 91.

should you be willing to serve Mrs Bennet[t] as mentioned—and it would be doing a great favor on a poor woman who unaided by her Husband has a large Family to support—that it would be better that any property the family may receive through your kindness should be given in the name of the eldest son Winstin, which may prevent the Husband of Mrs Bennet[t] coming forward and claiming it, as it is said he refused to support his Family.[118]

Subsequently these elaborate precautions proved needless. Only a few years later, in 1849, Vardamon suffered an untimely death, and Mary Bennett was left a widow.

Thus the Bennett women met their needs in the realm of domestic relations in a manner similar to that of the immigrants generally. In facing thorny and pressing problems of authority to marry, protection of persons and property upon separation, and divorce absolute to permit remarriage, they neither operated in a legal vacuum nor in complete compliance with the rules of the local jurisdiction. The expatriates drew on the local law only to the extent absolutely necessary. Instead, they did their best to order their present circumstances in a manner harmonious with the remembered law of the eastern and midwestern states from which they had come.

[118] Letter, Larkin to Padre José María Real, June 6, 1845, 3 LARKIN PAPERS, *supra* note 61, at 225.

10

Conclusion

The Anglo-American expatriates were unable to adapt well to Mexican California's legal system. The older residents, those who had arrived before the overlanders, had become naturalized citizens, had married California women, and had otherwise worked themselves into positions of prominence, nevertheless distrusted and deprecated the formal judicial structure. Although they were thoroughly assimilated into the California culture and had significant economic stakes in the current system of government, subconsciously they adhered to common law legal concepts. These merchants and sea captains tended, by preference, to adjust their disputes amongst themselves, especially where elements of complexity or commercial practice were involved.

Many of the later overland arrivals existed outside the legal system. Some arrived with families, thus barring intermarriage; most never learned Spanish nor made any other effort to assimilate. The majority of them lacked the Mexican immigration document legally necessary for their existence in California. Their continued residence was the combined result of traditional Californio courtesy and current military inability to uproot them en masse. Except for criminal violations and occasional petty litigation, these expatriates seldom entered into the flow of the official legal process.

Of course, some Americans and Englishmen did make use of the alcalde courts. For some litigation the nature of the controversy made the use of the regular courts almost inevitable. If a suit involved the validity of a land grant or a resolution of conflicting land descriptions, it is not surprising that foreigners conceded legitimacy to the official system to interpret its own acts. Then too, when the matter was straightforward and both parties lived within the territorial jurisdiction of the same alcalde or justice of the peace, there was a greater tendency to use the Mexican courts. If an American owed a Scotsman a small and certain sum, perhaps on a promissory note or account, or if an American merchant sought payment from a Californio for goods sold and delivered, a suit before the local alcalde might well follow, if litigation were necessary at all.

Some expatriates tried to hedge their legal bets, not knowing with certainty how their rights might be best enforced in the future. Very few expatriates created judicial contracts, whereby the judge examined the fairness of the agreement and himself wrote up its terms. But many Americans and British, having reached a written agreement out of court, then took their document to the *juez* for recordation pursuant to his notarial function. Moreover, it was common for commercial arbitration, with arbitrators drawn from among the local mercantile community, to begin by a referral from the local alcalde court.

When matters became more complicated or involved commercial practices or customs, there was a marked tendency to arbitrate. This was a common commercial practice in the nineteenth century. This avoidance of the legal system was specifically a common frontier practice among mercantile minorities. In territorial Wisconsin in the early nineteenth century, traders preferred to arbitrate among themselves rather than submit their disputes to justices of the peace,[1] as did the commercial community of British Detroit in the 1780s.[2]

It is not surprising, then, that the expatriate community turned inward to resolve all but the simplest commercial disputes. What is interesting is the hostility so many expressed for the local judicial system. It must remain conjectural, but it is nonetheless reasonable to believe that this was the result of two related factors: the great extent to which the common law norms and concepts had ingrained themselves into the American and British psyches, and the expatriates' inability, because of that successful acculturation to the common law, to understand the procedures, purposes, and cultural assumptions of the Mexican legal system. Even the thorough assimilation of the older residents was not deep enough

[1] Kommers, *The Emergence of Law and Justice in Pre-Territorial Wisconsin,* 8 Am. J. Legal Hist. 20, 28 (1964).
[2] 1 C. Burton & M. Burton, History of Wayne County and the City of Detroit, Michigan 195 (1930) (3 vols).

to root out this common law heritage and its presuppositions as to the correct manner to resolve disputes.

The overland agricultural immigrants, presumably less aware of legal concepts than the more sophisticated traders, were nonetheless able to employ accurately remembered notions of eastern law. They married by contract and divorced by rescission, thereby demonstrating a knowledge of the only then developing contractual theory of the marriage relationship. Other studies of these same immigrants' experiences while on the overland trail have likewise suggested their familiarity with property law and contract concepts and the great extent to which they were acculturated with the norms and assumptions of the common law.[3]

The use of law by the mercantile community was pervasive. In commercial quarrels the traders sometimes took the crass position of "might makes right" or justified questionable conduct on the basis of economic necessity. Generally, however, in their correspondence with fellow disputants they freely appealed to the "law," their "rights," or to the "contract" to justify their claims. Not only did law pervade their thinking but it energized their actions. Expatriate traders comfortably applied common law setoffs and merchants made technical, legalistic interpretations of their contracts. The common law was a part of the cultural understandings the Anglo-Americans brought with them to Mexican California, and it remained with them the rest of their lives.

What has developed as a result of this study is a portrait of the expatriates, overlanders and older residents alike, deeply imbued with the rugged, highly individualistic concepts of this period of the common law. Rights were absolute entitlements and duties their stern correlatives, owed unconditionally. No matter how onesided or unfair, a contract should be enforced strictly according to its terms. Courts should not rewrite agreements. If debts were owed or damages assessed, judgment should be rendered for immediate payment in cash, with no extensions and regardless of a defendant's personal needs or ability to pay. The common law would make the world safe for contract.

Furthermore, at common law rights were defined in accor-

---

[3] J. REID, LAW FOR THE ELEPHANT: PROPERTY AND SOCIAL BEHAVIOR ON THE OVERLAND TRAIL (1980) (property law); Reid, *Binding the Elephant: Contracts and Legal Obligations on the Overland Trail,* 21 AM. J. LEGAL HIST. 285 (1977) (contract law).

dance with complicated but neutral rules—the substantive law—
clearly stated and preferably written down for all to see. Disputes
were resolved by the ritualistic combat of adversarial trial, ideally
before a jury. The process produced clear winners and clear
losers, and there was no need, in fact it would have been un-
desirable in the current thinking, for a court to seek accommodation or the reconciliation of the antagonists. Of course, individual
jurists and litigants could hold more sophisticated views, but the
essence of Anglo-American law of the period was rugged individualism, let the chips fall where they might, and an attitude on the
part of litigants and the law alike of whole hog or none. It was
with these ideas in their background that the expatriates framed
their concepts of how a legal system ought to operate and by
which they judged the California scheme of things and found it
wanting.

These assumptions could not stand in sharper contrast with
the philosophy of Californio and Mexican jurisprudence. Some of
the contrast was noted by a federal district judge in 1894 as
follows:

From the earliest times the governmental systems of the Anglo-Saxon
and the Latin races have been widely different. Among Latin peoples
the chief thought has been for their welfare and advancement as a
collective entity. . . . Among Anglo-Saxons, on the contrary, the individual always remained the most prominent purpose in governmental conception. . . . The progress of the English-speaking people to
the highest form of civil and religious liberty is not adventitious or
accidental, but is due to this ennoblement of the individual in the
conceptions and practices of the English law.[4]

Although inaccurate and self-congratulatory, there is nevertheless a kernel of truth in the judge's perceptions. The philosophi-
cal focus of the Spanish and Mexican law was on the reconciliation of conflict and the accommodation of conflicting interests,
serving the greater interest in the community and its harmony. In
contrast, the common law ideas of absolute rights and a sharply
adversarial combat resulted in a clearly defined winner, serving
the interest of the individual.

The Mexican concern for accommodation and reconciliation is
seen most clearly in civil matters, but it appears even in criminal

[4]United States v. James, 60 F. 257, 262 (D. Ill. 1894) (Grosscup, J.).

cases. In criminal matters it was quite enough for the Californios to conduct a judicial, inquisitorial investigation of the facts, and there was little need for a formal trial with a parade of witnesses and the full panoply of the common law's adversarial process. The important element was the punishment, with its important issues of what ought to be done to protect society and to heal the scars of the societal disruption. Not surprisingly, it was only after guilt was determined that a defense counsel was appointed to represent the offender and to defend his interests in this most important matter of disposition. Perhaps the closest modern parallel is the juvenile court system as originally conceived, before the recent constitutionalization of juvenile rights by the United States Supreme Court.

Civil cases offer an even clearer view of the reconciliatory philosophy behind the Californio and Mexican jurisprudence. The very procedure itself was an earnest attempt to *avoid* litigation. This mandatory conciliation process through the use of *hombres buenos* was mandatory and resolved almost all litigation. The procedure was well suited to Mexican California and well regarded by the Californios. In contrast, conciliation was despised by the Anglo-Americans, who thought the procedure a mere waste of time that delayed the more appropriate clash of trial.

California domestic relations cases ostensibly filed to obtain a judicial separation seldom led to more than a temporary breach of marital unity. The number of reconciliations of spouses was enormous. In part, this reflects the Californio's Catholic view of the inviolability of marriage. It also casts light on the function of the separation suit itself. It appears to have been a social safety valve whereby one spouse, usually but not exclusively the wife, could put pressure on the other to reform errant conduct. It represented the ultimate step in placing a spouse in a position of public obloquy. For each separation suit actually filed, one can imagine that many more were threatened in private in an effort to make the fear of a public airing of grievances—and this in very small communities where almost everyone knew everyone else—reform the offending spouse's behavior. The use of a marital suit by the Californios to modify conduct and to reconcile is also seen in the process whereby the wife was removed from the husband and placed with another family once suit was filed. A petition of a husband to reclaim his wife from a safe house and an earnest judicial examination as to whether the improvement of a husband's conduct justified a reunion is eloquent testimony to the healing purpose of the Californio domestic relations law.

The effort of the law to smooth the troubled waters of discord is manifest in even the most common of civil suits, those seeking the payment of money for debt, goods sold and delivered, and damages for all kinds of torts or contracts. In suit after suit judges extended the time for payment or ordered that a judgment might be paid in installments, or that an obligation on its face to be paid in money might be satisfied in hides, wheat, soap, or whatever commercially viable commodity was available to a defendant. What common law judge would dare change the due date of an obligation, or the medium of payment, or issue an installment judgment? The purpose behind this accommodation was not to favor improvident borrowers or credit purchasers nor to relieve them of just debts, as many expatriate creditors sincerely believed, but to resolve an unsettled and antagonistic condition by fashioning a decree that could rest easily on all concerned and resolve the dispute without exalting a winner or crushing a loser.

With this approach to law, it is easy to see why the Californios were not much concerned with procedural devices such as attachment or execution. Most lawsuits would not survive conciliation, and of those that did, the closeness of the community would force a judgment debtor to reach an accommodation with his creditor. The desire for flexibility and fairness, as the judge might apply these concepts to a specific dispute, eliminated the need for detailed and readily available rules of positive law.

Those in whom the common law was inbred could not understand nor could they tolerate the relativism and ambiguity of this approach. Much of the expatriate criticism of the alcalde system was accurate. The courts were inefficient, at times unpredictable, and they lacked any semblance of effective enforcement techniques. California badly needed a sheriff to enforce judgments. But the depth of the Anglo-American criticism reflected differing cultural norms of what was wanted and expected from a legal system. The expatriates wanted certainty, predictability, and efficiency in enforcement of judgments. These expectations arose from a highly individualistic culture, pluralistic and diversified, and rested on a need for strong, state-supported sanctions. It was natural for these foreigners to see a lack of clear legal guidelines as lawlessness, and a lack of written laws coupled with judicial accommodation of debtors as necessarily implying corruption. For the Californios, individualized judgment, extension of due dates, and this accommodating spirit of judicial intervention were simple justice. Their ideas were derived from the tradition of the Spanish alcalde, the respected and almost revered village elder, who had been viewed as a father, lovingly and patiently reconciling his children's anger and resolving their disputes.

In contrast with the pluralistic, individualized Anglo-Americans, Spanish culture put its focus on community. In a predominantly homogeneous society, one sharing the same religion and, at least in California, congregating in small communities with few stark differences in social class, notwithstanding economic disparity, it was realistic for the Californios to believe that an alcalde or *juez de paz* might appropriately mete out highly specific justice tailored to the litigants. Nor was it unrealistic for them to assume that in their tiny villages and pueblos, in which almost everyone shared the same fiestas and fandangos, that community approbation could alone be an effective sanction for enforcement of judicial decrees for civil matters with a minimal military backup for criminal sanctions. The alcalde system worked well for the Californios. They enjoyed easy access to the judge, who was almost always a neighbor, a fast process of judicial hearing and determination, and a high community level of acceptance of the results.[5]

A striking parallel is found in the shifting fortunes of the eighteenth-century church courts of Massachusetts. The Congregationalists made efforts to resolve private disputes through church meetings, thereby avoiding the rigid structure of the common law courts. They sought the flexibility of a judgment among

[5] These are condensed and abbreviated descriptions of three of four factors Professor John R. Wunder proposed as tests to evaluate the effectiveness of local trial courts. J. WUNDER, INFERIOR COURTS, SUPERIOR JUSTICE: A HISTORY OF THE JUSTICES OF THE PEACE ON THE NORTHWEST FRONTIER, 1853–1889 (1979). Even in their fuller description the alcalde courts passed these three tests without question. Equally without question, the Californio courts failed the first of the four factors: whether judicial decisions were based on intelligent and legal reasoning, including a high degree of judicial education and access to written law. That test itself, however, reflects a common law bias. A good number of societies would not think access to written law was important and would regard a judge's understanding of community mores as far more important than his technical training.

their brethren in accordance with Jesus's admonition to seek reconciliation and avoid litigation, and specifically that "if your brother sins against you, go and show him his fault, just between the two of you. . . . But if he will not listen, take one or two others along. . . . If he refuses to listen to them tell it to the church."[6] As with the alcalde courts of California, these church courts lacked any coercive power of enforcement and depended upon group sanction and a defendant's desire not to be ostracized to effectuate their orders. So long as litigation was brought by residents within the same community and the town was homogeneous with few nonconforming or divisive elements, the church courts flourished. Defendants willingly obeyed their brethren's judgments. Once a community became diversified or the divisive influences of commercialism disturbed the tranquility of a pastoral homogeneity, the church courts declined and the official courts began to monopolize the litigation process.[7]

Although the Californio civil and criminal courts were never adjuncts of the church, the comparison with these Congregational tribunals is apt. Just as with these religious bodies in eighteenth-century Massachusetts, the Californio judicial system depended on the good will of the inhabitants, their compliant faith in the wisdom of the alcaldes, and the effectiveness of a small, cohesive community to enforce its decrees and effectuate the healing of breaches in the fabric of the body politic.

We have discussed the clash in values between the Anglo-Americans and Californios primarily in terms of legal tradition. That is appropriate. Nevertheless, beneath the legal values lies a more generalized historical reality. The Anglo-American legal values of predictability and individualism reflected not merely a legal tradition but also the needs and pluralistic views of an atomistic society in the midst of the Industrial Revolution, history's

[6]Matt. 18:15–17 (New International). *See also* Luke 12:57–59 (New International) ("Why don't you judge for yourselves what is right? As you are going with your adversary to the magistrate, try hard to be reconciled to him on the way, or he may drag you off to the judge, and the judge turn you over to the officer, and the officer throw you into prison. I tell you, you will not get out until you have paid the last penny.").

[7]*See generally* W. NELSON, DISPUTE AND CONFLICT RESOLUTION IN PLYMOUTH COUNTY, MASSACHUSETTS, 1725–1825 (1981); J. AUERBACH, JUSTICE WITHOUT LAW? 19–46 (1983).

greatest commercial, industrial, and social upheaval. The Mexican California legal values of community and conciliation, in turn, reflected not merely a legal tradition but also the needs and cohesive, inclusive views of a pastoral, precommercial, and homogeneous society.

Another analogy may help illustrate the point. In seventeenth-century Connecticut the towns were small and homogeneous. Attitudes were communal, and arbitration, although then completely voluntary and legally unenforceable, was popular. It offered participants a "method of resolving their differences that was intimately linked to the communities in which they lived. This bond between arbitration and community explains why the unenforceability of arbitration awards caused few problems in the first decades of settlement."[8]

Between 1700 and 1750 the communities changed in that they became less cohesive, less isolated, and less homogeneous. With the growth of commerce there were more disputes between persons residing in different towns. Thus there was a sharply decreased community interest in the process of dispute resolution. As the social relations between disputants became more attenuated and arbitration less communally based, two developments occurred that closely paralleled the expatriate criticism of the Mexican California legal system. First, arbitration judgments increasingly called for a simple payment of money rather than a modification of conduct or other judgment tailored to the specifics of the dispute. Second, more and more desire was expressed for a means of coercion to enforce arbitration awards.

In their basic assumptions about their legal system, the Californios ultimately proved to be wrong. The very existence of a large foreign population, and especially the unassimilated overlanders, was a cancer that pierced the homogeneity of the population and the commonality of their beliefs. Although individually more assimilated, the power of the expatriate commercial class to bring the discontent and material striving of the modern world into a peaceful, pastoral society destroyed the common consent that made the Californio legal system possible. The quickening of

[8]Mann, *The Formalization of Informal Law: Arbitration Before the American Revolution*, 59 N.Y.U. L. REV. 443, 455 (1984). The balance of the discussion of arbitration in colonial Connecticut is drawn from this excellent article.

the blood wrought by the commercial demand for hides and tallow brought greed and a heightened taste for the world's luxuries. Now an indebted rancher might flaunt a court's impotence to enforce its decrees, whereas in simpler days he would have yielded to a sense of community. For such a man and for the new era, more formal judicial structures with efficient powers of coercion would be needed. In fact, mainland Mexico was experiencing parallel commercial pressures and the breakdown of community. The legal requirement that *hombres buenos* be brought to the conciliation hearing was dropped in October 1846,[9] and the conciliation process was itself abandoned as a condition for suit in 1857.[10]

It is ironic that the expatriates, those most critical of the Californio judicial system, contributed the most, even by their very presence, to its dysfunction. At least one of these expatriates proved sensitive to the changes they had in large part themselves fomented. He was Thomas Oliver Larkin, the American consul and leading American merchant, whose activities we have closely observed. Just before the American invasion in July 1846, he had written Abel Stearns that "the times and the country are well enough for me."[11] After the conquest of California, its commercialization and entry into the common law world moved ahead with breakneck speed. After a decade, in 1856, Larkin looked back with nostalgia at the calmer days of the Californios. He again wrote his old commercial acquaintance Abel Stearns and expressed his yearning to return to the older days, the "times prior to July 1846 and all their honest pleasures and the flesh pots of those days. Halcyon days they were. We shall not enjoy there like again."[12]

[9] 3 J. FEBRERO, OBRA COMPLETA DE JURISPRUDENCIA TEÓRICO-PRÁCTICA 135 (Mexico City 1851) (4 vols.).

[10] Interpretation of 1857 constitution by Mexican jurist Matías Romero, *printed in* W. LOGAN, A MEXICAN LAW SUIT 43 (1895).

[11] Letter, Larkin to Abel Stearns, Apr. 27, 1846, FIRST AND LAST CONSUL: THOMAS OLIVER LARKIN AND THE AMERICANIZATION OF CALIFORNIA, A SELECTION OF LETTERS EDITED BY JOHN A. HAWGOOD 59 (2d ed. 1970).

[12] Letter, Larkin to Abel Stearns, Apr. 24, 1856, FIRST AND LAST CONSUL, *supra* note 11, at 104.

Appendices

Appendix A

Ranch Management Contract, 1845 [1]

Be it known to all men by these *Presents* that on this day *William Leidesdorff* and *Willard Buzzell* have entered into an agreement respecting the cultivation of a farm situated on the Sacramento and belonging to said Leidesdorff, as also the raising of cattle, sheep and c, or stock or any description which may be found productive, under the following *conditions*.

First. Said Buzzell agrees to proceed immediately to said farm and take charge thereof, with whatever stock, or property of any kind whatsoever that may be entrusted to him by said Leidesdorff, and to erect such buildings, Corales, etc. as may be necessary and that all his attention shall be paid, to the business specified in this contract without entering into any business with others during the time specified——

Second. Said Buzzell binds himself to keep an exact account of the disposal of all goods and utensils which are now delivered him, as also of the payments made to Indians, or other servants employed in said farm, noting the prices thereof as acostumed in the adjacent farms, and in case of purchasing beaver pelt or other produce, to remit the same to said Leidesdorff: also specifying in his account all and every article used in the erection of the necessary buildings improvements, as also the amount paid for labor on the same——

Third. Said Buzzell by these presents binds himself, to truly and faithfully for the term of four years from date, exert himself and do all in his power for the interest of the concerned,——

[1]Quoted from James F. Manning, "William A. Leidesdorff's Career in California," at 96A-100 (M.A. thesis, University of California at Berkeley, 1942). This thesis indicates that the original contract is in the Huntington Library, San Marino, California, but does not cite its location.

Fourth. Said Leidesdorff on his part binds himself to place on said farm during the present year as follows.

Three hundred head of meat cattle, or more if convenient
Thirty mares and the stud
Twelve tame horses
Two hundred sheep, and any stock which may be convenient———

Fifth. Said Buzzell also promises to exert himself in sowing all grain or seed which may be productive on the farm, of which he will, receive the same proportion as in other interests———

Sixth. For the full and strict compliance, with all the articles set forth in these presents on the part of said Buzzell, said Leidesdorff agrees to give him one third part of all increase of cattle, horses, and other stock as also of all produce raised in said farm; at the same time said Buzzell binds himself to deliver all produce to said Leidesdorff, without trading with others. He the said Leidesdorff crediting in account of said Buzzell the fair marked price for his proportion———

Seventh. At the time of entering on the farm; said Buzzell promises to take a correct list of all tools and utensils, that are now delivered to him, and which shall be appropriated to the use of the farm, and account for the same, in order that said Leidesdorff maybe able to ascertain the precise amount of expenditure in building, etc., on said farm———

Eighth. It is especially agreed on both parties, that no iron for branding cattle of any description, shall be used on the farm except the one given by said Leidesdorff, and on no account shall any division of cattle take place until the expiration of the term specified———

Ninth. Said Leidesdorff agrees to allow in account the usual wages for six indians for the first year, and for four the remaining years———

Tenth. That this contract may be dissolved previous to the time specified in case of deficiency on the part of said Buzzell or failing in compliance with all the articles of this contract, and in such case said Buzzell forfeits all rights to his said third part of increase———

Eleventh. In consideration that said Buzzell has the use of the necessary stock for the support of himself and family, it is agreed that whatever articles sent to this place, for the actual use of said

Leidesdorff shall not be charge in account, but in case of surplus the same to be accounted for———

Twelve. Said Buzzell promises to give at the expiration of each year an exact account of the property existing on said farm, and the amounts expended during the year———and to remit to said Leidesdorff, all the hides from cattle which it may be actually necessary to kill except what may be necessary, for the use of the farm which will appear in the accounts.———

Thirteenth. At the expiration of the term noted in this contract, all buildings or improvements to remain as the property of said Leidesdorff unless a new contract shall be made———

Fourteenth. For all articles made from wool grown on the farm, said Buzzell shall receive two thirds of the product, but otherwise one third———

Fifteenth. It is agreed that said Buzzell shall not receive families or persons, to become residents on the farm without previous consent of said Leidesdorff———

Sixteenth. In case of any misunderstanding or disagreement, it is mutually agreed that any question which may arise shall be settled by the usual mode of arbitration without recourse to law ——— And for the faithful compliance with all the Articles of this contract we mutually bind ourselves, this twelfth day of April in the year of our Lord, one thousdand eight hundred and forty-five, this document not being on sealed paper for want thereof, and in testimony of our agreement we place our hands and seals in duplicate in presence of witnesses———

Willard Buzzell (SEAL)
Wm. A. Leidesdorff (SEAL)

Witness:
Nathan Spear
Robert T. Ridley
William S. Hinckley

Appendix B

Mercantile Partnership Agreement, ca. 1836[1]

It is hereby mutually agreed, between Nathan Spear, William S. Hinckley and J. P. Leese that they will contract to carry on business at San Francisco in the following manner.

First, that said Hinckley & Spear shall furnish goods to said Leese for sales & returns, at the actual cost of importation, and that the profits on said goods shall be equally divided between the contracting parties.

Second, that said Leese shall keep an exact account by entering all goods received, or purchased of others, with the corresponding sales thereof, and also an account for all expenses whch appertain to the company.

Third, that the erection of whatever buildings that may be necessary for the favorable prosecution of business shall be taken as expense, and that each one of the contracting parties shall be owners of said buildings in equal proportion [no punctuation]

Fourth, that the two Launches which are in San Francisco shall be joint concern keeping exact account of their expenses and earnings.

Fifth, that any future article which may be added with detriment to the original contract shall have the consent of the contracting parties mutually [no punctuation]

Sixth, the three contracting parties hereby hold themselves bound to further the business in any way possible.

Seventh, that the capital supplied by said Hinckley & Spear shall be as near ten thousand dollars as the supply of goods

---

[1] Quoted from Spear, *Correspondence*, Box 2, Miscellaneous Papers, Item 2, on file with the Bancroft Library, University of California, Berkeley, California.

adapted to the market will permit, and that the amount may be exceeded at their option.

William S. Hinckley
Nathan Spear) by W.S. Hinckley
) power attorney
Jacob P. Leese

Appendix C

Store Management Contract, 1843[1]

This agreement made this 16th day of May One Thousand Eight hundred & Forty Three in Monterey upper california by & between Thomas O Larkin on the first part and Talbot H Green on the second part.

The said Larkin by these writeings puts into the charge of said Green his stock of goods now in his store and ware house's in Monterey & all his grain & provisions therein for the purpose of carring on the buisness of said Larkin in his store & primises in Monterey for the term of one year, and agrees to give said Green for his services, Four Hundred dollars, and five percent on all proffits that may be made from the said busness for the term of said year.

Said Talbot H Green on his part agrees by these writeings to take charge this day of the store and buisness in Monterey of said Larkin, for the term of one year and to do all in his power in collecting debts and carring on the trade & intrest of said Larkin for the time and term here mentioned and to deliver to said Larkin at the expiration of the time all he may have on hand _____ The amount of goods grain & provisions deliverd to said Green this day as pr Inventory being Four Thousand Two Hundred Ninety two dollars two reals (4292$2). Said Green is from time to time to purchace more goods for the store when he may be able to pay for them in produce at the time of purchace but not to purchace any on a credit.

As Witness our hands this 16th day of May A.D. One Thousand Eight hundred & Forty three.

Thomas O. Larkin (Rubric)   Talbot H Green (Rubric)

[1]Quoted from 2 THE LARKIN PAPERS: PERSONAL, BUSINESS, AND OFFICIAL CORRESPONDENCE OF THOMAS OLIVER LARKIN, MERCHANT AND UNITED STATES CONSUL IN CALIFORNIA 15 (Hammond ed. 1951–1968) (10 vols. & index).

Bibliography

MANUSCRIPT SOURCES

Alvarado, Juan Bautista. Historia de California. 5 vols. Bancroft Library, University of California. Berkeley, California.

Archives of California (transcripts and extracts). 63 vols. Bancroft Library, University of California. Berkeley, California.

Archivo de la familia Alviso. Bancroft Library, University of California. Berkeley, California.

Castro, Manuel. Documentos para la historia de California. 2 vols. Bancroft Library, University of California. Berkeley, California.

Castro, Manuel de Jesús. Correspondence and Papers, 1836–1863. Bancroft Library, University of California. Berkeley, California.

Fitch, Henry D. Documentos para la historia de California. Bancroft Library, University of California. Berkeley, California.

Larkin, Thomas O. Consular Records. Monterey County Historical Society. Salinas, California.

Monterey Archives. 16 vols. Monterey County Historical Society. Salinas, California.

Official Documents Relating to Early San Francisco, 1835–1857. Bancroft Library, University of California. Berkeley, California.

Osio, García. Cartas y documentos. Bancroft Library, University of California. Berkeley, California.

Pico, Pio. Documentos para la historia de California. 2 vols. Bancroft Library, University of California. Berkeley, California.

Pinto, Rafael. Documentos para la historia de California. 2 vols. Bancroft Library, University of California. Berkeley, California.

Prefect Records of Los Angeles. 3 vols. Henry E. Huntington Library. San Marino, California.
Reynolds, Stephen. Diary. Peabody Museum. Salem, Massachusetts.
Spear, Nathan. Correspondence and Papers. Bancroft Library, University of California. Berkeley, California.
Stearns, Abel. Stearns Collection. Henry E. Huntington Library. San Marino, California.
———, ed. Yndice juzgado la instancia de la ciudad de los Angeles, ramo criminal. Henry E. Huntington Library. San Marino, California.
United States District Court, Northern California. Records. U.S. Land Commission Case No. 361, Mary S. Bennett, Claimant. Bancroft Library, University of California. Berkeley, California.
Vallejo, Mariano G. Documentos para la historia de California. 37 vols. Bancroft Library, University of California, Berkeley.

PRINTED PRIMARY SOURCES

Arrillaga, Basilio José, ed. *Recopilación de leyes, decretos, bandos, reglamentos, circulares y providencias de los supremos poderes . . . todo el año de 1837.* Mexico City: J. M. Fernández de Lara, 1839.
Atherton, Faxon D. *The California Diary of Faxon Dean Atherton 1836–1839.* Edited by Doyce B. Nunis, Jr. San Francisco: California Historical Society, 1964.
Belden, Josiah. *Josiah Belden 1841 California Overland Pioneer: His Memoir and Early Letters.* Edited by Doyce B. Nunis, Jr. Georgetown, Cal.: Talisman Press, 1962.
Bennett, Winston. "Memoirs." *San Jose Pioneer,* May 26 and June 2, 1877.
Bidwell, John. *Life in California Before the Gold Discovery.* Palo Alto: Lewis Osborne, 1966.
Bryant, Edwin. *What I Saw in California.* New York: D. Appleton & Co., 1848. Reprint. Lincoln: University of Nebraska Press, 1985.
California Senate Committee on the Judiciary. "Report on Civil and Common Law," (1850), printed in *California Reports.* Vol. 1 (appendix). San Francisco: Nathaniel Bennett, 1852.
Castañares, Manuel. *Colección de documentos relativos al de-

partamento de Californias. Mexico City: Voz del Pueblo, 1845. Reprinted in Weber, David J., ed. *Northern Mexico on the Eve of the United States Invasion.* New York: Arno Press, 1976.

Cleveland, Richard J. *A Narrative of Voyages and Commercial Enterprises of the Sons of New England.* Cambridge, Mass.: 1842.

Clyman, James. *James Clyman, American Frontiersman, 1792–1881.* San Francisco: California Historical Society, 1928. Reprint. *Journal of a Mountain Man.* Edited by Linda M. Hasselstrom. Missoula, Mont.: Mountain Press Publishing Co., 1984.

Colton, Walter. *Three Years in California.* New York: A. S. Barnes & Co., 1850. Reprint. Stanford: Stanford University Press, 1949.

Dana, Richard H., Jr. *Two Years Before the Mast: A Personal Narrative of Life at Sea.* New York: Harper & Brothers, 1840. Reprint (2 vols.). Edited by John H. Kemble. Los Angeles: Ward Ritchie Press, 1964.

Davis, William H., Jr. *Sixty Years in California.* San Francisco: A. J. Leary, 1889. Reprinted as *Seventy-five Years in California,* San Francisco: John Howell, 1929.

Douglas, Sir James. "A Voyage from the Columbia to California in 1840." *California Historical Society Quarterly* 8 (June 1929): 97–115.

Dublán, Manuel, and Lozano, José María. *Legislación mexicana; ó colección completa de las disposiciones legislativas . . . 1687–1910.* Mexico City: J. J. Lara, 1876–1912.

Dye, Job. "Recollections of a Pioneer of California." *Santa Cruz Sentinel,* May 15, 1869.

Farnham, Thomas J. *Travels in the Californias, and Scenes in the Pacific Ocean.* New York: Saxton & Niles, 1844. Reprint. *Travels in California.* Oakland: Biobooks, 1947.

Febrero, José. *Obra completa de jurisprudencia teórico-práctica.* 4 vols. Mexico City: S. Pérez, 1850–1852.

Galvan Rivera, Mariano. *Colección de los decretos y órdenes de las Cortes de España, que se reputan vigentes en la Republica de los Estados Unidos Mexicanos.* Mexico City: Mariano Arévalo, 1829.

Galvin, John, ed. *The Coming of Justice to California: Three*

Documents. Translated by Adelaide Smithers. San Francisco: John Howell-Books, 1963.

García Diego y Moreno, Francisco. *The Writings of Francisco García Diego y Moreno: Obispo de Ambas Californias.* Translated and edited by Msgr. Francis J. Weber. Los Angeles: Archdiocese of Los Angeles, 1976.

Garner, William R. *Letters from California 1846–1847.* Edited by Donald M. Craig. Berkeley: University of California Press, 1970.

Halleck, Jabez, and Hartnell, William E. P. *Translation and Digest of such portions of the Mexican laws of March 20th and May 23rd, 1837, as are supposed to be still in force and adapted to the present condition of California.* San Francisco: Office of the Alta California, 1849.

Hastings, Lansford W. *The Emigrants' Guide to Oregon and California.* Cincinnati: George Conclin, 1845. Reprint. New York: Da Capo Press, 1969.

Hecox, Margaret M. *California Caravan: The 1846 Overland Trail Memoir of Margaret M. Hecox.* Edited by Richard Dillon. San Jose: Harlan-Young, 1966.

Kent, James. *Commentaries on American Law.* 4 vols. Second ed. New York: O. Halsted, 1832.

Lara, J. M., ed. *Colección de los decretos, y ordenes de interes común, que dicto el gobierno provisional.* 3 vols. Mexico City: J. M. Lara, 1850.

Larkin, Thomas O. *Chapters in the Early Life of Thomas Oliver Larkin.* Edited by Robert J. Parker. San Francisco: California Historical Society, 1939.

———. *First and Last Consul: Thomas Oliver Larkin and the Americanization of California.* Edited by John A. Hawgood. Second ed. Palo Alto: Pacific Books, Publishers, 1970.

———. *The Larkin Papers: Personal, Business, and Official Correspondence of Thomas Oliver Larkin, Merchant and United States Consul in California.* Edited by George P. Hammond. 10 vols. and index. Berkeley: University of California Press, 1951–1968.

Nidever, George. *The Life and Adventures of George Nidever.* Edited by William H. Ellison. Berkeley: University of California Press, 1937.

Rea, Vargas, ed. *Cinco documentos sobre la Alta California.* Mexico City: Biblioteca Aportación Histórica, 1944.

Robinson, Alfred. "Business Letters of Alfred Robinson." Edited by Adele Ogden. *California Historical Society Quarterly* 23 (1944):301–34.

————. *Life in California.* New York: Wiley & Putnam, 1846. Reprint. New York: Da Capo Press, 1969.

Rosamel, Joseph de. "California Prior to Conquest: A Frenchman's Views." Translated by William F. Shepard. *California Historical Society Quarterly* 37 (March 1958):63–77.

Ruschenberger, William S. *A Voyage Round the World During the Years 1835, 36, and 37.* Philadelphia: Carey, Lea & Blanchard, 1838. Reprint (California portion). Kemble, John H., ed., *Sketches in California 1836.* Early California Travel Series, vol. 13. Los Angeles: Glen Dawson, 1953.

Simpson, Sir George. *Narrative of a Voyage Round the World, During the Years 1841 and 1842.* London: Henry Colburn, 1847. Reprint (California portion). *Narrative of A Voyage to California Ports in 1841–42.* San Francisco: Thomas C. Russell, 1930.

Sutter, John A. *New Helvetia Diary.* San Francisco: Grabhorn Press, 1939.

Tarakanoff, Vassili Petrovich. *Statement of My Captivity Among the Californians.* Early California Travel Series, vol. 16. Translated by Ivan Petroff. Los Angeles: Glen Dawson, 1953.

Thompson, Alpheus B. *China Trade Days in California: Selected Letters from the Thompson Papers, 1832–1863.* Edited by D. Mackenzie Brown. Berkeley: University of California Press, 1947.

White, Joseph M. *A New Collection of Laws, Charters and Local Ordinances . . . of Mexico and Texas.* 2 vols. Philadelphia: T. & J. W. Johnson, 1839.

Wilkes, Charles. *Narrative of the United States Exploring Expedition. During the Years 1838, 1839, 1840, 1841, 1842.* 5 vols. Philadelphia: C. Sherman, 1844.

Wilson, R. A. "The Alcalde System of California." *California Reports.* Vol. 1 (appendix). San Francisco: Nathaniel Bennett, 1852.

SECONDARY SOURCES

Albertson, Dean H. "Jacob P. Leese, Californio." M.A. thesis, University of California (Berkeley), 1947.

Auerbach, Jerold S. *Justice Without Law?* New York: Oxford University Press, 1983.

Baade, Hans W. "The Form of Marriage in Spanish North America." *Cornell Law Review* 61 (November 1975): 1–89.

Bakken, Gordon M. *The Development of Law in Frontier California: Civil Law and Society, 1850–1890.* Westport, Conn.: Greenwood Press, 1985.

Bancroft, Hubert H. *California Pastoral,* in *The Works of Hubert Howe Bancroft.* 39 vols. San Francisco: History Co., 1874–1890.

———. *California Pioneer Register and Index, 1542–1848* (extracted from *History of California.*). Reprint. Baltimore: Regional Publishing Co., 1964.

———. *History of California.* 7 vols. In *The Works of Hubert Howe Bancroft.* 39 vols. San Francisco: History Co., 1874–1890. Reprint. *History of California.* Santa Barbara: Wallace Hebberd, 1963–1970.

Barker, Frederick F., and Cormack, Joseph M. "The Mercantile Act: A Study in Mexican Legal Approach." *Southern California Law Review* 6 (November 1932): 1–30.

Barkun, Michael. *Law Without Sanctions: Order in Primitive Societies and the World Community.* New Haven: Yale University Press, 1968.

Bean, Walton. *California: An Interpretive History.* New York: McGraw Hill Book Co., 1968.

Beers, Henry P. *Spanish and Mexican Records of the American Southwest: A Bibliographical Guide to Archive and Manuscript Sources.* Tucson: University of Arizona Press, 1979.

———. "The American Consulate in California." *California Historical Society Quarterly* 37 (Spring 1958): 1–17.

Beilharz, Edwin A. *Felipe de Neve: First Governor of California.* San Francisco: California Historical Society, 1971.

Beutel, Frederick K. "Colonial Sources of the Negotiable Instruments Law of the United States." *Illinois Law Review of Northwestern University* 34 (June 1939): 137–50.

————. "The Development of Negotiable Instruments in Early English Law." *Harvard Law Review* 51 (March 1938): 813–45.

Bloomfield, Maxwell. *American Lawyers in a Changing Society, 1776–1876.* Cambridge: Harvard University Press, 1976.

Borah, Woodrow, and Cook, Sherburne F. "Marriage and Legitimacy in Mexican Culture: Mexico and California." *California Law Review* 54 (May 1966): 946–1008.

Bowman, J. N. "History of the Provincial Archives of California." *Southern California Quarterly* 64 (Spring 1982): 1–97.

————. "Libraries in Provincial California." *Southern California Quarterly* 43 (December 1961): 426–39.

Burton, Clarence M., and Burton, M. Agnes. *History of Wayne County and the City of Detroit, Michigan.* 3 vols. Detroit: S. J. Clarke Publishing Co., 1930.

Caughey, John W. *California: A Remarkable State's Life History.* Third ed. Englewood Cliffs, New Jersey: Prentice-Hall, 1970.

Chapman, Charles E. "The Alta California Supply Ships, 1773–1776." *Southwestern Historical Quarterly* 19 (1916): 184.

Clagett, Helen L. "The Sources of the Commercial Law of Mexico." *Tulane Law Review* 18 (March 1944): 437–60.

————, and Valderrama, David M. *A Revised Guide to the Law and Legal Literature of Mexico.* Washington: Library of Congress, 1973.

Clark, Harry. "Their Pride, Their Manners, and Their Voices: Sources of the Traditional Portrait of the Early Californians." *California Historical Quarterly* 53 (Spring 1974): 71–82.

Cook, Sherburne F. *The Conflict between the California Indian and White Civilization.* Berkeley: University of California Press, 1943. Reprint. Berkeley: University of California Press, 1976.

————. *The Population of the California Indians, 1769–1970.* Berkeley: University of California Press, 1976.

Cowan, Robert G. *Ranchos of California: A List of Spanish Concessions 1775–1822 and Mexican Grants 1822–1846.* Los Angeles: Historical Society of Southern California, 1977.

Craver, Rebecca McDowell. *The Impact of Intimacy: Mexican-Anglo Intermarriage in New Mexico.* El Paso: Texas Western Press, 1982.

Culp, Maurice S. "Negotiability of Promissory Notes Payable

in Specifics." *Mississippi Law Journal* 9 (February 1937): 277–92.

Dakin, Susanna B. *A Scotch Paisano in Old Los Angeles: Hugo Reid's Life in California, 1832–1852 Derived from His Correspondence.* Berkeley: University of California Press, 1939. Reprint. Berkeley: University of California Press, 1978.

————. *The Lives of William Hartnell.* Stanford: Stanford University Press, 1949.

Dallas, Sherman F. "The Hide and Tallow Trade in Alta California, 1822–1846." Ph.D. dissertation, Indiana University, 1955.

Dillon, Richard. *Fool's Gold: The Decline and Fall of Captain John Sutter of California.* New York: Coward-McCann, 1967. Reprint. Santa Cruz, California: Western Tanager Press, 1981.

DuMars, Charles T., O'Leary, Marilyn, and Utton, Albert E. *Pueblo Indian Water Rights: Struggle for a Precious Resource.* Tucson: University of Arizona Press, 1984.

"Early American Arbitration: II. In Old Virginia." *Arbitration Journal* (n.s.) 1 (Summer 1946):174–76.

Ebright, Malcolm. "Manuel Martinez's Ditch Dispute: A Study in Mexican Period Custom and Justice." *New Mexico Historical Review* 54 (January 1979):21–34.

Elliott, J. H. *Imperial Spain, 1469–1716.* New York: St. Martin's Press, 1963.

Ellis, Richard E. *The Jeffersonian Crisis: Courts and Politics in the Young Republic.* New York: Oxford University Press, 1971.

Engelhardt, Fr. Zephyrin. *The Missions and Missionaries of California.* 4 vols. and index. San Francisco: James H. Barry Co., 1908–1916.

Fallers, Lloyd A. *Law Without Precedent: Legal Ideas in Action in the Courts of Colonial Busoga.* Chicago: University of Chicago Press, 1969.

Francis, Jessie D. *An Economic and Social History of Mexican California.* New York: Arno Press, 1976.

Friedman, Lawrence M. *A History of American Law.* New York: Simon & Schuster, 1973.

Geary, Gerald J. *The Secularization of the California Missions.* Studies in American Church History, vol. 17. Washington: Catholic University of America Press, 1934.

Geiger, Maynard, Fr. *Franciscan Missionaries in Hispanic Cali-*

fornia 1769–1848. San Marino, Calif.: Huntington Library, 1969.

Golbert, Albert S., and Nun, Yenny. *Latin American Laws and Institutions.* New York: Praeger Publishers, 1982.

Grivas, Theodore. "Alcalde Rule: The Nature of Local Government in Spanish and Mexican California." *California Historical Society Quarterly* 40 (March 1961): 11–32.

————. *Military Governments in California, 1846–1850.* Glendale, Cal.: Arthur H. Clark Co., 1963.

Guest, Fr. Francis F. "Municipal Government in Spanish California." *California Historical Society Quarterly* 46 (December 1967): 307–36.

Hammond, George P. *The Weber Era in Stockton History.* Berkeley: Friends of the Bancroft Library, 1982.

Hansen, Woodrow J. *The Search for Authority in California.* Oakland: Biobooks, 1960.

Haring, C. H. *The Spanish Empire in America.* New York: Harcourt, Brace & World, 1947. Reprint. New York: Harcourt, Brace & World, 1963.

Harlow, Neal. *California Conquered: War and Peace on the Pacific, 1846–1850.* Berkeley: University of California Press, 1982.

Hart, James D. *American Images of Spanish California.* Berkeley: Friends of the Bancroft Library, 1960.

Hartog, Hendrik. "The Public Law of a County Court; Judicial Government in Eighteenth Century Massachusetts." *American Journal of Legal History* 20 (October 1976): 282–329.

Hawgood, John A. "The Pattern of Yankee Infiltration in Mexican Alta California, 1821–1846." *Pacific Historical Review* 27 (February 1958): 27–37.

Hay, Douglas. "Property, Authority and the Criminal Law," in *Albion's Fatal Tree: Crime and Society in Eighteenth-Century England.* Edited by Douglas Hay. New York: Pantheon Books, 1975.

Hindus, Michael S. *Prison and Plantation: Crime, Justice, and Authority in Massachusetts and South Carolina, 1767–1878.* Chapel Hill: University of North Carolina Press, 1980.

Holmes, Oliver W., Jr. "The Path of the Law." *Harvard Law Review* 10 (March 1897): 457–78.

Horwitz, Morton J. *The Transformation of American Law, 1780–1860.* Cambridge: Harvard University Press, 1977.

Hunt, Rockwell D. *John Bidwell, Prince of California Pioneers.* Caldwell, Idaho: Caxton Printers, 1942.

———. "Legal Status of California, 1846–49." *Annals of the American Academy of Political and Social Science* 12 (November 1898):387–408.

Irizarry y Puente, J. "Functions and Powers of the Foreign Consulate—A Study in Medieval Legal History." *New York University Law Review* 20 (June 1944):57–100.

Jones, Oakah L., Jr. *Los Paisanos: Spanish Settlers on the Northern Frontier of New Spain.* Norman: University of Oklahoma Press, 1979.

Jones, William C. "An Inquiry into the History of the Adjudication of Mercantile Disputes in Great Britain and the United States." *University of Chicago Law Review* 25 (Spring 1958): 445–64.

———. "Three Centuries of Commercial Arbitration in New York: A Brief Survey." *Washington University Law Quarterly* 1956 (April 1956):193–221.

Kagan, Richard L. *Lawsuits and Litigants in Castile, 1500–1700.* Chapel Hill: University of North Carolina Press, 1981.

Kelsey, Rayner W. "The United States Consulate in California." *Publications of the Academy of Pacific Coast History.* Vol. 1. Berkeley: University of California Press, 1910.

Knaup, Kathianne. "The Transition from Spanish Civil Law to English Common Law in Missouri." *Saint Louis University Law Journal* 16 (Winter 1971):218–31.

Koegel, Otto E. *Common Law Marriage and its Development in the United States.* Washington: J. Byrne & Co., 1922.

Kommers, Donald P. "The Emergence of Law and Justice in Pre-Territorial Wisconsin." *American Journal of Legal History* 8 (January 1964):20–33.

Kuhn, Arthur K. "The Function of the Comparative Method in Legal History and Philosophy." *Tulane Law Review* 13 (April 1939):350–61.

Langum, David J. "Californio Women and the Image of Virtue." *Southern California Quarterly* 59 (Fall 1977):245–50.

———. "Californios and the Image of Indolence." *Western Historical Quarterly* 9 (April 1978):181–96.

———. "Expatriate Domestic Relations Law in Mexican California." *Pepperdine Law Review* 7 (Fall 1979):41–66.

———. "From Condemnation to Praise: Shifting Perspectives on Hispanic California." *California History* 61 (Winter 1983): 282–91.

Lecompte, Janet. "The Independent Women of Hispanic New Mexico, 1821–1846." *Western Historical Quarterly* 12 (January 1981): 17–35.

Llewellyn, Karl N. *The Bramble Bush: On Our Law and its Study.* New York: Oceana Publications, 1930.

Logan, Walter S. *A Mexican Law Suit.* Brooklyn: Eagle Book and Job Printing Department, 1895.

Lounsbury, Ralph. "Mexican Land Claims in California." Washington: National Archives, 1940 (typewritten report).

McAlister, Lyle N. *The "Fuero Militar" in New Spain 1764–1800.* Gainsville: University of Florida Press, 1957.

McCoid, John C., II. *Civil Procedure: Cases and Materials.* Saint Paul: West Publishing Co., 1974.

McEwen, Craig A., and Maiman, Richard J. "Mediation in Small Claims Court: Achieving Compliance Through Consent." *Law & Society Review* 18 (1984): 11–49.

MacLachlan, Colin M. *Criminal Justice in Eighteenth Century Mexico: A Study of the Tribunal of the Acordada.* Berkeley: University of California Press, 1974.

McMurray, Orrin K. "The Beginnings of the Community Property System in California and the Adoption of the Common Law." *California Law Review* 3 (July 1915): 359–80.

Mann, Bruce H. "The Formalization of Informal Law: Arbitration Before the American Revolution." *New York University Law Review* 59 (June 1984): 443–81.

Manning, James F. "William A. Leidesdorff's Career in California." M.A. thesis, University of California (Berkeley), 1942.

Margadant S., Guillermo Floris. *Introducción a la historia del derecho mexicano.* Mexico City: Universidad Nacional Autónoma de Mexico, 1971. English edition: *An Introduction to the History of Mexican Law.* Dobbs Ferry, New York: Oceana Publications, 1983.

Mattes, Merrill J. *The Great Platte River Road: The Covered Wagon Mainline Via Fort Kearny to Fort Laramie.* Lincoln: Nebraska State Historical Society, 1969. Second ed. Lincoln: Nebraska State Historical Society, 1979.

Merryman, John H. *The Civil Law Tradition: An Introduction to the Legal Systems of Western Europe and Latin America.* Second ed. Stanford: Stanford University Press, 1985.

Meyer, Michael C. *Water in the Hispanic Southwest: A Social and Legal History 1550–1850.* Tucson: University of Arizona Press, 1984.

Miller, Ronald L. "A California Romance in Perspective; The Elopement, Marriage, and Ecclesiastical Trial of Henry D. Fitch and Josefa Carrillo." *Journal of San Diego History* 19 (Spring 1973):1–13.

Miller, Ronald L. "Henry Delano Fitch: A Yankee Trader in California, 1826–1849." Ph.D. dissertation, University of Southern California, 1972.

Miranda, Gloria E. "Gente de Razón Marriage Patterns in Spanish and Mexican California: A Case Study of Santa Barbara and Los Angeles." *Southern California Quarterly* 63 (Spring 1981):1–21.

Moore, Lloyd E. *The Jury: Tool of Kings, Palladium of Liberty.* Cincinnati: W. H. Anderson Co., 1973.

Nelson, William E. *Americanization of the Common Law: The Impact of Legal Change on Massachusetts Society, 1760–1830.* Cambridge: Harvard University Press, 1975.

———. *Dispute and Conflict Resolution in Plymouth County, Massachusetts, 1725–1825.* Chapel Hill: University of North Carolina Press, 1981.

Northrop, Marie E. *Spanish-Mexican Families of Early California: 1769–1850.* 2 vols. New Orleans: Polyanthos, Inc., 1976 (vol. 1); Burbank, Cal.: Southern California Genealogical Society, 1984 (vol. 2).

Nunis, Doyce B., Jr. *The Trials of Isaac Graham.* Los Angeles: Dawson's Book Shop, 1967.

Ogden, Adele. "Boston Hide Droghers Along California Shores." *California Historical Society Quarterly* 8 (1929):289–305.

———. "Hides and Tallow: McCulloch, Hartnell and Company, 1822–1828." *California Historical Society Quarterly* 6 (1927):254–64.

———. "Alfred Robinson, New England Merchant in Mexican California." *California Historical Society Quarterly* 23 (1944):193–218.

———. "New England Traders in Spanish and Mexican California," in *Greater America: Essays in Honor of Herbert Eugene Bolton.* Berkeley: University of California Press, 1945.

———. *The California Sea Otter Trade, 1784–1848.* Berkeley: University of California Press, 1941. Reprint. Berkeley: University of California Press, 1975.

Pallares, Jacinto. *Curso completo de derecho mexicano.* Mexico City: I. Paz, 1901.

Pitt, Leonard. *The Decline of the Californios: A Social History of the Spanish-Speaking Californians, 1846–1890.* Berkeley: University of California Press, 1966.

Poldervaart, Arie W. *Black-Robed Justice.* Santa Fe: Historical Society of New Mexico, 1948. Reprint. New York: Arno Press, 1976.

Pound, Roscoe. "The Causes of Popular Dissatisfaction with the Administration of Justice." *American Bar Association Reports* 29 (1906):395–417.

Powell, Richard P. *Compromises of Conflicting Claims: A Century of California Law, 1760 to 1860.* Dobbs Ferry, New York: Oceana Publications, 1977.

Read, Frederick. "The Origin, Early History, and Later Development of Bills of Exchange and Certain Other Negotiable Instruments." *Canadian Bar Review* 4 (September & December 1926):440–59, 665–82.

Reid, John P. "Binding the Elephant: Contracts and Legal Obligations on the Overland Trail." *American Journal of Legal History* 21 (October 1977):285–315.

———. *Law for the Elephant: Property and Social Behavior on the Overland Trail.* San Marino, Calif.: Huntington Library, 1980.

Robertson, James R. "From Alcalde to Mayor: a History of the Change from the Mexican to the American Local Institutions in California." Ph.D. dissertation, University of California (Berkeley), 1908.

Sayre, Paul L. "Development of Commercial Arbitration Law." *Yale Law Journal* 37 (March 1928):595–617.

Schurz, William L. "The Manila Galleon and California." *Southwestern Historical Quarterly* 21 (1918):107–26.

Servín, Manuel P. "The Secularization of the California Missions: A Reappraisal." *Southern California Quarterly* 47 (June 1965):133–50.

Simmons, Marc. *Spanish Government in New Mexico.* Albuquerque: University of New Mexico Press, 1968.

Steele, Eric H. "The Historical Context of Small Claims Courts." *American Bar Foundation Research Journal* 1981 (Spring 1981):293–376.

Stein, Peter, and Shand, John. *Legal Values in Western Society.* Edinburgh: Edinburgh University Press, 1974.

Tays, George. "Commodore Edmund P. Kennedy, U.S.N., Versus Governor Nicholás Gutiérrez: An Incident of 1836." *California Historical Society Quarterly* 12 (1933):137–46.

Thurman, Michael E. *The Naval Department of San Blas: New Spain's Bastion for Alta California and Nootka, 1767–1798.* Glendale, Calif.: Arthur H. Clark Co., 1967.

Tucey, Mary, and Hornbeck, David. "Anglo Immigration and the Hispanic Town: A Study of Urban Change in Monterey, California, 1835–1850." *Social Science Journal* 13 (April 1976):1–7.

Underhill, Reuben L. *From Cowhides to Golden Fleece; A Narrative of California, 1832–1858.* Stanford, Calif.: Stanford University Press, 1939.

Unruh, John D., Jr. *The Plains Across: The Overland Emigrants and the Trans-Mississippi West, 1840–60.* Urbana: University of Illinois Press, 1979.

Vance, John T. *The Background of Hispanic-American Law: Legal Sources and Juridical Literature of Spain.* Westport, Conn.: Hyperion Press, 1979.

Weber, David J. *The Mexican Frontier, 1821–1846: The American Southwest Under Mexico.* Albuquerque: University of New Mexico Press, 1982.

Weinberg, Harold R. "Commercial Paper in Economic Theory and Legal History." *Kentucky Law Journal* 70 (1982):567–92.

Wigmore, John H. *A Treatise on the Anglo-American System of Evidence in Trials at Common Law.* 5 vols. Second ed. Boston: Little, Brown, & Co., 1923.

Wolaver, Earl S. "The Historical Background of Commercial Arbitration." *University of Pennsylvania Law Review* 83 (December 1934):132–46.

Woolfenden, John, and Elkinton, Amelie. *Cooper: Juan Bautista Rogers Cooper, Sea Captain, Adventurer, Ranchero, and*

Early California Pioneer, 1791–1872. Pacific Grove, Calif.: Boxwood Press, 1983.

Wright, Doris M. *A Yankee in Mexican California: Abel Stearns, 1798–1848.* Santa Barbara: Wallace Hebberd, 1977.

Wunder, John R. *Inferior Courts, Superior Justice: A History of the Justices of the Peace on the Northwest Frontier, 1853–1889.* Westport, Conn.: Greenwood Press, 1979.

Yankwich, Leon R. "Social Attitudes as Reflected in Early California Law." *Hastings Law Journal* 10 (February 1959): 250–70.

Young, John E. "The Law as an Expression of Community Ideals and the Lawmaking Functions of Courts." *Yale Law Journal* 27 (November 1917): 1–33.

Zainaldin, Jamil S. "The Emergence of a Modern American Family Law: Child Custody, Adoption, and the Courts, 1796–1851." *Northwestern University Law Review* 73 (February 1979): 1038–89.

Zollinger, James P. *Sutter, the Man and His Empire.* New York: Oxford Press, 1939.

Index